"*Deep Space Nine* extended the critical promise of *Star Trek* into our homes in an unprecedented way. Students of recent history, twentieth-century geographies, contemporary militarism, queer studies, and Afrofuturism should read *A Different 'Trek.'* David Seitz reopens this chapter in popular culture to remind us that staying in place—especially on a planet like ours, with its bloodstained maps and shifting tides of power—affords us every possibility to confront legacies of injustice and imagine radical futures."

—ANDRÉ M. CARRINGTON, author of *Speculative Blackness: The Future of Race in Science Fiction*

"A remarkable guide to a remarkable series. Equally versed in contemporary debates in Black studies and critical theory and in *Star Trek* lore—and equally skilled in explaining both to outsiders—not only does David Seitz make the case for the relevance of *Deep Space Nine* for Leftist thought. His critical yet generous stance also provides a model for future investigations into the ways that commercial entertainment can transcend its origins and speak creatively to the political dilemmas of its age."

—ADAM KOTSKO, author of *Neoliberalism's Demons: On the Political Theology of Late Capital*

"David Seitz displays a vast knowledge of *Star Trek* lore, storylines, and fandom and masterfully deploys a constellation of lenses—queer and critical race theory, Marxism, feminism, and psychoanalysis—to turn a penetrating but generous gaze on the *Trek* universe. He brilliantly explores the anticolonial and inter-imperialist struggles central to *Deep Space Nine* as an unstable allegory of neoliberal racial capitalism from the United States to Palestine."

—TIM MCCASKELL, author of *Queer Progress: From Homophobia to Homonationalism*

"Like the Orbs of the Prophets, David Seitz's *A Different 'Trek'* illuminates the deeper teachings of *Star Trek: Deep Space Nine*. An incisive analysis of DS9, Seitz gives us a compelling examination of how the stories of the series, while imperfect, go where no *Star Trek* has gone before, challenging the consequences of militarism, colonialism, and capitalism that are too often overlooked in the liberal utopianism of the franchise. Clear-eyed and thoughtful, *A Different 'Trek'* is the close read of *Deep Space Nine* that we have been waiting for, built on respect and recognition of the Black intellectual and radical work foundational to both the field of cultural studies and the art of generations of Black *Star Trek* actors."

—CHANDA PRESCOD-WEINSTEIN, author of *The Disordered Cosmos: A Journey into Dark Matter, Spacetime, and Dreams Deferred*

"This is a rich and conceptually diverse account of political possibility in the series *Deep Space Nine*. Through his characterization of racial capitalism at the heart of the *Star Trek* universe, David Seitz powerfully draws out the geopolitical tensions between the possibilities of 1990s U.S. liberal humanism and its constitutive violences. I now want to go back to the beginning of the series to re-view it in light of the insights and observations offered in the book."

—JO SHARP, professor of geography at the University of St Andrews, Scotland, and author of *Geographies of Postcolonialism*

A DIFFERENT *TREK*

**Cultural Geographies
+ Rewriting the Earth**

Series Editors
Paul Kingsbury, Simon Fraser University
Arun Saldanha, University of Minnesota

A DIFFERENT *TREK*

**Cultural Geographies
+ Rewriting the Earth**

Series Editors
Paul Kingsbury, Simon Fraser University
Arun Saldanha, University of Minnesota

A DIFFERENT *TREK*

Radical Geographies of
Deep Space Nine

David K. Seitz

University of Nebraska Press | Lincoln

Portions of the book have previously appeared in "Playing
with *Star Trek* in the Critical Geography Classroom: STEM
Education and Otherwise Possibilities," in "Teaching and
Learning Emotional Geographies," special issue, *Journal of
Geography in Higher Education* (2021), https://doi.org/10
.1080/03098265.2021.1978063, https://www.tandfonline.com;
"'Second Skin,' White Masks: Postcolonial Reparation in *Star
Trek: Deep Space Nine*," *Psychoanalysis, Culture & Society*
22, no. 4 (2017): 401–19; and "'Most Damning of All . . . I
Think I Can Live with It': Captain Sisko, President Obama,
and Emotional Geopolitics," in "The Geographies of *Star
Trek*," special issue, *Geographical Bulletin* 58 (2017): 19–28.

The University of Nebraska Press is part of a land-
grant institution with campuses and programs on the
past, present, and future homelands of the Pawnee,
Ponca, Otoe-Missouria, Omaha, Dakota, Lakota, Kaw,
Cheyenne, and Arapaho Peoples, as well as those of the
relocated Ho-Chunk, Sac and Fox, and Iowa Peoples.

Library of Congress Cataloging-in-Publication Data
Names: Seitz, David K. (David Kroening) author.
Title: A different trek: radical geographies
of Deep Space Nine / David K. Seitz.
Description: Lincoln: University of Nebraska Press, 2023. |
Series: Cultural geographies + rewriting the earth |
Includes bibliographical references and index.
Identifiers: LCCN 2022045028
ISBN 9781496227997 (hardback)
ISBN 9781496235428 (paperback)
ISBN 9781496236586 (epub)
ISBN 9781496236593 (pdf)
Subjects: LCSH: Star trek, Deep Space Nine (Series) | Television
programs—Social aspects—United States. | BISAC: SOCIAL
SCIENCE / Human Geography | SOCIAL SCIENCE /
Media Studies | LCGFT: Television criticism and reviews.
Classification: LCC PN1992.77.S7315 S45 2023 |
DDC 791.45/72—dc23/eng/20230112
LC record available at https://lccn.loc.gov/2022045028

Designed and set in Minion Pro by L. Welch.

For my teachers, and my students

People have referred to *Deep Space Nine* as this darker thing, in my mind it resembles us. . . . *Deep Space Nine* was talking about homelessness and terrorism and all of these things. Gender identity. *That's* us.

—Avery Brooks, *The Fifty-Year Mission: The Complete, Uncensored, Unauthorized Oral History of "Star Trek"*

The voyager is not the only active one. Origin and destination have lives of their own.

—Doreen Massey, "Some Times of Space"

Allegory is the scene of excess in which we live the failure of official/dominant archives, policies, and argots to grant the diverse conditions in which bodily practices, transcultural encounters, and national histories have met, meet, and might meet again, in the future. It is, indeed, an inheritance promising totality that needs to be split, to be simultaneously embraced and overcome. Therefore its spaces of anomaly open up the possibility for experiencing change.

—Lauren Berlant, "'68, or Something"

People have referred to *Deep Space Nine* as this darker thing, in my mind it resembles us. . . . *Deep Space Nine* was talking about homelessness and terrorism and all of these things. Gender identity. *That's* us.

—Avery Brooks, *The Fifty-Year Mission: The Complete, Uncensored, Unauthorized Oral History of "Star Trek"*

The voyager is not the only active one. Origin and destination have lives of their own.

—Doreen Massey, "Some Times of Space"

Allegory is the scene of excess in which we live the failure of official/dominant archives, policies, and argots to grant the diverse conditions in which bodily practices, transcultural encounters, and national histories have met, meet, and might meet again, in the future. It is, indeed, an inheritance promising totality that needs to be split, to be simultaneously embraced and overcome. Therefore its spaces of anomaly open up the possibility for experiencing *change*.

—Lauren Berlant, "'68, or Something"

Contents

Illustrations

Tables

Tables

Preface

Beyond Uhura, "Beyond Vietnam"

In her memoir, *Beyond Uhura: "Star Trek" and Other Memories*, the late artist and activist Nichelle Nichols (1994) recalled her now-celebrated 1967 encounter with Rev. Dr. Martin Luther King Jr. Filming had just wrapped on the first season of Gene Roddenberry's *Star Trek*, the American science fiction television program in which Nichols costarred as uss *Enterprise* communications officer Lieutenant Nyota Uhura. Against the backdrop of worldwide movements for decolonization and the Black freedom struggle in the United States, King saw something profound in the presence of Uhura, a Black woman in a significant role, on the *Enterprise* bridge.

Off-screen, Nichols had endured a long series of slights from Desilu and Paramount studio officials. Studio staff, anxious to minimize her role, disparaged her appearance and hid her voluminous fan mail. Nichols, who had sung with jazz great Duke Ellington and was already a successful entertainer, had had enough. Although she had good rapports with most of the *Star Trek* team, Nichols saw no need to endure further abuse from studio personnel. She had a Broadway contract offer in hand and was inclined to leave the *Enterprise* behind.

It was King, Nichols recounted, who changed her mind. In a chance meeting at a public event, the civil rights leader implored the actor:

You must not [leave]. Don't you realize how important your presence, your character is? . . . Don't you realize the gift this man [Roddenberry] has given the world? Men and women of all races going forth in peaceful exploration, living as equals. . . .

You have opened a door that must not be allowed to close. I'm sure you have taken a lot of grief, or probably will for what you're doing. But you have changed the face of television forever. You have created a character of dignity and grace and beauty and intelligence. Don't you see that you're not just a role model for little Black children? You're more important for people who *don't* look like us. For the first time, the world sees us as we should be seen, as equals, as intelligent people—as we *should* be. There will always be role models for Black children; you are a role model for everyone.

Remember, you are not important there in spite of your color. You are important there *because* of your color. This is what Gene Roddenberry has given us. (Nichols 1994, 158-59, original emphasis)

King argued that Nichols's presence on *Star Trek* was a matter of world-historical and universal significance, an intervention into how non-Black people see Black people in a moment of rising movements for Black self-determination in Africa and throughout the diaspora.

In the decades that have followed, Nichols's enduring presence—and King's validation of it—have become the cornerstone of the case for *Star Trek*'s liberal bone fides (Kanzler 2004). Nichols became a champion of people of color and white women in the sciences, working with the U.S. National Aeronautics and Space Administration (carrington 2016; Thompson 2019). She has been claimed as an inspiration by everyone from astronaut Mae Jemison to actor Whoopi Goldberg to former U.S. president Barack Obama, who hosted her at the White House in 2012, giving *Star Trek*'s famous Vulcan salute.

But what many liberal commentators have missed about Nichols's encounter with King is the context for their meeting. In some recollections, Nichols suggested the conversation happened at a fundraiser for the National Association for the Advancement of Colored People in Beverly Hills. In others, she was more tentative about the setting. But according to entertainment journalist Brian Cronin (2013), the Los Angeles event that most closely coincided with King's travels, Nichols's accounts, and *Star Trek*'s shooting schedule was King's speech to the Nation Institute at the Beverly Hills Hilton on February 25, 1967: "The Casualties of the War in Vietnam." In that speech, King (1967) lambasted the U.S. government's "paranoid anti-Communism," condemned Americans' collective "failure to deal positively and forthrightly with the triple evils of racism, extreme materialism and militarism," and warned that the country was "presently moving down a dead-end road that can lead to national disaster."

The speech that gave King occasion to cheer on Nichols also served as a rough draft for his only somewhat better-known "Beyond Vietnam" sermon, which he gave at the Riverside Church in Manhattan a little over a month later, on April 4, 1967. Acting at the urging of his close friend, the Vietnamese Buddhist monk and activist Thích Nhất Hạnh, King confronted the U.S. government even more boldly, linking the Black freedom struggle with opposition to U.S. imperialism: "I knew that I could never again raise my voice against the violence of the oppressed in the ghettos without having first spoken clearly to the greatest purveyor of violence in the world today: my own government" (King [1967] 2015, 204). Crucially, at stake for King were both the country's political-economic system and its soul. Warning of impending "spiritual death" in a nation that spent more on war than economic uplift, King called for "worldwide fellowship," a "revolution of values" grounded in a syncretic, transformative, "all-embracing and unconditional love" (216).

"Beyond Vietnam" offered a searing, salient diagnosis of the contradictions of U.S. empire, capitalism, and white supremacy and a prophetic call for a better world. It remains a largely buried aspect of King's radical legacy (C. West 2015; Singh 2017; Douglas and Loggins 2021). The sermon also made King a national pariah, not only among racist reactionaries, who already hated him, but also in the respectable halls of liberal public opinion, where many had come to sympathize with his civil rights advocacy (e.g., *Washington Post* 1967). The fallout from "Beyond Vietnam"—which advocated closer links between civil rights, antiwar, and labor movements— led to the circumstances of King's assassination exactly one year later, on April 4, 1968, during his visit to a sanitation workers' strike in Memphis,

Tennessee. Presented with Gene Roddenberry's optimistic, idealistic view of a twenty-third-century humanity without racism or capitalism, then, King insisted that a such a future might only emerge through blistering critique of and mass confrontation with the unjust material structures of his own time—confrontation anchored in a radical, prophetic love.

Returning Nichols's encounter with King to its place in the radical history of Black freedom struggles is indispensable in our own historical moment. In the post–civil rights, post-Obama era, liberals celebrate diverse representation in politics and popular culture as a good in and of itself, regardless of the political content or material effects of that representation on poor, racialized people everywhere. If we were to reduce this superficial form of politics to a slogan, we might do worse than "Let them eat representation." At the 2020 Democratic National Convention, for instance, Joe Biden, flanked by his running mate, Kamala Harris, invoked the words of Black revolutionary Ella Baker: "Give people light and they will find a way." But as historian Keeanga-Yamahtta Taylor (2020) points out, "Biden recognized Baker's person while ignoring her anti-capitalist politics."

Philosopher and activist Angela Y. Davis (2008) argues that the concept of diversity at once "equates racial and gender justice with color and gender blindness" at home and "provincializes the relationship of people within the USA to the world" (14). Organizers and scholars have come up with many names for the cynical use of diversity in this manner, but what these various incarnations share is an imperative to blunt the demands of mass movements for racial and economic justice and an end to empire—the very movements so important to both King and Nichols. What is called for, then, is a return to context, a critical reembedding of diverse and historic images in the histories, geographies, and visions for a better world that informed them.

This book is not principally about the *Star Trek* series in which Nichols costarred from 1966 to 1969, now known as *The Original Series* (TOS), but one of the franchise's less widely appreciated television iterations, *Deep Space Nine* (DS9). Airing from 1993 to 1999, DS9 starred Avery Brooks as Benjamin Sisko, *Trek*'s first Black commanding officer. An adventure from

1. A time-traveling Captain Sisko unable to resist the opportunity to meet Captain Kirk, as Lieutenant Uhura, the character responsible for their encounter in several respects, looks on ("Trials and Tribble-ations," season 5, episode 6, aired November 4, 1996).

DS9's fifth season concretizes the link between Brooks and Nichols by revisiting an iconic TOS episode, "The Trouble with Tribbles" (J. West 1996b; Pevney 1967). In DS9's "Trials and Tribble-ations," Sisko and his twenty-fourth-century crew pursue a time-traveling assassin, coming "back" to the twenty-third century to save Captain Kirk's *Enterprise*. The assassin plants a bomb in one of thousands of tribbles—campy alien furballs—that have taken up residence on the *Enterprise*. Although she has a minimal role in DS9's tribble reprisal, Uhura is in fact the episode's prime mover; it is she who brought the first tribble back to the *Enterprise* in the first place. Once the bomb is disarmed, Sisko cannot pass up the opportunity to meet the heroic Captain Kirk, ignoring strict orders to minimize interaction with people in "the past." Through a feat of careful editing, Uhura hovers behind the Kirk-Sisko meeting, at once haunting the encounter and indispensable to it, from her celebrated (and lamented) position on the *Enterprise* bridge (see carrington 2016; Nichols 1994).

A Different "Trek" argues that Nichols's presence was the first of an ongoing series of critical interventions into *Star Trek*, interventions that go far beyond the diversity and inclusion for which it is often rightly celebrated. This book takes seriously the social movements and the spiritual values that provided the context for King's message of encouragement to Nichols: material struggles against white supremacy, U.S. imperialism, heteropatriarchy, and capitalism and for other, better possible worlds. It returns to King—and to other critics of U.S. imperialism and what the late political theorist Cedric J. Robinson ([1983] 2000, 308) called "racial capitalism"—to make the case for DS9's underappreciated radical political and intellectual legacies. Although long marginalized in the *Trek* franchise and in scholarly criticism, this program's probing examinations of racial capitalism and empire, and its prophetic speculations about how a better world might yet be achieved, continue to challenge audiences' expectations of what *Star Trek*—and what life in the United States as we know it—are and could be.

to it, from her celebrated (and lamented) position on the *Enterprise* bridge (see carrington 2016; Nichols 1994).

A *Different "Trek"* argues that Nichols's presence was the first of an ongoing series of critical interventions into *Star Trek*, interventions that go far beyond the diversity and inclusion for which it is often rightly celebrated. This book takes seriously the social movements and the spiritual values that provided the context for King's message of encouragement to Nichols: material struggles against white supremacy, U.S. imperialism, heteropatriarchy, and capitalism and for other, better possible worlds. It returns to King—and to other critics of U.S. imperialism and what the late political theorist Cedric J. Robinson ([1983] 2000, 308) called "racial capitalism"—to make the case for *DS9*'s underappreciated radical political and intellectual legacies. Although long marginalized in the *Trek* franchise and in scholarly criticism, this program's probing examinations of racial capitalism and empire, and its prophetic speculations about how a better world might yet be achieved, continue to challenge audiences' expectations of what *Star Trek*—and what life in the United States as we know it—are and could be.

1. A time-traveling Captain Sisko unable to resist the opportunity to meet Captain Kirk, as Lieutenant Uhura, the character responsible for their encounter in several respects, looks on ("Trials and Tribble-ations," season 5, episode 6, aired November 4, 1996).

DS9's fifth season concretizes the link between Brooks and Nichols by revisiting an iconic TOS episode, "The Trouble with Tribbles" (J. West 1996b; Pevney 1967). In DS9's "Trials and Tribble-ations," Sisko and his twenty-fourth-century crew pursue a time-traveling assassin, coming "back" to the twenty-third century to save Captain Kirk's *Enterprise*. The assassin plants a bomb in one of thousands of tribbles—campy alien furballs—that have taken up residence on the *Enterprise*. Although she has a minimal role in DS9's tribble reprisal, Uhura is in fact the episode's prime mover; it is she who brought the first tribble back to the *Enterprise* in the first place. Once the bomb is disarmed, Sisko cannot pass up the opportunity to meet the heroic Captain Kirk, ignoring strict orders to minimize interaction with people in "the past." Through a feat of careful editing, Uhura hovers behind the Kirk-Sisko meeting, at once haunting the encounter and indispensable

Acknowledgments

This book, like the series it analyzes, is pedagogical. So it is only fitting that it is dedicated to my teachers—especially to teachers like Bob Strauss at Wilson Elementary School and Scott Morgensen at Macalester College, who took my interest in *Star Trek* seriously, and to the late Lauren Berlant, whose intellectual impact I continue to ponder almost every day. It is also dedicated to my fantastic students, particularly but not only my *Star Trek* and Social Theory students at Harvey Mudd College. That class, among others, has functioned as an ideal laboratory for the book's work.

In a broader sense, everyone I have encountered in my life is both my teacher and my student. This book could not exist independent of the communities and families, chosen and unchosen, that have formed me. My father, Dan Seitz, introduced me to *The Next Generation* (TNG), and my sister, Kadie Seitz, watched *Voyager* (VOY) with me after choir practice when we were kids. Special thanks are due to my mother, Kristie Kroening, for patiently abiding this obsession, even taking me to *Star Trek: The Experience* at the Las Vegas Hilton. Thanks also to Jake Kornely, Al Nichols, and Barb Seitz, for whom marrying into the family has meant, among other things, listening to me carry on about *Star Trek* on more than one occasion.

If my family of origin in the United States planted the seeds for *A Different "Trek,"* those seeds first began to sprout in Canada. Tim McCaskell knew that *A Different "Trek"* was a book before I did. He has been an insightful, generous reader of my work, including this manuscript, for over a decade, and I remain grateful indeed for his mentorship. Sunday evenings in Toronto with the iconic Mic. Carter sharpened my reading of DS9, as did ongoing conversations with the brilliant Beyhan Farhadi, Jordan Hale, Kyle Turner, and Adam Zendel. Special thanks to Adam for alerting me to the work of

Will Burrows, and to Will for graciously allowing us to use his fantastic DS9 agitprop on the book's cover. Jordan Hale, the closest thing I've got to a chief of operations in my working life, and Dustin McMurphy came to my rescue in preparing high-quality still images from DS9.

Mark Rhodes II, Fiona Davidson, and Hannah C. Gunderman deserve special thanks for organizing a 2016 session on the Geographies of *Star Trek* at the American Association of Geographers Annual Meeting in San Francisco, and for including my work in a rich 2017 special issue of the *Geographical Bulletin* on "The Geographies of *Star Trek*." That AAG panel also introduced me to the intrepid Steven Thrasher, who in turn referred me to andré carrington's pathbreaking work. Thanks to the *Geographical Bulletin* (Gamma Theta Upsilon), *Psychoanalysis, Culture & Society* (Palgrave MacMillan), and the *Journal of Geography in Higher Education* (Taylor and Francis) for permission to republish portions of previous articles on *Star Trek* here. Comments from reviewers for these journals and audiences at the AAG, the Science Fiction Research Association, and the Sexuality Studies Association all enriched that writing. Thanks to Arun Saldanha, Alison Sperling, David Valentine, and Ricky Varghese for organizing those events.

Since 2017 I have had the good fortune of being able to develop this project under the auspices of the Department of the Humanities, Social Sciences, and the Arts at Harvey Mudd College, a unique interdisciplinary community that values idiosyncratic scholarship and teaching. Thanks to the HSA department for so regularly allowing me to offer a course on *Trek*, and to Harvey Mudd College for funding a pretenure sabbatical to write the book. Deborah Laird, the HSA department's administrator, adeptly kept my research accounts in working order as I zealously obtained research materials unavailable through other means. Many thanks also to Alex Chappell, Kirsten Hansen, Nazia Islam, Adam Rosenkranz, and their colleagues at the Claremont Colleges Library, who not only patiently abided my numerous requests for interlibrary loan materials but were a wealth of knowledge in sources that informed *Trek*-related teaching and research. Thanks also to the Paley Center for Media.

Researching and writing this book has depended on a community of friends, interlocutors, and correspondents from near and far. Among them, those who deserve special mention include but are not limited to: Karin Aguilar San Juan, Anisha Ahuja, Stuart Aitken, Travis Alexander, Sabrien Amrov, Juliann Anesi, Trevor Anthony, Lucas Bang, David Blaney, Aaron Brosier, Wes Brunson, Kayla Burchuk, Madelaine Cahuas, Jon Cazarez, Vince Chan, Sofia Chang, Jih-Fei Cheng, Wendy Cheng, Jason Chu, Chris Clowers, Nikki Coletto, Julia Collins, Deb Cowen, Shaundra Cunningham, Ambereen Dadabhoy, Iyko Day, Susan De Gaia, Marianne de Laet, David Del Valle, Whitney DeVos, Tom Donnelly, Guillermo and David Douglass-Jaimes, Erika Dyson, Jessica Ellis, Shawki El-Zatmah, Kouross Esmaeli, Ken Fandell, Matthew Farish, Ramzi Fawaz, Sara Fowler, Lia Frederiksen, Richard Fung, Martin Gabriel, Samuel Galloway, Mylène Gamache, Anup Gampa, Lily Geismer, Dina Georgis, Jen Jack Gieseking, Eric Goldfischer, Steffanie Guillermo, Sharon Haire, Georgia Hartman, Yui Hashimoto, April K. Henderson, Emily K. Hobson, Natalie Holdren, Naeem Inayatullah, Kiandra Jimenez, Denise Johnson, Anna Joranger, Caroline Jorgensen, Leslie Kern, El-Farouk Khaki, Jessica Kizer, Josh Kopin, Alysse Kushinski, Youna Kwak, Philip Lance, Nicole Latulippe, Elsie Lewison, Hilary Malson, Derritt Mason, Kevin McGeough, Will McKeithen, Katherine McKittrick, Isaac Meister, Joshua Mendez, Jane Mi, Emily Milton, Donna Minkowitz, Leah Montange, Suzi Moore, Liz Murphy, Ryan Murphy, Taj Nabhani, MyLinh Nguyen, Joanne Nucho, Eve Oishi, Jeff Ono, Laura Palucki Blake, Alexandra Papoutsaki, Stacey Park, Savitri Persaud, Daniel Picus, Bala Ramamurthy, Adam Rosenberg, Farhang Rouhani, Erin Runions, Joey Russo, Danae Schulz, Joseph Serrano, Preeti Sharma, Brian Shuvé, Dany Sigwalt, Roberto Sirvent, Terry Sivers, Deondre Smiles, Christopher Smith, Christy Spackman, Paul Steinberg, Lisa Sullivan, Krys Tabujara, Athena Tan, Aparna Mishra Tarc, Eugene Ting, Zoe Tobier, Marc Tremblay, Kris Trujillo, Jonathan Valelly, Oriol Vallès Codina, Kathy Van Heuvelen, Ricky Varghese, Jamel Velji, Molly Walker, Nicole Wallens, Amanda Waugh Lagji, Chris Webb, Blake Wilkinson, David Wilson, Carlin Wing, Willie Wright,

Ralph Carl Wushke, Nick Yi, Angeline Zalben, Ron Zdroik, and no doubt many others who will hopefully forgive me for failing to list them here.

I am honored that this book contributes to the Cultural Geographies + Rewriting the Earth series at the University of Nebraska Press, which was my first choice as a home for the project. I have long admired the work of Arun Saldanha and Paul Kingsbury, and their editorial guidance has been rigorous and supportive. Bridget Barry has been both insightful and capacious in guiding this project to publication. Thanks also to the entire UNP staff for their hard work making this book a real object that circulates in the world. Once the manuscript was drafted, Fiona Davidson and Gerry Canavan, who have since revealed themselves to me, offered energizing and generative peer reviews. Alongside the press's peer review process, Harvey Mudd College generously funded a manuscript workshop. Here, too, I could not have asked for a better team of readers. andré carrington's sheer brilliance is matched only by his magnanimity. His comments on the relationship between race, class, and narrative have informed and improved almost every page of the manuscript, even and perhaps especially in areas where we do not fully agree. Jo Sharp pushed me to think beyond U.S. SF parochialism and to clarify the book's contribution to cultural geography, and she gave her honorarium to the community organizations that this book's royalties will also support. Alfred Flores, an insightful colleague and a great friend, rightly encouraged me to historicize futuristic allegories that extend much older imperial preoccupations. Darrell Moore "got" the project, and every single one of his comments has helped it to do what it wants to do more effectively. With line edits and good humor, Aimee Bahng invited me to zoom out and ask bigger-picture questions about the book's stakes. Stephanie Rutherford has been an unparalleled friend and mentor since we met in 2009, and I could not ask for a better read of the text than through her incisive Virgo eyes. This book is stronger because of all these reviewers. All limitations, of course, remain my own.

Next, a word on sources. I am especially indebted to two sources: Terry J. Erdmann and Paula M. Block's magisterial *"Star Trek: Deep Space Nine"*

Companion (2000) and the open-source fan encyclopedia Memory Alpha, lovingly maintained by thousands of Trekkers. Whenever I could access a primary or secondary source referenced in Memory Alpha myself, I cite it. Whenever I could not, I cite Memory Alpha. I am also beyond grateful for Mark A. Altman and Edward Gross's excellent, if cumbersomely titled, *The Fifty-Year Mission: The Complete, Uncensored, Unauthorized Oral History of "Star Trek"; The Next 25 Years, from "The Next Generation" to J. J. Abrams* (2016) and three excellent documentaries, Ira Steven Behr and David Zappone's *What We Left Behind: Looking Back at "Star Trek: Deep Space Nine"* (2019), William Shatner's *The Captains Close Up* (2013), and Brian Volk-Weiss's *The Center Seat: 55 Years of "Star Trek"* (2022).

I also continue to be impressed by the creativity, thoughtfulness, and potential for interdisciplinary rigor in *Star Trek*'s vast community of critical and scholarly interpretation. The discourse on *Star Trek* is so voluminous that I have largely elected to stick to academic literature, only dipping occasionally into fan message boards or podcasts—shout-outs to *Women at Warp*, *Soy Trek*, and *All the Asians on Star Trek*. Whenever I engage an interpretation that I know to be someone else's, I cite it. All other interpretations, for better and for worse, are my own. At the same time, I make no pretense of pure scholarly originality. For who could? *Star Trek* is among the most richly intertextual television franchises on the planet, loved and debated by millions of people. It is not only possible but likely that others, particularly *Star Trek* fans with similar political convictions, will find in these pages interpretations with which they agree *and* disagree. I hope so!

Finally, as the shout-out to fan media suggests, to conduct scholarly research on *Star Trek* is to benefit from the love and labor (paid and unpaid) of a vast community of other fans. I take community love and labor seriously, and it is part of why I am planning to split royalties for this book to community organizations connected to the book's political priorities, as elaborated in the conclusion. Special thanks to Jane Nguyen at Ktown for All, Sadé Swift at the Black Alliance for Peace, and D. Granberg at Jewish Voice for Peace for facilitating donations and, above all, for their urgently needed work.

Abbreviations

DIS   *Star Trek: Discovery* (2017–present)

DS9   Deep Space Nine, the name of the space station and the primary setting for the series

DS9   *Star Trek: Deep Space Nine* (1993–99)

ENT   *Star Trek: Enterprise* (2001–5)

FCA   Ferengi Commerce Authority

LD   *Star Trek: Lower Decks* (2020–present)

PIC   *Star Trek: Picard* (2020–present)

SF   science fiction or speculative fiction, a term that can encompass science fiction and other genres (e.g., horror, fantasy) extrapolating beyond known worlds

TAS   *Star Trek: The Animated Series* (1973–74)

TNG   *Star Trek: The Next Generation* (1987–94)

TOS   *Star Trek: The Original Series* (1966–69)

UFP   United Federation of Planets

VOY   *Star Trek: Voyager* (1995–2001)

Dramatis Personae

Bajoran Prophets A community of extradimensional beings who experience space and time as continuous rather than linear or corporeal. The Prophets have a spiritual connection and political commitment to the historically oppressed people of the planet Bajor, who worship them as gods. The Prophets live in an artificial spatial anomaly connecting the Bajoran sector (in the Alpha Quadrant) to the Gamma Quadrant, a distant region of space on the other side of the Milky Way galaxy. Secular Federation scientists call this anomaly "the Bajoran wormhole" and the Prophets "wormhole aliens." Bajorans refer to the anomaly as "the Celestial Temple" and home of the Prophets.

Bajorans Secondary protagonists of DS9, a community indigenous to the planet Bajor. A historically colonized and displaced people, the Bajorans have recently defeated the fifty-year, genocidal colonial Occupation by the Cardassian Empire, with armed resistance and spiritual guidance from the Bajoran Prophets. The postcolonial Bajoran Provisional Government has invited a small team of officers from the United Federation of Planets to assist with rebuilding, but whether Bajor will join the Federation remains an open, contested question. At the beginning of the series, many cells of the Bajoran Resistance to the Cardassian Occupation remain active.

Borg Collective Primary antagonists in other *Trek* iterations, the Borg are a coercive, expansionist, universalist formation of hybrid, cybernetic organisms. In TNG, the Borg abduct Captain Jean-Luc Picard and use his knowledge to nearly destroy the Federation. This attempted Borg invasion, culminating at the Battle of Wolf 359, is responsible for the murder of thousands, including scientist Jennifer Sisko, the late wife of Benjamin Sisko, the hero of DS9.

Cardassian Empire Primary antagonists of DS9. The Cardassian Empire is an extractivist, settler-colonial, interplanetary empire whose genocidal Occupation of Bajor has only recently been beaten back by the Bajoran Resistance. The Occupation was headquartered at the space station Terok Nor, which is repurposed as the Bajoran and Federation starbase Deep Space Nine. The Cardassians have also recently ended a military conflict with the Federation. The Cardassian military government and Occupation of Bajor were opposed by small but growing Cardassian dissident movements. Political conflict on Cardassia accelerates when its leaders join the Dominion.

The Dominion Primary antagonists of DS9. The Dominion is a political alliance of many planets and peoples with a clearly demarcated race and class hierarchy: the reclusive, elite, shape-shifting Founders (also called Changelings), the professional-managerial and diplomatic Vorta, and the Jem'Hadar ground soldiers. The Dominion controls access to territory and trade on the other side of the Bajoran wormhole, in the Gamma Quadrant, and looks to make commercial and territorial inroads in the Alpha Quadrant, the region of space where most of *Trek* takes place.

Federation or United Federation of Planets Primary protagonists of DS9 and the *Star Trek* franchise. A political alliance of many planets and peoples in the Alpha and Beta Quadrants, the Federation initially included humans, Vulcans, Andorians, and Tellarites, but it now encompasses hundreds of peoples. It remains headquartered in San Francisco on Earth. The Federation is predicated on liberal, secular, universalist, and democratic values and a postscarcity economy, largely championed in TOS, TAS, and TNG. These values are thrown into crisis by the events of DS9. The Federation uses its relationship with Bajor to seek a foothold in the Gamma Quadrant.

Ferengi Alliance The most unabashedly capitalist social formation in the *Star Trek* universe. Initially introduced as a primary antagonist in TNG, the Ferengi are reduced to comic relief in that series. DS9 offers a more sustained and complex look at the class and gender contradictions of Ferengi society.

Klingon Empire Primary antagonists in many other iterations of *Star Trek*. DS9 depicts the Klingons as a tradition-bound community in political-economic tumult and as on-again, off-again allies of the Federation.

Maquis A group of mostly ex-Federation citizens whose territorial claims have been sacrificed in a recent Federation peace treaty with the Cardassians. Both settler-colonial in their relationship to land and fiercely opposed to Cardassian fascism, the Maquis also includes a significant number of exiled members of the Bajoran Resistance.

Romulan Empire Primary antagonists in many other iterations of *Star Trek*. DS9 depicts the Romulan Empire as a secretive republic courted by both the Federation and the Dominion as a military ally.

Starfleet A hierarchical organization that serves the functions of military, scientific research, and space exploration for the Federation. Although the Federation is officially a postscarcity society, entry into Starfleet is highly competitive and coveted by many Federation citizens.

PRIMARY CHARACTERS

Benjamin Lafayette Sisko (Avery Brooks) The reluctant, brilliant hero of DS9 and the first *Star Trek* lead commanding officer played by a Black actor. Starfleet commander, eventually promoted to captain of Deep Space Nine, and leader of the Federation effort in the Dominion War. A human from New Orleans who is surprisingly named as Emissary of the Bajoran Prophets, Sisko's growing spiritual connection to Bajor and the Prophets provokes conflict with his secular Starfleet duties. Scarred by the loss of his first wife, Jennifer Sisko, in the conflict with the Borg. Son of Joseph Sisko. Widowed father of Jake Sisko. Lover of Kasidy Yates.

Ezri Dax (Nicole de Boer) A young Starfleet counselor and morale officer and a member of the symbiotic Trill species. The composite of young Trill woman Ezri Tigan and a three-hundred-year-old genderless symbiotic creature named Dax that has shared experiences, personalities, and lifetimes with numerous Trill hosts. Unlike Jadzia, who was well-prepared to join with Dax, Ezri joined with the Dax symbiont on short notice and remains disoriented and unsure of herself. Lover of Julian Bashir.

Jadzia Dax (Terry Farrell) A roguish young Starfleet science officer and joined member of the symbiotic Trill species, Jadzia has access to three hundred years of experience from the previous lives of the Dax symbiont, which has joined with both women and men. These experiences include those of the late Curzon Dax, a rowdy Federation ambassador and friend and mentor to Commander Sisko. Lover of Worf.

Jake Sisko (Cirroc Lofton) A talented writer with interests in journalism and creative writing. Jake loses his mother at a young age but has a special bond with his loving father, Benjamin Sisko, and his grandfather Joseph Sisko. Jake comes of age while living on DS9. Best friend to Nog.

Julian Subatoi Bashir (Alexander Siddig) A zealous, talented young physician from London with a chip on his shoulder. Eventual best friend of Miles O'Brien. Lover of many women on the station, notably including Leeta and Ezri Dax. Object of infatuation for Garak.

Kira Nerys (Nana Visitor) A major, later a colonel in the Bajoran Militia and the First Officer of DS9. A former Bajoran Resistance fighter with deeply anticolonial and spiritual sensibilities, Kira is skeptical of the Bajoran Provisional Government and of Federation presence. Surrogate mother to Kirayoshi O'Brien. Lover of Bareil, Shakaar, and Odo. NB: Bajorans list surnames first. Nerys is Major Kira's personal name.

Miles O'Brien (Colm Meaney) Federation engineer from Ireland. Former transporter chief on the *Enterprise-D* in TNG, O'Brien is promoted to chief of operations on DS9. An enlisted man rather than an officer, O'Brien was a soldier in the Federation conflict with the Cardassians before he married Keiko Ishikawa. Father of Molly and Kirayoshi. Eventual best friend of Julian Bashir.

Odo (René Auberjonois) A shape-shifter, or Changeling, found near the wormhole by a Bajoran scientist during the Occupation, Odo is regarded as an outsider and used as a mediator between Bajorans and Cardassians. He serves as a security officer on Terok Nor but is respected enough by Bajorans that he continues in this role on DS9 after Bajoran decolonization begins. Odo abhors weapons, instead using his shape-shifting abilities to confront suspects, and watches the avaricious restaurateur Quark

like a hawk. He eventually learns that he is a Founder of the Dominion and must come to terms with those origins. Lover of Kira.

Quark (Armin Shimerman) Ferengi proprietor of Quark's Bar, Grill, Gaming House, and Holosuite Arcade, both on Terok Nor during the Cardassian Occupation and on DS9 as decolonization begins. Always alert to Odo's surveillance. Quark employs his brother Rom, nephew Nog, and Leeta.

Worf (Michael Dorn) Chief of Federation Security on DS9. Another crossover from *TNG*, Worf comes to the station to help soothe tensions between the Federation and the Klingon Empire. Worf is the first and among the only Klingons in Starfleet. Surrogate son to Martok. Lover of Jadzia Dax.

RECURRING CHARACTERS

Bareil Antos (Philip Anglim) A progressive Bajoran cleric who is a political rival to Winn Adami. Lover of Kira.

Brunt (Jeffrey Combs) Investigator for the Ferengi Commerce Authority. He zealously intervenes in Ferengi political-economic life in the service of "free" enterprise and hates Quark, whom he regards as a mediocre entrepreneur.

Damar (Casey Biggs) A hard-drinking Cardassian leader and rival to Dukat who eventually comes out against the Cardassian alliance with the Dominion.

Dukat (Marc Alaimo) The primary antagonist of DS9. Cardassian prefect of Bajor during the final years of the Occupation. Dukat is constantly plotting ways to restore his position in the Cardassian Empire and to restore Cardassian domination over Bajor. Father to Tora Ziyal.

Elim Garak (Andrew J. Robinson) A cryptic, charismatic exiled Cardassian spy who works as a tailor on DS9. Like his enemy, Dukat, Garak dreams of returning to grace in the Cardassian Empire. Infatuated with Bashir. Friend to Ziyal.

Enabran Tain (Paul Dooley) Retired head of Cardassian intelligence. Largely disavowed father to Elim Garak.

Female Changeling (Salome Jens) An imperious Founder who leads the Dominion's efforts to conquer the Alpha Quadrant. The primary Founder interlocutor for Odo.

Gowron (Robert O'Reilly) Klingon chancellor. Born to an elite family, Gowron is presented as petty and reckless.

Ishka (Andrea Martin, Cecily Adams) An outspoken Ferengi (bourgeois) feminist who advocates equal rights to accumulate profit for women. Mother of Quark and Rom. Grandmother of Nog. Lover of Zek.

Jennifer Sisko (Felecia M. Bell) A civilian scientist, mother of Jake Sisko and first wife of Benjamin Sisko. Jennifer was killed in the Borg attack at Wolf 359 before the events of DS9 begin.

Joseph Sisko (Brock Peters) A beloved New Orleans restaurateur, chef, and widower who keeps in close touch with his intragalactic family. Father to Benjamin. Grandfather to Jake.

Kasidy Yates (Penny Johnson Jerald) A spirited, independent freighter captain who takes mutual aid seriously. Lover to Benjamin Sisko.

Keiko Ishikawa O'Brien (Rosalind Chao) An accomplished botanist and educator whose career is put on hold when she follows her husband, Miles O'Brien, from the *Enterprise-D* on TNG to DS9. Mother of Molly and Kirayoshi.

Kirayoshi O'Brien (Clara Bravo) Son of Keiko and Miles O'Brien. Surrogate son of "Aunt" Kira Nerys.

Leeta (Chase Masterson) A Bajoran hostess of a dabo gambling table at Quark's casinos who participates in efforts to unionize the establishment. Lover of Julian Bashir and Rom.

Martok (J. G. Hertzler) A grizzled, jocular Klingon military officer with a peasant background. Surrogate father of Worf.

Michael Eddington (Kenneth Marshall) A Federation security officer assigned to DS9 who defects to the Maquis.

Molly O'Brien (Hana Hatae) Young daughter of Keiko and Miles O'Brien. Fan of the O'Briens' cat, Chester, much to the ire of her mother.

Morn (Mark Allen Sheppard) A Lurian courier who frequents Quark's. He is reportedly verbose but, in a running gag, is never depicted speaking.

Nog (Aron Eisenberg) An adolescent Ferengi living on DS9 with his father, Rom. Doubtful of his own aptitude for business, Nog becomes the

first Ferengi to join Starfleet. Nephew of Quark. Grandson of Ishka. Best
friend of Jake Sisko.

Opaka (Camille Saviola) Spiritual mother of the Bajoran Resistance.
Opaka served as kai, or state religious leader, during the final years of the
Occupation as the decolonization movement gained strength.

Rom (Max Grodénchik) Insecure younger brother of Quark. Rom leads a
unionization drive at Quark's and quits working for his brother, pursuing
less exploitative work in the Bajoran engineering corps on the station.
Father of Nog. Lover of Leeta.

Shakaar Edon (Duncan Regehr) Bajoran Resistance leader who opposes
Winn's export-oriented agricultural production schemes and later serves
as First Minister. Lover of Kira.

Tora Ziyal (Cyia Batten, Tracy Middendorf, Melanie Smith) A budding
artist and daughter of Gul Dukat and Tora Naprem, a Bajoran woman
forced into military sexual servitude during the Occupation. She is a
source of political embarrassment to her Cardassian father and lives in
exile on DS9. Friend to Garak and Kira.

Vic Fontaine (James Darren) A holographic 1960s Las Vegas lounge
singer from Quark's holosuites who becomes sentient. Friend to many
members of the crew, particularly Bashir, Odo, and Nog.

Weyoun (Jeffrey Combs) An especially obsequious member of the
Dominion's Vorta class of diplomats, managers, and professionals.
Weyoun is among the primary liaisons with the Federation during the
Dominion War. Vorta are serialized clones, and we meet several itera-
tions of Weyoun over the course of the series.

William Ross (Barry Jenner) Starfleet admiral in charge of the Federation
war effort against the Dominion who often turns to Sisko and recruits
him to play a larger role in leading the war effort.

Winn Adami (Louise Fletcher) A Machiavellian Bajoran cleric who
instrumentalizes religious fundamentalism to a range of ideologically
inconsistent ends to advance her own political interests. She eventually
reaches the rank of kai, the head of Bajor's state religion, and even briefly
serves as interim First Minister.

Zek (Wallace Shawn) The aging Grand Nagus, or head of the Federal Reserve Bank, of the Ferengi Alliance. Lover of Ishka.

WRITERS AND PRODUCERS

Ira Steven Behr Staff writer, 1993–95; staff writer, executive producer, and showrunner, 1995–99

Hans Beimler Staff writer, 1995–99

Rick Berman Executive producer, 1993–99

René Echevarria Staff writer, 1994–99

Peter Allan Fields Coproducer and writer, 1993–94

Ronald D. Moore Staff writer, 1994–99

Michael Piller Executive producer and showrunner, 1993–95

Bradley Thompson Staff writer, 1996–99

David Weddle Staff writer, 1996–99

Robert Hewitt Wolfe Staff writer, 1993–97

A DIFFERENT *TREK*

A DIFFERENT *TREK*

Introduction
Reading Racial Capitalism from DS9

"We're All Stuck Here for a While"

During the week of January 3, 1993, nearly one in five U.S. households watching television tuned in to the debut of a different kind of *Star Trek* series. *Deep Space Nine*, the fourth installment in the popular science fiction franchise, enjoyed "the highest-rated series premiere in syndication history" at the time (Erdmann and Block 2000, 8).[1] To date, no *Star Trek* episode since *The Original Series* has received a larger share of live viewers than "Emissary," DS9's ambitious ninety-one-minute pilot.

But what audiences encountered in "Emissary" defied their expectations. Since its premiere in 1966, *Star Trek*, drawing inspiration from British imperial maritime novels and U.S. settler-colonial westerns, had been organized around the same geographical logic: outward-facing exploration (Bernardi 1998). Highly episodic and shunning serialization, save for the occasional cliff-hanger, *Star Trek* to date had been about one-off colonial encounters, "alien of the week" titillation, and tidy solutions dispensed at warp speed by the USS *Enterprise*, the flagship spacecraft of the United Federation of Planets. By contrast, DS9 was "stuck" in place, anchored at a space station near a recently decolonized planet, Bajor, which was celebrating hard-fought independence after fifty years of genocidal, extractive Occupation by the Cardassian Empire. The station's top Federation officer, Commander Benjamin Sisko (Avery Brooks), was a Black single father from New Orleans, a grieving widower who didn't want to accept his assignment helping the Bajoran Provisional Government rebuild after Cardassian withdrawal. Its Bajoran First Officer, Major Kira Nerys (Nana Visitor), was a former anticolonial revolutionary—Cardassians would say "terrorist"—

1

who now found herself reluctantly thrown into the role of postcolonial government official. Like many Bajorans, Kira is a devout follower of the Prophets, extradimensional beings who guide her planet's liberation struggle and who have a vision for Bajor—and for Sisko. The space station's crew was composed principally of Bajorans and other extraterrestrials. As film scholar Micheal C. Pounds (2009) puts it, "This *dramatis personae* clearly indicated that . . . DS9 was not going to be a *Star Trek* television series that would dwell on the wonders of future technology or being bold galactic explorers" (213).

Indeed not. Even the physical structure that these characters inhabited, a celestial port city, was itself a postcolonial, postindustrial ruin, intended by set designer Michael Okuda to resemble an offshore oil rig (Behr and Zappone 2019). A relic of the Cardassian Occupation, when it was known as the Terok Nor ore-processing facility and labor camp, the station was repurposed and renamed by the Bajorans during decolonization. Defeated by the Bajoran Resistance, embittered departing Cardassian colonizers trash the station on their way out, murdering Bajoran merchants and stripping the station (and the planet below) of "every component of value" (Carson 1993a). Instead of the glittering optimism of the *Enterprise* bridge, what U.S. audiences saw on the station's busted-up Promenade looked a lot more like their own tumultuous society (Pounds 2009; Raile 2014). Many recognized in DS9's wreckage the streets of Los Angeles, which in spring 1992 had been swept by a multiracial rebellion against racism, capitalism, state violence, and "organized abandonment" (Gilmore 2011; Camp 2016). The uprising was sparked by outrage at impunity for the beating of Black motorist Rodney Glen King by white police, and for the murder of Black teenager Latasha Harlins by a Korean American convenience store owner (C. Robinson 1993; Chang 1994; Stevenson 2015). Rodney King's plea to Angelenos to end the violence—"Can we all get along?"—is the most widely remembered part of the statement he made at the time. But his remarks closed with an explicitly geographical and existential reflection: "We're all stuck here for a while. Let's, you know, let's try to work it out. Let's try to work it out" (Serrano 1992; see Gooding-Williams 1993).

2. The Siskos' first glimpse of DS9 from the outside ("Emissary," season 1, episodes 1–2, aired January 3, 1993).

Star Trek is often hailed for its prophetic dimensions, both anticipating technological "innovation" and using allegory and optimistic visions of a utopian future to comment critically on war, racism, and capitalist inequality here and now. But *Trek* has almost always articulated this futurity through starships, explorers, and other images of mobility—and leaving places behind, as the late artist and critic John Berger (2001) observed, has a way of concealing consequences (102). DS9's stationary allegorical geography meant from the outset that it would be, as series writer Robert Hewitt Wolfe puts it, a "show . . . about consequences" (Altman and Gross 2016, 466). The series juxtaposes multiple clashing political, economic, and cultural perspectives embedded in a single contested place, one far from the glitz of the *Enterprise* or the manicured lawns of Starfleet Headquarters. It foregrounds contradictions between the Federation's comfortable core and its misunderstood and exploited Bajoran periphery, from the outside looking

3. The wreckage left on Deep Space Nine, formerly Terok Nor, by the departing forces of the Cardassian Occupation of Bajor ("Emissary," season 1, episodes 1–2, aired January 3, 1993).

in. Instead of an itinerant spacecraft, this was a place where consequences would have to be, as Rodney King suggested, "worked out" (see Hall 1997).

DS9 ran for seven seasons, from 1993 until 1999. Only one *Star Trek* series, TNG, surpasses its staggering total episode count of 176. More than any other *Trek*, DS9 insists on the importance of political, geographical, and cultural context for understanding action and character development. Its early seasons follow Bajor's postcolonial politics, routinely questioning whether the planet will remain politically and economically independent and whether Sisko's Federation officers are themselves a neocolonial presence. In the later seasons, the already fractious Bajoran sector becomes the setting for an intergalactic war between the Federation and the Dominion, an imperialist society from the other side of the galaxy that is marked by its own race and class stratifications. It is against this geopolitical backdrop that the show's protagonists and a web of intricately developed secondary characters go about their everyday lives: debating and scheming about politics, attending religious services, raising their children, hanging out with friends, making knowledge, eating, drinking, having sex, exercising, gambling, shopping on the station's Promenade. These characters attach a wide range of meanings to Bajor and to DS9 as places: unwanted, remote military posting; space of refuge from political exile; fecund site of commercial opportunity; coveted, "exotic" scientific assignment; gateway to a significant religious site; or home under threat of (re)conquest. Even when the crew does get a starship—the compact but formidably armed USS *Defiant*—at the beginning of season 3, the show remains defined by the specificity, contradictions, and dynamism of place.

DS9 has come to delight many critics. Its highly serialized and complex narratives and rich character development anticipated by several decades the contemporary popularity, even prestige of long, "bingeable" television plot arcs. Its political commentary—on capitalism, homelessness, religion, racism, imperialism, criminal justice, settler colonialism, terrorism, worker's rights, gender and sexuality, household labor, family, environmentalism, disability, and more—consistently took the franchise and syndicated television in new directions, and remains salient, and underappreciated, to this day. It featured a Black commanding officer fifteen years before the Obama presidency, and a same-sex kiss eighteen months before the famous coming-out episode on *Ellen*. In a thorough 2016 retrospective on *Star Trek's* first half century, *TV Guide* opined, "When we look back on this franchise in the future—and we will—DS9 will be considered the best acted, written, produced, and altogether finest of the [first] four *Trek* series. There, we said it. Now let the arguments begin" (Logan 2016, 71). The series embodies the best of what *Star Trek* and popular SF can be, bringing prophetic social critique and fabulous speculations about alternative modes of political life to wide audiences largely unreached by more rarefied works.

But DS9 initially confused and disappointed many longtime *Star Trek* fans, including many higher-ups in the franchise family. Well before its premiere, the premise of a place-based *Trek* series that departed from its predecessors' mobile, utopian optimism incurred anxiety, even dread. Screenwriter Susan Sackett, a longtime associate of Gene Roddenberry, claims that the *Trek* creator "*hated*" the DS9 concept and "did not want them doing it," but that the writers and the producers used Roddenberry's passing in 1991 to push ahead anyway (Altman and Gross 2016, 413, original emphasis). DS9's first showrunner, Michael Piller, received a letter from a grade-school class in the Midwest begging him not to stray from *Star Trek*'s hopeful ethos (Altman and Gross 2016, 421). For some, at least, such fears were borne out. Actor and activist George Takei (2007), celebrated for his TOS role as security officer Hikaru Sulu, once called DS9 "the polar opposite of Gene's philosophy and vision of the future," opining that "*Star Trek* lost its way."

Early assessments in academia and the chattering classes were only slightly more generous. Few put it more crudely than right-wing commentator Jonah Goldberg (2001): "Benjamin Sisco [*sic*] was one angry dude . . . did we really need Shaft in a Federation uniform?" Liberals, for their part, often reduced DS9 to a "dark," "postmodern" derivative or subset, rather than considering it on its own terms (e.g., Harris 2006; Barrett and Barrett 2017). Anthropologist Jon Wagner and sociologist Jan Lundeen (1998) lament that Sisko "is only nominally in control, more like the concierge of a dingy multiethnic hotel than the skipper of a British Man-of-War" (187), and minimize Major Kira's anticolonial nationalist politics, guided by the Bajoran Prophets, as an "inner conflict . . . more mundane than, say, Spock's Manichean struggle between human feeling and Vulcan reason" (188). As Black studies scholar Lisa Doris Alexander (2022, 43) points out, much otherwise quite thoughtful scholarship on *Star Trek* contains minimal discussion of DS9 (e.g., Bernardi 1998) or even excises the series from consideration altogether for fear that it might create complications (Relke 2006; Greven 2009). The disorientation and melancholy that DS9 seems to provoke for some critics recall the sentiments of "omnipotent" being Q (John de Lancie), a notoriously prejudiced and generally irritating *Trek* antagonist who pops up frequently on other series but appears on DS9 only once. Upon meeting Sisko for the first (and last) time, Q challenges him to a boxing match, repeatedly punching the reluctant, patient com-

mander, who finally knocks Q flat on his ass (Lynch 1993b). "You hit me," Q marvels. "Picard never hit me." Amused by the comparison with TNG's beloved captain (Patrick Stewart), Sisko doesn't miss a beat: "I'm not Picard."

The dynamic of either misunderstanding or occluding DS9 has hardly been lost on the people whose labor created it. Eclipsed for the entirety of its original run by "flagship shows" set on mobile spacecraft—*The Next Generation* for its first two seasons and *Voyager* thereafter—DS9 was the franchise's self-conscious "middle child" in the 1990s (Altman and Gross 2016, 469). Writer and executive producer Ira Steven Behr, who is widely credited as the core creative genius behind DS9, says this "forgotten-middle" dynamic enabled greater creative latitude: "If we were going to be the bastards, we were going to be inglorious bastards!" (Altman and Gross 2016, 471). Visitor, likewise, refers to DS9 as the proverbial "black sheep of the family" but links its marginalization with a belated aesthetic vindication. She recalls predicting on set with actor Armin Shimerman (Quark) that in a decade or two, recalcitrant Trekkers would come around: "That's proven to be true; people are discovering it now thanks to streaming. They're rediscovering the show and it's nice to see. *And* the show holds up" (Altman and Gross 2016, 545, original emphasis). Such forecasts have to a significant extent been validated, both by the show's enduring popularity on streaming services and by an excellent retrospective documentary, *What We Left Behind* (Behr and Zappone 2019), codirected by Behr and released on the twenty-fifth anniversary of the series premiere.

But if DS9 has been vindicated aesthetically, this book's central argument is that its prophetic critiques of 1990s U.S. politics, which in many ways deepened the foundations of our current crises, have been vindicated politically, to a degree most scholars and even many fans have yet to appreciate. DS9 still matters because it cut against the grain in the era when U.S. elites feted the putative end of global class struggle and embraced "free" trade, the "War on Crime," *The Bell Curve*, and attacks on queers and the welfare state. As policy makers boasted of a new world order and touted the United States as the "indispensable nation," DS9 reflected back to Americans an unaccountable security state and a "diverse" empire predicated on race and class inequality, and saluted Palestinian and other Indigenous struggles for self-determination and the role of liberation theologies in anticolonial movements. As centrist Democrats sneered that Black and union voters had "nowhere else to go" (Frank 2016), DS9 offered sympathetic portrayals of those criminalized and left behind and hailed unionizing service-sector workers. From the decolonizing Bajoran sector, where many of *Star Trek's* cardinal taboos—prohibitions against money, religion, eugenics, and interpersonal conflict—are not in effect, DS9 mapped the yawning distance between the 1990s United States and Gene Roddenberry's ideal future by presenting audiences with their own contradictions. It did so not as a matter of cynicism—or "realism," as the term is usually glossed by international-relations scholars—but of materialism, in the good old-fashioned Marxist sense. DS9 maps both contradictions and possibilities, speculating about "what we might need to give now" (Brown 2006, 41) for something like Roddenberry's utopian future to come about. Though not without the constitutive flaws one would expect of Hollywood SF, the series teems with what Black studies and religious studies scholar Ashon T. Crawley (2017) calls "otherwise possibilities," which "announce . . . the fact of infinite alternatives to what *is*" (2, original emphasis). In a moment when so many of the proverbial chickens of the 1990s have come home to roost, returning to DS9 might yet help us identify alternatives that remain available to us in the present.

A Different "Trek" gives additional voice, scholarly validation, and coherence to the interpretive possibilities that have made DS9 so attractive to many on the political Left. Consider, for instance, an interview that lawyer and journalist Briahna Joy Gray, who rose to fame as press secretary for democratic socialist Bernie Sanders's 2020 U.S. presidential campaign, gave on the podcast *Black Girl Nerds*. After a conversation spanning socialism, Black voters' frustrations with both major political parties, and a Green New Deal, Gray is invited to identify her favorite *Star Trek* captain. Recounting how her *Trek* tastes matured alongside her political trajectory from liberal to Leftist, Gray explains that her initial idealization of TNG's Picard, the perfect avatar of the Federation's rational Enlightenment liberal humanism, gradually gave way to greater admiration for Sisko. Praising

Sisko's gentle portrayal of Black fatherhood and noting the political challenges he confronted at the Federation's periphery, Gray argues that it is Sisko's "metaphysical, emotive, dreamer side" that made him a figure of radical hope for the Bajorans in their own struggle for decolonization (Black Girl Nerds 2019). Elsewhere, Gray—the Black woman who came damn close to being White House press secretary in a democratic socialist administration—has used DS9's Bajoran allegories to express solidarity with Palestinian human rights and self-determination (Littlefield NYC 2020). For a "dark," "postmodern" spin-off that threatened to disillusion a gaggle of midwestern schoolchildren in 1992, this is no small feat.

Even so, DS9 remains understudied in the academy, its intellectual and political contributions relegated to a minor niche within a fan subculture. As of this writing, scholarship referencing *Star Trek* almost always invokes TOS or the franchise in general (table 1). DS9's immediate predecessor, TNG, is mentioned in over four times as many peer-reviewed academic works, and it has been the subject of several excellent monographs and edited collections dissecting its treatments of gender and race (e.g., R. Roberts 1999; Harrison et al. 1996). VOY, which debuted during DS9's run, also surpasses its academic publication count, and recently saw an edited collection examining its politics of identity and futurity (Lively 2020). Even the more recent *Star Trek: Discovery* (DIS), which is still on the air, saw the release of an edited volume within three years of its premiere, despite the notoriously slow pace of academic publishing (Mittermeier and Spychala 2020).

Table 1. *Star Trek* scholarship by search term

TERM	GOOGLE SCHOLAR HITS (SEPTEMBER 2022)
"Star Trek"	80,900
"Star Trek: The Next Generation"	8,570
"Star Trek: Deep Space Nine"	1,940
"Star Trek: Voyager"	2,830

Source: Created by the author.

So why not *DS9*? Arguably the most politically intricate *Trek* series, its star, Brooks, was until recently the only lead actor in the franchise to hold a graduate degree, and he remains the only one to work as a full-time academic (Rutgers University Alumni Association n.d.). For all the franchise's discourse about the wisdom of Spock and Picard, it is Brooks who regularly invokes the corpuses of artists and intellectuals like Paul Robeson, Chinua Achebe, Octavia Butler, Samuel Delany, and Cornel West (Shatner 2013; Altman and Gross 2016; Bradford 2013). To point out Brooks's credentials is not a matter of elitism. For all his artistic dynamism, Brooks maintains an extremely humble, private persona, giving quite ample credit to *DS9*'s writers and producers and quipping that the work simply helped him to finance his children's education. Rather, noting his artistic and intellectual profile underscores the irony that *DS9*'s intellectual contributions, like *DS9* itself, have largely been either misunderstood or forgotten in its academic reception.

Thankfully, there are some important exceptions. As the first scholarly monograph devoted to a critical analysis of *DS9*, *A Different "Trek"* builds on excellent articles and book chapters, particularly in Black studies, gender and sexuality studies, and human geography. Although the book engages these works in detail in the following chapters, it would be remiss not to highlight the work of SF scholar andré m. carrington (2016), whose landmark study, *Speculative Blackness: The Future of Race in Science Fiction*, dedicates a rich chapter to Sisko, who carrington argues challenges *Star Trek*'s usual allegorical treatment of race by "replac[ing] allegory with history" (161). *A Different "Trek"* would be impossible if not for the examples set by scholars like carrington, Roger A. Sneed, Chanda Prescod-Weinstein, Steven Thrasher, Lisa Doris Alexander, Mark Anthony Neal, Micheal C. Pounds, Allen Kwan, De Witt Douglas Kilgore, Kathy E. Ferguson, Mark Alan Rhodes II, Fiona M. Davidson, Lincoln Geraghty, Gerry Canavan, Crystal Fleming, and others who took *DS9* seriously from the outset.

A Different "Trek" is by no means meant to be the final or comprehensive word on *DS9*. If anything, it is meant to amplify and proliferate ongoing conversations in which Black scholars continue to play a central role. As a white *DS9* scholar, I am mindful of the fact that some stories are not mine to tell, that some choices around legibility are not mine to make (Neal 2013), and that some messages are not decipherable to me (Iton 2008; Snorton 2014). Even so, as we saw in the preface and as Martin Luther King Jr. suggested to Nichelle Nichols, part of what's at stake in *Star Trek* is the political work that representations of Blackness do in the minds of non-Black people. The work of Black studies scholars makes clear that neither the dominant framing of *DS9* as a derivative, postmodern spin-off nor applauding Sisko as uncomplicated evidence of *Star Trek*'s liberal inclusivity does the character or the show justice. Taking cues from these critics, *A Different "Trek"* challenges static, decontextualizing, depoliticizing, and tokenizing views of Sisko and *DS9* and highlights the underappreciated intellectual and political contributions of an actor, a character, and a series whose social critiques and alternative visions have significant ramifications for how all people live.

Cultural Geographies of *DS9*

Interpreting the only *Star Trek* series that is grounded in an allegorical location requires an approach that takes the concept of place seriously. Flouting the boundaries between the humanities and social sciences, cultural geography is a field preoccupied with "how to disclose and respond to a heterogeneous world of differences" (Anderson 2020, 609). Committed to contextualization in space and time, it locates people, places, and things within the power structures and patterns that unevenly make the world. On its best days, cultural geography undertakes this mapping work without losing sight of an example's transformative potential *or* the heft of those power structures and patterns. With abiding commitment to the Marxism that has revolutionized contemporary human geography but careful attention to questions of difference, as well, cultural geography holds in loving, raucous tension the material and the metaphysical, the global and the local, class politics and identity politics, the universal and the particular. Doing justice to the complexity of *DS9*'s narratives, influences, world-building, character development, and aspects of its production history and reception requires taking advantage of cultural geography's intellectual promiscuity, drawing concepts and examples from a wide ambit. But at this book's foundations are core concepts well-known to human geographers: racial capitalism, imperialism, settler colonialism, place, and social reproduction.

This book contends that in its best moments, DS9 returns U.S. audiences to the material contradictions of what the late political theorist and Black studies scholar Cedric J. Robinson ([1983] 2000) called "racial capitalism" (308). Challenging more Eurocentric Marxisms, Robinson argued that racisms, from the early dehumanization of European groups to the transatlantic slave trade to the conquest of the Americas, have been fundamental to the emergence and maintenance of global capitalism. In search of an "ideology of liberation" (317) from racial capitalism, Robinson lifted up what he called Black radical tradition, the cumulative insight built up across the multigenerational long haul of Black freedom struggle. Crucially, this tradition goes beyond "a variant of Western radicalism whose proponents happen to be Black" (C. Robinson [1983] 2000, 73). Although central throughout *A Different "Trek,"* Robinson's critiques enable chapter 1 to illuminate the radical stakes of Brooks's turn as Sisko, analyzing in detail three Sisko-centric episodes that comment incisively on U.S. racial capitalism and imperialism in the twentieth century and beyond.

Robinson was also a tireless internationalist, highlighting the alternatives modeled by anticolonial movements in the Global South. His work emphasized the constitutive links between racism, capitalism, and imperialism at a global scale. Understood as a racialized class project, imperialism describes the maintenance of a global network of territorial and economic colonies via military bases, trade agreements, formal territorial annexation, political interference, dissemination of imperial culture, and other means (Immerwahr [2019] 2020). Imperialism also encompasses the project of settler colonialism, which the late anthropologist Patrick Wolfe (2006) defined as a system "premised on the securing—the obtaining and the securing—of territory" (402) by means of a "logic of elimination," entailing both the "dissolution of native societies" and "a new colonial society on the expropriated land base" (388). Indigenous studies scholar Glen Coulthard

(Yellowknives Dene) argues that racial capitalism requires both the exploitation of working-class labor and the ongoing, murderous accumulation of Indigenous lands (Coulthard 2014; Day 2016). By linking distinct but intertwined forms of racism that have facilitated exploitation and dispossession, globally and locally, over the past several centuries, critiques of racial capitalism, imperialism, and settler colonialism together challenge a facile U.S. liberal nationalism that offers limited, provisional inclusion and recognition to Black, Native, and racialized Americans but does little to dislodge deeper structures of domination and exploitation (Rodríguez 2008; K.-Y. Taylor 2016; Singh 2017; McAlister 2005; A. Davis 2008).

Approaching imperialism, including its settler-colonial dimensions, through this lens throws the core allegorical conflicts in *Star Trek*—between the Cardassians and the Bajorans and between the Federation and the Dominion—into different light. Chapter 2 offers a rare, sustained reading of Bajor's struggle against the Cardassian Occupation as an allegory for the struggles of Indigenous peoples against settler colonialism, with a particular eye toward the Palestinian struggles explicitly hailed by TNG and DS9 creators. Chapter 3 asks whether the strict race and class hierarchy at the foundation of the Dominion's imperialism might allegorize not an enemy of the United States but the U.S. empire itself, particularly its exploitation of poor and racialized military workers. Throughout, the book also questions whether *Trek*'s United Federation of Planets, widely interpreted as a stand-in for the United States, the West, or the United Nations, itself comprises an imperial force; it considers how vaunted images of "diversity"—including *Star Trek*'s famously multicultural Starfleet personnel—can serve as a legitimating tool for empire. Chapter 1 weighs competing interpretations of Sisko as both a "diverse" warmonger and a dissident Black soldier, and chapter 6 evaluates several of the show's queer characters as accomplices to Cardassian and Federation imperialisms.

Reviewing recent scholarship on racial capitalism, Black studies scholar Charisse Burden-Stelly (2020) observes that although many Leftists agree that racism and capitalism are inextricably connected, there remains considerable disagreement as to how, and as to what should be done. For

Burden-Stelly, analytical distinctions like universal/particular and material/cultural-metaphysical can offer the Left clear choices about its possible political directions. Black geographies scholar Katherine McKittrick (2011, 2021) offers an alternative here, modeling an approach that refuses to bracket culture from political economy. Following McKittrick, *A Different "Trek"* turns repeatedly to the work of Jamaican philosopher Sylvia Wynter (1992, 2003; Wynter and McKittrick 2015), who interrogates how parochial cultural European ideas about what constitutes human life have persisted across multiple epochal shifts, with deadly material effects. The book also follows McKittrick's careful readings of the work of geographer Ruth Wilson Gilmore (2002, 2007, 2011, 2015), whose farsighted political-economic analysis of labor, race, state violence, and social movements offers the building blocks for understanding *DS9*'s commentary on the deadly mechanics of U.S. racial capitalism. McKittrick, Wynter, and Gilmore decry unjust structures of knowledge and power, but they also point to the proliferation of alternative visions coming out of social movements—some Black led, some multiracial, both materialist and cultural-metaphysical—for a better world.

Together, these works help chapters 1 and 2 to evaluate what it means for Sisko, a Black man from New Orleans, to stand in for humanity in the eyes of the Bajorans, an allegorical colonized people. In "Emissary," Sisko's crew discovers a wormhole—an artificial, beautiful passage to a distant region of interstellar space—which many Bajorans immediately recognize as the prophesized Celestial Temple, home of the Prophets. Sisko and Kira travel to the wormhole with Kai Opaka (Camille Saviola), the revered leader of Bajor's state religion, to make contact. The Prophets do not experience linear time or corporeal embodiment—for them, being takes place in other genres altogether. Given Bajor's painful, decades-long Occupation by the Cardassians, the Prophets are suspicious of all "linear" beings except Bajorans. At first, this skepticism extends to Sisko. "You have no regard for the consequences of your acts," they tell him (Carson 1993a).

But unlike previous *Trek* captains, Sisko does not try to sell the Prophets on a tidy, teleological narrative of human progress beyond atrocities now safely relegated to the past. Instead, he gradually opens up, inadvertently showing the Prophets his own capacity to dwell ethically with consequences by revealing his ongoing grief at the loss of his wife Jennifer (Felecia M. Bell), who died in a devastating space battle called Wolf 359. This haunting loss cannot help but recall the maritime brutality of the transatlantic slave trade (Pounds 2009; Neal 2013). The Federation's adversary in that battle, the authoritarian Borg collective, abducted Picard, appropriating his military and technical expertise and killing eleven thousand Federation citizens, including Jennifer Sisko. Through the prism of this devastating personal/historical experience, Benjamin Sisko can see what other *Star Trek* protagonists cannot: the complicity of the Federation's high-tech Enlightenment humanism, personified in Picard's brilliance, with the very fascism and imperialism that its exponents repudiate (Reich [1946] 1980; Césaire [1955] 2000).

Sisko's palpable resentment of Picard in "Emissary" led some to worry that it would alienate TNG fans (Jones and Parkin 2003, 180; R. Britt 2022, 217–18). Yet it is Sisko's anger and grief, his "non-linear," nonpathological melancholy, that convinces the Prophets, with their profound care for Bajor, that he can be trusted (Sharpe 2016; Butler 2004). Sisko, for his part, recognizes that the Federation's secularist bias ignores the indispensable place the Prophets hold in Bajor's liberation struggle. Much to everyone's surprise, the Prophets name Sisko their "Emissary" to the world of all linear, corporeal beings, including Bajorans. Where previous *Treks* offered full-throated defense of European liberal humanism, DS9 lies, as Black studies scholar Fred Moten (2018) suggests of the Black radical tradition, "in apposition to enlightenment. Thrown shade, off to the side of its derivative, apposition remixes, expands, distills, and keeps radically faith with the forces its encounters carry, break, and constitute" (41). DS9 is not so much a repudiation of the human altogether as a relentless and hopeful questioning and supplantation of the dominant genres through which it has been imagined (Wynter and McKittrick 2015; McKittrick 2021). Neither a spin-off nor a subset, it offers a vital counterpoint, corrective, and critical intervention in the *Star Trek* franchise and U.S. popular SF (carrington 2016, 160; Canavan 2016).

DS9's radical interventions also raise the question of place, and the role that local conflicts can play in global struggles against racial capitalism, settler colonialism, and empire. Attention to place is, perhaps understandably, dismissed in some corners of the political Left as sentimental, nostalgic, and reactionary (Harvey 1993). Place-based struggles, so the thinking goes, can never hope to defeat global systems of capitalist exploitation that are notoriously wily and adept at producing and taking advantage of differences across space. Challenging this view, the late geographer Doreen Massey (1994) argued that places are dynamic, capable of holding multiple identities and meanings, and defined through their specific material and cultural relationships to other places. Massey's (2005) work resonates with long-standing themes in many Indigenous cosmogonies. The late theologian Vine Deloria Jr. (Standing Rock Sioux) (2003), for instance, linked the priority of time over space in Western thought to the West's outsized role in environmental destruction, and to mass alienation in capitalist societies. These more complex views of place urge careful attention to context as a prerequisite for evaluating the politics of localized political struggles. They enable chapter 2 to affirm the progressive, emancipatory character of Bajoran anticolonial nationalisms and the Prophets' nod to theologies of liberation, and they enable *A Different "Trek"* to evaluate the import of DS9's place-based intervention in *Trek*'s hypermobile spatial epistemologies.

Finally, *A Different "Trek"* attends to the politics of social reproduction in station life. Feminist geographer Cindi Katz (2001) explains that social reproduction entails "daily and long-term reproduction, both of the means of production and the labor power to make them work." It includes both "the acquisition and distribution of the means of existence, including food, shelter, clothing, and health care" and the education needed to reproduce a workforce (711). Often highly feminized and racialized, cultural assumptions about the work of social reproduction are central to its frequent devaluation and privatization—and if all such work were adequately remunerated, capitalism itself would collapse (Hashimoto and Henry 2017). An emphasis on social reproduction enables chapters 4 and 5 to evaluate the significance of DS9's (re)introduction of money (embodied in Ferengi capitalism) and interpersonal conflict (the domestic quarrels of the O'Brien family) to the *Star Trek* universe, in transgression of long-standing franchise taboos against both. Taking cues from the Black socialist feminist reading of systems of oppression as "interlocking" modeled by the Combahee River Collective (1983; see also K.-Y. Taylor 2012), these chapters refuse to bracket *Star Trek*'s allegorical economies, which have long been praised by progressive economists, from critiques of gendered and racialized divisions of labor. Chapters 4, 5, and 6 also challenge single-issue readings of gender, sexuality, and disability in DS9, insisting that race, class, and empire provide formative context for such struggles.

Here a little tour of the station's Promenade, inspired by Massey's (1994) approach to places as the dynamic products of complex geometries of power, illustrates how the book's final chapters bring all these core concepts together. DS9 is, first and foremost, a postcolonial place, a relic of the Cardassian Occupation, reinhabited and repurposed by a new Bajoran and Federation administration. Under the new Bajoran Provisional Government, the Promenade's Bajoran shrine proudly disseminates the Prophets' theologies of liberation. For a time, a free, public, secular Federation school is among the Promenade's other commons spaces.

But DS9 is also a postindustrial place. During the Occupation, the station served as an ore-processing facility and was fueled by brutally exploited Bajoran labor. Under the new Bajoran and Federation administration, its main purpose is no longer manufacturing but the exchange of goods and services. A space of interplanetary contact, the Promenade is home to vendors including a Klingon restaurant, a Vulcan restaurant, a Bajoran restaurant and a smaller Bajoran *jumja* stick stand, and a jewelry store (Memory Alpha n.d.n). Then there is Garak's clothiers, run by the sole Cardassian still on the station, who can, depending on the visitor, fix an inseam on a Starfleet uniform, fashion a beautiful dress, or obtain top secret intelligence information. Finally, of course, there's the Ferengi establishment Quark's Bar, Grill, Gaming House, and Holosuite Arcade, universally known simply as "Quark's." In the wake of the Occupation, the station becomes a destination for an eclectic group of Bajoran and off-world patrons, and for the people who entertain, heal, teach, and serve them.

But in some respects, the station's service economy is less a break from Occupation precedent than a continuation of it, particularly when it comes to the military sex trade. DS9 is, among other things, a base, and as international-relations scholar Cynthia Enloe (2014) cautions, "To analyze any base as if it were simply the sum of its budget, its equipment, its land, its chain of command, its legal basis, and its mission is to seriously underestimate all the power that is used to manage it, all the ideas that are devised to underpin it, and all the policies that are implemented to keep it running smoothly" (173). "Smoothly," Enloe notes, "usually serves to perpetuate patriarchal international relations" (173). Cardassian rule brought cohorts of Bajoran women to the station, forcing them into military sexual servitude. While Bajoran independence ended that odious practice, Quark's gambling facilities—the Ferengi roulette-style games of dabo and tongo, as well as a dartboard—are still tended by tall, buxom hostesses. These workers come from all over, but many are Bajoran war orphans who are often breadwinners for themselves and their surviving kin. Known colloquially as "dabo girls," these workers are tasked with titillating customers, distracting them from just how much money they're losing—with, to use Enloe's terms, smoothing the flow of gold-pressed latinum into the proprietor Quark's eager hands. In everyday station life, the term "dabo girl" circulates variously as a pejorative, a matter-of-fact description, and a reclaimed term of pride. Upstairs at Quark's, the holosuites serve many purposes, but chief among them is as virtual reality brothel. A handful of holographic *Trek* characters elicit considerable sympathy in their quests for recognition as sentient holograms, but the anonymous digital sex workers of the *Star Trek* universe do not fare nearly as well. Chapters 4 and 5 champion other "minor" characters—unionizing service workers at Quark's and the station's schoolteacher, Keiko Ishikawa O'Brien—who remind us that social and cultural struggle, rather than technological "innovation," is key to any prospect of an economically just future.

A Different "Trek" is not primarily concerned with intervening in the theoretical literatures on racial capitalism, social reproduction, or any of the core concepts detailed above themselves. Rather, these concepts facilitate the work of interpretation, opening up what is already present in *DS9*'s world-building, in the hopes of giving cohesion to what others, in and beyond the university, may also notice. Developed, as it was, through the work of teaching first-year undergraduate students who specialize in science and engineering, the book is pedagogical; it aims to provoke *Star Trek* fans who may not share its political attachments, particularly liberals, to further thought. *Star Trek* is often and rightly praised for its inclusive representations, but the concepts introduced here invite a more materialist reckoning with the *Trek* universe, and with our own.

Reading *Star Trek*

The contributions of *A Different "Trek"* to the academy, meanwhile, are twofold. First, it draws on concepts like place and imperialism to make a cultural-geographical intervention in the broader social sciences and humanities scholarship on *Star Trek*. A great many scholars have turned to *Star Trek* as illustrative of core tenets of their disciplines, and given its richness and sheer scope, the *Trek* megatext has obligingly yielded. But much of this scholarship reflects the university's predilection for disciplinarity, its habit of relegating questions of identity to cultural studies, issues of class to economics or sociology, and matters of geopolitics to political science or international relations. Refusing to relegate discussion of race, class, gender, sexuality, and empire to separate intellectual fiefdoms might be de rigueur in some corners of the academy or social movements, but much *Trek* scholarship, like mainstream U.S. political discourse, continues to either divorce class from identity or collapse them into one another, and to sidestep any critique of U.S. empire altogether. Although *A Different "Trek"* does not fully transcend that problem—what book could?—its debts to intellectually capacious fields like Black studies and cultural geography enable it to connect some threads that often remain separate in scholarly literature.

Film scholar Daniel Leonard Bernardi's (1998) landmark study of race in *Trek* films, television, and fandom provides a worthy example. Bernardi persuasively argues that *Trek* gives peoples and cultures of European descent an outsize role in humanity's future. While nonwhite humans unquestionably enter the charmed club of the human, they generally do so by assimilating to white European and American cultural norms and standards. In turn, stereotypes about racialized peoples are often redirected and projected onto extraterrestrials, who come to allegorize racial difference: "aggressive" Klingons, "shifty" Romulans, "greedy" Ferengi, and so on. Bernardi also criticizes U.S. imperialism, from the settler-colonial conquest of Indigenous lands to the use of the colonial "frontier" metaphor in Vietnam, Iraq, and outer space alike. Yet a fuller analysis of imperialism takes a back seat to a liberal nationalist framing preoccupied with "domestic" debates between U.S. neoconservatives and multiculturalists. Bernardi neglects the ways neoconservatives have cynically weaponized multiculturalism, to the detriment of nonwhite military workers and victims of U.S. empire around the world (McAlister 2005; Puar 2007; Melamed 2011; Singh 2017). And although critical of the racialized, uneven geographies of consumer power among Trekkers, Bernardi's critique of capitalism is largely suggested rather than developed.

A cultural-geographical engagement with a work like Bernardi's requires supplementing it with the work of political scientists and economists who praise *Star Trek*'s postscarcity economy (Gonzalez 2015; Ewing 2016; Saadia 2016), geographers and international-relations tracking mutations in *Trek*'s geopolitical allegories (Goulding 1985; Franklin 1994; Dyson 2015; O'Connor 2012; Dittmer 2019; Campbell and Gokcek 2019), and gender studies scholarship examining Starfleet's often frustratingly gendered divisions of responsibility and *Trek*'s queer and trans allegories and representations (R. Roberts 1999; Ferguson 2002; Song and Tan 2020). Many, though not all, of these works are tightly focused on the "proper object" of their discipline, to the exclusion of the others (Butler 1994). There remains considerable value to expertise in disciplinary forms, and this book identifies the fields that form many of the scholars that it cites to highlight opportunities for interdisciplinary dialogue. But *Star Trek* and the world it allegorizes are decidedly interdisciplinary, if not undisciplined (McKittrick 2021). However imperfectly, concepts like social reproduction and racial capitalism and fields like cultural geography and Black studies offer opportunities to bring some of these domains of expertise together.

Alongside its cultural-geographical intervention in more disciplined *Star Trek* scholarship, *A Different "Trek"* intervenes in debates within and beyond geography about the work of affective, emotional, and psychic life in how scholars interpret popular culture (Seitz 2017c; Ruez and Cockayne 2021). What is often most striking in critiques of popular cultural texts is the range of affective positions writers stake out toward their objects of analysis—the feelings they have about those texts and about the texts' other consumers.

Star Trek scholarship provides a case in point. Education scholar Karen Anijar (2000), for instance, performs a scathing, often quite funny exposé, a kind of "gotcha!" ethnography, of educators' reactionary attachments to and uses of *Star Trek* in the southeastern United States in the 1990s. Anijar's subjects laud *Trek*'s family values and find one another through rituals that she compares to those of Gnostic Christians. She argues that "The Federation is a glorious vision of the American dream that never was. That dream is a fantasy. *Star Trek* is another version of the fantasy" (217). Marked by a penchant for debunking and demystification, Anijar's approach masterfully embodies what the late literary theorist Eve Kosofsky Sedgwick (2003) called a "paranoid reading." Sedgwick drew on the work of late psychoanalyst Melanie Klein ([1946] 1975), for whom patients in the "paranoid-schizoid position" starkly bifurcate the world and themselves into hermetically separated, good and bad compartments, refusing any impurity, contamination, synthesis, or surprise. For Sedgwick, paranoia described not a psychological state but a habit of interpretation, one that leaves little room for interruption or transformation. In Anijar's case, the consumption and dissemination of *Star Trek* is almost always an occasion for uncritical, unthinking capitalist, racist, heteropatriarchal, imperialist complicity that demands to be exposed. Anijar's is a richly *contextualist* approach, in that she toggles between the reactionary aspects of the *Trek* text and the reactionary things people do with it.

Anijar's attention to *Star Trek* is so thorough, however, that it is hard not to read her as a kind of fan. Other scholars attempt to stake out an aloof distance, even disavowing the figure of the Trekker to bolster their performance of critical authority. Drama scholar Geraldine Harris (2006), for instance, worries that her readers may find it "bathetic to move from these 'real' and serious issues [postmodernism and globalization] to discussing *Star Trek*" (111) and concludes two dozen pages of close readings of *Trek* with the confession, "I fear I begin to sound like a 'Trekkie'" (135). Heaven forbid! The days when SF was widely dismissed as an unserious and unrigorous object of study are, thankfully, long gone (thanks to forerunners like Sobchack 2001). Scholarly consensus has embraced geographer Barney Warf's (2001) view that "science fiction is no mere plaything, it can be a tool of critical social analysis" (36). But there remains a palpable scholarly contempt for forms of SF that reach popular audiences. Although corners of the academic Left are understandably suspicious of the reactionary, consumerist, jingoistic aspects of majoritarian, middlebrow, and mass culture, such suspicion can also serve as an alibi for unexamined professional-class snobbery. For better and for worse, *Star Trek*'s promises of universalism provide millions of people with "resources for processing difference" (Li 2019, 105). Why snub us?

Still others—particularly some of those most attached to Roddenberry's liberal secular humanism—are remarkably defensive of the franchise, as if admiring *Star Trek*'s radical potential or aesthetic value required stubbornly minimizing its problems with racism or sexism (see also Barrett and Barrett 2017). Political scientist George A. Gonzalez (2015, 2017, 2018), for instance, has produced a series of books praising *Trek* as a near-perfect embodiment of the European Enlightenment, save, perhaps, for its limited environmental commentary. In contrast to Anijar's contextualism, Gonzalez's corpus is a proudly *textualist* one: "I rely almost entirely on the *Star Trek* text to make my argument" (Gonzalez 2015, 15). The presumption here—oddly reminiscent of that of so-called biblical literalists—is that the text of the

Trek "canon," itself quite a contested and heterogenous formation, can speak for itself (see Kotsko 2016).

There is much to admire in Gonzalez's work—in the hope that he wants to hold on to in *Star Trek*'s postcapitalist politics. Yet his work brusquely dismisses readings offered by feminist, antiracist, and anticolonial scholars—many of whom, he neglects to note, are also fans—as "shockingly (or willfully?) ignorant of the Star Trek text" (Gonzalez 2017, 17). Gonzalez defines racism and sexism so narrowly, as matters of individual "bias," that he cannot consider their formative, rather than incidental, roles in capitalist development or the ways they shape *Trek*'s production and consumption. For Gonzalez, the mere fact that nonwhite characters are included is evidence of *Trek*'s antiracist credibility. Not unlike neoliberal multiculturalists, he writes off any substantive critique of the *terms* of the inclusion and representation, perhaps unaware of the critiques made by some *Trek* actors themselves (see Nichols 1994; carrington 2016; Altman and Gross 2016), as "superficial." Such defensiveness misses an opportunity to strengthen Gonzalez's ostensibly Left project. His central claim—that "more than ever, we need to be inspired by the internationalism, optimism, anti-imperialism, anti-fascism, and social justice of *Star Trek*"—is invaluable (2015, 30). Yet the second term in his list—"optimism"—can also be weaponized to eschew the critical reckoning with colonialism and patriarchy needed for the other goals to be realized (see Berlant 2011). We might think of work in Gonzalez's defensive idiom as *itself* a kind of paranoid reading, what Klein called "manic denial," which can tolerate no ambivalence about the object of study upon which it depends (see Alford 1989).

To point out, as many do, that *Star Trek* reprises European and American colonial discourses is not a matter of ignorance, shocking or otherwise, but of open historical record. *Star Trek* did not emerge sui generis from the vacuum of space. Indeed, as geographer Deondre Smiles (Leech Lake band Ojibwe) (2020) reminds us, "outer space is not the first 'final frontier.'" The very emergence of the SF genre was conditioned by the technologies, nationalisms, and economic transformations of nineteenth-century empires, and contemporary mainstream U.S. SF film and television are the contradictory product of Southern California's striated geographies, the lovechild of the military-industrial-academic complex and Hollywood (Csicsery-Ronay 2003; Bahng 2018). Roddenberry, who created TOS and continued to play an important role in the franchise until his passing in 1991, named C. S. Forester's English imperial *Horatio Hornblower* novels and American settler-colonial westerns like the television series *Wagon Train* as his principal sources of inspiration (Rabitsch 2018). Prior to TOS, Roddenberry served as a U.S. Army Air Corps pilot and then as a Los Angeles Police Department officer. He worked as a speechwriter for notoriously racist LAPD chief William H. Parker—a cold, detached man with whom he often clashed. Roddenberry later remarked that it was Parker's infuriatingly hyperrational demeanor that inspired *Star Trek*'s Vulcan Mr. Spock (D. Alexander 1994, 131–32; G. Horne 1995). TOS premiered just a few years after U.S. president John F. Kennedy's moon speech, which positioned the space race with the USSR as the new "frontier" in U.S. expansionist ideology (Slotkin 1992; Bernardi 1998). The word "trek" itself derives from an Afrikaans word for a sojourn into a territory from a settler's point of view (Richards 1997, 36). In 1838 thousands of Dutch-speaking Boer colonists in South Africa embarked on the *Voortrek*, or "Great Trek," packing their wagons and relocating outside the reach of British imperial rule. Chief among the Boers' complaints was the British empire's abolition of slavery, an institution that the Boers wished to preserve (McClintock 1995, 370).

DS9 extends these settler-colonial legacies, with television westerns set in frontier towns, like *Gunsmoke* and *The Rifleman*, and the films of John Ford and Sam Peckinpah chief among the inspirations identified by its creators (Erdmann and Block 2000; Altman and Gross 2016). The show was even branded a "politically correct Western" by *Newsweek* (1993) upon its debut. As the late cultural theorist Stuart Hall (1981) pointed out, the imperialist roots of Euro-American "adventure" stories "have been distanced from us, by our apparently superior wisdom and liberalism. But they still reappear on the television screen" (39).

Given these inheritances, it is to *Star Trek*'s credit that it nevertheless imagined a peaceful future in which Russians, white American settlers,

Africans, and Japanese people harmoniously collaborated, and where both women and men held positions of leadership. The secular Federation had eradicated capitalism and racism, allowing all people to freely share in the abundance enabled by high technology. TOS's Vietnam War allegories gradually shifted from a defense of militaristic theories of the balance of power to a rejection of imperialism (Franklin 1994; O'Connor 2012), and Roddenberry, Takei, Leonard Nimoy, and others involved with the show publicly came out against the war. At a time when the capacity of U.S. liberal democracy to overcome white supremacy and capitalist inequality was under intensified scrutiny at home and abroad (Dudziak [2000] 2011), *Star Trek* proffered an optimistic future that was both recognizably American and distant enough to offer modest immanent critiques of the United States.

Rather than a hopelessly complicit trapping of a reactionary culture or a purely radical, redemptive text, *Star Trek* is perhaps best understood as a contradictory byproduct of the U.S. Cold War liberalism of the 1960s (O'Connor 2012). U.S. political historian Lily Geismer (2014) helpfully defines liberalism in this context as "'not radical,' and especially 'not conservative'" (7). Given this nebulous definition, it is not surprising that U.S. Cold War liberalism spanned an incoherent field of positions. Quick to disavow the Right but reluctant to embrace the Left, Cold War liberals supported labor unions and civil rights within the United States but often hesitated to condemn the anticommunist repression to which many Black and labor radicals were subjected. Cold War liberals opposed the socialism and communism that had helped ignite the radical imagination of racialized peoples struggling for decolonization, at times doing so even when it meant propping up right-wing dictatorships. In the wake of the Cold War, *Star Trek* identified new antagonists in new allegorical story lines (Sharp 1998; Davidson 2017). But its residual Cold War liberalism, articulating multicultural diversity *with* U.S. moral superiority and military primacy, has often persisted (Singh 2017). DS9 has arguably gone further than any other *Trek* installment in questioning the Federation's official myths about itself—and thus, in questioning the pretensions of U.S. empire. But even its critique is far from complete.

A Different "Trek," then, is not just a book about a different *Star Trek* series but a different way of reading and feeling about *Star Trek* as a contradictory product of liberal culture. As an alternative to paranoid readings that either unequivocally expose the complicity of their objects or struggle to defend the purity of those objects at all costs in a state of manic denial (Alford 1989), Sedgwick (2003) proposed what she called "reparative" reading, which asks after "the many ways selves and communities succeed in extracting sustenance from the objects of a culture—even a culture whose avowed desire has often been not to sustain them" (150–51).

The very notion of "reparative" reading often incurs scrutiny from radical scholars and activists, because its name seems to valorize limited, liberal, reformist efforts to rehabilitate toxic structures and attachments rather than transform them (Berlant 2011; Stuelke 2021). But reparation's skeptics would benefit from returning to Klein, whose "depressive" psychic position forms the basis for Sedgwick's reparative reading (Seitz 2017a, 2017c). Far from the "sappy, aestheticizing, defensive, anti-intellectual, or reactionary" motives often attributed to reparative readers (Sedgwick 2003, 150), Klein's depressive position is remarkably levelheaded about the limits of its objects of attachment. Despite its grim name, the depressive position sees something the paranoid position cannot fathom, something that remains latent in some objects of attachment and study—a kind of radical potentiality, what Crawley calls "otherwise possibilities" (2017). As carrington (2016), who also draws on Sedgwick, puts it, "All too often, we [SF critics] misrecognize the viable alternatives that sometimes present themselves to us" (18).

In my view, depressive/reparative attunement to otherwise possibilities aligns well with the role of the antiracist, socialist Left. The so-called reparative turn—the long citation trail of at times politically flaky scholarship invoking Sedgwick's call for reparative reading—has been understandably lamented by some radicals as an incrementalist withdrawal from revolutionary critique and politics (Stuelke 2021). Yet ironically, many of those very same radicals regularly participate in important dialogues on the Left about how to discern "revolutionary" reforms from "reformist" ones

(Gilmore 2007)—work that requires both hardheaded materialist analysis and an affective tolerance for ambivalence and contradiction that is well described by Sedgwick (if not by all of her followers) and especially by Klein. In this sense, depressive/reparative geographies *are* radical geographies, precisely because they map what geographer David Harvey (2000) called "spaces of hope" amid vast and violent contradictions, rather than fatalistically retracing those contradictions or stridently denying their very existence.

To be sure, not every object is worth repairing, particularly when it comes to the objects and implements of racial capitalism and empire. But part of the brilliance of Sedgwick's turn to Klein is that for Klein, the paranoid position and the depressive position aren't polar opposites, and one doesn't progress from one to the other, once and for all. Rather, one toggles between paranoid and depressive positions throughout one's life. Sedgwick (2003) observed that "it is sometimes the most paranoid-tending people who are able to, and need to, develop and disseminate the richest reparative practices" (150). What Sedgwick meant is that one need not discard one's radical politics, nor one's justified paranoia about the violence of racial capitalism and empire, to be capable of depressive, reparative insights. These insights are largely a matter of unexpected interruption, of pleasant surprise. Depressive/reparative reading need not discard a commitment to the project of demystification so core to critical work on SF to also be open to those surprises (see McGeough 2016).

Sedgwick's writing aptly describes the emotional work of studying *Star Trek* from the Left, because the franchise reiterates colonial discourse so routinely that simply exposing that reiteration isn't exactly breaking news. As international-relations scholar Naeem Inayatullah (2003, 74) reflects, "If one expects as I did, that popular culture would more or less faithfully reproduce the hegemonic order, then one can be surprised" (see also Goulding 1985, 88). The project of *A Different "Trek,"* then, is to lift up the moments of good surprise, some of them widely overlooked or misapprehended, when *DS9* interrupts that reproduction and makes bolder and much more critical commentary. These interruptions have everything to do with *DS9*'s emplaced, reflective character, a significant departure from *Trek*'s hypermobile gaze.

I readily concede that no object of analysis inspires love *for everybody*. There are many prospective readers, particularly on the antiracist and anti-imperialist Left, for whom core aspects of *Star Trek*'s problematic premises—a grating American exceptionalist optimism, colonial exploration, military hierarchy, casual depictions of violence, faith in so-called high technology, nods to European Enlightenment humanism, middlebrow aesthetics—or even the mere fact that it is a Hollywood television and film franchise make it a nonstarter. *DS9* both sustains many of these premises and radically challenges them, but this book will almost certainly fail to satisfy radical readers for whom *Star Trek* is a fundamentally bad attachment that can be dismissed out of hand. It may also frustrate fans who resent all things "PC" and want to enjoy *Star Trek* without "politicizing" it. But if you answer to either of those descriptions and have made it this far, you are welcomed, in good faith, to keep going. If the analysis doesn't manage to surprise you, or to meaningfully challenge your assumptions about *Star Trek* or politics at least once, then *DS9* almost certainly will.

Clearly, then, this book is not a formalist reading conversant in the conventions of television and film studies. If anything, its critical but generous orientation toward its object of analysis and its focus on *DS9*'s characters, narrative, and world-building may underwhelm or even vex more highbrow, literary types. Readers most interested in the show's music, set design, costuming, lighting, and sound or in *DS9* fan fiction, cosplay, video games, or comprehensive production history will likewise find little of interest here (see instead excellent works like Erdmann and Block 2000; Altman and Gross 2016; Reeves-Stevens and Reeves-Stevens 1994; Summers 2013; Pearson and Davies 2014). The book does not address these matters in detail, not because they are unimportant, but simply because they are beyond my expertise, and I encourage others to go where I cannot. Likewise, *A Different "Trek"* does not spend much time rehearsing the salient but obvious point that *Star Trek* is lucrative business and Paramount has a decidedly capitalist interest in continuing to make it. Leftists have been finding and exploiting the ironic, unwitting, and camouflaged radical possibilities in the allegories of capitalist mass entertainment since well before the publication of Walter Benjamin's landmark essay "The Work of Art in the Age of Mechanical Reproduction" ([1935] 2007), and this book follows suit (Halberstam 2011).

As a work of cultural-geographical interpretation, *A Different "Trek"* turns to DS9's narratives with both apprehension and curiosity about their potential "to trace relations between people, places, and things as part of a situated practice" of transformation (E. Cameron 2012, 575). Although some suspect that storytelling may well be *wholly disciplined* by power relations" (E. Cameron 2012, 575, original emphasis), cultural theorist Dina Georgis reminds us that "story is also the principle of freedom. In stories, we work out the events that change us. It is our means of becoming and the effect of our creative impulse. In this way, the story can change" (2). Although it engages in historical and geographical contextualizing work and theoretical readings both with and against the grain, an interest in story is at the heart of the research methods used to create this book.

Like queer studies scholar Jack Halberstam (2011), *A Different "Trek"* frequently engages in plot summary, "usually a rejected methodology in literary studies," because understanding what happens in DS9 is "actually a lot harder than it may seem" (59). For the most part, this means reinterpreting many of DS9's 176 episodes and the arcs across them. Although most discussions focus on an episode's primary, or A, plotline, B and C story lines often do much of the most important political world-building in SF (Hassler and Wilcox 1997). If *Star Trek* is, as film scholar Jeffrey A. Weinstock (1996) contends, a kind of ethnographic text, then these "minor" plots often provide the thickest descriptions. Chapters 4 and 5, in particular, turn to secondary story lines, which can serve as a revealing foil for an A story, keep a longer-term plot arc simmering, or provide revealing comic relief. In its tribute to a much-maligned secondary character, Keiko Ishikawa O'Brien, chapter 5 engages in a curated viewing of every episode in which the character appears—a method that can elicit sympathetic identification (Fawaz 2019). In other places, particularly chapters 1 and 6, beginning with story means turning to licensed *Star Trek* novels—both novelizations of television scripts and wholly new works—that extrapolate and extend DS9 into other media. These chapters follow carrington (2016), who argues that such novelizations are wrongly dismissed as derivative and demonstrates their originality and radical political potential (see also Guynes and Canavan 2022).

The entire book also reads the narratives and characters in DS9 episodes vis-à-vis their "intertexts," a term developed by philosophers Julia Kristeva (1980) and Roland Barthes (1977) to describe the web of meanings and texts that precede and inform the act of writing. If *A Different "Trek"* at times appears to privilege the perspectives of the show's writers, the principle of intertextuality complicates that privilege, because it insists that no story is purely original. Because *Star Trek* is notoriously self-referential, the intertexts in question are often other *Trek* installments. Yet making sense of DS9 has also required turning to the non-*Trek* films, novels, televisions programs, and plays that shaped it, principally mid-twentieth-century westerns, SF, and World War II films (Kreitzer 1996). As I wrote this book, John Wayne's menacing yet graceful stride stalked across my living room far more often than it otherwise would have. If I never see the Duke's face again, it'll be too soon. However, the benefit of turning to intertexts is the occasion it offers to ask how DS9 both repeats and transforms old stories—to ask whether, in the reprisal of colonial and imperial histories and encounters, there is any possibility of repetition with a transformative difference (Bhabha [1994] 2012; McKittrick 2021).

Alongside stories—episodic and long-term, of characters and of entire social formations—and the insights and muses of the writers who created them, the book turns to the actors who perform and interpret those tales. Actors, reflects Wallace Shawn, who plays Ferengi Grand Nagus Zek, are like writers in that they are replete with "otherwise possibilities" (Crawley 2017). Actors "understand the infinite vastness hiding inside each human being, the characters not played, the characteristics not revealed. . . . If the play we're watching is an illusion, if the baby who now wears the costume of the hustler in fact had the capacity to become a biologist . . . then the

division of labor, as now practiced, is inherently immoral, and we must somehow learn a different way to share out all the work that needs to be done. The costumes are wrong. They have to be discarded. We have to start out naked again and go from there" (Shawn 2009, 100–101).

Finally, in following Sedgwick's "move toward a sustained *seeking of pleasure* (through the reparative strategies of the depressive position)," this book takes inspiration from the consumptive agency of audiences, especially fans (2003, 137, original emphasis). Fandom is often reduced by outsiders to a freakish, appetitive subculture beset by a narcissistic desire for "relatable" images. But the best of fan and reception studies scholarship makes clear that what a great many fans bring to sf—even the most "mainstream" and middlebrow—is a desire for other possibilities for living (Thomas and Stornaiuolo 2019; Adare 2005; Jenkins 1992; Jenkins and Tulloch 1995; Penley 1997; Pounds 1999; Kanzler 2004). There can be both joy and political value in fans' creative (mis)readings, in making errant, inappropriate, or unexpected connections (Halberstam 2011; Chen 2012; Keeling 2019). Chapter 2 considers what people *do* politically with *Star Trek*, with an eye toward Bajor's allegories for Indigenous decolonization in Palestine and elsewhere. I anticipate and respect that many who created *ds9* may disagree with some or even many of the interpretations that follow in this book. But if, as geographer Jo Sharp (2000) contends, "the 'imagined geographies' created through all sorts of media are central to the geographies used by people when going about their daily lives," then fictive texts are "part of a social process," the effects of which, however patterned, cannot be fully known in advance (333).

Even as many fans relate to *Star Trek* on reactionary terms (Anijar 2000), this is by no means a universalizable claim. Many others offer critical and playful readings, drawing from the best of *Star Trek*'s utopian leanings while tethering them to even more radical futures. These interventions come from the franchise's many internal counternarrators (carrington 2016), from scholars, journalists, and artists active in contemporary political discourse, and from a myriad of Leftist Trekker social media communities. As examples from Rev. Dr. Martin Luther King Jr. to contemporary advocates for democratic socialism, peace, and racial justice like Briahna Joy Gray attest, *Star Trek* is as much about what people use it to imagine—and demand—as it is about the text itself. Chapter 2 highlights the reception and appropriation of *Star Trek*'s Bajoran story line by anticapitalist, antiracist, and anti-imperialist viewers, who often joke about *Star Trek* if it were written by Leftists instead of liberals.

Rather than racist *or* antiracist, then, *Star Trek* is best approached in a depressive/reparative vein, as both racist *and* antiracist, colonial *and* anticolonial, capitalist *and* anticapitalist, patriarchal *and* feminist, heteronormative *and* queer, all at once (Kanzler 2004). It is the specific, conjunctural articulations of these things together that cry out for analysis. DS9 presciently interrogates what it might mean to have queers in the military, a Black commander in chief, noncitizen soldiers, insurgent unionization in a colonial service economy, an "indispensable nation" guilty of war crimes—the contradictions of what literary scholar Chandan Reddy (2011) calls "freedom with violence" that characterize U.S. life. Instead of a project of condemnatory exposure or denialist defense, this book approaches DS9 with geographer Cindy Patton's question to Sedgwick (2003, 123) in mind: "Supposing we were ever so sure of all of those things—what would we know then that we don't already know?" Every time I've thought I had *Star Trek*, and especially DS9, figured out, I've gone back to the show itself, and it has brimmed with a complexity and with "otherwise possibilities" that will always elude capture by academic critique (Crawley 2017). If that complexity has made *A Different "Trek"* a challenging book to write, it has hopefully made the analysis—and the conversations that I hope follow—that much richer.

1   The Radical Sisko

"I'm Exactly Who I Was before the Fact"

In his fantastic performance as the twenty-fourth-century hero Captain Benjamin Sisko, artist and intellectual Avery Brooks drew on considerable experience playing heroes of the past (McKittrick 2017; Iton 2008). Brooks has portrayed the renowned Black American musician, communist activist, lawyer, and athlete Paul Robeson on stage since 1979 (Rhodes 2017, 34).[1] As the first Black person to earn a master of fine arts degree in theater from Rutgers University, Brooks followed in the footsteps of Robeson, who was Rutgers's third Black undergraduate student and first Black football player. Although Robeson endured smears and violent attacks during the McCarthy era and spent the rest of his life in exile and poor health, his legacy as a movement intellectual and an electrifying artist continues to compel the imaginations of people eager for a better world (G. Horne 2016; Rhodes 2016; Redmond 2020).

Thanks to Robeson's family and the efforts of artists and intellectuals like Brooks, Paul Robeson has, since the 1970s, regained a measure of mainstream renown. In the documentary *The Captains Close Up*, even William Shatner (2013), himself no radical Leftist, could ask Brooks about Robeson's impact on his life and work. Brooks explains that he was raised with a keen awareness of histories of Black struggle and an appreciation for the richness of Black cultures. He points to antislavery revolutionaries like Denmark Vesey and Nat Turner and pathbreaking actors like the late Brock Peters, a *Trek* veteran best known for his work in *To Kill a Mockingbird* and *Porgy and Bess* who portrayed Benjamin Sisko's, father, Joseph, on *DS9*. Brooks also credits red-baited activist artists like Paul Robeson and Canada Lee (see M. Smith 2004). Were it not for these forerunners, he speculates, he would not have been on *Star Trek*—or become a world-famous actor at all: "I am not in any way fooled, cajoled, by virtue of *Star Trek* or any other reality, that I am in some other place. I'm exactly who I was before the fact" (Shatner 2013).

Brooks contends that he wouldn't be on *Star Trek* without Robeson, just as in the preface, Nichelle Nichols made clear that she wouldn't have remained on *Star Trek* without Martin Luther King. Given the centrality of Nichols—and her history-making interracial kiss with William Shatner—to the franchise's liberal iconicity, is it not possible that without Nichols, without King's encouragement, there wouldn't have been a *Star Trek* revival at all? Building on these and other reassessments of the centrality of Black creative genius and political struggle to *Star Trek* (see carrington 2016), this chapter argues that Brooks's work as Sisko takes up the intellectual and political legacy of Black freedom struggles in ways that scholars have only begun to fully appreciate. What would we learn if we read *Deep Space Nine* through the lens of King's "Beyond Vietnam" sermon and through the antiracism, anti-capitalism, and anticolonialism of movement artists like Robeson? What if we read Black freedom struggles as an indispensable, if often minimized or domesticated, interlocutor for the *Star Trek* franchise itself?

To be sure, King's insistence in "Beyond Vietnam" on a fuller reckoning with the demands of global and local struggles for decolonization (Inwood and Tyner 2011, 453) is neither the only nor the most radical critique to emerge from Black freedom struggles across the diaspora. In turning to King, this book does not endorse a masculinist, individualistic "great man" theory of social transformation. Even as they persuasively read King as an insightful critic of racial capitalism and empire, Black studies and political science scholars Andrew J. Douglas and Jared A. Loggins (2021) note that King was challenged over the patriarchal assumptions limiting his polit-ical imagination by Black women organizers like Ella Baker and Johnnie Tillmon. Indigenous critics like the late Vine Deloria Jr. (2003) have like-wise noted King's relative silence on settler colonialism. It is by no means sufficient to limit critique to racism, capitalism, and militarism if we do not

The Radical Sisko

consider how closely connected they are to heteropatriarchy and ongoing settler colonialisms, matters central to the chapters that follow.

Nevertheless, King's "Beyond Vietnam" provides an invaluable lens for this chapter. As we have seen, King is *already* a crucial interlocutor for the *Star Trek* franchise. King's thought and legacy, and the movements that made it possible, remain poorly understood and subject to frequent co-optation. Yet his contemporary renown makes the radical, overlooked dimensions of his legacy all the more accessible. King grappled with the limits of mainstream political language, the way that nationalism and liberalism insist on seeing racism, capitalism, and U.S. imperialism as discrete, rather than connected and interdependent social forces. Refusing to stay in his proverbial lane, he recognized that even the limited experiments in multiracial working-class democracy that the U.S. War on Poverty had begun to make possible were being undermined by massive state investment in the war in Vietnam, and by a broader policy of intervention throughout the decolonizing world (King [1967] 2015). Enduring a severely repressive Cold War climate (Burden-Stelly 2020) and widespread condemnation, King nevertheless dared to ask, in faith and in love, "What can I say to the Vietcong or to Castro or to Mao as a faithful minister of this one [Jesus Christ]? Can I threaten them with death or must I not share with them my life?" (2015, 205). As Douglas and Loggins (2021) have argued, King's work evinces an exemplary, original synthesis of the materialist and cultural-metaphysical dimensions of struggles against racial capitalism, articulating together democratic socialist policies of redistribution, Black Christian prophetic fire, a capacious but unsentimental love, and a universalism forged in struggle from below (C. West 2015).

At the heart of this chapter's concerns lie the *geographies* of freedom and justice, in excess of the contradictory promises of the U.S. nation-state. Black studies scholars across a range of disciplines have read Benjamin Sisko's geographies through the lenses of the Middle Passage and the Black diaspora, challenging work that limits a reading of Sisko to a demand for African American inclusion in a domestic, nationalist frame (Pounds 2009; Neal 2013; L. Alexander 2016; carrington 2016; Sneed 2021). This chapter builds on that work by arguing that both Sisko and Brooks direct us to a political analysis explicitly linking struggles against racism, capitalism, and empire, an analysis suggested but not fully developed in scholarship to date. Taking a cue from King's refusal to be disciplined by liberal and U.S. nationalist geographical imaginaries that bracket race from class from empire, this chapter takes up King's interdependent triplets—racism, capitalism, and imperialism—to make sense of three Sisko-centric episodes of *DS9*: "Past Tense, Parts I and II," "Far Beyond the Stars," and "In the Pale Moonlight" (Badiyi 1995; Frakes 1995; Brooks 1998; Lobl 1998). All three episodes are widely beloved, regularly making "best" lists formulated by renowned critics (Couch and McMillan 2016; Bastién 2018a). "Far Beyond the Stars" also tops the lists of many involved with the production of the series, including Brooks himself (Memory Alpha n.d.f).

Yet in popular and scholarly criticism, the three episodes tend to be cast as *respectively* addressing capitalist inequality, usually glossed as poverty or homelessness ("Past Tense"), racism ("Far Beyond the Stars"), and U.S. imperialism ("In the Pale Moonlight"). This chapter complicates such readings, tracing how racial capitalism and American empire reinforce one another in each episode. Concretely, this practice takes the form of what legal theorist Mari Matsuda (1991) calls "asking the other question," or asking "where's the [missing element] in this?"—looking for race and empire in "the class episode," for class and empire in "the race episode," and so on.[2] In some instances, these episodes themselves offer far richer critiques than even many sympathetic interpretations fully recognize. In others, the episodes are better thought of as critical mirrors, reiterating imperialist, capitalist, or racist assumptions in ways that deliberately return audiences to our own contradictions. Let's begin, though, by briefly considering Sisko's geographies.

Musicologist and Black studies scholar Shana Redmond (2020) calls Paul Robeson an "everything man." With the highest esteem for Robeson and Redmond's important book on him, it could be argued that this ingenious label also applies quite well to Brooks's turn as the hero of *DS9*. Captain Benjamin Lafayette Sisko is a great many things to a great many people:

The Radical Sisko

Starfleet officer and commander, politician, chef extraordinaire, religious icon, military tactician, single father, widower, son, Emissary of the Bajoran Prophets, historical figure, lover, musician, comrade, (problematic) fan favorite, friend. Although an ill-fated Romulan senator once remarked upon meeting Sisko, "Somehow, I thought you'd be taller" (Lobl 1998), the protagonist of DS9 (who stands at six feet one, or 1.87 meters) is indeed an epic hero, larger than life. And as Brooks has pointed out, drawing on the work of the eminent late Nigerian writer Chinua Achebe, Sisko came at a time when even seeing a Black actor in a mainstream SF role without prostheses was itself an achievement. "One of the things that attracted me about *Star Trek* was that I did not have prosthetic makeup on my face, that in some way, some 400 years hence, that I would be human, completely human, and brown, too—see? That is a beneficent fiction born out of the imagination of how we can be" (Shatner 2013; see also Gallardo 2013; J. Russell 2013).

Black studies scholars and Black DS9 fans have been quickest to pick up on the stakes of Brooks's work as Sisko. These writers have noted the character's caring portrayal of Black single fatherhood and care for his own widower father (Neal 2013; Bastién 2018b), his middle-class upbringing in New Orleans (Kilgore 2014), his moving treatment of the existential pain of anti-Blackness (Sneed 2021), and his disdain for "postracial" liberal narratives that sanitize Earth's history of racism (L. Alexander 2016). In fine fan form, these readings have been meticulous in their attention to detail, noting Sisko's affinity for African diasporic art (Pounds 2009), love for baseball and especially the Negro Leagues (L. Alexander 2016), flare in preparing New Orleans cuisine from jambalaya to gumbo, and limited but noticeable use of African American Vernacular English (Pounds 2009), which previous *Trek* creators had counseled Black actors to avoid (Shrager 1997). These details matter, not only in the name of "accuracy," but because they speak to what McKittrick (2016) calls "Black livingness"—the dynamic complexity and ordinariness of Black people's lives, in excess of even the best-intentioned academic arguments about oppression and resistance (see Ware 2020). Black critics have praised DS9 for not sanitizing or censoring

Sisko's justified anger (Pounds 2009; Neal 2013; James 2020; but see Kilgore 2014) but lamented that it took so long for him to get a promotion to captain and a ship of his own, as well as the belatedness of his return to the iconic bald head and goatee that Brooks had sported as Hawk in *Spenser: For Hire* and *A Man Called Hawk* (Behr and Zeppone 2019).

Some (Greven 2009, 99; Geraghty 2003) have suggested that Sisko's caring fatherhood reflect a conservative choice to make the hero a respectable, devout patriarch, perhaps as an overcompensation for the demonization of Black families by anti–welfare state discourse.[3] Yet Black studies scholarship compels a different interpretation. Writers like Bastién (2018b) have emphasized the tenderness and vulnerability that characterizes widower Ben Sisko's relationship to his son, Jake (Cirroc Lofton). Following cultural theorist Hortense Spillers (1987) in her contention that a radically different grammar of gender and sexuality is required to understand Black life in the Americas in the wake of slavery, we might read Benjamin Sisko less as a Black copy of white family values than as a complex parental figure, even a "male mother" (Greven 2009), in excess of the white patriarchal frame.

This reading is corroborated by frequent *Trek* actor Tony Todd, who plays a grown-up version of Jake Sisko in season 4's heartrending "The Visitor" (Livingston 1995b). When Captain Sisko is trapped by a mysterious space-time anomaly, Jake dedicates his entire adult life to studying the anomaly to get his father back, sacrificing everything to reverse the event that separated him from his dad. Todd has movingly explained how the memory of his recently departed aunt, the woman who raised him, informed his interpretation of Jake's adoration for his father and dogged determination to rescue him, pointing to a more complex configuration of gender and care in the Siskos' father-son bond (Altman and Gross 2016, 498–99). As Brooks puts it, "All I'm interested in is telling the truth. It's so simple in another way, because I loved Cirroc Lofton [Jake Sisko] then and I love him now. Most of what you witnessed in the exchange between us, and indeed Tony Todd in the assistance, most of what you saw was *real*" (Altman and Gross 2016, 499). The Siskos evince a tenderness between father and son that the McCains, the white settler father-son protagonists

The Radical Sisko

4. Reunited after the tumultuous events of "Emissary," Commander Sisko and his son, Jake, embracing on the Promenade ("Emissary," season 1, episodes 1–2, aired January 3, 1993).

of *DS9*'s key influence, *The Rifleman*, could idealize as the "family values" of frontier masculinity but never fully explore (Sharrett 2005; see Bole 1995a). The bonds between Joseph, Benjamin, and Jake Sisko are also rare for *Trek* characters broadly, and for *Trek* men in particular, who tend to struggle with estrangement from their fathers, brothers, and sons (Sneed 2021).

Black studies scholarship has also offered crucial insight into Sisko's painful transatlantic geographies (Pounds 2009; Neal 2013; carrington 2016; Sneed 2021). Literary scholar Christina Sharpe (2016) writes that for Black people, starting from "the personal" can "illustrate the ways our individual lives are always swept up in the wake produced and determined, though not absolutely, by the afterlives of slavery" (8). When Sisko makes first contact with the Bajoran Prophets, they are immediately struck by his grief over the loss of his wife, Jennifer, in the massacre at Wolf 359 three years earlier. The Prophets remark that Sisko does not experience linear time but

The Radical Sisko

"exists" psychically at the time and place of her death. For popular culture scholar Mark Anthony Neal (2013), Sisko's return to this devastating space battle recalls "the inability of African Americans to distance themselves from the trauma of the transatlantic slave trade" (29). Yet as the modern institution of slavery invented the odious fiction of "black nonpersonhood," McKittrick (2017) observes, that fiction is "coupled with ongoing black struggles to assert and reinvent black humanity as fantastic" (98). Sisko's geographies—Wolf 359 and the Atlantic, New Orleans and Bajor, DS9 and nowhere—are at the heart of his own twenty-fourth-century "struggles to assert and reinvent black humanity" (Pounds 2009; McKittrick 2017, 98).

Sisko's geographies are also informed by Brooks's geographies. The captain's connection to the majority-Black city of New Orleans places him not far from Brooks's family history in Mississippi. The actor's family is storied in its educational, musical, and professional achievements. His parents, tool and die maker and union official Samuel Brooks and music educator Eva Lydia Brooks (née Crawford), left Mississippi for Indiana (Brooks 2002; D. Smith 2006; Ring 2012). Though he was born in Evansville, Indiana, Avery Brooks has credited Gary, home of the Jackson 5 and the 1972 National Black Political Convention, with making him who he is (Brooks 2008). Alongside his work as a tenured theater faculty member at Rutgers, Brooks has served as artistic director for the National Black Arts Festival. His extensive musical, theatrical, film, and television CV includes a reading at a tribute event for the acclaimed Black SF writer Octavia Butler (New York Public Library 2006).

Brooks's musicality is far from incidental to his work as Sisko—and not only because he sings beautifully in several episodes and supervised the music on Shatner's (2011) *Trek* documentary *The Captains*. For the late geographer Clyde Woods (1998), the Mississippi Delta region is home to a "blues epistemology," an aesthetic and political tradition of explanation that "returns the blues back to its roots as a critique of plantation social relations and their extension" (20). Woods argued that the blues epistemology emerges from a participatory and democratic "blues soundscape" made up of heterogenous sounds from people and animals at work and at play, in joy and in pain (288–89). We can hear the blues soundscape in the participatory, relational Black working-class consciousness that inflected Brooks's interventions on the DS9 set. Actors Cirroc Lofton (Shatner 2013) and Nana Visitor (Behr and Zappone 2019) have recounted that Brooks was one of the only people on set to know the names of every single cast and crew member. It must be noted, too, that the melancholic, blues-infused sense of capacious workplace democracy—the defiant, everyday insistence that everyone counts and everyone matters—that Brooks brought to the set was informed in part by pain endured on the Paramount lot itself, as Brooks has recounted being racially profiled by security on his way home from work (see Altman and Gross 2016, 504–5).

The blues also resound in Neal's (2013) observation that the ever-musical Brooks makes virtuosic use of gesture—"grunts, sighs, head nods, and stares become lexicons unto themselves"—in his performances, including on DS9 (22). Captain Kirk was a Starfleet legacy (his father was also a Starfleet captain), and Captain Picard was an archaeologist born to a family of winemakers, suggesting that some forms of property ownership have not entirely disappeared by the twenty-fourth century. But Sisko—whose father is the owner, operator, chef, and principal server at a small restaurant in New Orleans—is the first *Trek* lead for whom his Starfleet posting is approached as a *job*, as opposed to an inheritance or a calling. As will become clear, that job often proves to be a thankless rather than adventuresome one, its difficulty giving rise to both politically admirable heroics and instructively questionable deeds (Kilgore 2014; Meisfjord 2019).

"I'm Trying to *Save Your Life*!"

In 1994, as DS9's third season was filmed, the Republican Party campaigned for and ultimately retook both houses of the U.S. Congress on a reactionary "contract with America." This platform expanded incarceration, further criminalized immigration, and, in the words of the Democratic president who ratified much of the GOP agenda, "ended welfare as we know it." Amid this ominous ascendancy, DS9 aired a two-part episode, "Past Tense," that focused unhesitatingly on the consequences of policies that privatized basic human needs and punished people for the "crimes" of homelessness, joblessness, and, in many cases, simply being Black or Brown (Badiyi 1995; Frakes 1995).

On a routine visit to Earth, the crew of the *Defiant* experiences a transporter accident. Sisko, Bashir, and Jadzia Dax beam down to San Francisco, the capital city of the United Federation of Planets. But instead of 2371, they show up in the San Francisco of 2024, during a grim era in *Trek*'s future history. Bashir and Sisko are violently apprehended by local police and taken to one of the city's many "Sanctuary Districts." But these spaces of "organized abandonment" (Gilmore 2011) are a far cry from the sanctuary policies proposed by migrant justice movements. They are carceral, walled cities-within-the-city that provide, rather inadequately, for the minimal needs of homeless, jobless, and mentally ill people while keeping them out of sight of the city's affluent tech class.

Confessing his unfamiliarity with Earth's ugly "twenty-first-century history," Bashir is appalled by the scale of the unmet need in the district, noting that there is only one doctor to serve a population of ten thousand people in twenty cramped square blocks. Indicting centrist bargains with conservative austerity as much as conservatives themselves, Bashir charges, "Causing people to suffer because you hate them is terrible, but causing people to suffer because you have forgotten how to care? That's really hard to understand" (Badiyi 1995). Sisko, who, like Brooks, knows history very well, explains that many well-intended twenty-first-century Americans simply regarded race and class oppression as intractable, but eventually, organized uprisings within the districts led by a Black resident named Gabriel Bell forced the United States to undertake revolutionary political and economic reforms.

Meanwhile Dax, who had been separated from Sisko and Bashir in transport, is stumbled upon by Chris Brynner (Jim Metzler), a major tech executive akin to a Gates or a Zuckerberg. Brynner is as generous in aiding Dax, whom he labels a "damsel in distress," as he is clueless about the Sanctuary Districts, where Dax quickly surmises Sisko and Bashir have been taken. Although Brynner and his wealthy friends have little empathy for

The Radical Sisko

5. Sisko waiting with others detained in the processing center of San Francisco's Sanctuary District A, confronting the extent of organized abandonment on twenty-first-century Earth (Gilmore 2011) ("Past Tense, Part I," season 3, episode 11, aired January 8, 1995).

district residents or understanding of their city's extreme inequality, Dax manages to use Brynner's communications tech to help Sisko, Bashir, and others organizing in the district to communicate with the outside world.

Back in the district, Sisko and Bashir are rudely inaugurated into a violent, tripartite social structure that divides residents between dependent but respectable "gimmes," violent "ghosts," and mentally ill "dims"—all feasible pejoratives, given extant U.S. grammars of dehumanization. The two try to keep a low profile so as not to alter the course of history, a common consideration in *Trek* time-travel episodes. Nevertheless, they are attacked over a ration card by a predominantly white gang of ghosts led by a man named BC (Frank Military). When a benevolent stranger (John Lendale Bennett) intervenes to break up the fight, an enraged BC stabs and murders him. Horrified, Sisko realizes that the Good Samaritan who has just been killed is, in fact, Gabriel Bell, the history-making Black resident whose work helped abolish the Sanctuary Districts.

Sisko deduces that someone must take Bell's place to ensure that his insurgency and its historical legacy endure. His hunch is confirmed for the audience by the rest of the crew back on the *Defiant*, who notice all around them the disappearance of the United Federation of Planets from history, a change from which they are, curiously, inoculated. Still orbiting Earth in a transformed twenty-fourth century, they search frantically for their missing comrades across Earth's history, struggling to identify when exactly it all went wrong. By the end of Part I, district residents have mobilized and seized the local processing center, taking the staff hostage. In a cliff-hanger ending, Sisko assumes responsibility for having altered historical events, reluctantly posing as Bell himself.

In the second half of "Past Tense," tensions mount between residents and the National Guard over the hostage crisis. At the processing center, Vin (Dick Miller), an older white district security officer who is now among the hostages, antagonizes the insurgents, deriding them as a "bunch of losers" whose efforts are doomed to failure (Frakes 1995). Vin himself complains about the budget cuts and private subcontracting that set the district up to fail residents, yet he struggles to see the utility of a systemic critique. When Vin provokes the trigger-happy BC, who is among the hostage takers, Sisko intervenes, taking Vin aside. "I'm trying to *save your life*," he tells him, "and the lives of every hostage in that room. And mister, you are *not* making it easy. . . . You don't know what *any* of this is about, do you?! You work here, you *see* these people, *every day*, how they *live*, and you just don't get it."

"What do you want me to say?" Vin protests. "That I feel for them? That they got a bad break? What good would it do?"

"It'd be a start!" Sisko retorts.

Sisko challenges Vin to realize that his own fragile interests are in fact far closer to those of district residents than those of the city's glitzy tech elite. His words recall the insights of Black studies scholar Fred Moten (Moten and Harney 2013), who argues that cross-race working-class solidarity can only emerge when whites "recognize that it's fucked up for you, in the

The Radical Sisko

same way that we've already recognized that it's fucked up for us. I don't need your help. I just need you to recognize that this shit is killing you, too, however much more softly, you stupid motherfucker, you know?" (140–41). Moten draws on the example of the late Black Panther organizer Fred Hampton, who refused to write off working-class whites as hopelessly beholden to what the great sociologist W. E. B. Du Bois ([1935] 2021) called the "psychological wages of whiteness." These exchanges reverberate in a moment when prospects for multiracial working-class coalition are too often presumed dead on arrival, when popular proposals for political transformation that would stand to benefit all or most people ("I am trying to *save your life*") are met with cynicism from defenders of the status quo across the political spectrum. Behr has suggested that even the character of BC, the crazed and hateful white murderer of Bell, needs to be understood as a contingent product of an impoverished and racist environment, rather than "inherently a murderer" (Erdmann and Block 2000, 200).

Vin's cynicism contrasts markedly with the perspective of district social worker Lee (Tina Lifford), another of the hostages. That Lee, who is Black, is an especial target of BC's rage speaks to the perverse ways in which white resentment is often disproportionately directed at (real and imagined) Black agents of a downsizing welfare state (K.-Y. Taylor 2016; Haney López 2010). Ironically, Lee, like many Black public sector workers, adamantly opposes austerity, offering a robust structural critique. She confides to Bashir about risking her job to help a woman evade criminalization, allowing her to simply "disappear into the sanctuary." When Bashir insists that "someday there won't be any need for places like" the district, Lee responds immediately, "I hope you're right. Even though it'll mean I'll be out of a job."

At the end of "Past Tense," when the National Guard raids the processing center, Sisko, Dax, and Bashir see to it that Lee, Vin, and the other hostages survive, and that dozens of sanctuary residents can broadcast their indictment of district conditions to a global public. Their actions restore the transformative history that was Gabriel Bell's legacy: abolition of the carceral Sanctuary Districts and a guarantee of full employment to all Americans. Sisko ensures that the legend of Bell lives on, restoring the timeline of Earth's history, without having to sacrifice himself in Bell's place.

Behr has stated that "Past Tense" is in part a nod to the 1971 uprising at New York's Attica Correctional Facility, a highly organized, Black-led multiracial effort against the dehumanizing, racist conditions endured by incarcerated people that ended after brutal, gratuitous state repression (see Rhodes 2017; Camp 2016; O. Burton 2016). The Attica brothers, who took prison guards and other staff as hostages but exercised considerable care to protect their lives, were subjected to grievous distortions by state and media actors, distortions used to justify the uprising's deadly suppression. Perhaps "Past Tense" imagines an alternative ending to the Attica uprising—one in which incarcerated people change history by seizing direct control of their own representation—that remains true to the uprising's abolitionist horizon.

Writers René Echevarria and Behr have also described "Past Tense" as an indictment of big tech's complicity in economic inequality, and as a critique of mainstream SF's faith that "Silicon Valley is going to fix it all" (Raile 2014). Yet while it is set in San Francisco—a city that anthropologist Savannah Shange (2019, 39) appositely calls "gentrification's endgame"—"Past Tense" was conceived in response to the uneven and increasingly carceral geographies of Los Angeles (Dozier 2019). Wolfe, Echevarria, and Behr recall a chilling front-page story in the *Los Angeles Times* that moved them to critically address antihomeless public policy (Erdmann and Block 2000, 197; Rhodes 2017; Greene 2017). The article detailed then mayor Richard Riordan's bid, at the behest of the downtown business community, to "shuttle homeless people to an urban campground on a fenced lot in the city's core industrial area" (Daunt and Nguyen 1994). Noting bipartisan openness to the proposal, the story made clear that such camps would criminalize unhoused sleeping anywhere else in the city.

Perhaps because of its pointed social commentary, "Past Tense" initially elicited little media attention and mixed audience feedback. Some complained that the episode was too "liberal," failing to present "both sides" of the debate on criminalizing homelessness. Behr has made quick work of such critiques (Memory Alpha n.d.m). But in our own historical moment,

The Radical Sisko

so indelibly shaped by Occupy Wall Street, Black Lives Matter, and the uneven geographies of COVID-19, "Past Tense" has enjoyed a more favorable reception. Historian Robert Greene II (2017), for instance, has hailed it as *Trek*'s "most political episode." Indeed, in contemporary Los Angeles, where market analysts found that two thousand more people became homeless with every rent increase of 5 percent *before* COVID-19 began (Zillow 2017), the episode's grim predictions for 2024 feel all too relevant.

Still, even laudatory liberal treatments of "Past Tense" tend to regard it as a case study in homelessness, bracketing homelessness from its root causes in racial capitalism (Lancioni 2010). Even the excellent *What We Left Behind* documentary frames homelessness as a new, postindustrial problem, a claim belied by the much longer history of vagabondage driven by capitalism's contradictions (Behr and Zappone 2019; Lytle Hernández 2017). If anything, as Gonzalez (2015) argues, the episode's dystopian future is prophetic, forecasting predictable consequences of contemporary capitalism's dependence on commodified housing and structural unemployment (39–42, 48). "Past Tense" issues a bold challenge to "a political economy—and landscape—so brutal as to convince us that calling for a pogrom against homeless people is just" (Mitchell 1997, 328).

Yet the episode also reminds us that capitalism is, as Gilmore (2017) puts it, "never not racial" (225). Recall that Dax is stranded outside the district without identification but rapidly greeted as a "damsel in distress." Sisko and Bashir, for their part, wake up in the district at gunpoint, already presumed to be dims. Behr has been clear that he made this decision advisedly: "The simple fact [is] that a beautiful white woman is always going to get much better treatment than two brown-skinned men. That's the reality of life" (Erdmann and Block 2000, 197; Greene 2017; Kilgore 2014). As we approach the actual year 2024, Black Californians, some 6.5 percent of the state's population, comprise nearly 40 percent of its unhoused people (Cimini 2019), and poor and working-class Black and Brown Californians are also leading multiracial coalitions against eviction, market-led housing development, and gentrification (Dozier 2019; *Democracy Now!* 2020). In making Gabriel Bell, a Black homeless activist, a world-historical actor whose actions rupture the smug bourgeois consensus that the poor deserve their fate, "Past Tense" offers a salient critique not simply of homelessness or income inequality but of a racial-capitalist U.S. order.

"Past Tense" also leaves viewers with ethical and political questions about racism, progress, and revolution. When district residents seize the processing center and begin broadcasting their stories, for instance, questions come up about the politics of respectability and innocence, about whose narratives should represent them (Gilmore 2017). At the episode's core, though, lies an especially troubling question: What does it mean that Sisko must re-create the Bell uprising—an event in which Bell sacrificed his own life to save the processing center hostages—in order to ensure the future progress of humanity, including his own existence as a Starfleet commander? For Black studies scholar Frank B. Wilderson III, a key figure in a growing body of thought known as Afropessimism, modernity itself, the founding of white civil society, *necessitates* "Black death" (2010). Wilderson makes powerful arguments about the anti-Black psychic structure of how human subjects come into being in the modern world. From this perspective, DS9's insistence on the historical necessity of Bell's murder as a guarantor of progress for those defined as human would seem to support an Afropessimist reading. This interpretation recalls past critiques of *Star Trek*'s habit of making white American and European linguistic, cultural, and philosophical norms stand in for the human in general, even when casting is multicultural (Bernardi 1998; Kwan 2007).

But a different reading might come through the lens of Wynter (1992), whose work would direct attention not to the narrative *necessity* of Bell's murder under an unchanging anti-Black status quo but to its utter *contingency*, to the need for alternative narrative paradigms. As McKittrick (2011) argues, scholarship about the destruction of Black people and places often recycles "an old story—a linear tale of white survival—even as it struggles against it" (955). For McKittrick (2011) and Wynter (1992), the point of radical scholarship is to contest the apparent naturalness and inevitability of that story. When seen through this lens, the Bell uprising can be understood as a refusal of the putative necessity of Bell's death. "Past Tense" is

The Radical Sisko

about Sisko's efforts to restage not Bell's inevitable demise but his agency as a transformative, world-historical actor, a homeless activist assembling multiracial coalitions of poor and jobless people who refuse to be confined and abandoned. The uprising that abolishes the Sanctuary Districts is a direct outcome of face-to-face mobilization work, without the luxury of high-tech comm badges or other quick technical fixes. In this respect, "Past Tense" provides a far more substantively democratic view of social change than *Star Trek* typically offers (Hassler-Forest 2016; Kotsko 2015). Its narrative evinces less the necessity of Black death than the possibility of what Gilmore (2017), building on Du Bois, calls "abolition geography— how and to what end people make freedom provisionally, imperatively, as they imagine *home* against the disintegrating grind of partition and repartition through which racial capitalism perpetuates the means of its own revalorization" (238, original emphasis).

There remains, finally, a geopolitical quandary to reckon with here. Behr has explicitly linked the events of "Past Tense" to the 1992 mass uprising against impunity for both the brutal police beating of Black motorist Rodney Glen King and the murder of Black teenager Latasha Harlins by a convenience store owner who had falsely accused Harlins of shoplifting (Raile 2014; Stevenson 2015). The 1992 LA uprising is explicitly hailed by Sisko's reference in "Past Tense" to the Bell uprising as "one of the most violent civil disturbances in U.S. history" (Badiyi 1995). Yet the domesticating spatial frame that would locate the Bell or King uprisings within the space of the nation—"*civil* disturbance"—does not do the global stakes, scale, or significance of these uprisings justice. Rodney King's beating at the hands of the LAPD occurred just three days after the end of the first U.S. war on Iraq, a conflict celebrated by neoconservative ideologues as evidence of a revirilized U.S. empire at the helm of a "new world order" (Bush 1991). In an interview with rank-and-file LA cops conducted shortly after the beating, police not only defended the officers involved but compared Rodney King to the recently defeated Iraqi dictator Saddam Hussein (Marc Cooper 1994, 165).[4]

Such a comparison is hardly accidental. The end of the Cold War created new opportunities for democratic social movements to demand a so-called peace dividend, a redistribution of defense funds to meet basic human needs. In this moment, Cedric J. Robinson (1993) observed, the old, linked tools of racism and nationalism yet again took on new utility for an imperial ruling class looking to maintain legitimacy and expand its wealth. As Gilmore (2002) explains, "At the very moment when the nation is basking in foreign victory, the domestic turns hostile" (20). Thus, even if "Past Tense" doesn't always seem like an episode about the contradictions of U.S. empire, the historical conditions it addresses—an economy that puts profits and the global power to secure them over the needs of poor and racialized people—cannot be understood outside of them.

In *Star Trek*'s rendition of history, the Bell uprising intimidates U.S. elites, extracting concessions in the form of "non-reformist reforms" (Gilmore 2007): the abolition of Sanctuary Districts and the reinstatement of full employment (Rhodes 2017). These gains, "Past Tense" suggests, are prerequisites for a twenty-fourth century devoid of capitalist scarcity, racism, and war (Gonzalez 2015, 105). Wolfe explains that imagining the Bell uprising meant asking, "What was the spark? What was the thing that made people think, 'We've got to do better?' And that's what we tried to portray" (quoted in Memory Alpha n.d.m). Yet even after the uprising, *Star Trek*'s twenty-first-century timeline is marred by international conflicts over eugenics and environmental catastrophe that end in nuclear genocide, suggesting that simply sharing the rent that the U.S. empire extracts from the rest of the world is not enough to guarantee peace and economic justice for all people.

The past fifteen years have seen massive U.S. social movements, rooted in longer histories of struggle, that have arisen to confront the intertwined evils of capitalist economic inequality and the racist and classist carceral state. Yet as American studies scholar Manu Karuka (2019) laments, "The antiwar movement remains dormant" (200). Certainly, radical strands of the Movement for Black Lives have made rich transnational connections with activists in Palestine, Brazil, and elsewhere (A. Davis 2015), and Indigenous antipipeline organizers continue to lead the way in Left internationalisms (Estes 2019). But it is striking how little mainstream or even radical political discourse explicitly addresses contemporary U.S. imperialism, from NATO's complex but no doubt conditioning role in Russia's egregious assault on Ukraine to the ongoing Global War on Terror, from the role of U.S. trained soldiers in a growing number of coups d'état in West Africa to the eight hundred U.S. military bases worldwide (Vine 2015). Reflecting on the initial victories of the civil rights movement in the context of an imperial system, Martin Luther King Jr. asked his friend, the musician and activist Harry Belafonte, "Are we integrating into a burning house?" (C. West 2015, xi). The *Star Trek* timeline advises that even after the Bell uprising, the answer might well be yes.

With the lingering question of empire in mind, let's turn to another beloved Sisko-centric episode, "Far Beyond the Stars." Both "Past Tense" and "Far Beyond the Stars" were conceived in critical response to the 1992 LA uprising (Behr and Zappone 2019), and both emerged from the same embryonic episode premise (Erdmann and Block 2000). But if "Past Tense" is usually framed as an episode about the "domestic" problem of homelessness, "Far Beyond the Stars" is received as a "domestic" race episode. Yet those involved in its creation, particularly Brooks, who both starred in and directed it, have much more complex spatial and historical imaginations—imaginations that have yet to be fully accounted for in mainstream or even radical *Trek* criticism.

"What's Wrong with Men from Mars?"

Season 6's "Far Beyond the Stars" presents us with a Captain Sisko who is gravely troubled by matters of war. The Federation is now embroiled in a devastating military conflict with the Dominion, an imperialist power from the other side of the Bajoran wormhole. Facing a mounting death toll, Sisko is exhausted and plagued by doubts about whether to continue his leadership role in the war. The episode takes the form of an extended vision that Sisko receives from the Bajoran Prophets, a vision in which Sisko is a Black American SF writer, Benny Russell, living in New York City in 1953. In *Wizard of Oz*–like fashion, DS9's regular actors are rearranged, each playing different roles in this story within a story.

As a staff writer for the SF magazine *Incredible Tales*, Russell composes an ingenious series of short stories about life on a futuristic space station called *Deep Space Nine*, where the captain is a "Negro." The work is indisputably brilliant and praised by his left-leaning coworkers, particularly his progressive Jewish colleague Herbert Rossoff (Armin Shimerman/Quark). Yet the magazine's conservative editor, Douglas Pabst (René Auberjonois/Odo), resists it. He asks Russell and his white woman coworker, K. C. Hunter (Nana Visitor/Kira), to skip staff picture day, lest their readers learn that not all *Incredible Tales* writers are white men. After this infuriating day at work, Russell is harassed by racist white-ethnic police (Marc Alaimo/Dukat and Jeffrey Combs/Weyoun) who question his claim to artistry.

Russell's restaurateur fiancée, Cassie (Penny Johnson Jerald/Kasidy Yates), and his friend Jimmy (Cirroc Lofton/Jake Sisko), an informal economy worker, counsel him to leave the magazine and become an entrepreneur instead, citing the color line as an intractable barrier for Black artists. Adding pressure to Russell's precarity is the competition he faces for Cassie's affection from Willie Hawkins (Michael Dorn/Worf), a celebrated Major League Baseball player. Something of a ladies' man, Hawkins basks in adulation in the Black world, enjoying solace from the scorn that he endures in the "integrated" white one.

Despite discouragement from his employer, lover, friends, and romantic rival, as well as agents of the state, Russell persists in writing his Deep Space Nine stories. He is urged to carry on—to "walk with the Prophets"—by an enigmatic Harlem street preacher (Brock Peters/Joseph Sisko). Here "Far Beyond the Stars" expressly links the Bajoran Prophets to Black Christianity's prophetic tradition (Sneed 2021), which philosopher Cornel West (1982) describes as "guided by a profound conception and human nature and human history, a persuasive picture of what one is as a person, what one should hope for, and how one ought to act" (16). Russell's Deep Space Nine stories proliferate as he writes in an almost-hallucinatory dream state, and he grows increasingly convinced of the *reality* of Benjamin Sisko. Like the Black surrealist artists of the twentieth century, Russell undergoes a "revolution of the mind . . . unleashing the mind's most creative capacities, catalyzed by participation in struggles for change" (Kelley 2002, 191).

For a brief moment, things finally seem to be going well. One of Russell's Sisko stories is provisionally accepted. But as Russell and Cassie celebrate, their friend Jimmy—played by Lofton, who normally portrays Sisko's son Jake—is murdered in cold blood by the same racist police who harassed Russell earlier. In outrage and grief, Russell confronts the police, who do not hesitate to beat him within an inch of his life. After a long and incomplete recovery, Russell returns to the office, only to find that his Deep Space Nine story, and the entire issue of *Incredible Tales*, has been pulped by the magazine's white publisher.

Russell confronts his editor, resigning from the magazine. Addressing the entire staff of *Incredible Tales*, he continues to insist on the viability of his vision: "You can deny me all you want, but you can't deny Ben Sisko. He *exists*! That future, that space station, all those people—they exist in here! In my mind. I created it. And every one of you *knew* it. You *read* it. It's here. Do you hear what I'm telling you? *You can pulp a story, but you cannot destroy an idea.* Don't you understand? That's ancient knowledge— you cannot destroy an idea. *That future—I created it, and it's real!* Don't you understand? *It is real.* I created it. *And it's real! It's real!*" (Brooks 1998, original emphasis). Heartbroken, incensed, and worn out, Russell collapses, only to wake up in an ambulance that appears to be hurtling through interstellar space. The street preacher again appears and proudly congratulates Russell/Sisko for having "kept the faith," counseling, "You are the dreamer, and the dream." Sisko wakes up in a medical bed on DS9, his father, son, and lover Kasidy Yates (Jerald) at his side. He resolves to keep on fighting the Dominion, wondering whether Benny Russell is the dream or he is.

Repeat viewing of "Far Beyond the Stars" can leave one overwhelmed at how much is contained in a mere forty-five minutes of television. It is, in a word, profound, and it remains difficult to watch without tearing up

6. Both the dreamer and the dream, Sisko glimpsing Benny Russell returning his gaze in an office window ("Far Beyond the Stars," season 6, episode 13, aired February 11, 1998).

multiple times. So it is entirely appropriate that "Far Beyond the Stars" is among the most discussed DS9 episodes. Many involved with the series' production point to the episode as their favorite. Brooks has remarked that if anything, it should have been a two-parter (Erdmann and Block 2000, 537).

The dominant reception of "Far Beyond the Stars" tends to approach it through questions of state racism and the inclusion of Black people in American society, particularly in SF (Canavan 2014; Delany 1998). When scholars quote Brooks regarding "Far Beyond the Stars" (e.g., Rhodes 2017; Sneed 2021), they often refer to his comments on the persistence of racism as a psychological and cultural force: "If we changed the people's clothes, this could be about right now. . . . What's insidious about racism is that it is unconscious. Even among these very bright and enlightened characters . . . it's perfectly reasonable to coexist with someone like Pabst. It's in the culture, it's the way people think" (Erdmann and Block 2000, 536). Part of the brilliance of Brooks's approach to directing "Far Beyond the Stars"

is this focus on the quotidian ways that unconscious racism surfaces, even among consciously enlightened people.

Black religious studies scholar Roger A. Sneed (2021) is exemplary in his attention to the episode's emotional force, describing the cathartic experience of repeat viewing of the episode. Sneed finds in "Far Beyond the Stars" a balm in an anti-Black society that alternately ignores and spectacularizes Black suffering but rarely takes it seriously. He argues that the episode provides speculative departure points for theologies of Black pain and healing. A key phrase from the episode, "the dreamer and the dream," even inspires the title of Sneed's important recent book on the religious dimensions of Black SF. Although writing on the resonances of "Far Beyond the Stars" for Black audiences in grief exceeds my evaluative purview as a white scholar, *A Different "Trek"* is deeply indebted to the already quite rich discourse on this episode.

However, even this important work does not exhaust what "Far Beyond the Stars" teaches us about the geographies of racial capitalism, empire, and incipient alternatives. At stake here is a reading that will challenge *Star Trek*'s large non-Black liberal audience. A long line of scholars, from Sharpe (2016) to Frantz Fanon ([1952] 2008) to Saidiya Hartman (1997), have disputed the adequacy of a politics focused on non-Black recognition of Black pain, urging scrutiny of the political terms and conditions of recognition. Indeed, many comfortable non-Black liberals are all too ready to fathom Black suffering in the context of a literary salon but reticent to countenance the financial and psychological hit entailed in political transformations, from reparations to prison abolition to Medicare for All, that might begin to ameliorate that suffering.

"Far Beyond the Stars" surely exposes anti-Blackness as a persistent psychological force. But the episode also directs audiences to the contingent—and contested—political-economic and geopolitical dimensions of anti-Blackness. Just pages before his reflection on the psychology of racism, Brooks situates Benny Russell's suffering in space and time: "The people we saw in that office each had a very specific identity. I wanted to see who those people were, in order to investigate one of the most oppressive times of the twentieth century. They were living with McCarthyism and the atomic bomb and the Red Scare. . . . I mean, that was a *very* interesting period" (Erdmann and Block 2000, 534, original emphasis).

Brooks takes care to contextualize Russell's rage and grief, locating it in the everyday life of an ascendant but embattled racial-capitalist U.S. empire in the early days of the Cold War. It is surely not lost on Brooks that the events of "Far Beyond the Stars" take place just two years before the Bandung Conference in Indonesia, which launched the Non-Aligned Movement and gave hope to colonized people all over the world—a conference the U.S. government blocked both Robeson and Du Bois from attending. Brooks knows precisely how brutally Cold War repression came to bear on generations of Black and Leftist organizers, intellectuals, and artists, including Robeson himself (Burden-Stelly 2020; G. Horne 2016). "A *very* interesting period," indeed. Brooks is not simply asking for Black pain to be fathomed, then. He is also suggesting that such pain is a product of histories of racial capitalism and empire that must be reckoned with and might finally be transformed.

Consider, too, the scrutiny to which Herbert Rossoff, Russell's Jewish coworker, is subjected for speaking up in Russell's defense. When *Incredible Tales* editor Pabst dismisses Russell's story as implausible, unmarketable, and liable to "cause a race riot," Rossoff vituperates him as a "craven fascist." Pabst doesn't hesitate: "Herb's been angry ever since Joseph Stalin died" (Brooks 1998). But if both men land insults, it is Pabst, the employer, who is in the position to intimidate Rossoff, blunting the possibility of Black-Jewish solidarity by drawing on a vast anti-Semitic repertoire of meanings that associate Jewish people with international socialism.[5]

We might also note the contested political economy of the world "Far Beyond the Stars" presents, particularly the race- and gender-differentiated pay rates among *Incredible Tales* writers. Hunter, a white woman, and Julius Eaton (Alexander Siddig/Bashir), a brown-skinned British American man, each make two cents a word, but Rossoff, an Ashkenazi Jewish man, makes four cents. Russell negotiates three cents a word for his Sisko stories—provided he rewrites them as a dream—but three cents a word

The Radical Sisko

is presented as something of a high-water mark, suggesting that his usual rate might well be two cents, if not one. The pay rate for Albert Macklin (Colm Meaney/Miles O'Brien)—a white man who writes popular, politically uncontroversial stories about robots—is never revealed at all.

Pulping the month's issue of *Incredible Tales*, then, is not only a matter of exclusion from representation or deprivation of recognition—as important as those things are. It is also, and relatedly, a matter of dehumanizing deprivation of economic livelihood. As Brooks explains in a panel discussion with Black artists, educators, and art dealers: "It is difficult for anyone who calls themself 'artist' in this part of the world to stay alive, to keep the lights on, hmm? To hold a family, hmm? To do all the things that everybody does. People wanna fix potholes before they will buy art" (Brooks 2008). Both "Far Beyond the Stars" and Brooks thus speak not to the psychology of racism in some political-economic vacuum but also to the extractive, devaluing, and contested political economy of Black art making under (and in excess of) racial capitalism.

Finally, we might heed Russell's reply when his stories are dismissed as unmarketable: "What about W. E. B. Du Bois, Zora Neale Hurston, Langston Hughes, Ralph Ellison, Richard Wright? Did you ever hear of *Native Son*?" (Brooks 1998). Several of the writers whom Russell lists committed to antiracist, anti-imperialist, and anticapitalist political analysis and organizing, even at great personal cost. Du Bois and Wright, two of the three writers examined in Cedric J. Robinson's ([1983] 2000) field-changing study of the Black radical tradition, grappled centrally with racism's simultaneously psychological *and* political-economic dimensions. In the current moment, when corporate-diversity trainers tout best-selling paperbacks to help well-intentioned white people purify themselves of the moral stain of their psychological racism, Benny Russell continues to offer the beginnings of a vital alternative reading list.

Black studies scholars have also thoughtfully expounded on the diasporic geographies and political consciousness of "Far Beyond the Stars"—the ways it exceeds a framing as a "domestic" race episode. carrington (2016), for instance, has examined SF writer Steven Barnes's (1998) superlative novelization of the episode. Although it is common for *Trek* episodes to be adapted to the novel form with franchise authorization, such works are often dismissed as derivative. Challenging this view, carrington argues for Barnes's novel as an original work that reinterprets and transforms the television script (177–79; see also Baetens 2005; Guynes and Canavan 2022). In Barnes's narrative, Russell encounters a Bajoran Orb, used to contact the Prophets, at the 1940 New York World's Fair. The Orb, described as an artifact of the Dogon people, presents Russell with a vision of transhistorical continuity between Russell, Sisko, "ancestors struggling through slavery and the Middle Passage," and an ancient encounter in West Africa with an "injured pilot," presumably a Bajoran, who brings the Orb to the Dogon (carrington 2016, 189).

Barnes's novel contests *Star Trek*'s official narrative of "first contact" between humans and extraterrestrials. The dominant story (Frakes 1996) privileges the technological prowess of a white North American man, Zefram Cochrane, whose invention of a faster-than-light engine in 2063 attracts the attention of the benevolent, rational Vulcans and precipitates an era of unity and interplanetary cooperation. But Barnes points to an earlier encounter, between the Bajorans and the Dogon, two peoples with rich religious traditions and long histories of struggle against colonialism. Here it is African diasporic people who stand in for humanity as a whole, shattering a nationalist frame that can only understand Benjamin Sisko or Benny Russell as excluded African Americans. Achieving racial inclusion, on the narrow terms delimited by liberal U.S. multicultural nationalism, West (1982) argues, "would be better than the current dismal [situation], but it can hardly be viewed as Black liberation" (112). The Black radical imagination, historian Robin D. G. Kelley (2002) explains, demands "revolutionary transformation" that is "inextricably linked to the struggles of colonized people around the world" (62–63).

Breaking the domesticating frame of nationalism also helps us to remember that "Far Beyond the Stars" is an episode about war. In Sisko's vision, the Bajoran Prophets turn to Black freedom struggles to allegorize the Federation-Dominion war, suggesting that Dominion imperialism is of a piece with U.S. white supremacy, in the hopes of motivating Sisko to keep up the fight. This book examines the allegorical meanings of Bajoran decolonization and the Dominion War in the following two chapters. What is of utmost significance here, however, is that Benny Russell, like Captain Sisko, is a war-weary Black American veteran.

Few have noted the place of the U.S. Navy in Benny Russell's backstory, a detail mentioned only once in both the episode and Barnes's book (for brilliant exceptions, see carrington 2016, 166; Kilgore 2014, 42). But considering Russell's trajectory from sailor to SF writer provides crucial global context for his (geo)political expectations. When the United States reinstated a military draft in 1940, many Black Americans of Russell's generation were justifiably skeptical. In the brutal Red Summer of 1919, Black veterans returning from Europe and migrants to the urban North had endured (and fought back against) widespread white race riots and massacres (Woods 1998). With the historic abuse of Black veterans in mind, Black socialist labor and civil rights leader A. Philip Randolph called for a 1941 March on Washington to demand the integration of military and defense industry work, a serious threat to a president seeking to broker unity as war loomed (Greer 2019, 53–55). Ordinary Black people resisted the mandate to fight and work for a country that denied them full humanity, remaining delinquent in draft registration in significant numbers (Kelley 1996, 172). Barnes's Russell, reflecting on his upbringing in Harlem, recounts attending speeches by Randolph, Du Bois, and the great Pan-Africanist Marcus Garvey (Barnes 1998, 91). Given his milieu, Russell would have almost certainly participated in debates about how to approach a war against fascism abroad, given the ugly reality of Jim Crow capitalism at home.

Neither the script nor the novelization of "Far Beyond the Stars" says much about Russell's time in the navy, where Black sailors faced a segregated division of labor, relegated to manual and service jobs, until 1944 (Martin 2010). But a brief exchange between Benny and Cassie in both texts in 1953 intimates that he began writing SF—"amateur stuff"—nearly fifteen years prior, in the late 1930s or early 1940s, while serving (Brooks 1998; Barnes 1998). At the beginning of Sisko's first extended vision as Russell, his interest in SF is met skeptically by a newspaper vendor (Aron Eisenberg/Nog), who prefers World War II films like *From Here to Eternity*. "What's wrong with men from Mars?" Russell jocularly protests. He listens, both amused and uninterested, as the vendor gushes about Burt Lancaster's celluloid military heroics, and then silently hands the vendor a coin. Given Russell's experiences, is it not politically instructive that he would be more intrigued by "men from Mars" than by reliving the wartime dramas of a white movie star? If not as openly seditious as draft resisters, we must take seriously Benny Russell's everyday, creative, "amateurish" distractedness from harsh manual labor, his proneness to speculative fabulation, his susceptibility to dreams of "otherwise possibilities" (Crawley 2017), including dreams of Black self-determination in the twenty-fourth century.

That Russell pursued his creative dreams more fully upon the end of the war, then, must be understood as a defiant Black geopolitical act. World War II left the racially diverse working-class people whose labor fueled the war machine proud to have defeated fascism, but angry and full of questions about alternative collective purposes to which their efforts might yet be directed (Gilmore 1998; Loyd 2014). As the buildup of the U.S. war machine became permanent with the onset of the Cold War, these buzzing questions coalesced into the fabulous swarms of postwar social movements, and as historian Kimberley Phillips Boehm (2012) points out, "Black veterans became the 'foot soldiers' of the civil rights movement" (13). By reprising this history, "Far Beyond the Stars" at once critiques the whiteness of postwar SF and posits a continuity between the fictitious Benny Russell and other veterans turned SF writers, including Roddenberry, a U.S. Army Air Force veteran who became a vocal supporter of the civil rights and antiwar movements (O'Connor 2012; carrington 2016).

The radical import of "Far Beyond the Stars," then, encompasses Black demands for representation, empathy, and inclusion, as well as an urgently needed critique of racist police violence. But as vital as all those things are, the episode's message also exceeds them. We must take seriously that Black navy veteran Benny Russell could dream of "otherwise possibilities" (Crawley 2017), of "something else" amid demeaned, dangerous work on navy vessels—that upon discharge from the ascendant U.S. war machine,

with all its technical prowess and coordinated might, Russell would dauntlessly pursue alternatives, refusing common sense at every turn. It is telling, too, that Russell continued to heed the Prophetic words of a radical Black preacher, well after doing so was inconvenient for him—a marked contrast to the U.S. presidential legacy that the Sisko character also presciently anticipated (Kilgore 2014).

"How Do You Make This Palatable?"

If "Far Beyond the Stars" reprises the history of Black freedom struggles on Earth to shore up Sisko's resolve to fight the Dominion, "In the Pale Moonlight," which aired just over two months later, depicts a war-weary captain in crisis once again. The episode takes the form of a personal log entry by a troubled Sisko (Lobl 1998), a confession relaying unethical choices made from apparent desperation through a series of flashbacks. Sisko's story begins with the posting of yet another casualty list. Commiserating over the war's mounting Federation death toll, Dax and Bashir point out that many Dominion sneak attacks come from Romulan territory, a violation that the Romulan Star Empire appears willing to overlook. Sisko sees an opportunity, and he begins speculating about bringing the Romulans into the Federation's war against the Dominion. Dax counsels that for such an effort to succeed, Sisko would need hard evidence of nefarious Dominion intentions toward the Romulans.

The task of producing such evidence—or fabricating it—brings Sisko to Garak (Andrew J. Robinson), who, as a "former" Cardassian spy, "specializes in gaining access to places he's not welcome" (Lobl 1998). Garak warns the good captain that it "may be a very messy, very bloody business. Are you prepared for that?" Sisko insists that he is. Intrigued by Sisko's resolve, Garak agrees to help. But achieving their goal proves difficult, requiring Sisko to commit a series of unethical acts: bribery, forgery, selling key ingredients in biological weapons, lying to a Romulan senator to his face. Finally, he becomes an accessory to multiple murders at Garak's hands.

When he receives the news that even after all these crimes, their schemes may well fail, a furious Sisko locates Garak and begins wrathfully beating

7. Sisko sardonically toasting the Federation's new alliance with the Romulans against the Dominion, just before deleting his confession about the conspiracy to create that alliance ("In the Pale Moonlight," season 6, episode 19, aired April 15, 1998).

him. Garak implores Sisko to let up, insisting he has carefully manipulated events to ensure that the Romulans will join the war as Federation allies. In his work for Sisko, Garak acts as an enabling, invisible subordinate located outside the law, to whom illegal state violence can be conveniently outsourced (Agamben 2005). Sisko's guilty conscience, Garak advises, is a miniscule price to pay for the security of their entire region of the galaxy (Lobl 1998). Garak's plan works. The news should assuage and vindicate Sisko, but it only seems to make him feel worse. Enumerating his transgressions, Sisko concludes that, "most damning of all . . . I think I can live with it." He then orders his computer to strike the entire log entry from the record.

As we saw in the preface, Martin Luther King Jr. urged Nichelle Nichols to remain on *Star Trek* at the very moment that he began to publicly denounce

The Radical Sisko

the U.S. war in Vietnam. *Star Trek*'s history of Black representation, then, is intimately linked to the antiwar dimensions of Black freedom struggles. "In the Pale Moonlight" extends and complicates these links, reprising the 1964 Gulf of Tonkin incident—in which the Lyndon Johnson administration fabricated a military confrontation to justify escalating U.S. military presence in Vietnam—to examine the dilemmas facing a Black military and political leader (Erdmann and Block 2000, 556–57). If the dominant reception, however problematic, of DS9 frames it as a "dark" show, then "In the Pale Moonlight" holds status as the "darkest"—and best-loved— episode of them all. Erdmann and Block (2000) grant that "the episode comes close to breaking most of *Star Trek*'s rules" (555), but they are equally quick to note that it topped a *Sci-Fi Entertainment* magazine survey as fans' favorite. Many people centrally involved in the episode understood it as a direct critique of U.S. foreign policy.[6] Andrew J. Robinson (2019), who portrays Garak, argues that it exemplifies DS9's unique willingness to dispel the myth of American innocence.

Given the episode's popularity and consequential themes, scholarly discussion of it remains remarkably sparing. At the time of this writing, both "Past Tense" and "Far Beyond the Stars" have received over three times the scholarly coverage as "In the Pale Moonlight." The episode does receive some insightful engagement from political scientist Stephen Benedict Dyson (2015) and literary scholar Michael Barba (2010), as well as briefer discussion elsewhere (e.g., Kwan 2007; Kathke 2020). Lisa Doris Alexander's (2016) important article about Sisko's connections to Black history includes a gorgeous image from "In the Pale Moonlight," but does not examine the episode's narrative. And although "Past Tense" and "Far Beyond the Stars" are showcased in the recent DS9 documentary (Behr and Zappone 2019), "In the Pale Moonlight" is only alluded to, and even then, only for its camp factor (but see Volk-Weiss 2022). It would seem that the Benjamin Sisko at the center of a moving story of a Black writer's struggle for representation (as "Far Beyond the Stars" is usually glossed) has garnered far more academic attention than the Benjamin Sisko who outsources empire's dirty work to a network of spies and criminals.

Table 2. *DS9* scholarship by search term

TERM	GOOGLE SCHOLAR HITS (SEPTEMBER 2022)
"Far Beyond the Stars" + "Deep Space Nine"	92
"Past Tense" + "Deep Space Nine"	96
"In the Pale Moonlight" + "Deep Space Nine"	28

Source: Created by the author.

Perhaps the uneven academic reception of these equally acclaimed episodes reveals something about what American studies scholar Melanie McAlister (2005) calls "military multiculturalism"—a U.S. nationalism that celebrates a superficial rendition of diversity in a domestic frame but either shies away from critiques of empire or points to America's diverse polity and military personnel, their purported resemblance to the world, as evidence of empire's legitimacy (see Melamed 2011; Singh 2017). Among contemporary U.S. liberals—and most U.S. professors are better described as liberals than Leftists—feelings of affection and pride for a person of color, a white woman, or a white gay man in a position of structural power can ignite hope for a better future. At the same time, the very presence of such "diverse" personnel is routinely cited to blunt critiques of the systems built on racism, capitalist inequality, and heteropatriarchy over which those personnel preside (K.-Y. Taylor 2016; Rodríguez 2008).

On the optimistic side, Kilgore (2014) suggests that the Bajoran Prophets' turn to Captain Sisko as a figure of renewal offers us a prescient model for understanding the hope surrounding Barack Obama's first presidential campaign (45). Journalist Briahna Joy Gray puts the matter even more strongly, mentioning a close friend's claim that "without Benjamin Sisko, Barack Obama wouldn't have been president!" (Black Girl Nerds 2019). Whatever the limits of "Black faces in high places" (K.-Y. Taylor 2016), these writers credit images like Sisko's with helping make the very idea of a Black U.S. president, once unimaginable, more possible. But what about the military multiculturalism's more cynical underside—the side that instrumentalizes diversity as an alibi for imperialism? What resources might "In the Pale Moonlight" provide for a critical appraisal of the disappointing continuities, the violences that have endured, across cultural touchstones and U.S. presidential administrations (Seitz 2017b)?

We can glean some answers to this question from the film that Behr has said provided the episode's formal model: John Ford's (1962) western *The Man Who Shot Liberty Valance* (Erdmann and Block 2000, 558). Like "In the Pale Moonlight," *Liberty Valance* is a flashback. The film's narrative is a story told by Senator Ransom Stoddard (Jimmy Stewart) at the funeral of cowboy Tom Doniphon (John Wayne), his erstwhile friend and rival. The two men represent different class positions and waves of white settlement in the fictionalized western town of Shinbone. Both vie for the love of Hallie (Vera Miles) but share an enemy in the gangster Liberty Valance (Lee Marvin). In their final confrontation, Stoddard appears to shoot and kill Valance, only later learning that it was Doniphon, hidden out of sight, whose gun took him down. Crucially, Doniphon tells Stoddard "the truth" in a flashback *within* the film's longer flashback narrative, meaning the entire rendition of events is only told from Stoddard's point of view. With Doniphon's reluctant blessing—"I can live with it"—Stoddard converts his unearned celebrity as "the man who shot Liberty Valance" into a political career. As Doniphon retreats into obscurity and disappointment, Stoddard marries Hallie and has a very conventionally successful life, but he remains haunted by his debt to Doniphon.

Film scholar Abigail Horne (2012) emphasizes that *Liberty Valance*'s story depends on hidden Black and Native labor, notably that of "the man who tosses Tom the gun in the first place: Pompey, played by Woody Strode" (6). Strode—a Black, Niitsitapi (Blackfeet), Cherokee, and Muscogee (Creek) actor, model, and athlete with roots in New Orleans—portrayed Doniphon's valet. Behr (Erdmann and Block 2000, 558) says he wanted to put Sisko in Doniphon's shoes in "In the Pale Moonlight." But what could it mean to position Sisko, a Black man with a deep connection to New Orleans and to the Bajoran decolonization struggle, as heir not to Woody Strode's valet but to John Wayne's cowboy? Certainly, that Sisko is a Black protagonist, a captain rather than a domestic laborer, is progress by numerous important measures. But might the role of captain, cowboy, or president in a racial-capitalist and imperial society come with some baggage of its own?

Although John Wayne died in 1979, historian Garry Wills (1997) contends that the actor remains one of the most significant figures in U.S. culture and, perhaps especially, in U.S. politics. While the western has lost its twentieth-century perch as the U.S. film genre par excellence, both the western and Wayne, its greatest star, continue to loom large in the minds of generations of Americans, particularly but not only whites. Well after his death and well into *DS9*'s run, Wayne regularly ranked within the top ten American movie stars in polls. Wills contends that Wayne's personal characteristics alone do not explain this persistence. Rather, Wayne stood in for a set of values and myths—"misleading truths . . . but important ones" (26)—at the heart of U.S. settler colonialism and imperialism: "a politics of gender (masculine), ideology (patriotism), character (self-reliance), and responsibility" (Wills 1997, 29).

What, then, might it mean for Sisko to inherit such misleading but important truths? Brooks (2008) is especially fond of Paul Robeson's insight that "an artist's responsibility is to his people." Perhaps one of the many ways that Brooks lives up to this Robesonian responsibility to his people and to all people is to critically reflect, as Sisko, the contradictions and limitations of "diverse" leadership, of representation, within systems and institutions that remain imperialist and racial-capitalist. Reflecting on his work in "In the Pale Moonlight," Brooks suggests, "When we talked about this darker thing, or people have referred to *Deep Space Nine* as this darker thing, in my mind it resembles us. The writers were making a left turn for me [in this episode]. How do you make this palatable? How do you make this comfortable, especially for a man who doesn't want to be here in this situation?" (Altman and Gross 2016, 524–25).

If the Sisko character anticipates the Obama presidency, as Gray and Kilgore have suggested, then "In the Pale Moonlight" cautions that in U.S. politics, as in SF, colonial cowboy inheritances persist with a vengeance. Though not all have cited Wayne as explicitly as Richard Nixon and Ronald Reagan, all U.S. presidents are evaluated against the John Wayne ideal.

The Radical Sisko

Obama himself unfavorably compared Donald Trump to Wayne, belittling his successor's unmanly irresponsibility (Jeffrey Goldberg 2020). Obama, for his part, was accused by opinion makers both of "killing John Wayne" and "going John Wayne" (Reuters 2012; Dixon 2012). Wayne and Obama are also linked by references to Geronimo, the Chiricahua Apache leader and U.S. political prisoner. Another Ford film, *Stagecoach* (1939), positions Geronimo as a fearsome threat to John Wayne's character, while the U.S. military under Obama used the codename "Geronimo" in assassinating Osama bin Laden, extending a long history of metaphors of indigeneity in imperial warfare, from Tomahawk missiles to Apache helicopters (Singh 2017; Tuck and Yang 2012).

For Obama to "go John Wayne," then, continued a war against "Natives," on and off screen, both inside and at the frontiers of the U.S. empire. And Obama's administration did indeed "go John Wayne," expanding a two-front War on Terror to a seven-front one, keeping the prison at Guantanamo Bay open, and dramatically expanding the prosecution of journalists and whistleblowers. The point here is not to cast disproportionate aspersion on Obama but to follow the lead of Keeanga-Yamahtta Taylor (2017), Angela Davis (2008), Cornel West (2017), and others who have cautioned against liberal idealization of "diverse" U.S. leadership as necessarily offering a substantive break in continuity from imperial statecraft. As critical ethnic studies scholar Dylan Rodríguez (2008) sagely warned at the moment of Obama's ascendancy, dominant U.S. institutions can reproduce racial-capitalist and imperial social relations, regardless of the identities of the personnel at their helm or the hope that many invest in projects of representation.

But what might it mean, alternatively, to read "In the Pale Moonlight" as elaborating the contradictory positioning of ordinary Black soldiers, rather than military and political elites? Black studies scholar Khary Polk (2020) observes that Black soldiers and military workers have been central to the history and growth of the U.S. empire, "at turns resistant and compliant" participants in that project (12). If we recall that Starfleet is, for Sisko, a job, and if we read him as a stand-in for the Black rank and file, then Sisko's unsettled conscience, his agonized ambivalence, might mirror the real misgivings of generations of Black soldiers, including Benny Russell from "Far Beyond the Stars." In this light, Brooks's remark that Sisko "doesn't want to be here in this situation" might articulate not a protestation of bumbling American imperial innocence but the material and ethical dilemmas faced by the poor and racialized communities that are targeted for military recruitment and presented with few other options.[7] Historians Boehm (2012) and Judy Tzu-Chun Wu (2013) have demonstrated that disillusioned Black veterans and members of the foreign service have often played an outsized role in movements for economic and racial justice and in antiwar movements. Read in this light, it is perhaps fitting that DS9's finale delinks Sisko's fate from the Federation altogether, (re)uniting him with the Bajoran Prophets and Bajor's struggle for decolonization. We might also turn to *Hollow Men*, a remarkable original *Trek* novel by the noted SF author Una McCormack (2005), which expands on the events of DS9, imagining the immediate aftermath of "In the Pale Moonlight" (see carrington 2016, 177–79). McCormack's text envisages possibilities for democratic accountability for Sisko, including a belated confession to the higher-ups at Starfleet and a confrontation between Sisko, Garak, and antiwar protestors on Earth. Rather than a bad-faith confession that remains out of sight, then, Sisko's "guilty conscience" might itself be a starting point for political alternatives.

Finally, it must be asked whether Sisko is an entirely reliable narrator in "In the Pale Moonlight," much as film scholars have questioned Stoddard's reliability in *Liberty Valance* (Hale 2017; Nazarian 2018; A. Horne 2012). Both Inayatullah (2003) and literary scholar Marion Gymnich (2005) encourage skepticism of the stories that Federation political actors tell their extraterrestrial interlocutors, their crewmates, and themselves via narrative devices like the captain's log. Fans have long wondered whether Dax, Bashir, Worf, Garak, Quark, or some combination thereof manipulated Sisko into a conspiracy to bring the Romulans into the war (JackityJackson 2019). In previous scripts for the episode, Dax suggests forging evidence herself, unaware that Sisko is already doing so (Memory Alpha n.d.m). Such speculations and alternative renditions compellingly map complicity among a wider network of beloved characters who are cast in Sisko's version of events as innocent, if at times coy. If "In the Pale Moonlight" functions as a critical mirror, then Sisko's complicity in war crimes at once reflects, conceals, and intertwines with the crew's and the audience's own complicity. The same can be said of any U.S. president, white or Black, and U.S. citizenry. In a society with at least a veneer of liberal democracy, citizens bear a collective responsibility for what is done in our name, and although such complicity is surely unevenly distributed, it is nevertheless diffuse.

Literary scholar Cynthia Nazarian (2018) argues that the somber, funerary ending of *Liberty Valance* "might be interpreted not as private mourning, but as political failure" (220). Sisko's insistent repetition that he "can live with" the Federation's political and moral failures and his own likewise signals an unease, both individual and collective, that could once more give way to conviction and action against empire. The history of the cross-race, cross-class movement against the Vietnam War and the unprecedented mass demonstrations against the second U.S. invasion of Iraq suggest that a critical recognition and reckoning with complicity—coming together to declare, "Not in Our Name!"—remains possible. As Brooks puts it, "We miss the mark when we ask the film and television industries to do what we cannot do ourselves" (Logan [1994] 1995, 124).

This chapter began with the insistence that King's intertwined, giant, evil triplets—racism, capitalism, and imperialism—could help us to appreciate the political salience of Captain Sisko as both a critic and a critical mirror of these destructive forces. Black studies critics of *DS9* have been among the few to underscore the ethical and political significance of Sisko's diasporic geographies, which exceed the U.S. nation-state even as they critically address the ongoing anti-Black violence at its foundations. These scholars attend with great care to the critical links between the Black human freedom struggle and Bajoran decolonization in *DS9*, a matter taken up in the following chapter. Sisko's pursuits challenge any rendering of racism as discrete from capitalism as discrete from imperialism, despite the critical tendency to bracket these concerns from one another. Building on this work, reading it, engaging it, and making geographical connections via

King's triplets attests both to the genius of DS9's writing, and above all, of Brooks's interpretation.

Far more than just a diverse "first" or the star of a postmodern spin-off, the radical Sisko attests to DS9's willingness to linger in difficult and indispensable places that other *Trek* series tend to run away from at warp speed. At once rebel against "organized abandonment" (Gilmore 2011), dissident artist who dreams of "something else" (Loyd 2014), and complicit warrior whose moral failures unevenly implicate us all, Sisko conjures "otherwise possibilities" by at once inspiring and discomfiting (Crawley 2017), thus embodying and extending both the materialist and the Prophetic dimensions of Black freedom struggles (Sneed 2021).

The Radical Sisko

2 Cardassian Settler Colonialism and the Bajoran Struggle for Decolonization

"Lessons We Don't Ever Seem to Learn"

Among the most frequent gripes made about the early years of DS9 was that the show literally never went anywhere. Deprived of a starship for its first two seasons, the "peacekeeping" Federation crew were tasked with better understanding and managing the social relations between the newly independent Bajorans, their recently ousted Cardassian oppressors, and the peoples on the other side of the Bajoran wormhole. DS9's geographies departed from *Star Trek*'s default spatial modality of whizzing from planet to planet, problem to problem, long-term consequences be damned.

For some audiences, the minutiae of local Bajoran politics—the afterlives of the Cardassian Occupation, matters of decolonization, truth and reconciliation, reparations, reconstruction, and debates on resource extraction and Federation membership—were simply boring. Nana Visitor, who plays DS9's principal Bajoran, generously observes that "there's a hard-core group of people out there who are interested in Bajor and then there's a lot that aren't" (Erdmann and Block 2000, 256). Perhaps audiences accustomed to more hyperrational interlocutors—Vulcans or androids—were disappointed to be presented with people whose problems seemed so cannily terrestrial. Or perhaps the glib "whatever" ethos of neoliberal 1990s U.S. culture simply rendered many indifferent to DS9's intricate Bajoran political world-building. In any case, when market research indicated low levels of audience interest in Bajor, Echevarria recalls that creators had to resort to defying studios, sneaking in Bajoran political content when they could get away with it (Erdmann and Block 2000, 97).

DS9's attention to Bajoran politics also meant examining the complexities of Bajoran religion, which is prominent from *Trek*'s very first encounter with Bajorans, the noted *TNG* episode "Ensign Ro." Over repeated objections from her superior officers, Ro Laren (Michelle Forbes), the first Bajoran in Starfleet, defiantly integrates Bajoran earrings, an important component of her religious practice, into her Federation uniform, offering a clear allegorical rebuke to gendered Islamophobic anxieties about veiling (Landau 1991b; Yeğenoğlu 1998).

Yet *TNG* could comfortably "accommodate" Ro, the only Bajoran on board, while maintaining the Federation's premise of cosmopolitan secularism. While ship-based *Trek* series could catalog the religious particularities of various extraterrestrials only to leave them behind, a place-based program could not. On *DS9*, Bajorans and non-Bajorans alike consult the Prophets through prayer, scriptures, and a set of Orbs—sacred objects that facilitate visions. The Prophets even engage in acts of direct intervention, imploring Sisko to postpone Bajor's entry to the Federation and causing a massive incoming invasion fleet to simply disappear. Neither Bajor's post-Occupation trajectory nor the development of primary characters like Kira and Sisko make sense absent the Prophets.

The centrality of Bajoran religion comprised a major intervention in the *Trek* universe, as religion had been among the Federation's cardinal prohibitions. Literary scholar Michèle Barrett and writer Duncan Barrett (2017) posit that in *DS9*, a "rebellion against [*Trek* creator] Gene Roddenberry's secular spirit has triumphed" (201). Although Roddenberry's humanism evinced a playfulness and a generosity of spirit (American Humanist Association 1991) that can be hard to come by among contemporary New Atheists hell-bent on demonizing Islam, the Barretts are no doubt correct (but see Porter and McLaren 1999).

Fans and scholars continue to debate both the allegorical meanings and the normative rightness of *DS9*'s Bajoran plot arc. Who are the Bajorans—with their history of oppression and religiously inflected liberation struggle—meant to represent? What does the answer to that question say, in turn, about the Cardassians, the Bajorans' primary oppressors? Or about

Cardassian Settler Colonialism

the Federation, with its designs on both peacekeeping and integrating Bajor into its secular polity? Is *DS9*'s unprecedented exploration of religious story lines a bad thing for the franchise—a tragic abandonment of Roddenberry's "secular spirit" and a grim concession to a perceived reassertion of religion in global political life since the 1960s (e.g., Dyson 2015; Gonzalez 2018; Decker 2016)? Or might this turn offer a welcome acknowledgment of the role of religion in global movements for a planet liberated from war, racism, and exploitation—the very ideals that Roddenberry and many Trekkers have cherished?

If nothing else, this chapter outs me as part of Visitor's "hard-core group of people out there who are interested in Bajor." Although critics have produced numerous scholarly tributes to Visitor's Kira Nerys (Oglesbee 2004; Nussbaum 2008; Seitz 2017c), this chapter grounds Kira in her broader allegorical geography, making her our primary interlocutor for Bajor's anticolonial politics and political theologies. Departing from Eurocentric (Kapell 2000) and Orientalist (Richards 1997) readings of the Bajoran-Cardassian conflict dominant in *Trek* scholarship, it argues that *DS9*'s Bajoran story lines offer a sympathetic allegorical treatment of Indigenous challenges to settler colonialism, including, but not only, struggles for Palestinian self-determination. Although creators' decisions to cast predominantly white actors to play Bajoran roles must be problematized, there remains much to learn from reading *DS9* allegorically and affectively, for "partial and incomplete metaphors" (Gonzalez 2015, 60; see Georgis 2013, 5–6). Bajor's arc elaborates a coherent critique of Cardassian Occupation as settler colonialism and an affirmative depiction of the place of religion in anticolonial freedom struggles, while also raising questions about the Federation's "soft" imperialism.

Against pathologizing readings of Bajoran religion as reactionary religious nationalism or a "clash of civilizations," this chapter reads Kira and the Prophets as reminders that there can be capacious and emancipatory as well as conservative articulations of religion and place. Kira is a "particularist" in that she remains fiercely committed to Bajor, to religious orthodoxy, and to the principle of anticolonialism throughout *DS9*. Yet through encounters with what psychoanalytic theorist Deborah Britzman (1998) calls "difficult knowledge," Kira's heart and communities of solidarity grow tremendously, making her a salutary example of what cultural theorist Ramzi Fawaz (2019) refers to as particularism "with a heart for the universal."

As *DS9* begins, the Bajoran Resistance has ended the Cardassian Occupation, which caused between five million and fifteen million premature Bajoran deaths and polluted Bajor's soil through voracious extractivism (Gilmore 2002). The Occupation has also triggered a massive refugee crisis, such that Bajorans are introduced in *TNG* as a stateless, diasporic people (Landau 1991b). With Bajor and Cardassia still technically at war, the Federation establishes a small "peacekeeping" military presence in the sector at the request of Bajor's Provisional Government. Yet this government does not command legitimacy with all Resistance factions, which have heterogeneous geographical, political-economic, and ideological bases.

Much of *DS9* is concerned with working through the psychic, political, and economic legacies of Occupation. Much to its credit, the program's careful pacing depicts the work of reconstruction and the working through of historical trauma as a repetitive and gradual process fraught with contestation and full of painful revelation and belated insight. The Deep Space Nine station itself is a legacy of the Occupation. Built by coerced Bajoran labor as an ore-processing facility and operated under the Cardassian name Terok Nor, the station served as the military capital of Cardassia's Bajoran colonies and has only recently been repurposed as a Bajoran and Federation base. In "Civil Defense," the crew accidentally triggers an old alarm system designed to destroy the station rather than allow it to fall under control of insurgent Bajoran workers (Badiyi 1994). In "Necessary Evil," security chief Odo, the only station official to work under both Cardassian and Bajoran-Federation administrations, reopens a murder investigation he conducted during the Occupation. Odo realizes that his initial inquiry incorrectly exonerated Kira, who had carried out an assassination for the Resistance (Conway 1993b).

Cardassian Settler Colonialism

Given the Occupation's centrality to DS9, fans have long pressed TNG and DS9 writers and producers regarding which histories it allegorizes. When asked, writers typically refuse to specify any one reference point. Listing events in the Yugoslav region, South Africa, Haiti, Vietnam, the Russian Federation, Germany, Iran, and Black communities in the United States, creators imbue the conflict with a kaleidoscopic arbitrariness (Memory Alpha n.d.f).

But a 1994 exchange revealed something decidedly less arbitrary. Asked pointedly whether Bajor and Cardassia were comparable to Palestinians and Israelis, Piller joked that the writers "could take a day to answer" the question:

> If you go back to the beginning, when we were creating the issue of why the Federation was coming here and the franchise, that would create the continuing storylines that Bajorans would provide us, we saw in it, certainly, parallels to the Palestinians. We saw parallels to the Israeli formation. We saw parallels to the American Indians. We used our feelings, our knowledge of those events, and the troubles that seem—many of them are, unfortunately, lessons we don't ever seem to learn, we keep doing the same thing to people over and over again, in different places in different ways. But some of the lessons can be explored. And by giving it a little distance—by calling it Bajor instead of pick any of the ones that I've just said—you have an opportunity to look at it a little more objectively than you would if you were trying to tell somebody about Israel or the Palestinians or the American Indians. (Museum of Television and Radio 1994)

Piller's sophisticated remarks link the experiences of two peoples (Palestinians and Native Americans) and one historical event ("the Israeli formation") as the primary referents for the "feelings," "knowledge," and "troubles" that the Cardassian Occupation and its aftermath represent. Palestinians, Jews, and Native Americans have all endured vicious racial hatreds and catastrophic, genocidal violences. But as philosopher Judith Butler (2012) and progressive Jewish-led groups like Jewish Voice for Peace (2017) have insisted, "Israeli" and "Jewish" are not interchangeable or reducible to one another: many Israeli citizens are not Jewish, most Jewish people reside outside Israel, and Jewish people have a range of views on Israeli politics. Piller's specific choice of words—"the Israeli formation"—recalls long histories of devastating anti-Semitic violence, centrally including the Holocaust of six million Jews, which impelled millions of Jews to move to Israel, among other places. But it also invokes a specific political event, the 1948 creation of the state of Israel, which simultaneously caused the *nakba*, or forced expulsion of half of Palestine's prewar Arab population.

By establishing these particular links—between Palestinian and Native American experience and Israeli politics—Piller suggested that the Cardassian Occupation entails a process of *settler colonialism*. Education scholars Eve Tuck (Unangax̂) and K. Wayne Yang distinguish settler colonialism from other forms of colonialism, describing a process of "homemaking that insists on settler sovereignty over all things in their new domain" (2012, 5). The late anthropologist Patrick Wolfe (2006) explained that settler colonialism is a particular form of genocide, organized around a logic of replacing and eliminating Indigenous populations through a range of means, from cultural assimilation to forced resettlement to open mass killing. Although settler colonialism was first developed by Europeans, these scholars argue that it has in some instances been adopted by non-European societies as well. It is settler colonialism that links all three referents that Piller named, from the European conquest and homesteading of the Americas, to Hitler's admiring citation of the U.S. Indian reservation system, to the egregious living conditions in the Gaza Strip and Israeli settlements on Palestinian territory in contravention of international law. These are difficult links to make—not because they lack empirical evidence but because they implicate U.S. and Israeli audiences in profoundly uncomfortable, often politically unpopular ways, presenting us with "lessons we don't ever seem to learn." By turning to allegory, Piller suggested, perhaps the lessons of ethical cohabitation might finally begin to stick (Butler 2012).

Readings of the Bajorans as stand-ins for Jewish experiences of the Holocaust have been well developed in existing criticism, notably by the anthropologist and historian Matthew Wilhelm Kapell (2000). There is ample reason to make this link, as *DS9* is rich in intertextual references to film, literary, and philosophical responses to the Holocaust. In season 1's "Duet," among the very finest episodes in the series, Kira meets Aamin Marritza (Harris Yulin), a retired Cardassian military file clerk who is racked with guilt over his mundane complicity in the Bajoran genocide (Conway 1993a). (Evincing the colonial predilection for bureaucracy, Garak later dubiously brags that Cardassians taught the Bajorans how to keep records [Bole 1993].) Undergoing years of plastic surgery, Marritza poses as Cardassian Gul Darheel, the notorious overseer of a brutal labor camp, hoping that he will be tried and convicted in a Bajoran war-crimes tribunal and publicly embarrass the Cardassian Empire. As Kira uncovers Marritza's plan, she is moved by his willingness to sacrifice himself to bring the empire to shame for its atrocities. "Duet" reinterprets both Robert Shaw's play *The Man in the Glass Booth* (Shaw 1968), in which a Jewish Holocaust survivor is falsely accused of being a Nazi war criminal, and philosopher Hannah Arendt's ([1963] 1994) *Eichmann in Jerusalem* (Altman and Gross 2016, 461), which reports on the Israeli war-crimes trial of Nazi bureaucrat Adolf Eichmann.[1] The episode also begins a long arc in Kira's encounters—at times political alliances and even friendships—with Cardassian dissidents opposed to the Occupation.

Critics across a broad spectrum of political opinion have also acknowledged Bajor's allusions to the struggles of Indigenous peoples in general and to Palestinians in particular (e.g., Pounds 2009; Black 2020). Even the *New York Times*, hardly a bastion of the anticolonial Left, has compared Bajor to Palestine (Pareles 1996). Yet all of these acknowledgements are fleeting, suggested rather than developed, in contrast to Kapell's thoughtful article, which makes Bajor's Holocaust allegory its principal focus.[2] Worse still, some are clouded by a kind of Orientalist fog, obfuscating Bajor as "a place much like the Middle East, a place full of old peoples nursing ancient enmities. There the Cardassians and the Bajorans have a long-standing history of conflict, and the space station is frequently a place of intrigue and subterfuge" (Richards 1997, 189). As the late literary critic Edward W. Said (1993) and many others have demonstrated, the discourse of the

Middle East as beset by "ancient enmities" radically mystifies and decontextualizes conflicts that are in fact rooted in modern political history, rather than "ancient" religious hatreds—nuances abundantly reflected in *DS9*'s allegorical world-building as well.

This chapter asks what more we might learn when we read Bajor with an eye toward events beyond Europe in a focused, deliberate manner. There is no doubt a profound singularity, a horrifying specificity, to the Holocaust, to what the Third Reich did to Jewish people at such a massive scale. But to acknowledge an event's horrifying *singularity* does not require that one render it *exceptional*, a tendency present in Kapell's and other *DS9* criticism. As the late Martinican French politician and artist Aimé Césaire ([1955] 2000) famously argued, the racial thinking and practices of social control at work in Europe's capitalist imperialism, its genocides in the Americas and the Congo, among other places, laid the foundations for the Holocaust (36). Césaire's aim was not to minimize the horror of the Holocaust but to interrogate the racist, capitalist, and anti-Semitic geographies of the human that made it possible.

Césaire's observation compels people who oppose anti-Semitism and all forms of racism to concern ourselves with the *global* geographies of racial violence. His insight beseeches all of us, as Angela Davis (2015) asserts, to say "never again" to the European fascism behind the Holocaust, *and* to the racial capitalism and settler colonialism behind U.S. and South African apartheid regimes, *and* "to expand and deepen our solidarity with the people of Palestine" (60). What would it mean for *Star Trek* criticism to do the same—to privilege the struggles of Palestinians, Native Americans, and all colonized peoples as allegorical referents?

*

Given this chapter's critique of Cardassian imperialism, some may wonder why it does not dedicate more time to the Maquis Rebellion central to nineties *Trek*. In *TNG*, the Federation signs a peace treaty redrawing the Cardassian-Federation border, uprooting millions. The Maquis—a name drawn from the World War II French Resistance—are ex-Federation citizens

Cardassian Settler Colonialism

who remain on the "wrong" side of the new border rather than relinquish their homes. The Federation collaborates with the Cardassians to stop them.

Certainly, the Maquis oppose Cardassian imperialism. They comprise an inspiringly multiracial ("multispecies") social formation, including humans, Bolians, Vulcans, and Klingons (Sturgis 2013, 135). Many Bajorans are sympathetic to the Maquis, with whom they share a common enemy. Ensign Ro even joins (Stewart 1994). Geographer Fiona M. Davidson (2017) sees in the Maquis parallels to struggles in Palestine, Kurdistan, and other places abandoned or harmed by "great" foreign powers (see also Reeves-Stevens and Reeves-Stevens 1994).

Another plausible, sympathetic reading of the Maquis might consider their resonance with the Abraham Lincoln Brigade, a multiracial group of Americans who defied an isolationist U.S. government to defend Spain from German- and Italian-backed fascists in the 1930s (Kelley 1996; Featherstone 2012). Black Brigadiers and supporters, including Paul Robeson (G. Horne 2016), saw in European fascism the same colonial and racial-capitalist ideology that oppressed them in the United States, and sought to prevent it from spreading. The U.S. government opposed the Brigade, and the FBI spied on Brigadiers. Perhaps the Maquis resemble the Brigade in that they are proverbial canaries in the coal mine, rising up against the Cardassian Empire even when their own governments will not. Although many Maquis defend their homes from an arbitrary border, many others join out of ideological sympathy with the anti-imperialist cause. Like those proverbial canaries, the Maquis turn out to be prescient; the Cardassians become major Federation antagonists once more.

By this reading, Captain Sisko's lover, Captain Kasidy Yates (Penny Johnson Jerald) of the freighter *Xhosa*, might well be a latter-day Salaria Kea, a celebrated Black American nurse in the Lincoln Brigade (Kelley 1996; Featherstone 2012). "For the Cause" (Conway 1996) reveals that Yates is violating Federation law to engage in acts of solidarity and mutual aid, using the *Xhosa* (itself likely a reference to the antiapartheid struggle) to smuggle medical supplies to Maquis communities. Jerald is superb in her role as a conflicted Yates, in love with Sisko but committed to Maquis solidarity.

She keeps her Federation boyfriend guessing about her motivations and whereabouts. Yates spends six months in a Federation penal colony for her activities, rekindling her romance with Sisko upon her release. In her study of Black migrant women's lives in the early twentieth-century United States, literary scholar Saidiya Hartman (2019) writes of "waywardness: the avid longing for a world not ruled by master, man, or the police" (227). Hartman reconstructs poor Black women's spatial strategies of wandering, "rambling, roving, cruising, strolling, and seeking" (227). Although Yates's proprietary role as a freighter captain positions her differently from the women whose lives compel Hartman, her rebelliousness and inscrutability, and the *Xhosa*'s unsanctioned paths, quietly echo these wayward twentieth-century women in the twenty-fourth.

Yet we might also read most Maquis as settler colonists. A labor theory of property—having worked and put one's life into "improving" the land of previously "uninhabited" planets—is unmistakably central to the Rebellion's raison d'être (Locke [1689] 1884; Livingston 1994b). In this light, the Federation-Maquis conflict might recall an earlier phase of U.S. settler colonialism, when the federal government managed the "direction, pace and scale" of settlement, to "engineer the demography of the region in a manner that both secured and consolidated their territorial control" (Frymer 2017, 9; Dunbar-Ortiz 2015). Local settlers' conflicts with the federal government about the extent of settlement sometimes became violent, as in Bacon's Rebellion of 1676 (G. Horne 2018).

The Maquis also comprise a missed opportunity. TNG writers initially planned to introduce them as a community of Native North American Federation citizens in the seventh-season episode "Journey's End" (Allen 1994a). This plan was abandoned (Nemecek 2003), and the one-off Native American story that resulted has received a mixed reception at best from Indigenous audiences (Adare 2005). What could it have meant to instead introduce the Maquis *as* an Indigenous, or an Indigenous-led, multiracial society? What would it take to privilege the expertise of Indigenous writers, directors, and actors to develop such a story line (see, e.g., Memory Alpha n.d.q)?

Cardassian Settler Colonialism

As executed, the Maquis are ultimately most interesting for what they reveal about the contradictions of the Federation (Neumann 2001, 620). Sisko, in particular, goes to remarkably destructive lengths to apprehend Maquis leader Michael Eddington (Kenneth Marshall), whose "betrayal" he takes personally (Lobl 1997). One hopes that future *Star Trek* scholarship will pick up where this analysis leaves off—that others will be able to make something more coherent of the Maquis than I can. Fortunately, DS9's Bajor story line offers more robust allegorical resources for contemporary political critique.

"I Should've Killed Them All!"

After *TNG*'s introduction to the Bajorans as a sympathetic, displaced, stateless people (Landau 1991b), *DS9* pivots to the Bajoran homeworld itself, imagining life in the wake of the Occupation. Some commentators (e.g., Ono 1996) have criticized this shift to a place-based approach as a Eurocentric turn that reimagines Bajor as post–World War II Europe. To be sure, the Bajorans' statelessness speaks to the repeated displacements of Indigenous peoples, from the Trail of Tears to the *nakba*.[3] But *DS9*'s turn to Bajor enabled it to draw parallels between the territorial dimensions of Cardassian, Israeli, and U.S. settler colonialisms, and to examine the ways in which Bajorans, Palestinians, and Native Americans have endured and fought back in place, resisting their dispossession. Although *DS9* takes place after Occupation, it uses this "post" colonial temporality to address *ongoing* historical structures and traumas that are central to settler colonialism but that can be hard to name directly from within settler colonies.

The most chilling distillation of the Occupation's settler-colonial logic comes in an epic confrontation in season 6's "Waltz," an interrogative exchange between Sisko and Gul Dukat (Marc Alaimo), *DS9*'s grandiose, insecure, sadistic, smooth-talking archvillain. As Cardassian prefect of Bajor for thirteen years during the Occupation, Dukat is responsible for suffering and death at a staggering scale. Yet he insistently casts himself as a moderate, a maverick, "one of the good ones." In "Waltz," Sisko and Dukat are stranded alone on a remote planet and momentarily need one another to survive. The ever-insecure Dukat takes the opportunity to ask Sisko's opinion of him, pressing until the captain relents. Sisko grills Dukat on his conduct during the Occupation, charging that the man is "responsible for the murder of over five million Bajorans who died on your watch" (Auberjonois 1998).

Dukat protests, explaining that he had to answer to impatient Cardassian leaders' frustration that after four decades of Occupation, "the planet was still not ready for full-scale colonization." Dukat maintains that he sought to prevent genocide, reducing quotas at labor camps, improving medical care, and increasing rations. The Bajoran Resistance, he complains, interpreted such attempts at "peace" and "reconciliation" as a sign of weakness and struck harder than ever, with bombings and an assassination attempt on Dukat himself.

Sisko interjects, "Now let me get this straight: You're not responsible for what happened during the Occupation—the Bajorans are. . . . So why do you think they didn't appreciate the *rare* opportunity you were offering them, hmm?"

Dukat's answer reiterates the pose of burdensome, innocent superiority that political theorist Jeanne Morefield (2014) observes has long been fundamental to imperial rule. Bajorans, Dukat explains, "wanted to be treated as equals when they most definitely were not. Militarily, technologically, culturally—we were almost a century ahead of them in every way. We did not choose to be the superior race. Fate handed us our role. It would've been so much easier on everyone if the Bajorans had simply accepted their role." Instead, he laments, they fought back in acts large and small, stubbornly donning "their pride like some twisted badge of honor."

"And you hated them for it," Sisko surmises.

Abandoning any pretense of the bumbling, innocent imperialist, Dukat fully leans in. "Of course, I hated them! Their superstitions and their cries for sympathy, their treachery and their lies, their smug superiority and their stiff-necked obstinacy, their stupid earrings and their broken noses. Yes, I hated them. I hated everything about them!"

"You should've killed them all," Sisko offers, tongue firmly in cheek.

Cardassian Settler Colonialism

"Yes!" Dukat avers earnestly. "That's right, isn't it?! I knew it! I've always known it! I should've killed every last one of them and turned their planet into a graveyard the likes of which the galaxy had never seen! *I should've killed them all!*"

Sisko, although injured, manages to knock Dukat unconscious with a piece of debris. "And *that*," he muses, "is why you're not an evil man?"

Sisko thus exposes the genocidal colonial logics beneath Dukat's front of beneficence, effectively putting Cardassian settler colonialism on trial. Here again, Brooks's performance recalls Paul Robeson, who in 1951 helped deliver a grievance against the U.S. government from leading Black radical activists and intellectuals titled *We Charge Genocide: The Crime of Government against the Negro People* to the United Nations (Patterson 2020; G. Horne 2016). The captain's cross-examination makes clear that the Cardassian endgame in the Bajoran sector is not limited to its exploitation as a resource colony—mines, labor camps, orbital ore-processing—but extends to Cardassian *settlement*, what Dukat calls "full-scale colonization" (Auberjonois 1998).

Can Americans not hear echoes of Dukat's logic in the words of our own President Theodore Roosevelt, among many others? In 1886 Roosevelt remarked, "I don't go so far as to think the only good Indians are the dead Indians, but I believe nine out of every ten are, and I shouldn't like to inquire too closely into the case of the tenth" (Landry 2016). Can we not also hear echoes of Dukat's views in the words of former Israeli prime minister Benjamin Netanyahu? In 2018 Netanyahu dismissed critiques of the Israeli government's occupation of Palestine as "nonsense," proclaiming, "Empires have conquered and replaced entire populations and no one is talking about it" (*Jerusalem Post* 2018). Netanyahu also remarked that "the weak crumble, are slaughtered and erased from history while the strong, for good or for ill, survive. The strong are respected, and alliances are made with the strong, and in the end peace is made with the strong" (Prime Minister of Israel 2018).

The racism that Dukat expresses, moreover, isn't the result of some depoliticized "ancient enmity," but rather serves projects of expansion, extraction, and exploitation that are difficult to disentangle from both settler colonialism and the profit motive (Campbell and Gokcek 2019, 139). From the outset, *Star Trek* establishes the Cardassian Empire as economically and environmentally unsustainable (Landau 1991b; Carson 1993a; Conway 1993a; A. Robinson 2000; Memory Alpha n.d.c). The dominant way of life on the Cardassian homeworld so badly depletes the planet that Cardassian elites, refusing to reconsider their own economic practices, deem territorial expansionism and the exploitation of Bajoran labor an economic necessity. Cardassian settler colonialism alienates Bajorans from their own land, turning them from people at home into refugees and mobile, disposable "Bajoran workers," for Cardassian extractive industries. That Cardassians forced Bajoran workers to process ore on Terok Nor in chambers that reached up to 55°C (131°F), then, must thus be understood not simply as an act of racial hatred but as a simultaneously cultural, political, environmental, and economic evil (Badiyi 1994). Whether Bajor allegorizes the Indigenous Americas, Palestine, or elsewhere, American studies scholar Manu Karuka's (2019) observation applies: "Viewed from Indigenous places, capitalism began in an imperial mode. Capitalism *is* imperialism" (185).

"None of You Belonged on Bajor"

Unsurprisingly, then, there is ample evidence of Bajoran antipathy toward Cardassians in *DS9*, antipathy that endures well beyond the formal cessation of military hostilities. Such prejudice becomes painfully evident in "Duet," when Marritza, the Cardassian who poses as a war criminal in the hopes of putting his own people on trial, is stabbed to death by a Bajoran passerby on the station's Promenade (Conway 1993a). Kira, who is hardly given to forgive or forget the Occupation, asks the killer why. His reply—"He's a Cardassian. That's reason enough"—appalls her.

A former armed Resistance fighter—the Cardassians would say terrorist—Major Kira is the show's principal interlocutor for Bajoran decolonization. She is movingly performed by Visitor, a triple-threat actor, singer, and dancer with an extensive Broadway and television background. Visitor (2022), who has edited an unprecedented collection of the writings of

Cardassian Settler Colonialism

women *Trek* actors and writers, made feminist strides in her portrayal of Kira as an ass-kicking, outspoken revolutionary—so much so that higher-ups disapprovingly compared her walk to the iconic gait of John Wayne and added high heels to her Bajoran uniform (Visitor 2021). To Visitor's great credit, this imposed wardrobe change did little to attenuate Kira's swagger or fiercely defended convictions. The major's character arc is inseparable from Bajor's painful transitions between forms of political life, and she is beset by a near-constant stream of historical crises and ethical dilemmas. If Sisko is DS9's principal reluctant hero, Kira is its "moral center," as SF writer Abigail Nussbaum (2008) puts it, "the person who can always be counted on to speak the hard truths."[4]

Kira's unfailing political candor is established from our first encounter with her in "Emissary." Captain Picard assigns Sisko to liaise between Bajor's Provisional Government and the United Federation of Planets, facilitating the planet's presumed entry into the Federation (Carson 1993a). But if Picard is optimistic about Bajor's Federation membership, Kira is anything but. "I don't believe the Federation has any business being here," she tells Sisko. "I have been fighting for Bajoran independence since I was old enough to pick up a phaser. Finally, we drive out the Cardassians, and what do our new leaders do? Call up the Federation and invite them in." When her new boss offers that "the Federation is only here to . . ." she interrupts, "help us. Yes, I know. The Cardassians said the same thing sixty years ago" (Carson 1993a). Kira's retort resonates with the reminder offered by Said ([1978] 2003) during the second U.S. invasion of Iraq: "Every single empire in its official discourse has said that it is not like all the others, that its circumstances are special, that it has a mission to enlighten, civilize, bring order and democracy, and that it uses force only as a last resort" (xvi). American studies scholar Michele Casavant (2003) observes that this moment in DS9 is the first time that a sympathetic *Trek* character questions the latent expansionist assumptions of Federation ideology so plainly (89). Kira worries that Bajor is not truly exercising self-determination, that it remains caught between Cardassian and Federation spheres of influence, akin to what Pacific historian Augusto Espiritu (2014) calls "inter-imperial conflict." Espiritu explains that people and places caught in the middle of "ideological conflict, propaganda, diplomatic maneuvers, economic competition, territorial war involving two antagonistic empires" find a range of ways, both overt and subtle, to resist their positioning as dominoes (240). Here Kira opts for the overt.

More accustomed to the role of anticolonial freedom fighter than agent of a postcolonial state with which she often adamantly disagrees, Kira grows tremendously over *DS9*'s seven years. She is often described as letting go of her anger, trauma, and Bajoran nationalism in a tidy liberal narrative of overcoming. Yet it is perhaps closer to the mark to say that Kira's politics and values don't change, but her heart does. Grounded in historical experience and insights from the Prophets, Kira remains in some sense a particularist—resolutely place based, religiously orthodox, fiercely anticolonial. But she becomes, in cultural studies scholar Ramzi Fawaz's (2019) felicitous phrase, "a particularist with a heart for the universal," making Bajoran experience a departure point for insight, empathy, and solidarity with a range of oppressed peoples (11). Kira models an alternative form of cosmopolitanism, one out of step with pretensions of liberal imperialist universality and replete with possibilities for international/interplanetary contact and comradeship (Li 2019).

Anticolonialism is among the most enduring features of Kira's politics. Part of the Shakaar cell of the Bajoran Resistance in Dakhur, the agrarian province of her birth, Kira bombed Cardassian garrisons, ambushed and killed Cardassian soldiers, liberated a notoriously cruel labor camp, and even assassinated Bajorans who collaborated with the Occupation. Although she regrets some of her actions on an ethical level, she does not equivocate about the right of colonized people to armed self-defense. In "The Darkness and the Light," a reclusive Cardassian, Silaran Prin (Randy Oglesby), assassinates members of Kira's Resistance cell one by one. During the Occupation, Prin worked as a domestic servant for a Cardassian official responsible for arbitrary mass executions of Bajoran civilians and suffered a disfiguring wound during one of Shakaar's attacks. He now savors in long-awaited revenge. Realizing she's the next target, a very pregnant Kira goes on the offensive, hunting and confronting Prin.

"Don't you feel guilty?" he asks her. "Don't you feel ashamed of what you did?"

Even when facing death, Kira does not prevaricate: "We were at war, Silaran. Fifteen million Bajorans died during the Occupation and you want me to feel sorry for you? . . . None of us liked killing. We were fighting for our freedom. . . . None of you belonged on Bajor. It wasn't your world. For fifty years, you raped our planet and you killed our people. You lived on our land and you took the food out of our mouths, and I don't care whether you held a phaser in your hand or ironed shirts for a living. You were all guilty and you were all legitimate targets!" (Vejar 1997a).

Some may chafe at Kira's impenitent advocacy of anticolonial violence or her moral indictment of a (settler) civilian's complicity in Occupation. But we need not endorse Kira's actions to understand that they stem from neither "ancient enmity" nor a generic Bajoran chauvinism but a lucid critique of settler colonialism as an unjust social and spatial relation. For Kira, as for anthropologist Talal Asad (2007), "there is no moral difference between the horror inflicted by state armies (especially if those armies belong to powerful states that are unaccountable to international law) and horror inflicted by insurgents" (94, see also Putman 2013). Prin's focus on the personal trauma he endured at Bajoran hands, Kira insists, effects a false equivalence, ignoring the broader, structural asymmetries of settler-colonial violence, which stack the deck in favor of Cardassian affluence and against Bajoran survival and self-determination.

Yet Kira's Bajoran spirituality is also deep and abiding, both inseparable from her anticolonial politics and irreducible to it. Scenes of Kira's life off duty commonly depict her in prayer, either in her quarters or at the station's Bajoran temple. Kira, who lost both parents before she turned thirty, speaks frequently and stirringly about the centrality of the Prophets in surviving, fighting, and ending the Occupation and in working through its aftermath. The Prophets are insightful guides for grief, not least because they privilege geographical and psychical space over linear time. Prophetic visions are peppered with the refrain, "We are of Bajor," and devout Bajorans hold that "the land and the people are one" (Livingston 1993b). These

8. Kira in prayer at a Bajoran duranja, or lamp for the dead, in her quarters on Deep Space Nine ("Shakaar," season 3, episode 24, aired May 22, 1995).

are clear gestures to many Native American spiritualities, which the late historian and theologian Vine Deloria Jr. (Standing Rock Sioux) explained often eschew linearity and regard places "as having the highest possible meaning, and all their statements are made with this reference point in mind" (2003, 61). We might also consider resonances with Palestinian theologies of liberation spanning multiple religious traditions, including both Christianity and Islam; as Palestinian education scholar Munir Fasheh has pointed out, Palestinian Christianity is, in a sense, the only indigenous form of Christianity in the world (quoted in Robson 2010, 44). While this chapter will consider the problem of cultural appropriation in detail below, of utmost significance here is the Prophets' role in interrogating notions of progress that are destructive of people and places. A metaphysical sense of the irreplaceable value of Bajoran places and forms of life informs many of Kira's materialist critiques of both Federation and Bajoran agendas for post-Occupation development.

Cardassian Settler Colonialism

In season 1's "In the Hands of the Prophets," for instance, Winn Adami (Louise Fletcher), an ambitious cleric in Bajor's state religion, sees an opportunity to score political points after a secular Federation grade school opens on the station. Kira grows increasingly skeptical of Winn, who proves to be an opportunistic, devious charlatan. But she nevertheless argues that the school conflict raises valid questions about religion, science, and empire. When schoolteacher Keiko Ishikawa O'Brien (the hero of chapter 5) protests to Sisko, "I'm not teaching any philosophy. What I'm trying to teach is pure science," Kira retorts, "Some might say pure science, taught without a spiritual context, *is* a philosophy, Mrs. O'Brien."

Here some (e.g., Gonzalez 2015) might dismiss Kira as a retrograde Bajoran religious nationalist who is advocating teaching creationism or "intelligent design." But we can better understand Kira's stance when we consider both the place of Bajoran spirituality in anticolonial struggle and the active participation of Cardassian scientists in highly unethical Occupation experiments on incarcerated Bajorans (Livingston 1998b). Kira's sincere concern echoes histories of empire on Earth, in which both religion and scientism—the belief that science can be completely separated from its political-economic and cultural contexts and is purely rational, objective, and universal—can be exploited to serve colonial and imperial aims. Wynter (2003), for example, traces how centuries-old European Christian distinctions between the "chosen" and the "damned," so useful to Spanish imperialism, were recast in social Darwinist discourses on the genetically "selected" and "dysselected," repackaging old religious racism in a new, scientific wrapper. Wynter's aim is not a rejection of science per se, but a proliferation of liberatory sciences and philosophies that refuse to reproduce these deadly modes of social ordering.

The political stakes of Kira's hesitations about the Bajoran school also become clearer when we examine this episode's intertexts. Behr has stated that the school conflict was inspired in part by Jerome Lawrence and Robert Edwin Lee's play *Inherit the Wind* (Altman and Gross 2016, 462), which has been subjected to numerous film adaptations. Written during the second U.S. Red Scare, *Inherit the Wind* reprises the noted 1925 Scopes "monkey trial" over the teaching of Darwinian evolution in Tennessee public schools. The trial pitted Chicago liberal Clarence Darrow, a defender of evolution, against economic populist and former U.S. secretary of state William Jennings Bryan, a devout Presbyterian who opposed teaching evolution on religious grounds.

Although it can be tempting to map contemporary ideological fault lines onto the Scopes trial, historians caution against it (Larson 1997). They note that the textbook that triggered the lawsuit openly advocated racial eugenics, and that neither Bryan, who supported Jim Crow, nor Darrow, who both praised and criticized eugenics, offered a coherent antiracist position (Numbers 1986; Moran 2003). Yet Bryan, for all his considerable flaws, became a vocal opponent of U.S. imperialism, a sentiment echoed in *Inherit the Wind*. Condemning urban elites partial to eugenics and other forms of scientism, the Bryan character warns jurors, "I have been to their cities, and I have seen the altars upon which they sacrifice the futures of their children to the gods of science. And what are their rewards? Confusion and self-destruction. New ways to kill each other in wars. I tell you, gentlemen, that the way of science is the way of darkness" (Kramer 1960).

Though Bryan's primary referent is the mass sacrifice of (white) U.S. soldiers in World War I, Kira's suspicions about "pure science" reflect a related set of misgivings, but from the point of view of an allegorical colonized people. This is a nuance that Benjamin Sisko readily picks up on. When Jake, who is frustrated by Winn's disruptions at his school, dismisses Bajoran religion as "dumb," his father counters, "No, it's not. You've got to realize something, Jake. For over fifty years, the one thing that allowed the Bajorans to survive the Cardassian Occupation was their faith. The Prophets were their only source of hope and courage. . . . It may not be what you believe, but that doesn't make it wrong" (Livingston 1993c). If Jake Sisko stands in for the secularist leanings of many Trekkers here, his father gently reminds audiences that religion can have liberatory valences, as well as conservative ones.

Cardassian Settler Colonialism

"You're on the Other Side Now"

Both political experiences and Prophetic interventions also surprise Kira, forcing to question her prior assumptions. If there is a name for the rule that seems to govern many Kira-centric episodes, it might well be the law of "nonnecessity," or the relentless questioning of the expectation that social forces, identities, intentions, and desires will line up in tidy, predictable ways (see Sedgwick 1993). Where forms of politicized identity, like Kira's anticolonial Bajoran nationalism, use group identity as a stand-in for more complicated, structural histories of oppression and injury (Georgis 2013), nonnecessity invites us to reconnect with the complexity that identity refuses. People rarely encounter the "difficult knowledge" offered by nonnecessity gracefully (Britzman 1998). Yet the hope of reconnection with complexity is not to undermine the justice-seeking aims of politicized identity but to regain access to vital, painful, beautiful parts of the condition of being alive—parts that historical injury must not be allowed to foreclose.

"Duet" exemplifies Kira's encounters with nonnecessity. In meeting Marritza and hearing what's at stake for him, Kira realizes that some Cardassians—rare, though they may be—are truly committed to genuine atonement and reconciliation with Bajor. Clear as she remains on her political and spiritual values, Kira occasionally finds that the patterns through which she expects to be able to discern good from bad and friend from enemy just don't hold on an individual scale.

One of Kira's most deeply shaking encounters with nonnecessity comes in "Second Skin," when she wakes up on the Cardassian homeworld and is mortified to see the face of the enemy staring back at her (Landau 1994c). Kira is informed that she is, in fact, a Cardassian spy who was implanted with false memories and surgically modified to surveil the Bajoran Resistance under deep cover. Her hosts even display the uncanny corpse of the "real" Kira Nerys, whom they claim she replaced.

A despondent Kira refuses to collaborate with her intelligence "colleagues," but she tolerates the kindness of the Cardassian who claims to be her father, an elder statesman named Tekeny Ghemor (Lawrence Pressman)

9. A horrified Kira contemplating her Cardassian visage, as Tekeny Ghemor, her would-be father, looks on ("Second Skin," season 3, episode 5, aired October 24, 1994).

whose daughter has long been missing. When Kira realizes Ghemor is a Cardassian dissident who opposed the Occupation and is at risk of exposure and imprisonment, they escape together to DS9. Although Bashir confirms that Kira is, in fact, Bajoran—an ending that writers considered leaving more ambiguous (Erdmann and Block 2000, 77)—the exile Ghemor and the war orphan Kira form an unexpected bond, akin to that of parent and child.

In "Ties of Blood and Water," an ailing Ghemor returns to the station to share intelligence about their common enemies and die with "family" at his side. Kira is reluctant to participate in this vigil, both disturbed by recent revelations about Ghemor's bloody military record and reminded of the excruciating experience of narrowly missing the death of her own father, Taban (Thomas Kopache), during the Occupation. To her own surprise, Kira ultimately comes through for Ghemor, expressing relief that she could be there for her "father"—both of them—this time. Kira never verbalizes

Cardassian Settler Colonialism

anything resembling forgiveness for Ghemor's past. But she also refuses to view him as disposable (hooks 2018), recognizing that he now comes to her in solidarity, and that for better and for worse, they are a kind of kin.

Some humans also pleasantly surprise Kira, despite her misgivings about Federation presence. Kira's relationship with Sisko grows more complex after the Prophets astonish everyone by naming him as their Emissary. From DS9's outset, Sisko's is a "doubled body," invested with two distinct political-theological charges: (secular) Federation liaison to Bajor and Prophetic Emissary to all corporeal beings (Santner 2011). For Kira, this makes him at once commanding officer and figure of penultimate spiritual significance. The expressly theological character of Sisko's second charge—and the reverence that it inspires in Bajorans, including Kira—is at first extremely awkward for Sisko. Although he does not put up a front of frosty rationalism like Spock or Picard, Sisko's beliefs do not initially seem to depart much from secular humanist Starfleet norms. Like other Starfleet personnel, he refers to the Prophets in the secular scientific language of "wormhole aliens," language that makes many Bajorans, including Kira, bristle.

Yet Sisko gradually falls in love with Bajor and Bajorans, taking up passionate interests in Bajoran archaeology, religion, language, history, and architecture. Although he remains in close contact with his father in New Orleans, he pines for Earth less and less, saluting DS9 as "this place where I belong" and planning to retire on Bajor (Kroeker 1997). Within their first year of working together, Kira and Sisko become unlikely friends. "When I first met you, Major," Sisko reflects, "I thought you were hostile and arrogant. But I was wrong. Bajor needs you, and I need you. I like you" (Landau 1993a). When Sisko is badly injured and stranded far from a hospital, it is Kira, insistent that the Emissary cannot die, who keeps him conscious long enough to prevent a coma, praying, laying on hands, and telling him Bajoran fables (Singer 1995c).

African diasporic experience is far from incidental to Sisko's links to Bajoran spirituality. In an interview about the series pilot, Brooks reflected, "If you think 400 years hence and then look far back at the history of African people, there has always been a connection to the divine, to the spiritual. So, this Kai Opaka [leader of Bajor's state religion], this exchange Sisko has with her, is fascinating" (Memory Alpha n.d.e; see also De Gaia 2003, 146). As numerous religious studies scholars have demonstrated, Black people in the Americas have fundamentally remade the Christianity that Europeans sought to impose on them in slavery, creating and smuggling in knowledges, ceremonies, stories, and songs that affirm and sustain Black humanity and inflecting worship with African Islam and traditional African religions (e.g., Rivera 2021; Edwards 2013; Crawley 2017). With that history in mind, both Brooks and Sisko recognize that religion is a righteous, emancipatory force in Bajoran life, in ways that stridently secularist lenses miss. Although Sisko takes years to become comfortable with the reverence that Bajorans, including Kira, show him, he recognizes from the outset that accepting the role is not simply a job requirement but a contribution to a liberation struggle.

As Kira revises her initial judgments of some Cardassians and humans, she also questions her idealizations of some other Bajorans. In "The Collaborator," her lover, the unorthodox cleric Vedek Bareil (Philip Anglim), gives up his bid to lead the Bajoran state's official religion in order to hide a painful secret about a celebrated colleague's collaborations with the Cardassian Occupation (Bole 1994). Worse still, in "Wrongs Darker than Death or Night," Kira receives a devastating Prophetic revelation—her own mother, Meru (Leslie Hope), was forced into military sexual servitude for the odious Cardassian leader Gul Dukat for years after Kira thought her dead (J. West 1998).[5] The news forces Kira to reassess Meru, whom she had romanticized as an anticolonial heroine who died defying Cardassian captors. Kira is aghast seeing her mother accept gifts of food and clothing from her loathed oppressors—to say nothing of sleeping with the enemy. What sort of gods, one wonders, would show their most devout followers such horrible things? Yet Kira also comes to understand that she herself could not have survived childhood in a refugee camp without her mother's remittances. Under conditions of forced servitude, her mother made a sly material contribution to the Bajoran decolonization struggle: keeping her children alive to fight another day.

Cardassian Settler Colonialism

As Kira reassesses the memory of her mother, she also grows more critical of dominant idealizations of the Bajoran motherland. In season 1's superlative "Progress," the Provisional Government tasks Kira with evicting Mullibok (Brian Keith), an irascible elderly farmer who fled a Cardassian labor camp for a lush Bajoran moon (Landau 1993a). The government targets the moon for energy mining to heat hundreds of thousands of Bajoran homes, rendering it uninhabitable for a small population of subsistence farmers. Kira is reluctant to remove Mullibok, who has spent most of his life on the moon and would rather die than leave. Mullibok asks how the Resistance beat the Cardassians. "We beat them because—because we hung on like fanatics," she offers. "Hung on like fanatics," he grins cheekily, "I got to remember that" (Landau 1993a).

Increasingly ambivalent about her investiture as a government agent, an anxious Kira repeatedly removes her Bajoran militia jacket, only to put it back on (Santner 2011).[6] She questions whether the moon's other residents really left voluntarily, as the government claims, and proposes alternative, less environmentally destructive forms of energy generation. But her government contact is adamant that only the most expedient methods will do. When she counters that Bajoran extractivism repeats the same violence the Cardassians perpetrated, the remark jeopardizes her job. Here Sisko intercedes: "You have to realize something, Major. You're on the other side now. Pretty uncomfortable, isn't it? . . . [Mullibok's] fate is already decided. Yours isn't" (Landau 1993a).

Mining Bajor's moon to provide heat to needy families might seem like a rational, innocent-enough public purpose. But it parallels the devastating effects of dams and other state-supported infrastructure and energy projects on the foodways and self-determination of Earth's Indigenous communities (Estes 2019). Sisko, then, isn't just giving Kira a pep talk. He's also speaking for the Federation, naturalizing the destruction of a Bajoran form of life in the service of a particular and contested vision of Bajoran development. Kira reluctantly complies, setting Mullibok's home on fire and beaming him off the moon. A licensed DS9 novel that extends the events of "Progress" envisages a happily resettled Mullibok forgiving Kira

10. Unwilling evacuee Mullibok resisting Major Kira's attempts to comfort him as his home burns ("Progress," season 1, episode 15, aired May 9, 1993).

(see carrington 2016; Friesner 1994). But perhaps it is more instructive to ask whether Kira can forgive herself.

Similarly, in "Sanctuary," a matriarchal community of refugees displaced by a war on the other side of the wormhole petitions for asylum in an underpopulated Bajoran region devastated by the Occupation. Kira befriends Haneek (Deborah May), a refugee leader whose religious teachings foretell a place much like Bajor as a site of peaceful, prosperous cohabitation between two historically oppressed peoples. One of Kira's Bajoran friends surmises, correctly, that the refugees' petition is dead on arrival. "Aren't you being a little premature?" Kira resists. "These people have lost everything" (Landau 1993b). But the Provisional Government, citing the toll exacted by the Occupation, turns the refugees down, sending them elsewhere. "Fifty years of Cardassian rule has made you all frightened and suspicious," Haneek charges, leaving a haunted Kira once again unreconciled with Bajor's "post"

Cardassian Settler Colonialism

colonial trajectory (Gordon 2008). Episodes like "Progress" and "Sanctuary" are significant precisely because their outcomes are disappointing. Kira makes a compelling interlocutor for Bajoran politics and Federation presence because she remains alive to alternatives to the dominant vision of "progress," alternatives her government seems intent on foreclosing. Like philosopher Walter Benjamin's ([1942] 2007) evocative figure of the angel of history, Kira sees in Bajor's past the accumulated wreckage of unacknowledged "otherwise possibilities" (Crawley 2017).

Season 2's epic premiere puts Kira in the opposite position, scrambling to defend a Provisional Government she dislikes from a right-wing coup d'état (Kolbe 1993a, 1993b; Allen 1993). With help from Bareil and a cryptic Prophetic vision, Kira takes down the Circle, a xenophobic Bajoran faction looking to reclaim "Bajor for the Bajorans." Puzzled that the Circle seems better organized than the government, Odo, Kira, and Dax discover the ironic source of its power: weapons and funding from Cardassians eager to reinvade a politically isolated Bajor. Circle leader Jaro Essa (Frank Langella) claims that the Prophets are, in fact, on his side, denouncing Kira as "an outspoken opponent of the Provisional Government, of reason, of progress, and now finally, of me." But Kira and Dax, undercover as Bajoran clerics, sneak into the halls of government with proof of Cardassian involvement in the Circle, undermining the coup (Kolbe 1993b). DS9 creators have noted that this three-part episode, which was then unprecedented in the franchise, irritated the studio and some audiences, becoming exhibit A in the case against more Bajor stories (Behr and Zappone 2019). Yet its intricate story line—including a jab at the Reagan administration's illegal funding of right-wing counterrevolutionaries in Nicaragua and a nod to the revolutionary role of liberation theologies in Latin America—anticipated the highly serialized, complex political storytelling that DS9's later seasons would more fully embrace.

Ultimately, Kira does challenge the Bajoran state from its left, even taking up arms to oppose her government's extractivist development vision (J. West 1995). By season 4's "Shakaar," Winn Adami has become Bajor's state religious leader and is on track to become First Minister in the secular government as well. Winn stakes her electoral campaign on a dubious plan to dedicate an entire province to export-oriented agriculture and interstellar commerce. But the plan depends on public farm equipment already on loan to Kira's former Resistance comrades, who are now subsistence farmers. Winn sends a reluctant Kira to retrieve the equipment, but Kira is moved by the cause of subsistence over profit and takes the farmers' side in a confrontation with the state. A politically embarrassed Winn withdraws from the election, and Kira's old friend Shakaar Edon (Duncan Regehr) announces his candidacy on an economic-populist platform.

Wolfe has attributed the premise for "Shakaar" to Felipe Cazals's (1970) *Zapata*, a biopic of the Mexican revolutionary Emiliano Zapata Salazar (1879–1919), who led a peasant uprising for land reform (Gross and Altman 1996, 97; Brunk 2008). As the episode was filmed, the Zapatista Army of National Liberation, a contemporary Mexican revolutionary autonomous movement in the state of Chiapas, was putting Zapata's example to radical (and headline-grabbing) work against the Mexican state and the North American Free Trade Agreement. We can hear ricochets of both Zapata and the Zapatistas in the episode's critique of the use of state power to secure the conditions of an export-oriented economy over meeting people's basic needs.

Kira even comes, finally, to rethink her relationship to spirituality. Though her belief in the Prophets is never in doubt, she does not regard all their would-be intermediaries with equal credulity. Alongside her distaste for Winn Adami, which only deepens, Kira wryly questions the decrees of Akorem Laan (Richard Libertini), a long-lost, long-revered Bajoran poet who emerges from the wormhole claiming to be the Prophets' true Emissary (Landau 1996a). At first, Kira, Sisko, and most Bajorans afford Akorem the benefit of the doubt, even when he calls for a return to a pre-Occupation kinship-based caste system (see Trivedi 2022). When Kira attempts to take up her designated "true" calling as an artist, she rapidly fills her quarters with botched attempts at sculpture, concluding that art cannot possibly be her Prophetic destiny. When the Prophets intercede to clarify that Sisko is indeed their Emissary, a reassured Kira gifts him a poorly sculpted bird to celebrate his return—"a Kira Nerys original."

None of Kira's encounters with nonnecessity result in an abdication of her anticolonial politics or her enduring religious beliefs. For instance, when Gul Dukat, nostalgic for the Bajoran women he forced into sexual servitude during the Occupation, seeks a reconciliation with Kira in the hopes of boosting his political reputation and kindling a romance, she sees through his bad-faith efforts and decisively repudiates him (J. West 1996a, see Prescod-Weinstein 2019). But Kira's encounters with nonnecessity, combined with her anticolonial values, do lead her to expand her communities of solidarity to include people quite different from her. She befriends and mentors Tora Ziyal (Cyia Batten, Tracy Middendorf, Melanie Smith), Gul Dukat's estranged half-Bajoran daughter, who is shunned by Bajorans and Cardassians alike. And when Cardassian elites join forces with an even more powerful and oppressive empire called the Dominion (see chapter 3), Kira helps Cardassian dissidents overthrow them, articulating an anticolonial nationalism that is compatible with Left internationalism. These alliances are anything but easy. When the Dominion executes Cardassian civilians in retaliation for their guerilla attacks, dissident leader Damar (Casey Biggs) wonders naively, "What kind of state tolerates the murder of innocent women and children? What kind of people give those orders?" As a living witness to the Cardassian Occupation of Bajor, Kira does not hesitate to school him: "Yeah, Damar, what kind of people give those orders?" If Kira shares Damar's anger, she is also appalled by its belatedness and racialized selectivity (Vejar 1999c).

Kira remains righteously angry about the Occupation and its aftermath. But as her heart grows, the circle of what angers her grows, too: evictions, extractivism, land enclosure, xenophobic exclusion, religious oppression, genocidal violence—inflicted on her own people, sometimes in the name of Bajoran interests, and on others, including even Cardassians. Sisko's counsel to Kira in "Progress"—"You're on the other side now"—proves to be prescient in a perhaps-unintended sense. Though fiercely proud of her Bajoran identity, Bajoranness is not, for Kira, a "wounded attachment"

(Brown 1995). Being both historically oppressed and "on the other side now" leaves Kira with a heightened awareness of her own complicity in some of the very forces she has spent her life opposing. Kira learns that the oppressed can remain in some sense oppressed while also becoming the oppressor—that identity matters, but hard-to-name complexities and structural power imbalances matter, too. In this way, she breaks the perilous cycle of "lessons we don't ever seem to learn," the logic that Piller located at the heart of the settler-colonial societies that inspired *Trek*'s Bajoran allegory (see Rose 2007).

Some critics have painted Bajoran nationalisms with a broad brush, interpreting them as signs of arrested development, unfortunate side effects of Occupation that will presumably be overcome with Federation membership and secularization (e.g., Gonzalez 2018; Decker 2016; Wagner and Lundeen 1998). Yet *DS9*'s multivalent portrait of Bajoran nationalism suggests that nationalisms have many possible articulations (see Georgis 2013, 70–72), from the xenophobic schemes of the Circle to the anticolonial liberation struggle that Kira advances. As on our own world, sustained attention to context and questions of power are required to determine the difference. And Federation membership, moreover, is hardly an inevitability. At the Prophets' behest, Bajor indefinitely postpones its application for Federation membership, remaining independent as the series ends. Decades later, Behr reflects that keeping Bajor out of the Federation was "the one thing that we did that I know I'm proud of, and I think we're all proud of" (Behr and Zappone 2019). The Bajor arc thus challenges both the Cardassians' impenitent imperial domination and the Federation's posture of beneficent universality in ways that prompt critical reflection on the moral legitimacy of the actions of a range of settler-colonial states that tout themselves as beacons of democracy, including the United States and Israel.

The inextricable role of Bajoran religion in *DS9*'s story line has also elicited critical concern, even leading some to align the series with the late political scientist Samuel P. Huntington's (1993) infamous "Clash of Civilizations" thesis. With the end of a Cold War that pitted secular socialism against a liberal capitalist bloc, Huntington imagined that international politics would

Cardassian Settler Colonialism

revert, organizing itself around putatively older, metaphysical conflicts between a dynamic, liberal West and a number of other "civilizations" (some spanning entire continents!) with distinct cultural identities. Among the most thoughtful readers of DS9 as a clash of civilizations is Dyson (2015), who observes that "for the first time in *Trek*, religious beliefs and practices are taken seriously as cultural constructs that drive history" (100).

Huntington's thesis has been widely criticized, notably by Said (1993), who shredded its paternalistic assumptions of Western superiority and static conception of culture. If nothing else, however, the clash of civilizations is useful as an artifact, indexing anxiety among U.S. policy elites about finding new justifications for imperial interventions in the 1990s. As Sharp (1998) observes, such anxieties were also widespread in 1990s Hollywood, because containing the USSR had been fundamental to depictions of American identity and masculinity in action and adventure films for decades. Without an "evil empire" to fend off, Hollywood scrambled to reorient (pun intended) audiences toward a chaotic cast of new foes— the greedy drug lord, the irrational Muslim fundamentalist, even the U.S. government itself, cast as both tyrannical and ineffectual.

But if DS9 alluded to this "new" multipolar geopolitical landscape by moving away from a singular arch enemy (like the Klingons in TOS), it also cast anticolonial freedom fighters with religious motivations in a far more sympathetic light than many of its Hollywood peers. Allegory enabled DS9 to salute the liberatory role of religions and cosmogonies broadly, without having to pinpoint a single religious referent—an appropriate choice, given the religious and metaphysical heterogeneity of Palestine and many Indigenous communities in the United States. Echevarria recalls that the only thing that vexed the studio more than episodes focused on Bajoran politics were those focused on Bajoran religion (Erdmann and Block 2000, 319). Unlike Huntington or mainstream Hollywood producers, DS9's allegories imagined that religion could play an emancipatory role in global politics, as well as a reactionary one—that it could in fact provide support for the material struggles against racism, war, and exploitation that might one day achieve a more utopian future.

"Subversive Gestures Never Allowed in Any Realistic Program"

From a Left perspective, then, perhaps the most salient criticism of DS9's Bajor arc is that it failed to interrupt another pernicious Hollywood tendency: the whitewashing of anticolonial SF (J. Russell 2013; Saunders 2015). Yes, the occasional Black or Brown Bajoran face appears in DS9. But the vast majority of Bajorans, certainly the overwhelming majority of Bajorans with speaking roles, are played by white actors. Thus media studies scholar Kent A. Ono (1996) asserts that by casting mostly white actors to play Bajorans, *Star Trek* removes "terrorism" from existing histories of anticolonial struggle, making on-screen terrorists easier for white audiences to accept but also easier to dismiss as self-indulgent or apolitical (175).

Visibility matters here, because we *see* so much of Bajorans and the actors who play them on DS9. Although portraying a Bajoran requires an actor to wear a nose bridge prosthesis—referred to in on-set vernacular as "nose jobs"—and earrings, it leaves the rest of an actor's face in sight (Reeves-Stevens and Reeves-Stevens 1994, 11). Although more arduous than the makeup requirements for human or Betazoid characters, Bajoran prostheses conceal far less than Cardassian, Ferengi, Klingon, Founder, Vorta, or Jem'Hadar masks.

The decision to minimize Bajoran makeup requirements stems from producer Rick Berman's admiration for TNG actor Michelle Forbes, who portrayed Ensign Ro. Berman reportedly told Michael Westmore, the celebrated makeup supervisor on TNG and DS9, "We've hired a pretty girl and I want to keep her that way. Think of something that we can take and make her look a little alien, and still get the idea she's from another planet, but she's still gorgeous" (Memory Alpha n.d.a). Forbes, whose full name is Michelle Renee Forbes Guajardo, is of English, Welsh, and Mexican American descent and has dark-brown hair, light-brown eyes, and fair skin. The point here is not to scrutinize Forbes, a brilliant actor and a refreshingly thoughtful Leftist voice in Hollywood's sea of inchoate liberals. Rather, it is to note that the Bajorans as we know and see them are a product of Berman's valuation of fair-skinned beauty, of his directive to make that beauty visible.

Cardassian Settler Colonialism

Casting white actors in the roles of colonized peoples is by no means a problem unique to the Bajorans, DS9, or *Star Trek*. The whitewashing of anticolonial allegory is a defining crisis of mainstream American SF. International studies scholar Robert A. Saunders (2015) remarks that such a habit "inverts the genuine threat that Euro-American imperialism has posed to the non-white people of the world" (2). Anthropologist John G. Russell (2013) argues that such racial camouflage in SF is a cynical move that protects writers and studios from both critiques of appropriation and right-wing reaction while cashing in on the palatability of whiteness with global audiences.

Well-meaning gestures to the cosmogonies of colonized peoples, such as the Bajoran Prophets' resonances with Native American spiritualities, can be no less pernicious. Historian Philip J. Deloria (Standing Rock Sioux) critiques a postmodern form of settler-colonial multiculturalism that imagines "self-creative cultural free play" as "the prerogative of individuals," having "little to do with the relations between social groups or the power inequities among them" (1998, 172). Deloria and other Indigenous critics have grounded the appropriation of Native American identities and spiritualities in a so-called New Age in the longer, bloody history of American settlers displacing and murdering Native peoples, only to mourn and impersonate them.

But alongside questions of studio greed, cultural appropriation, and racist audience desire, it must be acknowledged that any objective discussion of the human rights and self-determination of Palestinians faces serious threats of concrete political repression in the United States. "Repression," to be clear, refers neither to a conspiracy nor to pernicious tropes about Jewish people and the media but to an ensemble of concrete practices—from state regulation of public employees' political speech to evangelical audience backlash—hostile to pro-Palestinian speech in the United States. Although DS9's creators have made clear that Bajor is not *only* an allegory for Palestine, they were certainly taking a risk in offering a nuanced, sympathetic portrait of violently displaced, often devoutly religious colonized people who use a range of tactics, including violence, to keep their homeland, and in publicly naming Palestine as a key point of inspiration. To be sure, *Star Trek* writers have always responded to historical conditions made by people, including by social movements. Palestinian American historian Rashid Khalidi (2020) recounts that during the First Intifada (1987–93), ordinary Palestinian civilians savvily took to transnational media to highlight the disproportionate use of Israeli military force against them, resulting in an increase in global and even U.S. public sympathy. In this sense, that the Bajorans exist at all is also to the credit of ordinary Palestinians, who made themselves thinkable on the global stage as sympathetic victims of settler colonialism in the 1980s and 1990s. Yet Khalidi notes that even during the First Intifada, as now, the rhetorical equation of "Palestinian" with "terrorist" continues to leave little room for nuance in many Americans' views (120). As Said ([1979] 1992) reflected, "However much one laments and even wishes somehow to atone for the loss of life and suffering visited upon innocents because of Palestinian violence, there is still the need, I think, also to say that no national movement has been so unfairly penalized, defamed, and subjected to disproportionate retaliation for its sins as has the Palestinians" (xxi).

It is also difficult to imagine that the Bajoran story lines on TNG and DS9 would have been acceptable, even as whitewashed allegory, had they been pitched to studios just a few years later. The attacks of September 11, 2001, led to a proliferation of jingoistic nationalist entertainment in the United States and to the "cancellation" (*avant la lettre*) of many antiwar and progressive entertainers and commentators. Indeed, *Trek* itself took a decidedly neoconservative turn in the early 2000s (Greven 2009). Whether in 1993, 2003, or 2023, more direct allegories for Palestine would almost certainly be faced not only with audience dismissal as obvious or didactic but also with the very real threat of censorship. As Israeli journalist Gideon Levy (2018) has observed more recently, "In the heavy-handed reality that has seized control over dialogue in the United States, there's no room for expressions that may offend the Israeli occupation." Ironically, while many Israelis of good conscience speak out against the racist and colonial actions of their state, Americans are the ones who often cannot follow suit.

In such contexts, it makes sense to read SF not only for racial representation but for allegory, for "partial and incomplete metaphors" (Gonzalez 2015, 60) that express sympathy or solidarity with anticolonial struggle. It seems all the more crucial to revisit Bajor's Palestine allegory in a moment of belated but growing recognition in the United States that speaking out against the specific, illegal, settler-colonial actions of a racist Israeli government in Palestine is not only *not* an anti-Semitic act but a moral imperative for everyone (Butler 2012; Erakat 2019; Jewish Voice for Peace 2017). That the Israeli regime is the single-largest recipient of U.S. military aid—to the tune of $4 billion a year—puts an onus on all U.S. citizens who care about racial justice to ask what is done in our name in Palestine. This recognition has come first and foremost thanks to the organizing of progressive Palestinians and Jews (including Palestinian Jews) across diasporas. It has also been facilitated by links between Palestinian and Black freedom struggles (A. Davis 2015), and by the international solidarity of contemporary Indigenous social movements, from Standing Rock to Mauna Kea, reminding the United States of our own unreconciled and contested settler-colonial present (Estes 2019; Gregory 2004).

By holding critiques of appropriation and racial camouflage in SF in tension with a grim awareness of the constraints on more direct support for Palestinian human rights in the United States, it becomes clear that *DS9* deserves at least modest credit for depicting religiously inflected resistance to settler colonialism as sympathetic and legitimate, even if that depiction is partial, problematic, and for the most part, camouflaged. A depressive/reparative reader—a typically "paranoid" Leftist reader who is invited by good surprises to revise harsh judgment (Sedgwick 2003)—would also remain curious about whether such messages are being decoded, hacked, and remixed by marginalized and radical audiences, whom fan studies scholars have shown to be nothing if not capacious and inventive (see Jenkins 1992; Jenkins and Tulloch 1995).

Here we might consider the example of historian and Indigenous studies scholar Maile Arvin (Kanaka Maoli) (2015). Arvin persuasively critiques James Cameron's film *Avatar* (2009) as a "distorted image of indigeneity" (114), but she also notes how Palestinian activists have used the film's popularity, "dressing up in 'blueface,'" to protest "the erection of an Israeli separation barrier near a Palestinian village." Arvin is careful not to attribute intentions to the demonstrators. But she nevertheless argues that the protest can be understood as "*both* an attempt to be visible to a Western audience that only sees settler colonialism in the distant past, the Amazon, or an intergalactic future, *and* a critique of the ways the West exoticizes and fetishizes indigenous peoples" (114, original emphasis). Arvin models how one can both critique the contents of a problematic cultural text and remain curious about what people might unexpectedly use that text, in all its contradictions, to do.

On this front, there is growing evidence that at least some Trekkers have picked up on the radical subtext of the Bajoran story line. Consider journalist Donna Minkowitz, a queer-feminist socialist Trekker and a vigilant observer of the Far Right. In 2002, against the climate of a censorious U.S. nationalism hell-bent on a second U.S. invasion of Iraq, Minkowitz wrote appreciatively of *Star Trek*'s 1990s incarnations:

> Science fiction routinely gets away with subversive gestures that would never be allowed in any realistic program. Thus it is that people who don't watch *Star Trek* are probably unaware that its vision of our future is socialistic, anti-imperialist and passionately committed to expanding the list of sentient life forms who are judged to have rights and acknowledged to be persons. (If you think this question applies only to hypothetical androids and blobs and has nothing to do with you, you haven't been watching *Star Trek*, which makes it clear that its disfranchised beings are surrogates for people of color, colonized workers, Palestinians—yes, there was an entire plot arc devoted to Palestinians—disabled people and others.) (2002)

Some two decades later, Minkowitz is far from alone. Leftist Trekker social media communities indicate that many *DS9* fans are seeing through Bajorans' racial camouflage. Social media accounts with thousands of followers—like Will Nguyen the "Star Trek Communist," "Star Trek Socialist," "Deep Space Socialist," "United Federation of Leftist Memes," "Star Trek Screen-

Cardassian Settler Colonialism

shots with Revolutionary Quotes Overlaid on Them," "Attention Bajoran Workers," and "Trekkie for Justice," which has fought censorship by Instagram over its outspoken solidarity with Palestinians—make frequent use of Bajoran allusions in support of anarchist, socialist, anticapitalist, antiracist, anticolonial, feminist, and queer messages. These accounts pair photos of Major Kira with the words of fighters for Kurdish independence and Palestinian self-determination, and with messages calling for the abolition of Immigration and Customs Enforcement and white supremacy. Certainly, allegory can be trivializing, even offensive. But it can also be a meaningful vector for unexpected, solidaristic practices of (dis)identification (Muñoz 1999).

Consider, finally, a thoughtful, extensive interview given by Forbes, whose appearances as Ro Laren introduced the Bajorans and their decolonization struggle to the world, to Leftist broadcasters Katie Halper, Briahna Joy Gray, Leslie Lee III, and Jack Allison. Forbes expresses regrets about her work on jingoistic television productions such as 24, describes her upbringing by a poor immigrant single mother and grandmother, and jokes about early iterations of the Bajoran nose prosthesis that resembled a vulva. When Forbes's young Leftist hosts explain that they see in the Bajoran story line a source of radical hope, one that inspires and encourages their own outspokenness on the still-taboo question of Palestine, she enthusiastically affirms these readings. She describes how Star Trek writers' "little morality tales" informed her already-developing Leftist consciousness as a young artist: "That original introduction of the character of Ensign Ro was the perfect metaphor for the Palestinians . . . and to be dropped into that, yes, of course it changed me, of course it shaped me. I mean, I was already shaping, but it certainly helped" (Littlefield NYC 2020). She goes on to lament the difficulty of publicly criticizing unjust Israeli government actions in the United States, recounting the horror she experienced watching videos of the eviction of elderly Palestinians from their own homes at gunpoint in areas slated for illegal Israeli settlement, and insists that empathy and solidarity with Palestinian self-determination must not be equated with anti-Semitism (see Butler 2012).

In one of the interview's lighter moments, Leslie Lee asks whether Visitor's Kira or Forbes's Ro would win in a hypothetical fight. Forbes, who turned down the role that became Major Kira, did not hesitate. Conceding that Ro had left a Bajoran refugee camp and secured access to Federation abundance at a young age, Forbes expressed respect for Kira's persistence on Bajor, her fight for survival under conditions of Occupation and its aftermath: "I would go with Kira, because she was there longer." With the highest respect for Ro Laren, Forbes is right. It is Kira's stubborn commitment to place—to religious and geographical particularity—as a departure point for inclusive and emancipatory struggle that makes her character and Bajor's anticolonial allegory so formidable and relevant to this day.

Cardassian Settler Colonialism

3   Jem'Hadar Marronage and the
      Dominion "Order of Things"

"The Carrot-and-Stick Empire"

When *The Next Generation* ended in 1994, and with *Voyager* set on the other side of the galaxy, DS9's creators soon found themselves in full control of the politics of the Alpha Quadrant, the galactic region where most of *Trek* takes place. As post–Cold War Hollywood scrambled to imagine new enemies against which to define U.S. geopolitical identity (Sharp 1998), the show's writers sensed an opportunity to create a different kind of *Trek* antagonist. For all *Star Trek*'s commitment to diversity—TOS popularized the Vulcan maxim, "Infinite Diversity in Infinite Combinations"—the franchise's "bad guys" prior to DS9 had often been imagined as highly homogenous societies. TOS and TNG largely fretted over antagonists that were depicted as sharing a racialized cultural identity (Klingons, Romulans, Cardassians, Ferengi) with few glimpses, if any, of internal race and class struggle. Even the authoritarian Borg collective, although comprised of heterogeneous peoples, is coercively universalist, forcibly integrating those peoples into a single hive mind (P. Jackson and Nexon 2003) and famously advising that "resistance is futile." But whether its enemies are homogenous or aggressively homogenizing, it is against these foils that the Federation's multicultural liberal democracy seems infinitely more legitimate in its claims to universality.

In the Dominion, a complex society that appears nowhere else in *Star Trek*, the Federation encounters a different kind of enemy, more akin to an evil twin. As Wolfe puts it, the Dominion were, "like the Federation, a collection of different races. But unlike the Federation, they were bound together by fear and extortion, whereas the Federation is bound together by noble thoughts and love and friendship and all that good stuff. So in a lot of ways, they were the mirror image of the Federation" (quoted in Memory Alpha n.d.d). Following Wolfe, this chapter develops an interpretation of *DS9*'s Dominion less as a foil or a negative resource for U.S. self-definition than as a mirror, a potential occasion for critical self-reflection.

Both multiracial *and* racist, the Dominion is ruled by a reclusive, xenophobic class of elites known as the Founders. The Founders, or Changelings, are shape-shifters, gelatinous beings capable of changing their material form, who live on a "rogue" planet in the Great Link, a utopian transindividual sea. Convinced of their own racial and moral superiority, the Founders see it as their mission to "bring order to the galaxy." Occasionally, a Founder leaves the link, often to gather intelligence; the capacity to assume the form of any person or thing makes Founders formidable spies. For the most part, however, the Founders' orders are carried out by two distinct, racialized subordinate classes: the Vorta—an intermediary, professional-managerial class of diplomats, scientists, and military commanders—and a lower class of soldiers, the Jem'Hadar, who serve as shock troops. Both groups are, at least according to Dominion propaganda, genetically engineered to worship the Founders as gods—a narrative that consolidates the Dominion's image as the polar opposite of the resolutely antieugenicist Federation.

Founders regard Vorta and Jem'Hadar life as utterly disposable. Vorta are serialized clones who retain their predecessors' memories and are programmed to commit suicide if captured (Posey 1998). Jem'Hadar are trained as warriors from infancy and grow to adult size within days of birth. They are instructed to go into battle as though already dead, fighting to reclaim their lives. Jem'Hadar are controlled in part through the narrative that they are born with an unbreakable addiction to Ketracel-White, a drug removing the need for water, food, and sleep that is strictly rationed and distributed by their Vorta commanders. Jem'Hadar soldiers rarely live to the age of fifteen (L. Burton 1996b). Although they refer to one another as "men," there are no Jem'Hadar women, only soldiers mass-produced in "birthing chambers." Even casting choices seem to reiterate the Dominion's

Jem'Hadar Marronage

race and class structure. To the best of my knowledge, both the Founders and the Vorta are almost exclusively portrayed by white actors, whereas a significant number of Jem'Hadar are played by Black actors.

The Dominion's evil, then, derives from neither a homogenous, racialized essence nor the forced imposition of a common culture but from what is referred to as "the order of things": the theologically prescribed, scientifically naturalized unequal social relations among its heterogeneous members. It is this rigid race and class hierarchy that enables the Dominion to dominate the politics, territories, and economies of so many other planets and peoples. As Wolfe outlines, "The Dominion was the Carrot-and-Stick Empire. The businessmen, the Vorta, were the negotiators, the friendly guys who show up with the Carrot. 'Hey, we're your friends. Have some phaser rifles, or space travel, whatever the hell you want. We'll arrange it. All you'll have to do is owe us.' Then, if you don't toe the line, they kick your ass with the Jem'Hadar" (Erdmann and Block 2000, 154). So although the Jem'Hadar are easily the most subordinated of the Dominion's three pillars, it is crucial to note the ground on which those pillars rest: economic domination, territorial annexation, and at times genocide of a host of other peoples (Memory Alpha n.d.d; Auberjonois 1996a).

Some critics (e.g., Napolitano 2012) see in the Dominion and its galaxy-ordering mission a purely racist social formation, devoid of any profit motive or other economic imperative. Yet as Gonzalez (2017, 34) astutely observes, the Dominion's racism and its extractive economic logics are intimately intertwined. The very first mention of the Dominion comes in "Rules of Acquisition," which follows Ferengi attempts to expand "synthehol" booze sales into the Gamma Quadrant. When Quark presses a trading partner for details about this mysterious "Dominion," she grows circumspect, counseling, "Let's just say if you want to do business in the Gamma Quadrant, you have to do business with the Dominion" (Livingston 1993d). When Bajor later signs a nonaggression pact with the Dominion to prevent a redux of the Cardassian Occupation, the Dominion isolates the planet from all external trade (Vejar 1997b). And the Dominion war machine relies heavily on intensive resource extraction, notably for mineral ingredients for Ketracel-White, which directly informs its territorial interests (Gonzalez 2018, 74; Williams 1997). Even the Founders' gelatinous default state—their shape-shifting abilities—allegorizes not only the phantasmatic mobility of whiteness but that of capital as well.[1]

At first, the Dominion seems content to repel Bajoran and Federation activity from the Gamma Quadrant, the side of the Bajoran wormhole that it already controls. But by season 5, the Dominion gains a territorial foothold in the Alpha Quadrant when the Cardassian Empire joins its ranks under the controversial leadership of Gul Dukat. Seasons 6 and 7 chronicle Federation, Klingon, and eventually Romulan efforts to resist a full-scale Dominion and Cardassian invasion. Given this arc, it is not surprising that extant scholarship almost uniformly interprets the Dominion as a stand-in for an external enemy of the United States (Dyson 2015, 100; Campbell and Gokcek 2019, 139). American studies scholar Stefan Rabitsch (2018), for instance, perceptively argues that by casting the eugenicist and expansionist Dominion as Nazis, *DS9* contributed to the torrent of 1990s good-war propaganda celebrating the fiftieth anniversary of Allied victory in World War II (39–40; see also Engelhardt 2007; Pauwels 2002). Kapell (2000), likewise, notes that when the Federation defeats the Dominion, a triumphant Admiral William Ross (Barry Jenner) quotes a victory speech by U.S. general Douglas McArthur, who commanded the Southwest Pacific theater in World War II and became de facto ruler of U.S.-occupied Japan.

Another line of inquiry examines what the Federation's often-problematic conduct in the Dominion War might tell Americans about ourselves, highlighting the Federation security state's repeated abuses and excesses. In "Home Front" and "Paradise Lost," Sisko brings down his own mentor, Starfleet admiral James Leyton (Robert Foxworth), after Leyton falsifies evidence of Dominion attacks to justify suspending civilian authority and implementing martial law (Agamben 2005) on Earth, the Federation's precious capital (Livingston 1996; Badiyi 1996). Gonzalez (2015) rightly asserts that these episodes "presage the Bush Administration contention that the al-Qaeda threat required greater political/legal latitude for the military-security apparatus" (158). To prevent Founder infiltrations, the

Federation undertakes draconian security measures, notably including blood screenings, on the faulty assumption that "bloodless" Changelings' samples will simply revert to their gelatinous state.

Meanwhile, a thrilling Bashir-centric plot arc introduces Section 31, a shady Federation intelligence agency. Comparable to many of the ever-proliferating number of U.S. espionage agencies (Tran 2018), Section 31 surveils Federation citizens, discredits foreign politicians it regards as opponents of Federation interests, and even develops (and uses) a biological weapon meant to eliminate the Founders (see Napolitano 2012). Actor William Sadler, who portrays conniving Section 31 agent Luther Sloan on *DS9*, points to Reagan administration apparatchik Colonel Oliver North as an odious muse.[2] Sadler had already played a character much like North, who illegally funneled tens of millions of dollars to brutal right-wing counterrevolutionaries in Panama and Nicaragua, in *Die Hard 2* (Harlin 1990). The actor explains that Sloan "breaks all the rules, all the rules of the Federation, in order to keep the Federation safe, or so he thinks and deeply believes. . . . The Federation, this honorable group, these honorable people for all these years, had this little worm in there who's been changing history for decades" (Sadler 2010). Little else about the Dominion arc suggests analogies to the U.S. Dirty Wars in Latin America. But the continued opacity and cruelty of the U.S. intelligence apparatus, which have only deepened in the decades since *DS9*, have made Section 31 a recurring vehicle for critiques of state violence in subsequent *Trek* iterations, particularly *DIS* (Tran 2018; Mittermeier and Spychala 2020).

But both existing criticism and Sadler's insightful commentary assume that the Dominion is "them," not "us." A rare departure from this assumption comes from a Trekker quoted by Anijar (2008) who compares the Dominion's bid for "permanent hegemony" to that of U.S. neoconservatives, quipping, "George W. Bush would have made a fine Vorta" (223). Likewise, Gonzalez (2018) compares the Dominion to the U.S. billionaire and political classes, who enjoy enormous wealth while sending "disposable" people to die in foreign wars (93). Wolfe, a self-professed history buff, also sees parallels to other Western imperialisms, particularly the Roman Empire's flexible approach to maintaining dominance (Erdmann and Block 2000, 167). Building on this latter line of interpretation, this chapter asks what happens when we read the Dominion neither as an "axis of evil" nor as an external Other who "forces" us to act out of accordance with our own values but as holding up a critical mirror to the U.S. empire. Even if it is consciously intended as an allegory for the United States' external Others, what might the Dominion, as the creation of American writers, index about the United States itself?

Where Wolfe frames the Dominion as an evil foil for the Federation's goodness, we might also observe what psychoanalyst Melanie Klein called "projective identification" ([1946] 1975). Projective identification describes an unconscious process whereby good and bad aspects of one's self-image are divided in two, kept separate and oppositional from one another, with the bad parts projected onto an object exterior to the self. Going beyond simple projection, projective identification actively molds and incites its object to take on the image of unwanted or disavowed parts of the self. For U.S. *Star Trek* writers and audiences, this might mean identifying with the goodness and light of Federation propaganda, while keeping the underside of American racial capitalism and imperialism at bay by infusing it into an enemy like the Dominion. The Dominion's evil, which in part reflects our own, then justifies Federation actions that depart from its own beneficent self-image.

For Klein, people constantly move between processes of splitting and projection, on the one hand, and the emotionally difficult work of integrating the good and bad aspects of our objects and ourselves, on the other. Recognizing that our seemingly good objects are in fact contaminated by truly horrific bad parts is a necessarily painful process, one that Klein calls "de-idealization" ([1963] 1975). This chapter reads the Dominion as a repository for the repressed content of U.S. exceptionalism and imperialism— content that is disavowed by neoliberal multiculturalist narratives only to be projected onto external Others. When we read the Dominion as an external enemy, its stark hierarchy and belief in Jem'Hadar and Vorta disposability reiterates the racist trope about enemies of the United States

and the West—that "they" do not value life as "we" do. But when we read the Dominion as a critical mirror or a vehicle for projective identification, it also reflects back to us the logics of U.S. racial capitalism itself, inviting the audience to confront our own contradictions.

Crucially, though, DS9 also shows us the fault lines in the Dominion's seemingly rock-solid "order of things." Although the Dominion's official line holds that the Founders are gods who have flawlessly engineered the Vorta and the Jem'Hadar to obey them, DS9's narratives and world-building cast considerable doubt on this narrative. Continuing the depressive/reparative project of A Different "Trek"—lifting up moments of interruption and surprise as they challenge our own paranoid judgment—this chapter attends to episodes that fracture, if not rupture, received truths about the Dominion's naturalized and sacralized race and class hierarchies. It highlights the freedom struggles of marooned and fugitive Jem'Hadar, and dissident Founders who reckon seriously with their complicity in empire. Through a depressive/reparative lens, we might see in the Dominion both critical reflection of the U.S. empire and glimmers of internal resistance.

*

Some may wonder why this book privileges the (geo)politics of the Cardassians and the Dominion over other DS9 antagonists. Historically, scholarship on Trek's extraterrestrial political allegories has focused largely on Vulcans, Klingons, and the Borg. Of those, only Klingons receive notable airtime on DS9. Why not a Klingon chapter, then?

Most scholars agree that in TOS, Klingons allegorized the USSR as the principal rival to the Federation's U.S. or West. Yet as Bernardi (1998) explains, "Even as Communists and Soviets, they [Klingons] are an amalgam of signifiers, a condensation of Othering intertexts, including darkened skin and sinister Fu Manchu goatees" (131; see also Bishop 2019; Summers 2013). After the Cold War, Anijar (2001) notes, "Klingons began to change, mutating into something (someone) else entirely"—they "became taller and more muscular. And their faces changed considerably (due in part to a large makeup budget)" (184–85). More Black actors were hired to play Klingons, with Worf actor Michael Dorn doubling as a Klingon lawyer in *Star Trek VI* (Meyer 1991). Klingons continued to draw on a mix of stereotypes about Japanese, Native American, and Muslim "honor" and "warrior" cultures (Vande Berg 1996, 59; Gonzalez 2015, 63), but this repertoire increasingly incorporated tropes of Blackness as well (see Ott and Aoki 2001, 399–403; Weinstock 1996, 334; J. Russell 2013). Here again, recall Gilmore's (2002) insight that "at the very moment when the nation is basking in foreign victory, the domestic turns hostile" (20). A permanent security state requires a permanent supply of enemies, internal and external, and *Trek* has often played along.

Critics have rightly questioned Lieutenant Commander Data's (Brent Spiner) matter-of-fact assertion on TNG of "a genetic predisposition toward hostility among all Klingons" (Iscove 1989). The claim parallels the contemporaneous pseudoscientific discourse on Black youth as "superpredators," a malevolent story that numerous Black studies scholars have contested (Wynter 1992; D. Roberts 1997). During a 1991 visit to the TNG set, Ronald Reagan remarked of Klingons, "I like them, they remind me of Congress" (quoted in Rogoway 2015). The trope of Klingon aggression made it easy for Reagan to depoliticize Congress's legitimate grievances with his administration—over social welfare, civil rights, South African apartheid, and Iran-Contra—as predictable, petty intransigence.

DS9's main interlocutor for Klingon politics is TNG's beloved Worf, who joins the crew in season 4 to manage the Federation's relationships with erratic Klingon chancellor Gowron (Robert O'Reilly) and grizzled General Martok (J. G. Hertzler). Actor Michael Dorn's comic timing as Worf is impeccable. His record as the *Trek* main cast member with the most franchise appearances is to be treasured. SF luminary Ursula K. Le Guin's ([1994] 1995) retrospective essay on TNG swoons, "Worf . . . was my first love. That voice, Richter 6.5—that forehead—those dark, worried eyes—those ethical problems! . . . Worf, caught between two worlds, was a powerful figure, tragic" (124–25). Le Guin sees in Worf a Shakespearean tragic figure of the first order, and in the Klingon Empire a rich world of familial and palace intrigue.

But as Starfleet's first Klingon officer, Worf is the Federation's point man on the Qo'noS file, forced into the tokenizing position of native informant, despite being an orphan who was raised on Earth by humans (Vande Berg 1996). Dorn has joked that Worf "is *always* pissed" (Altman and Gross 2016, 493, original emphasis). Given how much political pressure he's under, it's easy to understand why. In Worf's four years on D$9, Klingons go to war with the Cardassians, then the Federation, then join the Federation's war against the Dominion, only to be infiltrated by the Dominion. In the final season, Worf is asked to lead a Federation-backed coup installing Klingon leadership more cooperative with the joint war effort—replacing Gowron, whom Worf had also helped the Federation to install earlier (Vejar 1999c; Carson 1991). Worf's Federation colleagues respect him personally, but with the exceptions of Sisko and Jadzia Dax, they either fear Klingons or lecture them on their putatively endemic corruption problem, a classic imperial move. Whether Klingons are Russian, "Mongol," Japanese, Native, Arab, or Black American, the late communications scholar Leah R. Vande Berg's (1996) point stands: "The relationship between the dominant Federation culture (here the colonizer) and Klingon culture (here Worf) is never seriously problematized on anything but a personal level" (66). I'd be pissed, too.

D$9 offers rich, nuanced portraits of individual Klingon characters—Worf, his brother Kurn (Tony Todd), Worf's son Alexander (Marc Worden), Martok, Gowron, and others. Yet by my reading, when it comes to Klingon politics, it rarely shows us the contradictions of Klingon social formations on terms that suggest historical contingency, dynamism, or amenability to alternatives, and instead naturalizes those contradictions as morally or biologically innate. Fortunately, the same cannot be said of the Dominion.

"I Suggest You Stay on Your Side of the Galaxy"

For most of season 2, the Dominion is not seen but heard, the topic of ominous whispers. In the season finale, a wholesome Gamma Quadrant camping trip goes awry when Commander Sisko and Quark are captured by Jem'Hadar, leaving Nog and Jake stranded (Friedman 1994b). Talak'talan (Cress Williams), a formidable Jem'Hadar leader who stands an imposing

11. Jem'Hadar soldier Talak'talan casually breaking out of a containment field, which a panicked Chief O'Brien had set up around him in Ops, the station's command deck ("The Jem'Hadar," season 2, episode 26, aired June 12, 1994).

six feet five (1.96 meters), taunts the prisoners, then visits DS9 unannounced. He boasts of Sisko's capture, of the massacres of a litany of Federation and Bajoran vessels and communities in the Gamma Quadrant. "Unless you wish to continue to offend the Dominion," he warns, "I suggest you stay on your side of the galaxy" (Friedman 1994b).[3] A small fleet of Federation vessels rescue Sisko, Quark, and the boys. But the episode concludes with an unexpected Jem'Hadar suicide attack on the retreating USS *Odyssey*, a ship identical in make to *TNG*'s flagship *Enterprise-D*. Extending the cliché that U.S. enemies simply value life less than "we" do, Sisko grimly deduces, "They're showing us how far they're willing to go."

From our very first glimpse of the Jem'Hadar in the season 2 finale, their prosthesis is meant to establish the characters as fearsome, animalistic, racialized Others. Although Wolfe's initial proposal of a "fierce warrior race

Jem'Hadar Marronage

with skins like rhinos" struck Berman as "comic-booky," makeup director Westmore turned to nature photography to craft a subtler, rhino-inspired look: "If you'd put a horn on it, viewers would say, 'Oh—rhinoceros.' But what makes *Star Trek* so interesting is that you give the creature the same feel and meanness by putting little horns around his face. It makes them dangerous—if you bump into one, you're going to bleed. So you know automatically that you never get close to the Jem'Hadar" (Erdmann and Block 2000, 153).

The rationale for the Jem'Hadar look draws on long-standing Western misconceptions about the rhinoceros—an animal indigenous to Africa, South Asia, and Java—as inherently aggressive. Since sixteenth-century Portuguese colonialism in South Asia, visual studies scholar Lisa Uddin (2015) explains, Western representations have "rendered the creature utterly strange to its European audience, nourishing a persistent and versatile pattern of linking non-human natural histories to human beings identified as other than white" (196). German painter and printmaker Albrecht Dürer, who had never seen a rhinoceros himself, took liberties with Portuguese eyewitness sketches, transforming rhino skin into a menacing "coat of armor" (195). This Western way of seeing persisted into twentieth-century U.S. cinema, which cast rhinos as "irrational violence incarnate" (210). In fact, although fights *among* rhinoceros are not uncommon, experts estimate that rhino attacks on people are limited to about two annually and are rarely, if ever, fatal. Rhinoceros have far more to fear from human poachers than the other way around. Yet Dürer's fantasies retain a formative place in Western imaginations.

Such histories matter because, as literary scholar Ximena Gallardo (2013) observes, mainstream SF has a habit of extending them, repackaging images of "exotic" places and people as animalistic "while officially imparting a politically correct narrative where humans of all colors interact with no problems" (230). As noted above, although the Founders and the Vorta are played principally by white actors, a significant number of Black actors, as well as white ones, portray Jem'Hadar. Gallardo argues that SF employs "the alien mask (prostheses, rubber suits, and other disguises to create the illusion of an extraterrestrial creature) as if to veil the connection between the otherness it represents and the socio-historical reality of the black actor beneath the image" (229).[4] But heeding Gallardo's powerful critique need not prevent us from remaining curious about the narrative agency of actors, directors, and writers to take SF tropes in unexpected directions (carrington 2016). SF's general tendency toward masking as mystification makes the Jem'Hadar significant, precisely because of the efforts made, particularly by Black DS9 directors and actors, to infuse these characters with a measure of sociohistorical reality, refusing to allow the alien mask to complete its veiling work. What happens when we read DS9 against the grain, in a manner that challenges the dominant, racialized construction of the Jem'Hadar, rather than taking it for granted or simply exposing it?

*

If season 2's finale establishes the Dominion as a fearsome opponent, it tells us less about its social structure. A more revealing—and disturbing—look at the Dominion's internal race and class hierarchies comes in season 3's "The Abandoned," when an orphaned extraterrestrial infant mysteriously turns up on the station (Brooks 1994b). Never given a name, the baby rapidly develops into a child and then an adolescent Jem'Hadar within a matter of hours. Marveling at the child's metabolism, Bashir concludes that he must be the product of sophisticated Dominion genetic engineering. Although the young Jem'Hadar initially eats solid food, he soon craves Ketracel-White, and Bashir manages to synthesize a supply.

Ketracel-White aside, the child has little use for the adults on the station, most of whom seem to fear him. He defers only to Odo, and even then only because Odo is, by birth and appearance if not ideology, a Founder: "I know in here that I am inferior to you," the child explains to Odo, "but that everyone else here is inferior to me" (Brooks 1994b). Odo, who was raised outside the Dominion, was himself "discovered" and studied by Bajoran and Cardassian scientists and has come to resent the polite condescension of scientific experts and handlers. The constable pleads with Sisko that the boy be allowed to remain in his care and tutelage, rather than face a similar

Jem'Hadar Marronage

fate in a Federation laboratory. Kira is skeptical of Odo's plan, warning, "You are listening to your heart, not your head. That boy was created in a laboratory. His body, his mind, his instincts are all designed to do one thing. To kill." Odo counters that "each of us"—Kira the revolutionary, Odo the Founder—"chose to be something different," and that the boy, too, deserves a chance (Brooks 1994b).

Attempting a liberal pedagogy of citizenship, Odo preaches equality and individual agency, encouraging the child to reflect on his own desires for his future. The child describes violent urges, which Odo permits him to take out on holographic rivals in Quark's entertainment suites, rather than real people. When the child asks to learn more about his Dominion origins, Odo reluctantly agrees, advising that "sometimes the truth is not very pleasant" (Brooks 1994b). But once the child learns more, he demands to leave the station, to return to the Gamma Quadrant, to "be with my people." Odo persuades Sisko to let the child go, rather than subject him to Federation scientific study that would cost the young man his dignity, if not his life. Odo, the well-intentioned liberal and would-be adoptive parent, feels defeated by his failure to rehabilitate the child. Meeting Kira after the young man's departure, a dejected Odo confesses, "Major, about the boy. You were right."

Unmistakable in "The Abandoned"—which aired mere days before a major right-wing victory in the 1994 U.S. midterm elections—are references to racist and classist anxieties about drug addiction, physical strength, and crime among poor Black and Brown youth. The episode was produced against the backdrop of the media myth of the "crack baby," the scientifically unsupported idea that children of mothers—particularly Black mothers—who use crack cocaine while pregnant grow up to be criminals, addicts, and dependents. Legal scholar Dorothy Roberts (1997) has rightly taken media and political elites to task for using the "crack baby" image to justify slashing social safety nets and criminalizing poor Black mothers, rather than addressing the root causes of homelessness, poverty, and addiction in poor communities of color. "The powerful image of childhood innocence," Roberts writes, "does not seem to benefit Black children. Black children are

12. Sisko gently cradling an abandoned infant Jem'Hadar in his arms ("The Aban-doned," season 3, episode 6, aired October 31, 1994).

born guilty" (21). In "The Abandoned," the Jem'Hadar child refracts these uneven geographies of innocence. The character is played by two African American actors, Hassan Nicholas and Larry C. "Bumper" Robinson III. And Ketracel-White, often referred to simply as "White," shares a color and a nickname with both crack and powder cocaine (Barrett and Barrett 2017, 119). The connection is readily apparent to Russell (2013), who briefly reads the Jem'Hadar as a fraught metaphor for Black drug addiction (203). But if "The Abandoned" is addressing the War on Drugs, what is it saying, exactly?

One plausible interpretation is that the episode validates a "natural"—more accurately, *naturalizing*—account of who the Jem'Hadar "really are." In this view, this unnamed child, who is born addicted but separated from all the typical Jem'Hadar socialization, nevertheless rapidly proves to be incor-rigibly aggressive and violent, despite the best intentions of the adoptive parent. As Wolfe puts it, "The Jem'Hadar are basically killing machines . . .

Jem'Hadar Marronage

and it's not their fault. They're just drawn that way. It's the reality of who they are" (Gross and Altman 1996, 86).

But it is imperative to refuse such naturalizing accounts of addiction and violence, be they of mythical Jem'Hadar "killing machines" or of mythical "crack babies." These explanations neglect the formative role of what Wynter, drawing on the work of Martinican psychiatrist Frantz Fanon ([1952] 2008), calls *sociogenesis*, the principle that "we are not purely biological beings!" (Wynter and McKittrick 2015, 34).[5] For Wynter, the problem with reducing a person's conditioned attributes and behavior to genetics—in the Jem'Hadar's case, addiction to Ketracel-White, loyalty to the Founders, and violent contempt for everyone else—is that genetics are merely our "first set of instructions" (Wynter and McKittrick 2015, 26). This first set of instructions "*neurochemically implement[s]* the 'second set of instructions,'" Wynter's term for "nongenetically chartered origin stories and myths" (Wynter and McKittrick 2015, 26). What makes humans unique is that our shared stories and myths—about race, class, place, gender, sexuality, nation, kinship, religion, ethics, and the good life—dynamically interact with our genes, which carry out the orders of those stories.

Wynter contrasts human beings with bees and other social insects, whose social roles "are genetically *preprescribed for them*. Ours are not, even though the biocentric meritocratic IQ bourgeois ideologics, such as the authors of *The Bell Curve*, try to tell us what they/we are" (Wynter and McKittrick 2015, 34, original emphasis). Wynter challenges racist pseudoscience that argues the current distribution of prosperity in society is a natural reflection of genetic and moral superiority. Her insistence on "nonbiological causality" (Wynter and McKittrick 2015, 71) means that the world could yet be otherwise, that our performed racialized and classed social roles can be reimagined and reconfigured.

Because the Jem'Hadar are a metaphor for humans excluded from dominant concepts of humanity, Wynter's ideas show us what is at stake in a second interpretation of "The Abandoned." Consider the reading offered by Brooks, who directed the episode alongside playing Sisko: "For me, it was very much a story about young brown men, and, to some extent, a story about a society that is responsible for the creation of a generation of young men who are feared, who are addicted, who are potential killers. . . . Odo knows that this is still a child. . . . And for him to give up and just let the boy go—what kind of a statement would we be making? That these people are expendable, that we don't really care about them? Those are the hard questions to answer" (Erdmann and Block 2000, 180). For Erdmann and Block (2000), the link that Brooks identifies to our own world is merely metaphorical (180). But as Wynter insists, stories and metaphors *matter*, including on a neurochemical and genetic level. In contrast to Wolfe, for whom the Jem'Hadar are "just drawn that way," or Erdmann and Block, for whom links to our own unjust world are "mere" metaphor, Brooks emphasizes *potentiality*, not inevitability, refusing the narrative condemnation of young, poor Black and Brown men (Wynter 1992).

Following Wynter and Brooks, we might understand the Jem'Hadar child's departure from DS9 not as a sign of incorrigible and inherent violence but as a response to deep social alienation from a station where he is feared on sight (Fanon [1952] 2008). And if young Jem'Hadar are born addicted—a premise that subsequent episodes go on to challenge—then that addiction is not the fault of the imaginary bad Black mother whom Roberts defends but of the Founders and the Vorta, of the white-dominated capitalist and professional-managerial classes, who narratively and chemically poison Jem'Hadar youth. Earlier *Star Trek* allegories for racism have tended to decontextualize it, reducing it to a transparently silly irrationality easily disavowed by liberal audiences (J. Taylor 1969; Golumbia 1995). By contrast, Brooks's interpretation and direction highlight "normal" station residents' alienating fear of the young Jem'Hadar, uncomfortably implicating many audience members ourselves.

"The Founders' Ability to Control the Jem'Hadar Has Been Somewhat . . . Overstated"

If "The Abandoned" introduces the Dominion myth of genetic dependence on Ketracel-White, season 4's "Hippocratic Oath" begins to question it. The episode focuses on a fierce disagreement that erupts between close friends

Bashir and O'Brien when they are captured by Jem'Hadar soldiers. It soon becomes clear that this group of Jem'Hadar are no longer affiliated with the Dominion—that they have formed a breakaway, maroon community. The shipwreck, the maroon, and military desertion have long been staples of SF, rich with possibilities for imagining the contradictions between soldier and state, the predicaments and potentiality of abandonment and exile. But the figure of the maroon also has especial connotations in the history of Black freedom struggles, and Black SF creators have long put SF genre conventions into conversation with that history (see Scott 2022). Political scientist Neil Roberts (2015) explains that the practice of marronage—"a group of persons isolating themselves from a surrounding society in order to create a fully autonomous community"—has been central to Black and Indigenous struggles for freedom and self-determination against white settler plantation regimes in the Americas for centuries (4).

Some readers may question the extension of the concept of marronage to the Jem'Hadar, since the actors who play Jem'Hadar principally include both Black and white actors. Yet the late Cedric J. Robinson himself pointed out that in practice, maroon communities at times included poor whites who realized that they shared common enemies with Black and Indigenous maroons, whites who preferred to live in multiracial, Black-led communities (Robinson and Robinson 2017, 3–4). Black geographies scholar Willie Wright (2020), likewise, argues that the practice of marronage "exists in other forms, spaces, and conditions of control as various repressed groups have made attempts to retain autonomy in the face of countless spatial, laborious, libidinal and ideological forms of capture commensurate with capitalism's global expressions" (1136; see also Bledsoe 2017). At issue, then, is not an appropriation of marronage but rather a recognition that in a world in the throes of racial capitalism, Black and Indigenous freedom from capitalist enclosure is vital to everyone's freedom from capitalist enclosure.

We see in "Hippocratic Oath" the very practices of isolation for autonomy that scholars of marronage describe: a break from the Dominion's death-dealing "order of things," predicated on the Jem'Hadar's induced dependence on Ketracel-White. The maroon community's leader, Goran'Agar (Scott

MacDonald), explains to Bashir that he has deliberately led his soldiers back to this specific unnamed planet, where he was previously stranded for over a month with only three days' worth of White: "I was ready to die. But death never came. . . . Being here, on this planet, cured me" (Auberjonois 1995c). Goran'Agar reasons that Ketracel-White addiction—which Dominion lore figures as God-given, genetically preprogrammed, and impossible to overcome—might in fact be environmentally contingent. He orders Bashir to investigate geographical factors in Ketracel-White dependence in the hopes of finding a replicable cure for his soldiers.

Noticing the shock on Bashir's face, Goran'Agar muses that the doctor is "surprised because a Jem'Hadar soldier might want something more than the life of a slave" (Auberjonois 1995c). He continues to challenge Bashir's received knowledge about the Dominion throughout their encounter, illuminating the cracks in the Dominion's race and class hierarchies, which had previously seemed rock-solid. Goran'Agar's primary antipathy is toward the Vorta, his immediate managers. But he also questions the Dominion's fundamental political theology—the racist belief in Founder supremacy—by placing it in a comparative frame: "I have fought against races that believe in mythical beings that guide their destinies and await them after death. They call them gods. The Founders are like gods to the Jem'Hadar. But our gods never talk to us, and they don't wait for us after death. They only want us to fight for them—and to die for them" (Auberjonois 1995c).[6] Bashir is moved by Goran'Agar's quest for Jem'Hadar self-determination and conducts the research that his captor demands in earnest.

O'Brien is appalled by Bashir's cooperativeness, which he regards as hopelessly naive. Bashir pitches his research as a matter of Federation security, a potential weapon that could deprive the Founders of an army. But O'Brien remains wary of the prospect of Jem'Hadar autonomy, muttering, "At least the Dominion keeps them on a short leash." Bashir counters that the Jem'Hadar "are not animals. They're people being used as slaves," with "the potential to become something more" (Auberjonois 1995c). As their disagreement escalates, Bashir, who is younger than O'Brien but outranks him, orders his friend to assist. O'Brien complies but later mounts an escape,

Jem'Hadar Marronage

destroying Bashir's research equipment to force him to join. Goran'Agar reluctantly permits the two to leave. He elects to remain with his soldiers, who will likely die, rather than come along with Bashir as an exceptional Jem'Hadar medical subject. On their way home, Bashir and O'Brien continue to argue vehemently. Although their friendship recovers, we are left to wonder whether the same can be said of Goran'Agar and his men.

The dour conclusion of "Hippocratic Oath" makes it easy to write the episode off as complicit in the very process of "narrative condemnation" to inevitable death that Black radicals like Wynter (1992) urgently philosophize against. But reading the episode through its intertexts illustrates how the story interrupts and defies colonial common sense. As the script for "Hippocratic Oath" was in development, producers and writers referred to it as "*The Bridge on the River Kwai* story" (Erdmann and Block 2000, 266). The episode's resemblance to and divergence from David Lean's (1957) epic World War II film, based on French writer Pierre Boulle's ([1952] 2007) novel of the same name, prove to be instructive.

Lean's film follows British prisoners of war who are ordered by Japanese imperial prison commandant Colonel Saito (Sessue Hayakawa) to construct a railway bridge connecting Thailand and Myanmar. The Japanese state has placed considerable pressure on Saito to complete this project and will execute him if it is not completed on time. The prisoners are led by Lieutenant Colonel Nicholson (Alec Guinness), who resolves to build the bridge competently and without sabotage as a display of superior British engineering—his way of turning "defeat into victory" (Lean 1957). Nicholson's decision is met skeptically by the camp's doctor, Major Clipton (James Donald). At the film's iconic conclusion, a team of British, Canadian, and American operatives blow up the completed bridge, killing Nicholson and Saito. Watching from a distance, Clipton condemns the whole affair as "madness."

Comparative literature scholar Hirakawa Sukehiro (1999) argues that Boulle's novel and Lean's film are premised "on the illusion that the West still had a monopoly on technological skill," falsely depicting Japanese engineers as inept and Saito as weak (46–47). After Britain's painful 1942 defeat in

Singapore, Sukehiro asserts, "*The Bridge on the River Kwai* deals with the recovery of faith in British virtues of perseverance and inventiveness. In short, it is a glorification of the superiority of Western civilization" (46). "Hippocratic Oath" reverses the roles in the Nicholson-Clipton dispute, pitting a skeptical engineer against a forthright doctor. But although O'Brien and Bashir disagree over whether to cooperate with Goran'Agar, they share an assumption of Federation scientific expertise, a technological superiority explicitly linked to moral superiority. Even Goran'Agar seems to share this premise, as in his charge to Bashir: "As a Federation doctor, I know you are trained to feel compassion and sympathy for those in pain. These men are suffering now, but it is nothing compared to what will happen if they are not freed from the drug before our supply runs out" (Auberjonois 1995c). Jem'Hadar suffering and ineptitude provide a vehicle for Bashir's personal development and ascendancy as an ethical professional and liberal multicultural Federation citizen.

But alongside a familiar Orientalist "detour through the other" as a mode of Western self-making (Said [1978] 2003; Yeğenoğlu 1998), the episode's nod to *The Bridge on the River Kwai* can tell us something else, something unexpected. In compliance with his superiors, Saito uses Clipton's British technical expertise to implement the infrastructural agenda of the Japanese empire, fulfilling Orientalist stereotypes of Japanese obedience, as well as the technical ineptitude that Sukehiro contests. By contrast, "Hippocratic Oath" presents us with Jem'Hadar soldiers who appropriate Federation resources to contest the Dominion's racist class structure, division of labor, and division of expertise. Goran'Agar is not an incompetent engineer. He has been told his entire life that scientific research was beyond his purview, best left to the Vorta—that as a soldier already marked for death, his life belongs to the Founders (Puar 2007). In defiance, he leads his unit back to this obscure planet with its strange and beneficent environment, off the grid of the Dominion. He is a producer of scientific knowledge, providing Bashir with a hypothesis about the planet's possible emancipatory role in transforming Jem'Hadar physiology. Goran'Agar needs Bashir's technical expertise and is willing to use both force and moral appeals to access it.

But unlike Colonel Saito, Goran'Agar faces death for *defying* his elites, not for failing them.

Bashir exhaustively examines Goran'Agar's DNA, testing for numerous environmental determinants, but finds nothing. The doctor suggests an alternative theory: "What if nothing happened to you on this planet? What if you were never addicted to the drug in the first place? . . . Maybe you didn't need it" (Auberjonois 1995c). Bashir goes on to chalk up Goran'Agar's experience to a random DNA mutation. But his research, initiated by Goran'Agar's own hypothesis, could also suggest that the environmental condition that made the difference was freedom from the Dominion—that the whole scheme is, at least to some extent, as Wynter (following Fanon) would have it, "sociogenic" rather than biological in origin (Wynter and McKittrick 2015). Gonzalez (2017), too, sees in Jem'Hadar defiance the possibility that the core Dominion myth of "genetic conditioning" is, in fact, ideological indoctrination (85). Up against an exploitative and life-destroying myth of Founder supremacy, a racist and classist division of intellectual labor, and a tightly controlled Ketracel-White economy, Goran'Agar produces scientific hypotheses and appropriates the means of knowledge production to his own, emancipatory ends. Although O'Brien's suspicions and conservative desire for security and home (Blair 1997) seem to undermine this experiment in Jem'Hadar marronage, this is not our last glimpse of such experiments.

As the Dominion War arc advances, conflicts between the Jem'Hadar and the Vorta grow increasingly acrimonious. "To the Death," directed by the legendary TNG actor LeVar Burton (1996b), forces Sisko to momentarily join forces with the Dominion to stop a band of "rogue" Jem'Hadar. The fugitives seize an Iconian gateway, an ancient device enabling instantaneous travel anywhere in the galaxy. Dominion leaders fear that these independent Jem'Hadar could lead a fuller insurrection and become an unstoppable, autonomous, roving military force. The Vorta Weyoun (Jeffrey Combs) pitches the mission to Sisko in the name of shared security. Distrustful, Sisko asks why the Founders couldn't simply order the Jem'Hadar to surrender. "The Founders' ability to control the Jem'Hadar has been somewhat . . .

overstated," Weyoun confides. "Otherwise, we never would've had to addict them to White" (L. Burton 1996b).

Burton cast the late actor Clarence Williams III, star of *The Mod Squad*, as Omet'iklan, the leader of the loyal Jem'Hadar assigned to work with Sisko (Erdman and Block 2000, 347). Despite serious misgivings, Omet'iklan and Sisko come to establish a begrudging mutual respect. Their joint mission to suppress Jem'Hadar autonomy in "To the Death" is a bloody, reactionary, and racist one, and nearly a minute of the episode's combat scenes were censored in the United Kingdom for violence (Pesola 2021). But the episode's ending also suggests that autonomous Jem'Hadar formations will see another day. Having completed the mission, Omet'iklan shocks everyone by promptly killing Weyoun, his Vorta commander, "for questioning our loyalty." One of Omet'iklan's soldiers, Virak'kara (Scott Haven), swiftly confiscates Weyoun's supply of Ketracel-White, almost chuckling: "The Vorta will have no further use of this." Omet'iklan and his soldiers turn down Sisko's offer to take them to the nearest Dominion outpost. "There're still disloyal Jem'Hadar on this planet," Omet'iklan offers, and the two crews part ways, leaving the audience to wonder whether Omet'iklan and his soldiers will themselves go their own way (L. Burton 1996b).

"To the Death" also provides insight into the Vorta, thanks to another inspired casting choice. "With the ubiquitous, inimitable, multitalented Jeffrey Combs," Behr remarks, "we finally had a Vorta who sold the Vorta" (Erdmann and Block 2000, 347). Sell, indeed. Combs explains that Weyoun "is the snake of the universe . . . the smiling car salesman who'll tell you anything to make you feel as if you're the most important thing in his life just to get you to buy his product" (Erdmann and Block 2000, 347). Combs's vision for Weyoun came in part from Stanley Kubrick's epic *Barry Lyndon* (1975), a biting satire of eighteenth-century English imperialism: "There's a sequence at the court with all the proper sort of etiquette. Everyone has it out for everyone else, but they say things with such grace and kindness! That's the way I wanted to approach Weyoun, half car salesman and half court fop" (Erdmann and Block 2000, 348). Just as *Lyndon* lampoons the pettiness and avarice of English courtiers living off the transatlantic slave

13. Jem'Hadar leader Omet'iklan losing patience with Weyoun's insinuations about his disloyalty ("To the Death," season 4, episode 23, aired May 13, 1996).

trade and the colonization of India, the Americas, and Ireland, Combs's Weyoun gives banal evil a memorable, comical obsequiousness (Pramiaggone 2014; Arendt [1963] 1994).

But perhaps the most troubling image of Vorta-Jem'Hadar antagonism comes in season 6's "Rocks and Shoals," another, decidedly less emancipatory shipwreck story (Vejar 1997b). Sisko and company commandeer a Jem'Hadar warship but are shot down and stranded on an unknown planet. They soon realize that a Jem'Hadar unit has crashed there as well, with its Vorta commander, Keevan (Christopher Shea), badly injured.

What is unmistakable in "Rocks and Shoals" is that Keevan knows his men loathe him—and the feeling is mutual. During a fragile truce, Keevan confides that although he has Sisko's people outnumbered and outgunned, he has far too little Ketracel-White left to maintain control of his soldiers: "When it's gone, my hold over them will be broken, and they'll become nothing more than senseless, violent animals. They'll kill everyone they can. Me, you, the rest of your men, and finally turn on each other" (Vejar 1997b). Doctor Bashir approaches Keevan to examine him, but several Jem'Hadar block his way. "They're not here to protect me," Keevan sneers. "They've just never seen what the inside of a Vorta looks like."

Keevan offers to set his own soldiers up, ordering them to attack Sisko and his crew from a position that will make them easy to kill. In exchange, Keevan asks only that Sisko's people capture him alive. The proposal appalls Sisko, who repeatedly appeals to the Jem'Hadar leader, Remata'Klan (*Trek* veteran Phil Morris), telling him stories about marooned Jem'Hadar who turned on the "manipulative, treacherous" Vorta who led them. But Remata'Klan is unfazed, insistently adhering to the Dominion's prescribed "order of things." Remata'Klan is not at all surprised by Keevan's treachery. "Despite what Keevan may think," he tells Sisko, "the Jem'Hadar are often one step ahead of the Vorta." But he makes clear that he would rather die as a Dominion soldier than live as a medical ward of the Federation. The attack on Sisko proceeds as planned; all of the Jem'Hadar soldiers are killed, as well as a single Federation soldier, and a furious Sisko takes Keevan into custody.

Reflecting on Remata'Klan, actor Phil Morris compares the character "to a samurai warrior who is loyal only to his feudal lord, and that's how I played him. His willingness to die, despite Sisko's offer of an alternative, is his most honorable moment" (Memory Alpha n.d.p). If Morris's interpretation recalls timeworn tropes about noble-savage Japanese warriors, his reading also reflects a keen understanding of the episode's genealogy. DS9 writer Ronald D. Moore, beloved for his work on *Star Trek* and subsequent reboot of *Battlestar Galactica*, has named the World War II film *None but the Brave* (Sinatra 1965) as a key intertext for "Rocks and Shoals" (Memory Alpha n.d.p). The film follows the bonds and hostilities between Japanese and American soldiers stranded on a remote, uninhabited Pacific island—hostilities that tellingly leave every Japanese soldier and all but a few Americans dead.

Some critics have hailed *None but the Brave* as an "antiwar epic" from the tail end of director Frank Sinatra's Hollywood liberal phase, noting

Jem'Hadar Marronage

that it was a joint production with a Japanese studio (Cotter 2019). The film closes with the intertitle "NOBODY EVER WINS." Yet shortly after that intertitle leaves the screen, we learn that *None but the Brave* was made in consultation with the U.S. Department of Defense, the Hawaiian National Guard, the U.S. Marine Corps, and the U.S. Navy.[7] The film's sympathetic Japanese lead, Lieutenant Kuroki (Tatsuya Mihashi), is troped as a decent man who is tragically unable to fully Christianize, modernize, or overcome the honorable warrior in his blood.

"Rocks and Shoals" does not offer potentially emancipatory glimpses of Jem'Hadar marronage, as do "Hippocratic Oath" and even "To the Death." It might be argued that by engaging a kind of suicide by Federation gun, Remata'Klan and his men engage in a kind of self-freeing from both Dominion enslavement and Federation capture, recalling the fraught history of suicides by enslaved persons. Numerous artists have confronted and reimagined such histories, the late literary eminence Toni Morrison (1987) being perhaps the best-known example, in order to illuminate Black people's efforts to shape their own realities under even the most oppressive conditions. Yet by my reading, both Morrison and historians of suicide among enslaved people in North America (e.g., Snyder 2015) advise a caution in attributing singular meanings to such acts. Given the stakes, I am reticent to advance such an interpretation (McKittrick 2011).

What nevertheless compels attention about "Rocks and Shoals," however, is the primary plot point upon which it deviates from *None but the Brave*. Although both Kuroki and Remata'Klan remain loyal to their soldiers till the end, "Rocks and Shoals" introduces the character of Keevan, who sacrifices his soldiers in exchange for his own life. Whatever "honorable" choice Remata'Klan might be making, or might not feel he has, Keevan's calculations are deeply cynical, individualistic, disloyal even to the Founders. When Keevan is wounded, he sneers to Remata'Klan the words of a self-satisfied elite who has only momentarily fallen below what he perceives as his rightful station: "This must be quite gratifying for you. But I've decided not to give you the pleasure of watching me die in this foul-smelling cavern. I intend to live" (Vejar 1997b). Keevan fulfills that intention, and he does so at the expense of the lives of Remata'Klan and nine soldiers under his command.

Keevan later gets his comeuppance in spectacular fashion, albeit at Ferengi rather than Jem'Hadar hands (Chalmers 1997). Yet although none of the Jem'Hadar episodes make for easy viewing, "Rocks and Shoals" always hits the hardest. Can we not see in the Dominion elements of the very United States called out by King's "Beyond Vietnam"? King decried a society that would send its poor young men, outsized numbers of them Black and Brown, "eight thousand miles away to guarantee liberties in Southeast Asia which they had not found in southwest Georgia and East Harlem" ([1967] 2015, 204). Think, too, of the early days of COVID-19. One cannot help but see Keevan in the outsourcing of as much in-person responsibility and vulnerability as possible—from meatpacking to grocery shopping to firefighting—to an army of low-waged, often racialized essential workers. As the pandemic threw the global economy into crisis, firms like Amazon repressed essential-worker organizing for safer conditions, and court intellectuals like economist Larry Summers warned that cash relief to Americans facing job losses and evictions would "overheat" the economy (Horti 2020). Whether in the name of anticommunism, patriotism, or the "free" market, U.S. elites evince what Gilmore (2007) calls "a frightening willingness to engage in human sacrifice while calling it something else" (44). In making sacrifices of the Jem'Hadar (Gimore 2017), Keevan reflects back to Americans our own "order of things."

"Finding Out Who Your People Are Doesn't Tell You Who *You* Are"

If Keevan is craven and cynical to his last breath, the same cannot be said for Odo. An orphaned Changeling who longs to return home but abhors the Dominion, Odo's narrative arc focuses on a critical reckoning with his Founder inheritances. As the station's chief of security, Odo shares the Founders' preoccupation with order and justice. A rare holdover from the Cardassian Occupation, when he worked on Terok Nor as an investigator, Odo prides himself on a neutrality that earned him the trust of both Cardassians and Bajorans. The late René Auberjonois, a storied actor known for his long stage and television career, cited both John Wayne and Clint Eastwood as character models, and Odo's sensibilities can correspondingly tend toward the reactionary (Memory Alpha n.d.l). Yet even Odo is mortified by the Founders' authoritarianism and racism.

After the Federation's initial, unpleasant introduction to the Jem'Hadar in season 2, Sisko and company set out to speak with the Founders themselves. This first contact proves to be painfully disappointing for Odo, who was raised outside the Dominion and is now reuniting with his people for the first time (Friedman 1994c; Frakes 1994a). A Founder known only as the Female Changeling (Salome Jens), who goes on to lead the Dominion invasion of the Alpha Quadrant, explains the Dominion's national origin myth to Odo, rooting it in a deep sense of Founder persecution and injury: "The Great Link tells us that many years ago our people roamed the stars, searching out other races so we could add to our knowledge of the galaxy. We went in peace, but too often we were met with suspicion, hatred, and violence. . . . The solids [a Founder pejorative for outsiders] feared our metamorphic abilities, so we were beaten, hunted, and killed. Finally, we arrived here. And here, safe in our isolation, we made our home" (Frakes 1994a). Yet making home did not prove sufficient for the Founders—that home had to be vigilantly guarded, the surrounding space secured, neighboring peoples controlled and exploited. What may have begun as a refuge for the persecuted became an empire in its own right. The Female Changeling savors the irony: "The hunted now control the destinies of hundreds of other races."

If there is any hope for the Founders to break out of the paranoid state of injury (Brown 1995) that recursively authorizes their will to power, it seems to lie with its small diaspora, a group of children, known as "the Hundred"—including Odo—who are dispersed across the galaxy. Although the Founders have largely relinquished off-planet travel, leaving it to their Vorta and Jem'Hadar subordinates, the Hundred are seen as sources of knowledge that will gradually enrich the Great Link. What the Founders don't seem to expect, however, is that their children might return with dissident perspectives on how to share space with others differently, on more reciprocal and consensual terms (see Butler 2012). Having yearned for years to return to a home he did not remember, Odo now finds the worldview dominant in that home to be racist, unforgiving, and cruel. As Wolfe puts it, "Odo expected that finding his people would give him all the answers. . . . But [in the episode], we were basically saying, 'It's not that easy. Finding out who your people are doesn't tell you who *you* are'" (Erdmann and Block 2000, 163).

As Odo prepares to return to DS9, the Female Changeling cautions him, "We will miss you . . . but you will miss us even more" (Frakes 1994a). Although the Founders are wrong about a great many things, the Female Changeling is certainly right about the sense of melancholy in exile that lingers for Odo. In "The Adversary," Odo kills a fellow Founder who attacks his shipmates (Singer 1995b). For the Founders, who regard all lives as disposable save for their own, Odo has violated a fundamental ethical axiom of solidarity to his race and class—that "no Changeling has ever harmed another." As punishment, in "Broken Link," Odo's people remove his ability to change form altogether, trapping him in a human body and expelling him from nation and home (Landau 1996b; Georgis 2006).

Welcomed home only to be horrified and disavowed by his people, Odo attempts to forge an alternate home in diaspora, with other Changelings outside the Great Link. But these efforts are also frustrated. In "The Begotten," Odo is charged with raising a sick infant Changeling, another of the Hundred. Tragically, the infant succumbs to its illness, though not before generously restoring Odo's ability to change form (Treviño 1997). In "Chimera," Odo meets another one of the Hundred, Laas (J. G. Hertzler), who exhibits much of the same contempt for "solids" as the callous Female Changeling (Posey 1999a). Although Laas, too, abhors what he learns about the Founders, he exhibits a frightening conservative, vitalist, and neoprimitivist streak, spouting racist and misanthropic views and acting on them, to deadly effect.

Odo's friends on the station attempt to engage Laas in conversation, asking him about the planet where he lived for decades before he took to wandering the galaxy. Laas responds snidely that "it's just like any other

Jem'Hadar Marronage

14. The Founders expelling an agonized Odo from the Great Link ("Broken Link," season 4, episode 26, aired June 17, 1996).

planet that's overrun with humanoids. Cities and farms everywhere, other lifeforms displaced from their habitats. I once migrated to the southern continent with a herd of *volg*. By the time we returned to the breeding grounds the next summer, they'd been fenced off. The herd died out within two generations. It's the same on any planet where humanoids thrive. They disrupt the natural balance. . . . The truth is, I prefer the so-called primitive lifeforms. They exist as they were meant to, following their instincts. No words to get in the way, no lies or deceptions" (Posey 1999a).

Laas's romantic elegy to lost ecosystems—a loss that he generalizes as an inevitable outcome of human(oid) thriving anywhere—uncannily resembles contemporary claims that "we" now live in a geological era called "the Anthropocene," in which destructive "human" activity has had the most defining influence on the environment and climate. The Anthropocene concept has been roundly criticized by Black, Indigenous, Marxist, feminist, and other scholars for its sloppy generalizations, its assumption that racial capitalism—a peculiar, contested, destructive form of political, ecological, and economic life—somehow stands in for human-environment activity in general. Such sweeping claims, these critics point out, enable a lazy, all-encompassing misanthropy while ignoring asymmetries of power and culpability (Whyte 2017; H. Davis and Todd 2017; Swyngedouw and Ernston 2018; Karera 2019).

In playing Laas, Hertzler recounts that he "wanted to find a way to keep this character sort of annoyingly judgmental, because of his politics. . . . He felt that these humanoids were so far beneath him that it was like talking to dogs. His proenvironmentalist point of view, feeling that humanoids *ruin* things" (Erdmann and Block 2000, 657, original emphasis). Although Laas has certainly experienced genuine alienation and persecution as a Changeling, and although his empathy for nonhuman(oid) beings is commendable, his experiences congeal into a particularly noxious circuit of cynicism, *ressentiment*, and racism, not unlike that of the Founders themselves (Brown 1995).

We also soon see that Laas's seemingly generalized misanthropy targets certain humanoids in particular—and brutal—ways. In contrast to the more guarded Odo, who generally changes forms in his personal quarters, Laas changes forms wherever he pleases, taking great pleasure in a performative indifference to the reactions of humanoids. In what Quark irreverently describes as "a Changeling pride demonstration," Laas casually "becomes fog" on the Promenade of Deep Space Nine, disorienting hundreds of people. This action provokes a confrontation with an embittered Klingon soldier who has lost many comrades in the Dominion War. Laas insults the soldier and Klingons in general, and the soldier stabs Laas, who as a shape-shifter easily morphs and remains unharmed. Producing a sword of his own with the flippant remark, "Mine's bigger!" (Posey 1999a), Laas cavalierly stabs and kills not the attacker but his Klingon companion, who is essentially a bystander.

That Laas can at once grieve the destruction of nonhumanoid animals' habitat and casually murder a humanoid—and at that a Klingon, an extra-

Jem'Hadar Marronage

terrestrial often racialized as Black—with a glib, erotically charged remark paints a picture of a decidedly anti-Black and ecofascist sensibility, one all too salient in our own times. Philosopher Axelle Karera (2019) advises that, "unless Anthropocenean ethics and its apocalyptic imaginaries are willing to wrestle with the challenge that disposable blackness entails, it is unclear to me as to why this emerging ethics should continue to rely so firmly on the concept of life" (51). And journalist Naomi Klein (2019) warns of emergent ecofascist political formations that recognize the threat of climate change but oppose the "wealth distribution, resource sharing, and reparations" necessary to equitably address it. Indeed, we see quite decisively that only some lives matter in Laas's rendition of environmentalism.

Odo—in my view, quite wrongly—permits Laas to leave the station, fearing that a Klingon murder trial will result in his execution. But he adamantly refuses Laas's offer to travel the galaxy with him in search of other Changelings, his project of forging a new Great Link. Until the very end of the series, when the Founders are defeated, Odo must find home in difference, rather than in the Great Link or the Changeling diaspora. Ironically, for all his longing for home elsewhere, Odo's tenure on the station is second only to Quark's in duration. Odo knows the station better than almost anyone, a point that he routinely raises with Sisko whenever a Federation security officer angles for his job.

Postcolonial theorist Dina Georgis (2006) argues that queerness and diaspora share in their alienation and expulsion from home—exile from the heteronormative family for queers, and from the homeland or heteronormative nation for diasporic subjects. Odo always presents as a man when he takes the form of a humanoid, and Major Kira is his primary love interest. But might we not read him as queer in Georgis's metaphorical sense?[8] Both the Female Changeling and Laas routinely question and mock Odo's preference for his friends on the station over his people, casting affinities outside "one's own kind" as improper and frivolous, even a sign of arrested development, and doomed to inevitable failure. And although Odo is rejected by the Founders, some Federation elites treat him no better. In DS9's final arc, we learn that the secretive Federation intelligence agency Section 31 has created a biological weapon, a virus that slowly kills the Founders—and that they have surreptitiously used Odo as patient zero in the hopes of killing off his people altogether (Dorn 1999; Posey 1999b). Thanks to O'Brien and Bashir, this plan is eventually foiled (see chapter 6). But the fact that Odo's pathos and the painful lesions he suffers as a result of the Changeling virus are so bound up with his desire for belonging will strike a chord with anyone whose life has been touched by the uneven geographies of HIV/AIDS.

But if Odo is queer, he remains a queer of a particular, privileged sort. He is indeed alienated, cast out from home, the only one of his kind on the station—and yet the community from which he hails is one of extreme wealth and power, one whose persecutory anxieties authorize an ideology of race and class supremacy. What could it mean, then, for privileged queers like Odo to fail (Halberstam 2011), or refuse, to reproduce the cultural and political logics of his "own people"—especially if those logics are oppressive and cruel?

Auberjonois (2011) remarked that Odo's "very purpose" as one of "the Hundred" made it fitting that "he would ultimately be the creature that would return to his world to bring it back to sanity and to stop this terrible paranoid destruction." For U.S. citizens, both real and imagined violence toward the national family with which we are presumed to identify has authorized violence at scales incommensurable with the original events. Perhaps those of us in whose name such violent projects continue to be waged, those of us who most benefit from them, queer or otherwise, can learn something from Odo. Although he continuously longs to rejoin the Great Link throughout the series and is momentarily seduced by the promise of return in season 6, Odo ultimately refuses to do so until the Founders have been forced to relinquish their claims to supremacy. Odo very nearly dies in fighting *against* the Dominion, and it is, in the final analysis, his willingness to defy his own people that saves them from themselves.

This chapter has offered a reading of the Dominion that likely diverges wildly from the intentions of many of DS9's creators. But its conclusion affirms their creation as an original, provocative, and welcome contribution to the *Trek* metaseries. Read through a Left lens, the Dominion reflects back to Americans some of the core contradictions of racial capitalism in our own imperial context. Both multiracial and racist, the Dominion values life according a racialized and classed hierarchy that is rationalized both theologically and (pseudo)scientifically (Wynter 2003). Its economic and political elites use a range of means to guarantee political-economic dominance, including a highly racialized military. And although the Founders seem to live indefinitely, and the professional-managerial class Vorta enjoy a form of immortality as serialized clones, the racialized Jem'Hadar are subject to "the state-sanctioned . . . production and exploitation of group-differentiated vulnerability to premature death" (Gilmore 2007, 247). The Dominion is not some external Other but a vehicle for what Melanie Klein ([1946] 1975a) called "projective identification," a repository of content split off and externalized by the ideal self-image of the United States. The Dominion's evils, which make the Federation's illiberal departures from its "good-guy" image seem acceptable, are in fact our own.

Yet the depressive/reparative reading that this chapter has sought to perform also points to fractures, challenges to the Dominion's racial and economic "order of things." Jem'Hadar like Goran'Agar and Omet'iklan mutiny and form maroon communities, producing alternative scientific knowledges and seizing Federation- and Vorta-controlled means of (re) production to pursue alternative, autonomous forms of life. In rather different ways, these men refuse the Dominion story that their exploitation and disposability are natural and inevitable, and they dream of other ways to be.

And at the other end of the Dominion's hierarchy, privileged dissident Changelings like Odo queerly refuse to rejoin the Great Link, failing to reproduce the Founders' imperialist cultural logics. Odo also rejects alternative communities that indulge the same toxic circuits of misanthropy, *ressentiment*, and a racist will to power on display in Founder imperialism (Brown 1995). If anything, the Dominion is most damning in its portrayal of the Vorta as a craven, obsequious, and treacherous professional-managerial class, although one Weyoun iteration does deserve credit for defecting to the Federation in protest of the war (Posey 1998).

In the B plot of "Hippocratic Oath," Worf tells Captain Sisko, "When I served aboard the *Enterprise*, I always knew who were my allies and who were my enemies." The captain advises, "Let's just say DS9 has more shades of gray" (Auberjonois 1995c). Perhaps what is most "gray" about DS9 is the unsettling resemblance between its complex, heterogeneous "bad guys" and our own society. DS9 upends *Star Trek*'s predictable vectors of identification, challenging the propagandistic need to keep the "evil" of U.S. empire and racial capitalism repressed, separate, and oppositional. More clearly than any other *Star Trek* series, DS9 invites a reckoning with such evil content, which "good" liberal multicultural narratives attempt to sweep under the rug (Puar 2007).

Summing up her concept of deidealization, Melanie Klein ([1946] 1975) drew attention to a remark made in analysis by one of her patients: "The glamour has gone" (305). Although many have long seen the United States for what it is, if there is any hope for a more beautiful, truly free and democratic way of life in this world, then deidealizing the U.S. empire, even when it wears the comforting mask of liberal multiculturalism, surely has a crucial role to play. As reactionaries insist that only the most reverential accounts of our own "Founders" be taught in schools, sidestepping histories of slavery and Indigenous genocide, do we not see the untenability of the U.S. "order of things"? Perhaps it is this painful but productive invitation to deidealization, however limited, that explains why DS9's ornate world-building is so frequently passed over—and why, decades later, it still behooves us to consider it.

Jem'Hadar Marronage

4 Defetishizing the Ferengi

"Ferengi Are Us"

DS9's allegorical geography—set between Bajor and the wormhole—enabled it to richly elaborate on Bajoran struggles for decolonization and to envisage in the Dominion a new, more complex antagonist and mirror for the Federation. But if Bajor's location at an "inter-imperial" (Espiritu 2014) galactic crossroads attracted attention from Federation, Cardassian, and Dominion elites, it also lured a petite bourgeoisie hungry for commercial opportunities. Making the station a dense node of galactic trade enabled the series to transgress *Star Trek*'s long-standing money taboo, getting up close and personal with the most unabashedly capitalist (and among the most unabashedly patriarchal) extraterrestrial social formation in the *Trek* universe: the Ferengi Alliance.

For the Ferengi, no profit-bearing business, however disreputable, is beyond consideration. Casinos, brothels, war profiteering, piracy, bribery, and genetic engineering are all fair game. "Taxes" and "unions" are dirty words; even uttering them could lead to repression by the Ferengi Commerce Authority (FCA). Ferengi women, obnoxiously referred to as "females," cannot conduct business, leave the house, or even wear clothing; their lives are dedicated to housework, children, and massaging their husbands' ears, an eroticized practice called *oo-mox*. Men, for their part, are expected to be successful entrepreneurs, humiliated if they lack the "lobes" for business. Ferengi eat larvae known as tube grubs, consider flaked blood fleas a delicacy, and snort Hupyrian beetle snuff as a narcotic. While the Bajorans and the Dominion elicit interest principally from small, devoted groups of DS9 fans, the Ferengi tend to provoke much stronger reactions of revulsion and affection from a broader audience. Even many enlightened characters (and fans) share the view expressed by the ever-candid Major Kira: "They're greedy, misogynistic, untrustworthy little trolls, and I wouldn't turn my back on one of them for a second" (Livingston 1993d).

Introduced in TNG as a menacing, even cannibalistic antagonist, the Ferengi were a major flop. They were also funny. Diminutive, avaricious, and prurient extraterrestrials who hiss and scream when threatened, Ferengi were, as SF writer Keith DeCandido (2011) observed, "far too comical to be taken in any way seriously as the threat the script desperately wanted them to be." Realizing that they had laid an egg, TNG creators relegated the Ferengi to occasional comic relief. But DS9 offered writers and actors the chance to bring texture to extraterrestrials that had initially struck many as little more than caricature (Behr and Zappone 2019; Memory Alpha n.d.g, n.d.p). In Armin Shimerman's Quark, *Trek* had its first Ferengi main character, and the station had its foremost entrepreneur in all matters licit and illicit. Behr describes Quark as "a Ferengi, but not your typical cringing Ferengi" (Altman and Gross 2016, 446). But few of DS9's Ferengi, including numerous recurring characters, are as simplistic as those in TNG.

This chapter argues that DS9's more sustained, layered elaboration of the Ferengi refashioned them to create a rich satire of racial capitalism's neoliberal ethos in the 1990s. For many social scientists (e.g., Harvey 2005), neoliberalism describes the vengeance with which the capitalist class has remade the world since the 1970s through policies of global economic integration, market deregulation, privatization of public goods, and upward wealth redistribution at an unprecedented scale. But neoliberalism is also what historian Lisa Duggan (2003) calls "a kind of secular faith" (xiii). Theologian Adam Kotsko (2018) explains that neoliberalism does not stop at rules governing markets but aspires "to be world-ordering ambition of theology, which relies on people's convictions about how the world is and ought to be" (7). If the Bajoran Prophets comprise a righteous anticolonial force, and the Dominion's "order of things" a racist and classist political theology of empire, then Ferengi civic religion makes neoliberalism's theological pretensions explicit (Cowan 2010). Its sacred text, *The Ferengi Rules of Acquisition*, consists of 285 axioms, including such gems as "The justification for profit is profit" (the 202nd Rule), "Expand or die" (the 95th), and "Deep down, everyone's a Ferengi" (the 284th) (Behr 1995). The conceit that "everyone's a Ferengi" parallels neoliberalism's claims that markets express a universal human nature. But it also implicates *Trek*'s non-Ferengi characters and audiences, to a degree not fully appreciated in *Trek* criticism.

*

Because this book critically examines *DS9*'s reiteration and interruption of capitalist, racist, and colonial discourses, this chapter's praise for the Ferengi may surprise some readers. It is commonly observed, sometimes unfavorably, that *DS9*'s sustained look at the Ferengi returned capitalism to a metaseries cherished for imagining a future without it. Many Leftist Trekkers are fond of Captain Picard's lecture on Federation life for a twentieth-century financier who has just woken up from a long cryogenic sleep: "People are no longer obsessed with the accumulation of things. We've eliminated hunger, want, the need for possessions. We have grown out of our infancy" (Conway 1988). With such needs eliminated, Picard explains, the challenge of life is simply "to improve yourself." Left-leaning economic thinkers have praised the Federation as the embodiment of Marx's classless society (Gonzalez 2015; Ewing 2016), an emancipatory postscarcity economy (Benanav 2020), or, at the very least, a Keynesian meritocracy (Saadia 2016).

Yet cultural studies scholar Dan Hassler-Forest (2016) observes that while *Trek*'s postcapitalist utopia is occasionally described at a theoretical level in *TOS* or *TNG*, the implications of such a political economy are rarely investigated (386–87; see also Kotsko 2015; Altman and Gross 2016, 487–88). By contrast, *DS9*'s location on the periphery of Federation, Cardassian, and Dominion spheres of influence makes the series—particularly its Ferengi characters—incisive interlocutors for numerous allegorical economies, including the Federation's. If the Ferengi restore capitalism to *Trek*, they also suggest that it may have been there all along.

Consider the B plot of season 1's "Progress," which chronicles Kira's contentions with Bajoran post-Occupation development (see chapter 2).

The episode's secondary arc follows Jake Sisko and Quark's nephew, Nog (Aron Eisenberg), who form a business partnership, unbeknownst to the station's grown-ups. As Nog instructs Jake in Ferengi economic practice, their endeavors uncover the Federation's tacit but powerful standardizing and mediating role in Bajoran economic life. As the station transitions from Cardassian to Bajoran and Federation rule, Quark adjusts his restaurant inventory to cater to a different consumer base. During the Occupation, most residents of the station were imprisoned Bajoran workers, but most paying customers were Cardassian soldiers. Now, Quark is saddled with some "five thousand wrappages of Cardassian yamok sauce," a condiment that only Cardassians "could stomach," and only one Cardassian customer, the exiled Mr. Garak, to eat it (Landau 1993a).

Nog senses an economic opportunity, offering to take the unpalatable surplus off Quark's hands. "Progress" follows Jake and Nog across the circuits of exchange value as they trade the sauce for something they can convert to that coveted, delightfully tacky Ferengi currency: gold-pressed latinum. Calling themselves the Noh-Jay Consortium, the two boys negotiate deals and piece through a maze of import procedures and shipping codes. They exchange the sauce for one hundred gross of "self-sealing stem bolts," which they swap for a parcel of land on Bajor and sell, through Quark, to the Bajoran government.

Along the way, Noh-Jay encounters a droll but revealing hiccup: if yamok sauce is well-known but desirable only to Cardassian consumers, no one seems to know what self-sealing stem bolts even *are*, much less what their use-values could be. Looking to keep their business activities under wraps and to seem in the know, Nog and Jake obliquely ask Chief O'Brien, "Why does *anybody* use self-sealing stem bolts?" as if the answer were self-evident. To their surprise, O'Brien concedes frankly, "I wouldn't know. I've never used them. . . . I've never even seen one." Even the late Peter Allan Fields, who wrote "Progress," confessed he hadn't "the foggiest idea" how he came up with the bolts (Erdmann and Block 2000, 52).

As random or innocuous as the bolts may seem, however, the B plot of "Progress" parallels to an uncanny degree the centrality of technological

Defetishizing the Ferengi

15. Jake Sisko and Nog, proprietors of the Noh-Jay Consortium, puzzling over a self-sealing stem bolt ("Progress," season 1, episode 15, aired May 9, 1993).

standards to U.S. imperialism as a material project. Anticolonial *Trek* scholars have made much of the "universal" translator, with its assumption that translation is a solvable, purely technical problem that can readily yield transparent meaning (e.g., Inayatullah 2003). But as historian Daniel Immerwahr ([2019] 2020) demonstrates, U.S. imperialism has also imposed a universal language through the standardization of commonplace tools and technologies, from bricks to screw threads, from stop signs to nursing degrees.

For the engineers, entrepreneurs, and military officials seeking to coordinate the allied effort in World War II, such concerns were neither boring nor a laughing matter. Because combining nonstandard, incompatible parts could result in the failure of combat vehicles and equipment, the United States "spent $600 million sending spare screws, nuts, and bolts overseas to compensate for the incompatibility" between British screws, then threaded at fifty-five degrees, and American ones, threaded at sixty (Immerwahr [2019] 2020, 307). Engineers sought "the integration of the entire process into a smooth flow like a great river system" (quoted in Immerwahr [2019] 2020, 307). After the war, as decolonization movements rose up against European empires, the United States still took direct possession of new territory where it could, notably in Oceania. But across much of the world, it opted to govern indirectly, through an extensive network of hundreds of military bases, over eight hundred of which persist to this day (Vine 2015). Technologies like the standardized screw thread helped the U.S. empire attain "domination without annexation" (quoted in Immerwahr [2019] 2020, 315).

Chief O'Brien's puzzled unfamiliarity with the self-sealing stem bolt thus tells us something important about the Federation's structuring, even imperial role in setting the economic standard for Bajor after Cardassian Occupation. If the Federation is not so vulgar as to make latinum its medium of exchange like the Ferengi, its material dominance in Bajoran space is unmistakable, rendering self-sealing stem bolts an obscure currency indeed. Like Cardassian yamok sauce, the bolts figure as a niche commodity, drag on the easy flow of universal exchange.

Behr says he based the Noh-Jay Consortium on the plucky war profiteer character Milo Minderbender from Joseph Heller's World War II novel *Catch-22* (1961) (Gross and Altman 1996, 52). Geographers Deborah Cowen and the late Neil Smith (2009) likewise turn to *Catch-22* to theorize the messy entanglements of imperialism and global capitalism, noting that Minderbender "sold weapons to the enemy for the eminently rational reason that it could make windfall profits" (42). Although Nog and Jake don't go that far, when they realize that they cannot look to Chief O'Brien, the bearer of universal Federation technical standards, to understand or unload the bolts, they pursue local routes to accumulation, contacting "the Bajoran who ordered them in the first place" (Landau 1993a).

Much like the A plot of "Progress" discussed in chapter 2, the episode's B story also presents us with resistance to Bajor's seamless, Federation-brokered economic integration, friction against Immerwahr's ([2019] 2020) "smooth flow," or what Nog, in a Ferengi idiom, calls the "Great River" or "Great Material Continuum" (Posey 1998). These resistances are marginalized as quirky, local, and anachronistic, and often ultimately absorbed into that river's current. But there are moments of excess and incommensurability, too; several seasons later, Quark still has the bolts in storage, suggesting that the land deal falls through when Noh-Jay is exposed as a business venture led by children (Auberjonois 1995a). The Ferengi, precisely in their grubby, acquisitive machinations, ultimately provide us with more reason to scrutinize the Federation's postcapitalist pretensions. This scrutiny does not tear down the postcapitalist utopia elaborated by Picard so much as it invites us to consider the social relations that haunt utopian pronouncements, and to contemplate more materialist visions for how to get there from here.

*

Others, meanwhile, understandably object to the Ferengi's ostensible racialization. The Ferengi "look"—short stature, sharp teeth, bulbous foreheads, ridged noses, and gigantic ears that double as an erogenous zone—and their insatiable greed have led many to read them as reprising anti-Semitic (e.g., Casavant 2003) or Orientalist (e.g., Wilcox 1992) stereotypes about Jews and East Asians as devious, rootless capitalists. The *New York Times* once called the Ferengi "the Shylocks of Space," referencing the character in Shakespeare's *The Merchant of Venice* ([1605] 2004) whose very name has become an anti-Semitic cipher (Pareles 1996; Coodin 2017).

Though not wholly incorrect, such critiques are also not the whole story about the relationships between anti-Semitism, Orientalism, and capitalism. Scholars like the late historian Moishe Postone and literary theorist Iyko Day argue that blaming the inequalities endemic to racial capitalism upon a particular cultural group, rather than the capitalist class, is an act of *fetishism*. Fetishism has many connotations in critical social theory. For Marx, the fetish conceals the labor that gives value to all commodities. For Freud, it describes excessive libidinal attachment toward an inert object. But in both traditions, to fetishize something is to exclusively attribute a phenomenon to a particular component of the system that produced it, ignoring the role of the system as a whole.

Postone (1980) thus argued that Nazi anti-Semitism took the form of a romantic, nostalgic anticapitalism that pretended to take the side of "ordinary" German workers against Jews, who were conflated with the abstract, rootless, and ruthless dimensions of global capital. This anti-capitalism was not, in fact, anticapitalist—the Nazis enjoyed enthusiastic support from German and global business classes—but it was effective in blaming economic inequalities on Jews. Day (2016) has drawn on Postone's argument to show how racism against East Asians in Canada and the United States has taken a similar form, blaming white unemployment on "industrious" East Asian workers, merchants, and financiers, rather than a broader racial capitalist system that tends toward crisis, structurally requires unemployment, and exploits uneven global labor standards to trigger a race to the bottom between workers everywhere.[1] Neither Postone nor Day argues that anti-Semitism and Orientalism are reducible to their economic determinations. Cultural antipathies to both Jews and Asians have odious histories and presents that precede and exceed capitalism. But capitalism is often minimized in mainstream discussions of these forms of hatred, and Postone and Day helpfully highlight capitalism's formative, conditioning role.

These scholars illuminate where many critiques of the Ferengi fall short. Staunch defenders of capitalism (e.g., Jonah Goldberg 1999), for whom anti-Semitism is an entirely cultural affair, emphasize the Ferengi's anti-Semitic cultural valences, altogether deflecting questions of political economy. Liberal multiculturalists (e.g., Casavant 2003) acknowledge that the Ferengi offer a critical depiction of capitalism but link it only to capitalism's worst excesses, its nineteenth-century form, rather than the putatively progressive capitalism of the 1990s. Different as they are, both of these camps need to preserve capitalism as a "good" or at least redeemable object, and they particularize the Ferengi as an irrelevant, purely cultural caricature in order to do so. Finally, Leftist critics (e.g., Davidson 2017) recognize that the Ferengi stage a solid demonstration of capitalist social relations but rightly

Defetishizing the Ferengi

charge that *Trek* creators make the grave, racist error of attributing capitalist exploitation exclusively to a single extraterrestrial social formation. Yet all of these critiques effectively leave the fetishistic structure more or less intact. What happens if we *refuse* to fetishize or particularize the Ferengi, reading them as a more general commentary on the capitalist classes, and on racial capitalism as an everyday social relation, on Earth?

The late TNG writer Herbert J. Wright and director Rob Bowman say they created the Ferengi as a critique of the rapacious finance capitalism of the Reagan-era United States (quoted in Memory Alpha n.d.g). And Wolfe notes that the very name "Ferengi" derives from the Arabic word *al firanj* and the Persian word *farang*, which originally described "Franks" or medieval European traveling merchants (quoted in Memory Alpha n.d.g). In this light, the Ferengi stand in not for Jews or Asians but for Christian Europe from the perspective of its Others.

Also worth noting are the identities and political sensibilities of the writers, producers, and actors who created the Ferengi, particularly in DS9. Many of these artists are liberal, progressive, or socialist Jewish Americans who are well aware of the grisly history and persistence of anti-Semitism and who are also thoughtful critics of capitalist inequality. Shimerman has served in several leadership positions in the Screen Actors Guild–American Federation of Television and Radio Artists. In a 1993 appearance as Quark on *Live with Regis and Kathie Lee*, he describes the Ferengi as "the capitalists of the universe. We're out to make a buck. We're out to accumulate as much money as we can. I think of ourselves as the robber barons. We're the Carnegies, Rockefellers, people like that" (Shimerman 2020). If the Ferengi are an accusation, then Shimerman points the finger at neither Asians nor Jews but at America's titans of industry, its white Protestant bourgeoisie.

Some might argue that in directing scrutiny at the 1 percent, Shimerman distributes responsibility for capitalist inequality a bit too narrowly. Behr also sees in the Ferengi a much broader social commentary on neoliberal capitalism as a diffuse, everyday social relation that engenders familiar neuroses: "Ferengi are us. That's the gag, the Ferengis are humans. They're more human than the humans on *Star Trek* because they're so screwed up and they're so dysfunctional. They're regular people" (Whalen 2016).

And then there is Wallace Shawn, who makes seven fantastic appearances as Zek, the Ferengi chief economist, or "Grand Nagus." Perhaps best known for *The Princess Bride* (Reiner 1987) and *My Dinner with André* (Malle 1981), Shawn uses acting to support his calling as a playwright and essayist. He is also a proud socialist. Shawn's wide-ranging essays (2009, 2017) are accessible and lively in their criticisms of capitalism, racism, anti-Semitism, apartheid, the U.S. Dirty Wars in Central America, and the occupation of Palestine. Candid about his own privileged upbringing and struggles with self-contempt, Shawn (2017) is a champion of "unlucky people," particularly those demonized as terrorists or criminals. His performance as Zek suggests not that Jewish people are somehow uniquely to blame for capitalist inequality but that each of us contains multitudes, that racial capitalism as a social relation forecloses the "otherwise possibilities" that are everyone's birthright (Crawley 2017) for all but a "lucky" few.

These reflections recall the insight of psychoanalyst Sigmund Freud, who himself fled anti-Semitic persecution from Vienna to London in 1938. Analyzing an anodyne joke about a Jewish man who borrowed money only to purchase a delicious, expensive meal, Freud ([1905] 2002) remarked, "Only the accessories are Jewish, and the heart of the matter universally human" (39). Insofar as the Ferengi do draw upon or refer to anti-Semitic tropes, then, the thoughtful and progressive Jewish artists creating Ferengi characters are redeploying those tropes in the service of broader social critique, aimed not at Jews but at contemporary racial capitalism itself (see Bell and Valley 2013).

Economist Manu Saadia (2016) says that he "can definitely understand the disapproval of historians and scholars, as well as the offense of some fans" at the Ferengi. He agrees that the Ferengi do indeed "sometimes hew uncomfortably close to age-old anti-Semitic stereotypes" (188). Yet Saadia, the grandson of a Holocaust survivor, confesses that he also "adores" the Ferengi, who "reveal themselves to be much more than money-grubbing maniacs and lecherous leprechauns" (188). Indeed, as we will see, the Ferengi implement a transformative series of economic and social reforms over the course of DS9, some of which ought to inspire hope on our own planet. If the "Ferengi are us," broadly conceived, then they both return audiences to the cruelty of our own patriarchy and racial capitalism and suggest, at times quite humorously, how things could be otherwise.

"I Don't Want to End Up Like My Father!"

Saadia (2016) observes that the Federation's postwork, postscarcity economy makes scientific, military, and diplomatic positions in Starfleet coveted sources of meaning and status, rather than livelihood, for Federation citizens. Starfleet might well comprise something like what the late socialist feminist writer Barbara Ehrenreich called the "professional-managerial class" of the Federation, those few who are able to pursue the "joy of chosen work," while everyone else wants for nothing but must find other routes for personal development ([1989] 2020, 332).

But what about non-Federation citizens? As a citizen of the Ferengi Alliance, Nog finds himself born into in an inferior position in what George W. Bush would later call an "ownership society." Nog's father, Rom (Max Grodénchik), is Quark's younger brother and most abused employee. As eldest son, Quark enjoys privileged status in his family and owns the family business. He is a successful merchant, albeit highly anxious about his perceived entrepreneurial failures. But Rom and Nog have drawn far worse lots in a system that guarantees no social solidarity to its citizens and denies citizenship itself to women.

Quark's conduct toward his brother and nephew follows the 111th Ferengi Rule of Acquisition: "Treat people in your debt like family—exploit them" (Behr 1995). Nog grows up seeing his father constantly emasculated for his lack of business acumen. Quark remunerates Rom so poorly to serve drinks and repair equipment at his bar that when a rival establishment briefly opens on the station, Rom gladly accepts a better-paying job there (Livingston 1994a). Ludically invoking rich traditions of Jewish humor, Quark's penchant for self-deprecation frequently incorporates aggression toward Rom as well, evinced by his self-description as "just some bartender with a domineering mother and an idiot brother" (Brooks 1996). Rom's path to the good life in an ownership society consists of little beyond hoping to inherit the bar, either through Quark's death or through the expansion of his business.

Given this bleak picture, Nog aspires to a career in Starfleet, an unheard-of path for a Ferengi. For Nog, Starfleet is an exit route, a path to postscarcity economic security and autonomy and to meaningful work. Nog begs Captain Sisko to support his application to Starfleet Academy. When a skeptical Sisko presses Nog for his motivations, the Ferengi confesses, "Because I don't want to end up like my father!" Nog explains that Rom has "been chasing profit his whole life" to no avail; his father has considerable engineering skill but lacks business smarts, which makes him an utter failure by Ferengi standards. Nog identifies with his father, enough to know that he doesn't have "the lobes for business" either, but insists he has the technical inclination and the drive to make something of himself in Starfleet (Singer 1995a).

For Saadia (2016), Starfleet liberates Nog from the repressive "cultural norms of Ferengi society," which are mired in "tradition" and "amount . . . to gross economic malpractice" (43). Saadia argues that Nog abhors the Federation's planned economy but is drawn to a world where work is "no longer a necessary burden" and instead endowed with "life-affirming power" (45). Media studies scholar J. Emmett Winn (2003), meanwhile, interprets Nog's investment in Starfleet as a matter of internalized racism, a byproduct of growing up on a predominantly Bajoran station where Ferengi are profiled as thieves and widely disliked. For Winn, Nog's arc is one from racialized child to model minority. Like Saadia, Winn regards work in Starfleet as meaningful, professional-class work, and he analyzes fan debates about whether Nog's entry into Starfleet parallels affirmative action programs.

This chapter takes a somewhat different view. Winn is no doubt correct that Nog offers a case study in model-minority psychology. Starfleet service becomes a way for the diminutive (five-foot or 1.52-meter) Nog to grapple with racialized emasculation, what Asian American studies scholar David L. Eng (2001) has called "racial castration." Nog navigates suspicion from non-Ferengi and contempt within his family as the only son of a failed entrepreneur. It is profoundly painful to witness his father so routinely degraded by his uncle, and Nog wants out.

Yet this humiliation is an artifact not simply of "backward" Ferengi culture but of the interleaving of a cultural form (family) and a social relation (capitalism). As a Keynesian economist, Saadia wants to defend "good" capitalism from "bad" Ferengi family values, rendering Ferengi patriarchy as "economic malpractice." But as feminist scholar Miranda Joseph (2002) contends, capitalism "articulates 'the family' as a site of value" (149). People's identifications with family and community can facilitate forms of coercion and exploitation—from family businesses to underpaid or unpaid nonprofit work—upon which capitalism, in fact, depends. As Joseph explains, "The fetishization of family—our ability to forget that our attachments to our families are economic—occurs only in very particular political/ideological moments" (165). The ideal of the family as an apolitical haven in a love-less world, somehow beyond the reach of the economic, is unsustainable for Nog. Behind the stereotype of Ferengi as wealthy and unscrupulous entrepreneurs, *DS9* suggests that many, perhaps most Ferengi men aspire to "have the lobes for business" but do not. The function of the Ferengi entrepreneurial ideal, then, is essentially to sublimate class and familial conflict into masculine self-loathing, consigning these men to poverty, compensatory misogyny, and a privatized sense of failure and shame.

Starfleet offers Nog not a purely cultural vector of liberation or assim-ilation but a form of economic emancipation from constraining Ferengi capitalist and patriarchal structures of inheritance. If anything, we might read Nog the Starfleet cadet not as a professional-class affirmative action hire but as a working-class military recruit from a racialized community, engaged in a form of what Cowen (2008) calls "military workfare." Observ-ing that "there is a dearth of scholarship that investigates the soldier as a *worker*," Cowen (2008, 18, emphasis added) traces the long history of Western social citizenship's predication on military service, from early German experiments in a limited welfare state and the GI Bill to the con-temporary landscape of neoliberal austerity, in which military service is for many the only route to public provisioning for health care, education, and housing. As noted in chapter 1, one of the primary reasons that today's U.S. military boasts such a "diverse" workforce is that it offers a rare and elusive path to both legal and social citizenship for communities dispossessed by racial capitalism, austerity, settler colonialism, and imperialism. Read in this light, we might see Nog's Starfleet application as a constrained bid by a working-class, emasculated, racialized noncitizen for social solidarity, reducible neither to flight from "backward" tradition nor to self-loathing cultural assimilation. Thus when Quark panics that Nog's entry into Starfleet marks "the end of Ferengi civilization as we know it," Rom reassures him, "Relax, Brother. Nog isn't going to destroy the Ferengi way of life. He just wants a job with better hours" (Auberjonois 1995b).

Like all forms of citizenship—which both empower citizens and subject them to a higher authority (Berlant 1997)—Starfleet service comes at a cost for Nog. As an aspirant model minority, Nog has a knack for converting his fetishized "difference" into an asset, echoing a recurring theme in histories of Asian American military service (e.g., Wong 2005). Sisko's very first task for the would-be cadet puts Nog to work inventorying cargo containers, returning us to the nexus of empire and trade that we encountered in "Progress." Ferengi reportedly have very acute hearing; when the communications system on the *Defiant* falters, Nog fills in, relaying announcements from the command bridge to the engineering deck (Lobl 1997). Nog also calls upon the Ferengi belief in a "Great Material Continuum," serving as a quartermaster for Chief O'Brien and helping Jake track down a coveted Willie Mays baseball card for his father (Posey 1998; Dorn 1997). Nog even uses his short stature to his advantage, impressing Klingons with his willingness to enforce station noise restrictions against warriors twice his height (Friedman 1997). When he threatens to arrest General Martok and his rowdy drinking buddies, the general chuckles, "Courage comes in all sizes."

But interspersed with these lemons-into-lemonade moments, Nog, like many recruits from racialized and working-class backgrounds, faces serious hardships within the military and as a consequence of service. He experi-

ences something akin to what Du Bois (1903) called "double consciousness," second-guessing whether cliquish Starfleet cadets are standoffish because he's a Ferengi or simply because he's not in their in-group (Livingston 1996).

DS9's final season shows us just how high a price Nog pays for his ticket to the Starfleet good life. In "The Siege of AR-558," Captain Sisko, Nog, Ezri Dax, Quark, and Bashir help a beleaguered cohort of Starfleet soldiers hold a captured Dominion communications outpost (Kolbe 1998). The outpost feels worlds away from the well-lit, open port of DS9 or the pristine grounds of Starfleet Academy, where food and medicine abound. But Nog is initially giddy, idealizing a seasoned warrior, Reese (Patrick Kilpatrick), who sports a necklace of Ketracel-White tubes from the Jem'Hadar soldiers whom he has personally killed. Reese gruffly instructs a chatty Nog to "shut up and listen" for Jem'Hadar, and Nog once again puts his vaunted Ferengi ears to use in locating an enemy encampment.

The mission succeeds, but Nog and his comrades are ambushed on the way back to base. Nog gets shot in the leg, letting out what the script calls "a CRY of pain" and Netflix subtitles describe as a "high-pitched scream" (Kolbe 1998). Nog's piercing cry, not uncommon when Ferengi appear under duress, also recalls the dominant American image of the Asian man "as something that when wounded, sad, or angry, or swearing, or wondering whined, shouted, or screamed 'aiiieeeee!'" (Chin et al. [1974] 2019, xxvi). Decades of Asian American studies scholarship have both critiqued this image and challenged Asian American attachments to heteropatriarchal masculinity as a reaction to racist emasculation (e.g., Eng 2001).

Nog's scream diverges considerably from the brave model-minority front that he puts on for his fellow soldiers—a disavowal that both troubles and seeks to secure his model-minority status. Nog's bravery on the mission wins approval from Reese—"the kid did alright"—and Sisko. Back at the outpost field hospital, Bashir somberly reports that although he will be able to replace Nog's leg at a proper hospital, he will have to amputate it below the knee for now. Blissed out on pain meds, Nog smiles up at Sisko from his field hospital bed, "It doesn't hurt. You'd think it would, but it doesn't." Yet even here, Nog is ambivalent, asking Sisko about their mission: "It's worth it, right?" A shaken Sisko can only tell Nog, his son's best friend, "I hope to God it is" (Kolbe 1998).

Historians recount that 1990s Hollywood films like *Saving Private Ryan* sought to glamorize the U.S. role in World War II as an antidote to public disillusionment with expensive foreign wars after the U.S. defeat in Vietnam and the end of the Cold War (Wills 1997; Engelhardt 2007; Pauwels 2002). Although *DS9* often reiterates that "Good War" message, "The Siege of AR-558" is different, particularly in its placement of civilian Quark, newbie Nog, and care workers like counselor Ezri Dax and Dr. Bashir on the front lines. "If we'd used Kira, Worf, and Sisko, we'd have *The Dirty Dozen*," Ira Behr explains (Erdmann and Block 2000, 626). Rather than an ensemble of tough-as-nails fighters, like Robert Aldrich's (1967) star-studded World War II film, Behr sought to examine war's horrific effects on characters who are relatable in their ordinary vulnerability. Against the backdrop of its times, as well as our own, the episode is refreshing in its willingness to deidealize Nog's naive dreams of Starfleet war heroics. Nog spends the remainder of the battle supine on his field hospital bed, staring at the blanket over his phantom limb, replaying a cover of the nostalgic 1938 American song "I'll Be Seeing You" (Darren 1999) by holosuite star Vic Fontaine (James Darren), a rare sentient hologram who hosts a 1960s Las Vegas nightclub program.

In "It's Only a Paper Moon," Nog returns to DS9 a traumatized man (Williams 1998). Although twenty-fourth-century technology has replaced his amputated leg with an appendage virtually indistinguishable from the original, Nog's bodily, psychic, and social environments remain frustratingly out of synch. At AR-558, everyone expected him to feel pain, and he quickly disavowed it. Now Nog defies his doctors' orders by continuing to walk with a cane: "I don't care what they say. It hurts all the time" (Williams 1998).

Nog's reticence to incorporate his new limb offers a metaphor for his own ambivalent, partial (re)incorporation into the charmed ambit of Federation belonging and social solidarity. For Eng (2010), "the minority subject must, in the vein of the fetishist, simultaneously recognize and not recognize the material contradictions of institutionalized racism that claim his inclusion even as he is systematically excluded" (22). This structure of simultaneous avowal and disavowal aptly describes Nog's relationships to both Starfleet, which at once assimilates him into the chain of command and fetishizes his difference (ears, quartermastering), and his new leg, which doesn't hurt when it should and hurts when it shouldn't.

Placed on medical leave, Nog's only wish is to return to the physical and psychic position he occupied at the field hospital—lying in bed on his back, endlessly replaying Fontaine's "I'll Be Seeing You" (Darren 1999). Like the World War I veterans who informed Freud's early accounts of trauma ([1911] 1922), Nog is in a state of relentless psychic return to the scene of injury, including horrified flashbacks to the shot that wounded him and to his own high-pitched scream.

When this behavior both worries and irritates his best friend and room-mate, Jake Sisko, Nog seeks out Fontaine, the hologram whose song offered him such succor. Nog and Vic become fast friends, and Nog takes the unusual step of living full-time in one of the station's holosuites, running Vic's program continuously. In *DS9*'s final two seasons, many crew members take a liking to Fontaine's holographic club. Others, notably Captain Sisko, are skeptical about a fantasy of mid-twentieth-century Vegas that reimagines it as "postracial" (Kwan 2007; L. Alexander 2016; Vejar 1999a). But for Nog, "postracial" whiteness seems to be part of the appeal. He sees in Vic a jocular, mid-twentieth-century, white-ethnic American father figure.

Nog and Vic bond in part over American western films, discussing whether *Shane* (Stevens 1953) or *The Searchers* (Ford 1956) is a better movie. Vic makes an ideal interlocutor for Nog's fascination with mid-twentieth-century U.S. popular culture, as actor James Darren is a teen heartthrob film star of that period. Nog watches these films intently and repeatedly on Vic's black-and-white television. "Noggles, take it easy—it's only a movie," Fontaine counsels (Williams 1998). But Nog's obsession with westerns as a vehicle for staging and remaking injured manhood—even his preferences among these films—makes perfect sense in his predicament. Both *Shane* and *The Searchers* focus on the pedagogical dynamic between a boy or young man and an older man who educates him in a white frontier masculinity, a dynamic common to the western genre, including DS9's genealogies in *The Rifleman* (Sharrett 2005). *Shane* follows a young settler boy who idolizes a friendly, enigmatic rancher who helps the boy's parents in a land dispute. *The Searchers*, by contrast, pairs a young man of mixed white and Cherokee ancestry, Martin (Jeffrey Hunter, later Captain Pike on TOS), with a bigoted, bloodthirsty ex-Confederate soldier, Ethan (John Wayne), as they seek out loved ones kidnapped by Numunuu (Comanche) warriors.

Nog dislikes *Shane*, finding its lack of graphic violence unrealistic, and prefers *The Searchers*. This remark might suggest an identification with Martin, Ethan's "white but not quite" pupil (Bhabha [1994] 2012). Ethan's palpable hatred of Black and Indigenous people certainly echoes in Reese, who collected Ketracel-White tubes from slaughtered Jem'Hadar as souvenirs. But we could also read Nog's cathexis in these films, his interest in the dynamic between grizzled veterans and "innocent" youths, as a way of working through the traumatic discontinuity between his present and former selves. In this light, Nog is both Martin and Ethan, young, racialized outsider and aggrieved citizen-veteran. Indeed, Nog presents a classic case of so-called John Wayne syndrome, describing "the soldier's internalization of an ideal of superhuman military bravery, skill, and invulnerability to guilt and grief" (Slotkin 1992, 519–20).[2]

But even as Nog seems to burrow further into John Wayne masculinity as a defense, he is also keen to develop parts of himself racialized as Ferengi. When Vic frets about the club's finances, Nog offers to help, confidently assuring Vic that for Ferengi, business is "in our blood." Nog helps Vic get a tax refund, and pushes him to expand his holographic business. As in Starfleet, Nog engages in a model-minority "auto-Orientalism" here—what literary scholar Rey Chow (1995) called, "an Oriental's orientalism" (171). Though he had earlier confessed he lacks the "lobes" for business, here Nog repurposes stereotypes about Ferengi to his advantage, despite Vic's apparent unfamiliarity with them.

As thanks, Vic gifts Nog with an extravagant cane resembling those used by both western star Errol Flynn and the Ferengi Grand Nagus. Itself a fetish object, the cane effectively condenses Nog's cathexes during his treatment. In a kind of "cure by montage," Nog's leg pain gradually tapers off during his stay with Vic, and counselor Ezri Dax slyly convinces Vic that it is time to cut the cord. Although Nog resists when Vic boots him from the holosuite, he soon reintegrates into station life and returns to duty. In gratitude, Nog arranges to have Vic's program run indefinitely, gifting his holographic friend with the experience of ongoing conscious existence.

Disability studies scholars might argue that Nog's recovery from post-traumatic stress in a single, self-contained episode corresponds with an ableist bias toward "cure" narratives that rehabilitate or "fix" disabled people, assimilating them into the "mainstream." Several scholars have persuasively criticized another DS9 episode, "Melora," for indulging such a narrative (Monteith 2017; Kanar 2000). Yet such works tend to approach disability as a discrete identity, analogous to other identities, and would benefit from considering how racial capitalism and empire provide formative context for how disability is experienced and imagined (Combahee River Collective 1983; M. Russell 2019; Erevelles 2011; David Mitchell and Snyder 2015). SF and disability studies scholar Kathryn Allan (2013) argues that rather than simply critiquing cure narratives, scholars might ask what cure narratives *do* in particular contexts (9). Despite a predictably curative ending, "It's Only a Paper Moon" discloses something important about Nog's relationship to the Federation. Wounded by his father's racialized and classed emasculation, Nog is further wounded in his bid for fulfilling, meaningful work and economic security as a Federation citizen-soldier, which he had assumed would augment his masculine bodily integrity and self-efficacy, not threaten it. Although the episode's arc wants to recuperate Nog as a good, "abled-disabled" model minority for the Federation war effort—what disability studies scholars David T. Michell and Sharon L. Snyder (2015) call an "ablenationalist" subject—his body, including his unconscious mind, continues to insist that things simply aren't that easy.

"We've Been Exploited Long Enough"

Nog is not the only Ferengi who seeks an exit from Ferengi capitalism. We have seen how Nog frames his father, Rom, as intractably mired in Ferengi patriarchal tradition and class oppression, a static foil to his own dynamic desire for upward mobility. Yet Rom, too, seeks a form of social solidarity outside of familial exploitation—not in the Federation but in multiracial, working-class solidarity between Bajoran, Ferengi, and other workers at his brother's bar.

At the beginning of "Bar Association," among *DS9*'s finest episodes and another directed by LeVar Burton (1996a), Rom nearly dies of an ear infection that his callous employer brother refused to permit him time to have examined. When Bashir admonishes Rom for not seeking care sooner, Rom explains that Ferengi contracts grant bosses total control over workers' whereabouts. These contracts also seem to permit bosses to harass employees, as Quark speculates wildly about Bajoran dabo girl Leeta's (Chase Masterson) intimate life in front of her fellow workers. Although Leeta does not hesitate to tell Quark where to go, that Quark would feel entitled to engage in such speculation provides a revealing glimpse of the ugliness of everyday gendered class relations at the bar.[3] Appalled by Rom's contractual constraints, Bashir idly muses that Rom and his coworkers should form a union.

Although Rom doubts that the other Ferengi waiters would be open to unionization, he soon embraces Bashir's suggestion. The last straw is Quark's cynical use of the Bajoran Cleansing Festival, the month when Bajorans abstain from drinking and gambling, as an excuse to implement altogether unnecessary austerity measures, cutting wages by a third. Here we see explicitly that while the Federation might have transcended wage labor, post-Occupation Bajor most certainly has not. When Leeta—whose people, we must remember, have only recently beaten back the decimating fifty-year Cardassian Occupation—exclaims in horror, "I can't afford a pay cut!" at stake for her is not spending money or personal fulfillment but survival. (Leeta's remark also throws *DS9*'s many liaisons between wage-dependent Bajoran dabo girls and secure "postcapitalist" Starfleet officers into a different economic light.) But Quark's exploitation of his "idiot" brother turns out to be a double-edged sword for the restaurateur. Rom knows the ledgers of his brother's business well enough to call bullshit.

Rom's proposed union, the Guild of Restaurant and Casino Employees, is greeted by Bajoran dabo girls but meets hesitation from Ferengi staff. "Ferengi workers don't want to stop the exploitation," Rom laments, "we want to find a way to become the exploiters" (L. Burton 1996a). The waiters' hesitation is not a matter of static "culture" but a product of the clear and present danger of a promarket, interventionist Ferengi state agency—the FCA—as a repressive actor. "Bar Association" is the second of actor Jeffrey Combs's eight appearances as Inspector Brunt, an overzealous FCA agent who loathes Quark's entire family. Combs, who also plays the Vorta Weyoun, describes Brunt as "a completely right-wing devout Ferengi" and "the IRS guy from hell . . . the guy who just kept coming back to make your life miserable, audit after audit after audit" (Memory Alpha n.d.b). Even saying the word "union," waiter Grimp (Jason Marsden) worries, could lead to the seizure and closure of all a Ferengi man's financial accounts by the FCA—a permanent, emasculating exile from economic personhood.

But Rom is all in, summoning a confidence we have never before seen in him. "If they're going to come after us," he tells his comrades, "let's give them a good reason! . . . We've been exploited long enough. It's time to be strong, take control of our lives, our dignity, and our profits" (L. Burton 1996a). His confidence proves contagious. The Guild presents its demands to Quark, who rejects them out of hand. The Guild goes on strike, bribing customers not to patronize Quark's—labor organizing with Ferengi characteristics!

Inside the bar, a shocked Quark scrambles to replace workers with holographic versions of himself, but the holograms are buggy and keep crashing. This hilarious scene offers an important corrective to the premise that twenty-fourth-century technology will eliminate "low-skilled" work (e.g., Saadia 2016). Dream as capitalists might about replacing workers with cheap, efficient, obedient machines, threats to automate away work are often seriously exaggerated, an age-old rhetorical tactic to depress wages (Henwood 2015). In truth, the absence of a willing workforce presents Quark with a serious threat. As feminist geographers Yui Hashimoto and Caitlin Henry (2017) contend, "Capitalism depends on social reproduction being

16. Flanked by his comrades, Rom presents the demands of the DS9 Guild of Restaurant and Casino Employees to his brother, the management ("Bar Association," season 4, episode 16, aired February 19, 1996).

free or very cheap," and "raising its value shakes the foundations of such a system, one that is racist, anti-poor, patriarchal, and heteronormative."

Quark and his eponymous holograms attract few customers during the strike, but they do elicit sympathy from a surprising source. Though he is no friend to Quark, Constable Odo is also a Changeling; the Founders' history of persecution leaves Odo deeply averse to "mob" persecution, and he sees in this incipient working-class democracy the tyranny of the majority. But Odo's alacrity to intervene on Quark's behalf is reined in by Captain Sisko, who forces Quark to negotiate in good faith with the Guild, threatening to change the terms of Quark's station lease agreement. In chapter 1, we saw how Avery Brooks's Black working-class sensibility shaped DS9, both on set and on-screen. In an era when centrist Democrats ratified "free" trade and snubbed unions and Black voters as having "nowhere else to go," Sisko

Defetishizing the Ferengi

shows the difference it can (still) make to have agents of the state willing to intervene on behalf of labor instead of capital (Frank 2016).

Rom and his comrades also get encouragement from Dr. Bashir and Chief O'Brien, who are themselves descendants of survivors of English imperialism. O'Brien shares the example of his distant relative, Sean Aloysius O'Brien, who died leading a successful coal workers' strike in Pennsylvania in 1902 that won wage increases and a decrease in the length of the working day.[4] Bashir and O'Brien even get into a brawl with Worf after he crosses the picket line.[5] Unable to replace workers with automation, enlist law and order or the administrative state on his side, attract regular customers, or pit Ferengi workers against non-Ferengi, Quark resorts to bribing his brother, who is by this point excitedly poring over *The Communist Manifesto* and utterly unmoved (Marx and Engels [1848] 1919).[6]

The strike at Quark's is only broken by the violent intervention of the FCA, which sends Nausicaan Pinkertons to rough up Rom's family. Ironically, this means attacking Quark, who also happens to be management, demonstrating the FCA's zealous commitment to disciplining labor, even when it means hurting capital in the process. Here the FCA lampoons a core irony of neoliberal statecraft, which is often heavily interventionist, particularly in its commitment to law and order, despite laissez-faire pretensions (Peck and Tickell 2002; Harvey 2005). Moved by his brother's suffering, Rom reluctantly agrees to formally disband the union, just long enough to get the FCA off the case. In return, Quark meets the Guild's demands: increased wages, shorter hours, and paid sick leave. In a way, the settlement reverberates with the story of the "alt-labor" movement, which organizes sectors like agriculture and domestic work where unionization is impossible due to (often racially motivated) legal constraints.

The strike is also transformative for Rom and his comrades personally. As anyone who has participated in strikes knows, they can be exhausting, frustrating, and at times, frankly, boring. But strikes can also be exhilarating experiences of solidarity, raising workers' expectations for ourselves, our comrades, and the possibility of better worlds (McAlevey 2014). Rom's time spent with Leeta on the picket line kindles a romance between them. His newfound confidence also leads him to leave his job at Quark's. Refusing to live solely for the possibility of inheriting the bar, Rom uses his technical skills to secure a steady public sector job as a Bajoran station maintenance engineer. "If the strike taught me anything," he tells Quark, "it's that I do a lot better when you're not around."

"Bar Association," then, is a wonderful exception to Hassler-Forest's (2016) observation that *Star Trek* rarely fleshes out the democratizing implications of its postcapitalist premise. Ironically, refusing to follow *Trek* rules and simply banish money enabled DS9 to critique capitalism, in the twenty-fourth century and in the twentieth. Shimerman has praised the episode for addressing class contradictions that mainstream television often elides: "People think of this as a comic episode. And it is, of course. But in truth, it's really about union-management problems. The irony of it is that I play *management* in the episode. So I thought that to make Rom have a reasonably hard job as a union organizer, I would have to be tough about it, to show the struggle to the audience. Although you don't see it on TV very often, this is something that goes on in America all the time" (Erdmann and Block 2000, 315). Rather than some distant future in which technology smoothly outsources so-called "repetitive, energy-intensive, low-skill, high-output labor" to machines, "Bar Association" critically reflects the rise of a service economy in the United States, returning us to the contradictions of our own world and the struggles to transform it (Saadia 2016, 83).

"I'm Broke. Ruined. Destitute. A Pariah. How Are Things with You?"

Where Nog and Rom improve their lives by escaping from Ferengi capitalism, Quark is in an endless scramble to maintain his privileged class and familial position, anticipating threats to his profits from workers, relatives, customers, business partners, station leaders, and his nemesis, Constable Odo. As the embodiment of Ferengi entrepreneurialism, Quark is, like capitalism itself, in a constant state of crisis. He is at once one of DS9's funniest and most morally reprehensible characters: hysterical, neurotic, irreverent, hypocritical, lecherous, exploitative, unethical, and self-effacing.

Defetishizing the Ferengi

In the aptly titled "Prophet Motive" (Auberjonois 1995a), Quark is horrified to discover that the Bajoran Prophets, in their infinite wisdom, have transformed Grand Nagus Zek into a virtuous altruist. Zek sets up a Ferengi Benevolent Association, heavily revises the Rules of Acquisition, and kicks his beetle snuff habit: "It might be fun for you and me, but it's no fun for the beetles!" Zek even undermines one of Quark's retail deals, referring his client to a cheaper wholesaler (see Cowan 2010). Incensed, Quark smells a rat. It turns out that Zek had contacted the Prophets, assuming that their nonlinear perspective could help him anticipate future profit opportunities. Quark seeks an audience with the Prophets himself, demanding that the original Nagus be restored. The Prophets agree, but they first explain that they were horrified by Zek's capitalist "barren existence." Searching the continuum of Ferengi history, they found alternative moments when the Ferengi's "acquiring nature was not so pronounced." They tell an astonished Quark, "You have not always been as you are now," suggesting that Ferengi "nature" and "culture" are far more contingent than many readings presume (Auberjonois 1995a).

In "Body Parts," another particularly strong episode directed by Avery Brooks (1996), Quark returns to the station after a visit to the Ferengi homeworld. He cheerfully announces that according to an exorbitant for-profit doctor named Orpax, he has one week to live. Rom suggests that his brother get a second opinion, taking advantage of the Federation's health-care system, which is free, even for noncitizens. Quark is skeptical: "Bashir? How good can *he* be? He doesn't even charge!" In keeping with Ferengi economic practice, Quark arranges to sell disks containing small amounts of his vacuum-desiccated remains to the highest bidder upon his death. Elated at the prospect of Quark's death, FCA inspector Brunt buys up the entire stock.

But a belated visit to Bashir makes clear that Quark is not, in fact, dying. Bashir's diagnosis initially excites Quark, as it gives him grounds to sue the wealthy Orpax for malpractice. But it also puts him in the difficult position of either arranging his own early demise or committing the cardinal sin of reneging on a contract, violating the 17th Rule of Acquisition: "A contract is a contract is a contract—but only between Ferengi" (Brooks 1996).

Brunt makes clear that he has every intention of collecting on the sale of Quark's remains. Resigned to death but proud of his prospective wealth in the afterlife (a Protestant attitude if ever there were one), Quark arranges for a willing Garak to kill him (Cowan 2010). But Quark can't go through with that deal either. In a dream, he meets Gint (also Max Grodénchik), the first Grand Nagus and the author of the Rules of Acquisition, who confesses that the rules are "nothing but guideposts, suggestions," their perceived authority "a marketing ploy."

Quark breaks the contract with Brunt, validating the inspector's opinion of him as "another loser in a long line of failed Ferengis." But the consequences of Quark's transgression are not limited to name-calling. By breaking a contract, Quark has given the FCA grounds to nullify his economic personhood and confiscate his assets. When Brunt is through, Quark's restaurant, bar, and casino look as empty as a ransacked house in Dr. Seuss's *How the Grinch Stole Christmas*. Rom checks in on Quark, who surveys the eerily vacant space. "How am I?" Quark sighs. "I'm broke. Ruined. Destitute. A pariah. How are things with you?" (Brooks 1996).

But Quark's luck turns around soon enough. Bashir drops by, donating booze given by a patient, which he finds "undrinkable" and cannot ethically accept (free Federation health care really means *free*). Dax, too, comes bearing hideous drinking glasses, an unwanted gift from her sister. Suddenly, Sisko and a dozen crew members enter with furniture, citing a need for a "place to store some extra furniture for the next few months." Quark assents, a momentary sparkle of gratitude in his eyes, before he informs Sisko he'll be charging him a small "storage fee," to which an amused captain gruffly agrees. Within minutes, Quark's regular Morn (Mark Allen Sheppard) appears, claiming a chair.

The touching ending of "Body Parts" thus literalizes Joseph's (2002) claim that community supplements capitalism, and hints at the collective and public roots of many of the putatively self-generating private enterprises that dominate our own world. Where liberal and even Leftist critics of the Ferengi see a caricature of capitalism so extreme that it can easily be disavowed, we might find in "Body Parts" a cautionary tale in the limits

Defetishizing the Ferengi

wn neoliberal market fundamentalism. The apparent normalcy of Quarks extraction of value from his own "body parts" and the incompetence of his for-profit doctor mirror the ubiquity of plasma donation centers in poor, often racialized neighborhoods and the nightmare that is U.S. health care in general. In another episode, Quark quips, "I should've gone into insurance. Better hours, more money, less scruples" (Landau 1994b).

Quark gets a chance to restore his economic standing and shore up Ferengi patriarchy all at once in "Ferengi Love Songs" (Auberjonois 1997). Despondent at his economic exile, he returns to his childhood home, hoping his mother, Ishka (Cecily Adams, played earlier by Andrea Martin), affectionately known as "Moogie," will cheer him up. The visit does not go as Quark had hoped. Much to Quark's horror, it turns out that his mother is dating Grand Nagus Zek—and worse still, she is also the true power behind Zek's throne. Quark had already been aghast to learn that contrary to family lore, his father was a lousy businessman, and he inherited his "lobes" from his mother. In "Family Business," Ishka revealed she had become a highly successful online trader, using a virtual avatar to overcome masculinist exclusion from the marketplace (Auberjonois 1995b). But now it turns out that Zek (in yet another sly *DS9* dig at the Reagan administration) is suffering from memory loss, and Ishka has effectively taken the reins of the Ferengi Federal Reserve.

Enter Brunt. Ever the interventionist in the defense of such "natural" systems as capitalism and heteropatriarchy, the inspector has long kept the couple under surveillance. Brunt offers to reenfranchise Quark if he can break off his mother's liaison with Zek. Quark agrees, feeding the Nagus conspiracy theories about Ishka's secret plans to funnel her wealth into a feminist uprising (see Women at Warp 2015). The plan works, and the couple momentarily splits. But Quark recants when he realizes the harm that he has caused his mother—and that Brunt's endgame is to unseat Zek and install himself as Nagus. Quark's return to Ferengi economic personhood will have to wait another day.

Both the neurotic Quark and the right-wing Brunt fear that Ferengi women's economic empowerment, or what the excellent *Trek* podcast

Women at Warp (2015) has termed the "Ferengi feminist revolution," will undermine Ferengi capitalism itself. But DS9's Ferengi arc paints a much more ambivalent, contradictory picture of the relationship between feminism and capitalism. In "Rules of Acquisition," for instance, Quark is alarmed to realize that Pel (Hélène Udy), his gifted new business associate, is in fact a Ferengi woman passing as a man (Livingston 1993d). But Pel is hardly the sort of socialist feminist that Quark and Brunt so fear. She takes a job waiting tables at Quark's in order to get access to the boss and go into business with him. Quark quickly notices Pel's initiative, asking after the new worker's ambitions. Pel responds, "I don't plan on being a waiter forever" (Livingston 1993d). Her remark expresses a "girlboss" feminism that values aspirational identification with the Ferengi (male) bourgeoisie over working-class feminist solidarity, a "lean-in" feminism rather than what socialist feminist scholars Cinzia Arruzza, Tithi Bhattarcharya, and Nancy Fraser (2019) have called a "feminism for the 99 percent."

We get an even more instructive look at bourgeois feminism's contradictions in "Profit and Lace" (Siddig 1998), perhaps the single most controversial—if not most hated—Ferengi-centric episode in DS9. At Ishka's urging, Zek finally implements a suite of political-economic reforms affording Ferengi women the most basic of rights: the right to wear clothing, the right to access public space, and the right to conduct business. These reforms, modest as they are, result in Zek's deposition and banishment. To make matters worse, the reactionary Brunt is named Zek's soon-to-be-permanent replacement. Desperate to regain the confidence of the Ferengi capitalist class, Zek forms a government-in-exile on DS9, arranging a secret meeting with Nilva (Henry Gibson), CEO of the profitable and influential Slug-o-Cola. Zek plans to make Ishka the centerpiece of his capitalist case for women's economic enfranchisement, but a vicious argument with Quark strains her heart, forcing her into bed rest.

To atone for causing his mother's heart attack, Quark agrees to perform an entrepreneurial Ferengi femininity in her stead. In a miracle of twenty-fourth-century medicine, Bashir performs sex reassignment surgeries on Quark—including the equivalent of facial feminization on those ears—with

Defetishizing the Ferengi

17. Quark, as Lumba, fending off the unwanted advances of Slug-o-Cola CEO Nilva ("Profit and Lace," season 6, episode 23, aired May 13, 1998).

seemingly instant recovery.[7] Quark, introduced as a woman named Lumba, makes the pitch. Nilva is persuaded—and almost immediately begins sexually harassing Lumba. Brunt shows up expressing doubt as to Lumba's "real" femininity. Lumba defiantly exposes her breasts, then returns to fleeing Nilva's advances. Once Nilva's confidence gets Zek reinstated as Nagus, Bashir rapidly transforms Lumba back into Quark, who expresses a short-lived contrition for having sexually harassed the dabo girls in his employ.

Feminist, queer, and trans *Trek* fans continue to criticize the flippant treatment of sex reassignment surgery, essentialist view of feminine authenticity, and boys-will-be-boys outlook on sexual harassment in "Profit and Lace"—and rightly so (e.g., Hodge 2013; mario_painter 2015). To say it holds up poorly is an understatement. Nevertheless, the episode also sheds light on the formative context that Ferengi capitalism provides for the articulation of gender and sexuality, context that is suggested but not developed in many fan debates. This chapter opened with Behr's insight that the Ferengi offer a satire of contemporary neoliberalism, not an aspirational ideal for twenty-fourth-century life. If we look to "Profit and Lace" for feminist, queer, or transinclusive representation, we will surely be disappointed. But what if we take Behr's words seriously and read the episode as a critical reflection of the exploitative ways that capitalism instrumentalizes and naturalizes gender and sexuality—its tendency to pay lip service to equality and empowerment while undermining more liberationist feminist, queer, and trans aims?

A closer look suggests that Zek's rationale for Ferengi women's economic enfranchisement cannot even be called bourgeois feminist—it is capitalist, first and foremost. "Face it," he tells Quark, "for thousands of years, Ferenginar has allowed a valuable resource to go to waste. . . . They make up 53.5 percent of the population and contribute virtually nothing to gross planetary income. I say it's time they started pulling their own weight." Zek could use a serious dose of feminist economics here, such as scholar Marilyn Waring's (1999) efforts to "make women's work count," to include unpaid social reproduction in the gross domestic product. He would also benefit from questioning whether gross income is a suitable measure of economic well-being at all (Hickel 2020). But Zek's words reverberate with the ways that corporations, banks, and development agencies have sought to expand capitalism by targeting historically redlined, excluded populations—particularly women in the Global South and poor, racialized women in the Global North—for all manner of subprime loans. Historian Keeanga-Yamahtta Taylor (2019) calls this deceptive, pseudoemancipatory practice "predatory inclusion."

In moments, Zek's economic plan sounds like Fordist-era demand-side economics, like when Lumba claims that "Ferenginar will be expanding its workforce and its consumer base at the same time." But what goes unaddressed is the unpaid work of social reproduction, which will likely continue to fall on Ferengi women. Perhaps this elision is not surprising, since the plan has been conceived of by men, save for Ishka, who now has Zek's butler Maihar'du (Tiny Ron) at her disposal. Expanded consumer power for Ferengi women—by no means equivalent to economic democracy in the home or the planetary economy—is, above all, an opportunity for patriarchal Ferengi capital to find new markets. Chiding Nilva for marketing Slug-o-Cola solely to men, Lumba suggests the drink's high algae content will appeal to a naturalized feminine vanity, offering, "Drink Slug-o-Cola and keep your teeth a sparkling shade of green." Nilva is thrilled by this tagline. But seeing Ferengi women as consumers who can be induced to experience new demands does nothing to halt his sexual harassment of them.

Understandably desperate to fend off Nilva's advances, Lumba tries everything, even undermining her own sales pitch. "I hate Slug-o-Cola!" she confesses. But Nilva doesn't hesitate, replying with gleeful sadism, "So do I!" Psychoanalyst Jacques Lacan ([1965] 2002) enigmatically described love as giving something you don't have to someone who doesn't want it. Ferengi capitalism's embrace of women as consumers modifies the formula, giving something patriarchal Ferengi capitalists don't want (Slug-o-Cola) to Ferengi women who don't have it but can be incited via the "inclusive" enclosure of naturalized feminine desire to want it.

If the Ferengi are not a comfortably irrelevant caricature but a satirical, immanent critique of neoliberalism in the 1990s United States, then many aspects of the Ferengi feminist revolution in fact offer a satire of neoliberal, faux-feminist inclusion. You can see this satire in a nutshell in Ishka's bourgeois-feminist dream that "one day, a female will enter the Tower of Commerce, climb the forty flights of stairs to the Chamber of Opportunity, and take her rightful place as Grand Nagus of the Ferengi Alliance." This is a worthy dream. But what's most interesting is the way it is set against the naturalization of women's putative consumer desires, capabilities, and bodily states. "Profit and Lace" is not a utopian horizon but a critical mirror, reminding us that contemporary capitalism thrives through those very naturalizing moves.

But DS9 also suggests that women's economic enfranchisement, even if it is not envisioned on particularly feminist terms, can have unintended, emancipatory consequences. By the time Zek announces his retirement as

Grand Nagus, it seems that Ferenginar's cultural and political-economic transformation has accelerated. Zek calls the station, updating Ishka's sons on his plans. Building on the success of previous reforms and under Ishka's guidance, Zek and the newly formed Ferengi Congress of Economic Advisors have instituted a progressive income tax and a ban on monopolies, and now publicly provide wage subsidies for the poor, retirement benefits, and health care (Brooks 1999).

Mocking this "new workers' paradise," Quark is startled to learn that Zek has named him as his successor—or so he thinks. Zek's call is badly garbled by pollution in the Ferengi capital. When Zek and Ishka arrive on the station to announce the new Nagus, Quark is affronted to learn that *Rom*, his "idiot brother," is the pick. (Imagine a U.S. politician of either major party naming a plainspoken, grassroots labor union organizer as head of the Federal Reserve and you can begin to appreciate Quark's disbelief.) A defiant, resentful Quark publicly pledges that his bar will serve as "the last outpost of what made Ferenginar great." Quark parodies TNG's Captain Picard's grandiose anti-Borg speech in *Star Trek: First Contact*, declaring, "The line has to be drawn here. This far and no further!" (Frakes 1996). "He's not taking it very well," Zek frets. But Ishka shrugs, and the celebration of Rom—whom Zek calls "a kinder, gentler Nagus"—proceeds.

"The Person Who Lives among Us That We Don't Fully Understand"

Television scholar M. Keith Booker (2018) argues that "given the state of American politics in the Trump era, the United States has now assumed the role, not of the Federation, but of the Ferengi" (121). An analysis that defetishizes the Ferengi compels both agreement and disagreement with Booker. On the one hand, Trump certainly shares an unvarnished, petty criminality with the worst of Ferengi profiteering practices, and his vile treatment of the women in his employ is consistent with the 113th Rule of Acquisition: "Always have sex with the boss" (Behr 1995).[8] But on the other hand, U.S. liberals' principal failure during the Trump era (which, alas, did not end with his 2021 exit from the White House and Twitter) has been to obsess over his foul idiosyncrasies without substantively questioning the

Defetishizing the Ferengi

structures that created him—structures that are at once political-economic and cultural.

What is rightly hated in Trump, like what is hated in the Ferengi, in truth implicates a system that is bipartisan, to say the least. The very founding of the United States—a plantation economy fueled by kidnapped and coerced African labor and built on stolen Indigenous lands and the genocide of Indigenous peoples—would seem to embody the 52nd Rule of Acquisition, itself a political theology of accumulation by dispossession: "Never ask when you can take" (Behr 1995; Harvey 2005). Likewise, the rise of a permanent military-industrial complex in the United States after World War II—a thoroughly bipartisan affair that has also militarized U.S. police departments—exemplifies the 35th Rule: "War is good for business" (Behr 1995). Faced with contemporary economic and public health crises, both major parties rush to take care of corporate donors and neglect the multiracial poor and working classes, heeding the 162nd Rule: "Even in the worst of times, someone turns a profit" (Behr 1995). These contradictions cannot be pinned on Trump, nor even on the Republican Party, alone. To suggest as much is to fetishize both Trump and the Ferengi, rather than heed the occasion for thoroughgoing critical reflection and more transformative political commitment that both offer.

If anything, as religious studies scholar Douglas E. Cowan (2010) has argued, the Ferengi come out somewhat better than U.S. elites. When Quark and Sisko are captured by the Jem'Hadar in the season 2 finale, the Ferengi entrepreneur finds himself in the position of having something that the generally honorable, respectable captain needs: lockpicking skills. Quark agrees, but he takes the opportunity to needle Sisko:

QUARK: You know, Commander, I think I've figured out why humans don't like Ferengis.

SISKO: Not now, Quark.

QUARK: The way I see it, humans used to be a lot like Ferengi. Greedy, acquisitive, interested only in profit. We're a constant reminder of a part of your past you'd like to forget.

SISKO: Quark, we don't have time for this.

QUARK: But you're overlooking something. Humans used to be a lot worse than the Ferengi. Slavery, concentration camps, interstellar wars. We have nothing in our past that approaches that kind of barbarism. You see? We're nothing like you. We're better. Now, if you'll excuse me, I have a lock to pick. (Friedman 1994b)

The exchange is peppered with diversions and deflections from Sisko—"Not now," "We don't have time for this"—that attempt to sweep fundamental race and class contradictions between the Ferengi and the Federation under the rug, in the name of a united front against their Jem'Hadar captors. Sisko himself, as we have seen, needs no reminder of the exclusions that have historically attended the category of "human." But in this exchange, the commander finds himself in the role of a liberal universalist, suppressing difference to meet the crisis of the moment. If, as *DS9* suggests, even the Ferengi contain "otherwise possibilities" (Crawley 2017), then perhaps there is a modicum of hope for our own planet as well. But such hope will come not from impatiently brushing race and class contradictions aside in the name of yet another emergency, but from laboring to understand and alter them.

It would be unreasonable to expect that *A Different "Trek"* will put to bed concerns about the Ferengi as an Orientalist or anti-Semitic trope—nor should it. The past few years have seen a significant uptick in attacks on Jews and Asian Americans, and events like the 2018 Pittsburgh shooting, the 2021 Atlanta shooting, and the bipartisan rush toward a new U.S. cold war with China should trouble us all. Insofar as the Ferengi traffic in stereotypes tied to this violence, we must continue to critique them.

But there is also value in taking seriously what thoughtful liberal, progressive, and socialist Jewish artists like Behr, Shimerman, and Shawn *do* with these stereotypes in the service of broader critical commentary (see Bell and Valley 2013). These artists remind us that what anti-Semitism *wrongly* projects exclusively onto Jews, what Orientalism *wrongly* projects exclusively onto Asians, are in fact general evils of racial capitalism. With

Defetishizing the Ferengi

all due love and respect to Major Kira, condemning the Ferengi as "greedy, misogynistic, untrustworthy little trolls" allows the structure of the fetish to remain intact, and obscures what is greedy, misogynistic, and untrustworthy about social relations that implicate us all, even as they differentiate us. Rom, Leeta, and the rebel waiters and dabo girls at Quark's are clearly alive to alternative social and cultural models for caring for their guests and for each other. Ishka's bourgeois feminism and Nog's soldier-citizenship respond to the same constraints of heteropatriarchal capitalism, even if we read their pursuits as misguided bargains with power. Neither pitying these characters as held at bay by backward cultural "tradition" nor dismissing them as self-loathing assimilants to Federation norms does justice to the class character of their responses to political-economic conditions that are far from foreign to our own planet.

Shimerman recounts frequent queries from fans: "In America, people ask, 'Do the Ferengi represent Jews?' In England, they ask, 'Do the Ferengi represent the Irish?' In Australia, they ask if the Ferengi represent the Chinese. . . . The Ferengi represent the outcast. . . . It's the person who lives among us that we don't fully understand" (Whalen 2016). If the "Ferengi are us," then Shimerman's insight suggests we also do not fully understand ourselves (Kristeva 1988). Perhaps, then, there remains a measure of hope in the Prophets' comment to Quark: "You have not always been as you are now" (Auberjonois 1995a). The point here is not to embrace a nostalgic, romantic anticapitalism—remember, the Prophets do not experience time as linear—but to remain alive to this reminder of the always-immanent character of "otherwise possibilities"—of alternatives to the Ferengi status quo, and to our own (Day 2016; Crawley 2017).

5 O'Brien Family Values

"Weren't You One of the Little People?"

As *DS9*'s world-building richly elaborated on societies introduced in *TNG*—the Bajorans, the Cardassians, the Ferengi—it also reprised and fleshed out some of *TNG*'s "minor" characters. On his sole visit to *DS9*, the irritating, "omnipotent" extraterrestrial being Q (John de Lancie) asks Miles O'Brien, "Do I know you?"

Miles reminds Q that he had previously worked on the *Enterprise-D* under Captain Picard, a frequent target of Q's hijinks.

"*Enterprise*. Oh, yes," Q sneers. "Weren't you one of the little people?" (Lynch 1993b).[1]

If Q's remark stings, it is in part because it lands. Miles, transporter chief on the *Enterprise-D*, gets a considerably more interesting job as chief of operations on *DS9*. But his promotion—and the move to the Federation's periphery that it requires—comes at a significant cost: it means relocating his wife, Professor Keiko Ishikawa O'Brien (Rosalind Chao), and their young daughter, Molly (Hana Hatae), halfway across the galaxy, and that Keiko is out of a job. This chapter springs from a single question: If Miles is one of "the little people," how does it feel to be "the trailing spouse" of such a person?

To begin, consider a scene from *TNG*'s "In Theory," when the O'Briens are still newlyweds living on the *Enterprise-D*. In this episode, Lieutenant Commander Data (Brent Spiner), the ship's android chief operations officer, awkwardly experiments with a romantic relationship with his human colleague, security officer Lieutenant Jenna D'Sora (Michelle Scarbarelli). The O'Briens join the couple for a double date. In the way that people sometimes tease their romantic partners in front of friends, Keiko recounts a skirmish in the O'Briens' adjustment to cohabitation: "Every night, Miles leaves his socks on the floor. When we got married, I made the mistake of picking them up a few times. Then I realized, if I kept it up, I'd be doing it the rest of my life. So I stopped, figuring he'd get the point and do it himself. One night goes by, two, a week, ten days. By now there's a pile of socks half a meter high. . . . After two weeks, I couldn't stand it anymore. I bundled them up and put them in the cleaning processor. And I'm still doing it!"

"And a very good job she does of it, too," Miles adds (Stewart 1991).

D'Sora jocularly replies that Keiko's frustration reminds her of the predicament that Data faces. She confesses that she, too, is somewhat untidy, and that Data has taken to cleaning up after her. This light, momentary exchange juxtaposes Keiko and Data—an Asian woman and a sentient machine—as those to whom responsibility for household cleaning falls. The pairing might seem incidental, but it recalls a long history. Orientalist discourses have routinely cast Asians as affectless, compliant automatons well-disposed to enduring exploitation and domination (Day 2016). As SF scholar Aimee Bahng (2018) reminds us, the Asian woman and the robot converge in the Western "fantasy of docile Asian technoscience, gendered and sexualized to perform a service role" (126).

Keiko's very presence as a crew member's civilian spouse—the character is introduced on her wedding day—complicates the masculinist fantasy of a high-tech, swashbuckling future that has "innovated" away all the messy human aspects of social reproduction. Yet laudable scholarship on political economy and gender in the *Star Trek* universe has had little to say about such work. Economist Manu Saadia (2016), for instance, contends that replicators and other twenty-fourth-century gadgets have entirely done away with the need for many dimensions of social reproduction, particularly those involving "repetitive, energy-intensive, low-skill, high-output labor," enabling people to prioritize the "high-skill, low-output end of the curve" (Saadia 2016, 83; see also Gonzalez 2015, Ewing 2016). Meanwhile, a rich *Trek* criticism in gender studies has tended to focus on the sexist mistreatment of women on the job in Starfleet and the feminist potential of women's leadership, drawing parallels to the contradictions faced by professional-class women in spaces of "productive" work (e.g., R. Roberts 1999; Dove-Viebahn 2007). But *TNG*'s innocuous banter suggests that by eliding social reproduction as a form of gendered labor, both approaches miss out on what political theorist Melinda Cooper (2017) calls "the actual historical intricacies of economic and sexual politics" in the *Trek* universe (23).

And although scholars have thoughtfully investigated the homosocial relationship between Miles and the brash young doctor who becomes his best friend, Julian Bashir (Geraghty 2003; Howe 2017), the O'Briens' marriage and everyday family life have been subject to little scholarly discussion in their own right (in contrast to moving fan tributes, see Yeh 2022). *Star Trek* has shown us single-parent families before—the Crushers on *TNG* and the Siskos on *DS9*. But the O'Briens are both the franchise's first long-term couple with children and the first *Trek* family whose conflicts over gendered divisions of labor of all kinds regularly come to the fore. Moreover, as Bernardi (1998) briefly notes, Keiko's relationship with Miles is the first depiction of a sustained romantic relationship between differently racialized human characters in *Trek* (130). Given the interest that the franchise has attracted from economics, gender studies, and critical-race scholarship alike, the lack of scholarly attention paid to this relationship is all the more curious.

In the hopes of remedying some of these omissions, this chapter follows the O'Brien family to *DS9*, examining its politics of social reproduction while giving sustained consideration to Keiko's perspective, as well as her husband's. It highlights Keiko's underappreciated efforts to collectivize social reproduction on the station, as well as the travails of her engineer husband. Keiko reminds us that even in the putative postscarcity utopia of the Federation, someone still has to pick up the socks, and only social struggle, rather than technological "innovation," can transform gendered and racialized social divisions of labor.

The chapter's task is complicated by the fact that Keiko remains one of the most wrongly maligned characters in *Star Trek* and certainly one of the most wrongly maligned on *DS9*. A fan survey from the indispensable feminist *Trek* podcast *Women at Warp* found that 64 percent of respondents "loved" Miles and that only 6 percent "disliked" or "hated" him. By contrast, only 20 percent of respondents "loved" Keiko, with a nearly equal number, 17 percent, either "disliking" or "hating" her (Michelle 2017). Most respondents, 54 percent, reported mixed views of Keiko, with many defending actor Rosalind Chao over *Trek* writers' decidedly limiting choices for her. Google autocompletes "Keiko O'Brien" with "hate," and words like "grating," "annoying," and "nag" circulate frequently in online fan discussions of the character, as do what Mr. Spock might call "colorful metaphors" (L. Nimoy 1986). Even Chao herself, who is perhaps best known for her work in the film adaptation of *The Joy Luck Club* (Wang 1993), has joked about Keiko's "nagging" (Yu 2020b).

But if Keiko widely elicits such reactions, it behooves us to ask why. The late cultural theorist Lauren Berlant (2013) reminded us that the systematic study and analysis of artistic works "is one of the few places we learn to recognize our emotions as trained and not natural." If audiences are habituated both by race and gender biases and by Keiko's positioning in secondary B or C plots to regard her as a "minor" source of intermittent annoyance, then an alternative interpretive method is needed to try to consider life from her perspective. Popular culture scholar Ramzi Fawaz (2016) uses the term "affective curation" to describe a pedagogical practice of deliberately assigning students to read provocative cultural texts in order to better understand the strong reactions those texts can elicit. Taking inspiration from Fawaz, this chapter is based on a curated, systematic viewing of a particular subset of the *Trek* franchise: watching all twenty-seven of Rosalind Chao's appearances as Keiko on TNG and DS9 in order. Although doing so does not redeem writers' often-uninspired approach to writing the character (Michelle 2017), it can elicit stronger feelings of identification with her and illuminate the political stakes of some of her dilemmas and choices.

My fellow Keiko defenders have already pointed out that for all the O'Briens' conflicts, they clearly love each other, enjoy each other's company, and still have sex, which is not unimpressive, given that the show follows the first eight years of their marriage and the birth and early lives of their two young children. Indeed, as one thoughtful feminist analysis put it, the O'Briens' mutual "affection is so omnipresent, in fact, that many viewers simply fail to notice it" (Michelle 2017).

But to defend Keiko as a loving wife—or to shield her from antipathy that is often plainly misogynistic, racist, or both—does not do full justice to the character's significance. A civilian aboard the *Enterprise-D*, Professor O'Brien holds advanced degrees in botany and runs the *Enterprise*'s plant biology lab, a job she relinquishes in the move to DS9. It remains disappointing that writers did not make more inventive use of Keiko's botanical expertise, since extraterrestrial plants that can move, communicate, govern themselves, kidnap, or even kill are no strangers to the *Star Trek* universe (e.g., Sutherland 1973).[2] The writers' "bible" for DS9 hinted that Keiko's scientific expertise would come in handy for collaborations with Dax and other crew members, but this vision was rarely realized (Berman and Piller 1992).

Nevertheless, Keiko offers salient insight into the people whose care work makes the adventures of our seemingly carefree *Trek* heroes possible. As Miles, Bashir, and the rest entertain Trekkers with their not-infrequent brushes with death, there remain the kin of whatever kind who stay at home worrying, shouldering the burden of administering household economic and emotional life. Such burdens understandably generate ambivalent, contradictory feelings for characters like Keiko. Yet our introduction to the character casts her as inexplicably capricious. In "Data's Day," Keiko gets cold feet before her wedding to Miles, calling off the ceremony before deciding to go through with it after all. Keiko's vacillation is played for comic effect because it puzzles Data, the episode's hyperrational narrator (Wiemer 1991). As Berlant (2008) observed, "Popular culture is terrible at dealing with mixed bags and mixed feelings when the register is ideological and the topic is intimate, and women remain the default managers of the intimate" (xi). Here Data's very incapacity to make sense of Keiko's "mixed feelings" about the "mixed bag" of marriage—as the wedding ceremony concludes, he muses in an interior monologue, "There are still many human emotions

O'Brien Family Values

I do not fully comprehend"—might be read as a self-aware comment on the writers' part, in line with Berlant's point about pop culture's limits.

Keiko's mixed feelings are also presented as amusingly opaque to Worf. Like the O'Briens' wedding, TNG plays the birth of their first child, Molly, for comedy. When a disaster immobilizes the *Enterprise-D* and cuts the crew off from one another inside the ship, a very pregnant Keiko is stranded in Ten Forward, the ship's restaurant and bar famously tended by the iconic, well-hatted Guinan (Whoopi Goldberg). Keiko starts having contractions in Ten Forward, but the closest equivalent on hand to a midwife is Worf, who has just put his rudimentary field medic training at Starfleet Academy to work setting the bone of an injured crew member. When Keiko informs Worf that she is going into labor, the frightened security officer insists, "You cannot! This is not a good time, Keiko," to which she retorts, "It's not open for debate! Like it or not, this baby is coming" (Beaumont 1991). Keiko's body stubbornly reminds the more disembodied geek boys in TNG's action-adventure audience that, "like it or not," some forms of embodied labor—including labor and delivery—cannot be disappeared by "innovative" technology. Yet once Molly is born, Keiko is ecstatic, thanking her reluctant Klingon midwife, "You were wonderful, Worf. I couldn't have done it without you." When Keiko's second pregnancy is announced, a panicked Worf announces he plans to be on another planet at her due date (Landau 1996a).

To take Keiko's presence seriously is also necessarily to grapple with questions of race, ethnicity, and nationality. Screenwriter David Gerrold ([1984] 2016) recalls that the National Broadcasting Company, citing Cold War geopolitical imperatives, specifically prohibited Chinese characters from TOS in the 1960s, making Chao's very presence as a Chinese American actor playing a Japanese character on TNG and DS9 worth noting (147). The figuration of race, nation, and ethnicity in the O'Briens' relationship is complex and largely indirect. The script makes clear that Miles is from Ireland and Keiko is from Japan. But while Colm Meaney is, in fact, Irish, Rosalind Chao is Chinese American, and she does not affect a Japanese accent in her performance as Keiko. Chao, wary of playing yet another

Hollywood Chinese character named "Mei Li," reassured *TNG* creators they did not have to change the character's ethnicity after they cast her (Yu 2020b).

Where race does seem to surface in the O'Briens' relationship—and fans' reception of it—is in conflicts and compromises over food. Literary scholar and former restaurant critic Kyla Wazana Tompkins (2012) uses the term "racial indigestion" to describe how quotidian feelings about food can become a proxy for visceral racial attitudes. Tompkins's theories ring all too true in the *Trek* universe and fandom. To name but a few examples, the Sisko family's intimate relationship with Louisiana creole cuisine has been rightly celebrated by fans, *raktajino* (Klingon coffee) is a staple of daily life on DS9, Romulan ale remains an illegal but coveted spirit, and Klingon and Ferengi tastes for live insects are the stuff of fascination and disgust for many Federation citizens and fans alike. Our first glimpse of the O'Briens as newlyweds showcases negotiations over meal plans, between what the script presents as Keiko's standard twenty-fourth-century Japanese childhood breakfast—"kelp buds, plankton loaf, and sea berries"—and Miles's preferred options, "muffins or oatmeal, or corned beef and eggs" (Chalmers 1991). As the O'Briens' relationship develops, the two accommodate one another, taking note of the other's favorite meals and catering to those tastes, particularly on special occasions. But Keiko's gastronomic tastes nevertheless have incurred the scrutiny of some Trekkers, as in a post (in this case, from a self-professed Keiko fan) titled "Why Is Keiko So Resistant to Non-Japanese Food?" (BigYangpa 2018).

Such scrutiny has a long history, a history that echoes loudly in Keiko's reception. Asian American studies scholars Robert Ji-Song Ku, Martin F. Manalansan IV, and Anita Mannur (2013) remark that "the linkage of Asian Americans and food has been a dominant motif in American materiality and imaginary," and Chao herself is the daughter of Orange County restaurateurs (Hodgins 2008). Theater scholar Ju Yon Kim (2015) observes that "from the nineteenth century to the present, everyday scenes of eating, working, shopping, and studying have buttressed competing views of Asian Americans as ideal and impossible Americans" (3). Although Keiko is presented as Japanese, not Japanese American, *Trek*'s U.S. liberal multiculturalism sets the background norms against which Keiko's culinary choices register as a problematic, "forever foreign" Japaneseness (Takaki 1998).

Kim also points to a more specific history, of "Japanese women who immigrated to the United States in the postwar era as wives of American servicemen" and became objects of mainstream media fascination for "their adoption of American lifestyles" (11). The perceived disconnect between these women's adherence to white American norms, on the one hand, and their racialized bodies, on the other, persisted in the dominant gaze no matter what they did. Thus, when Keiko *does* prepare Miles's Irish meals, another fan laments that "she complains the whole time" (MatthiasRussell 2012). For some Trekkers, it seems that Keiko, much like the Japanese American "war brides" whom Kim discusses, can't win, whether the food she prepares is Japanese, Irish, or Klingon.

"I Don't Need Favors from You. I Just Need to Be Useful!"

Aside from the more quotidian squabbles over picking up the laundry and what to eat for dinner, most of the O'Briens' serious conflicts on TNG are eventually pinned on some outside force. When the crew is caught in a mysterious spatial rift and slowly driven to paranoia, Miles baselessly accuses Keiko of carrying on an affair with one of her scientist colleagues (Landau 1991a). On another occasion, hostile energy-based beings take possession of several crew members, including Miles, who terrifies his wife, taking her as a hostage. There is also trouble in paradise when a transporter accident momentarily shrinks Keiko, giving her the physiology of a twelve-year-old girl, confusing Miles as to how to relate to his wife, with whom sharing a bed now "feels wrong somehow" (A. Nimoy 1992). All of these incidents take place within self-contained, one-off episodes and are presented as forgiven and forgotten by the final act.

On DS9, however, the O'Briens clash much more intensely over crises of formal work and the work of social reproduction. Keiko's first appearance on DS9 makes it apparent that moving the family to the station put Miles's career advancement over her own and that she is frustrated by the absence of meaningful work for a botanist on the station. As a Federation citizen who is not in Starfleet, Keiko seems to want for nothing in the material realm. But it is clear that the absence of stimulating work is a betrayal of her expectations and ambitions for her own life. Miles offers to apply for a job transfer, or to ask Sisko to post Keiko to a local survey mission. Keiko is put off by these well-meaning but paternalistic suggestions, and she insists on finding a job on her own terms: "I don't need favors from you. I just need to be useful!" (Lynch 1993a). Departing from a Roddenberry-era prohibition of interpersonal conflict in *Trek* scripts (Altman and Gross 2016), here Keiko's understandable resentment of the role of trailing spouse is crystal clear.

Shortly after venting her frustrations, Keiko notices Nog and Jake Sisko getting into trouble on the station's Promenade, cracking up as they torment Bajoran strangers with bizarre and irritating, albeit harmless, insects. If Keiko's frustration, her sense of redundancy and need for usefulness, constitutes a surplus, she soon identifies a crisis of social reproduction on the station that calls her to meaningful work. "What this place needs," she declares, "is a school!" (Lynch 1993a). Keiko notes that there are over a dozen children on the station, from ages eight to sixteen, and insists that these young people need "structured activity." Commander Sisko, embarrassed by his son's prank, is instantly supportive of the idea, providing Keiko with space, furniture, and computers.

In some respects, the conceit behind the founding of the station's school—that a person with several advanced degrees who has taught botany at a university level and is also a parent can instantly become an elementary school teacher—brushes over the considerable, specific credentials and skills required of primary and secondary school teachers, in ways that reinforce the devaluation of teachers' labor. It is also worth noting that Keiko's own qualifications seem to get diminished in this process; although she is sometimes referred to as "Professor O'Brien," her students on DS9 call her "Mrs. O'Brien." But the station school reverberates differently in the era of COVID-19, when giant tech corporations and neoliberal politicians openly float the grim prospect of permanent at-home online learning, of

O'Brien Family Values

doing away with school buildings—and unionized education workforces—altogether (N. Klein 2020). "Don't you miss the schools you used to go to, Jake?" asks Keiko. Jake initially protests, but he then concedes that "studying alone on the computer, it gets kind of boring sometimes." He soon becomes one of the school's prize pupils (Lynch 1993a). Here *DS9* suggests that even in the twenty-fourth century, online learning is no substitute for the social interaction, expertise, empathy, and care work of an in-person teacher, and a school community with adequate resources to offer free education to a diverse public. In her pathbreaking essay "What Would a Non-Sexist City Be Like?" urban planner Dolores Hayden (1980) provides examples of urban design schemes that would enable neighbors to voluntarily collectivize childcare and other household tasks, lightening the often highly gendered burden that can make life in nuclear families so exhausting. Much as Hayden recommends, Keiko appropriates space and resources to contest the privatization of social reproduction, the consignment of the station's children to individualized study in their quarters under the supervision of their nuclear families.

Not every parent on the station, however, is as open to enrolling their child in the school as Commander Sisko. "Little lady," Rom queries patronizingly, "what do you know of Ferengi education?" Keiko, who has done her research, makes a pitch to Rom on terms convergent with dominant Ferengi ideology: "Consider the advantage your son will have over other Ferengi once he's learned about other cultures, once he learns how others run their economies, conduct business, negotiate. . . . Knowledge is power, Mister Rom." Although Rom remains skeptical, not least because Keiko is a woman, Nog enrolls. Nog's performance in school is uneven, particularly when "Mrs. O'Brien" leaves Miles in charge as a substitute during a three-week visit to Earth (Livingston 1993a). But Nog eventually thrives, and it is difficult to imagine his entry to Starfleet Academy—or Jake Sisko's later career as a brilliant writer—without Keiko's pedagogy.

But the greatest resistance that Keiko's teaching incurs comes from neither a parent nor even a student but from the ambitious Bajoran religious leader Winn Adami (Louise Fletcher), who later becomes the kai, the head of Bajor's official state religion. In the season 1 finale, "In the Hands of the Prophets," Winn interrupts one of Keiko's lessons, making a scene about "blasphemy" when Keiko refers to the Bajoran Celestial Temple in the secular Federation vernacular of "the wormhole" and to the Bajoran Prophets as "wormhole aliens" (Livingston 1993c). Polite but increasingly vexed by Winn's questioning in front of the entire class, Keiko quips, "I don't teach Bajoran spiritual beliefs. That's *your* job. Mine is to open the children's minds to history, to literature, to mathematics, and to science" (Livingston 1993c). If one of *DS9*'s main faults is that it only made two women regular cast members, the conflict in this episode, foregrounding a philosophical and political debate between a woman cleric and a woman scientist and educator about the place of religion in public education, offers a welcome departure from that pattern, passing the Bechdel test with flying colors (Hodge 2014).

Keiko soon realizes that she has made a powerful enemy. For Winn, the school is a means to an end, a way to raise her profile as an orthodox cleric and manipulate and endanger one of her political opponents (Cowan 2010). Everyday life on the station turns unpleasant for the O'Briens. One of Winn's more zealous followers even bombs the school, although it is thankfully empty at the time, and no one is hurt. Bajoran parents on the station initially heed Winn's call to boycott the school. But the violence of her followers alienates them, and when the school is rebuilt, Keiko returns to a full classroom.

Even when classes resume at the rebuilt school, though, it does not put an end to the O'Briens' struggles over formal work and the work of social reproduction. When a short-lived right-wing Bajoran government covertly backed by Cardassians attempts to expel all non-Bajorans from the sector (see chapter 2), Miles elects to stay with his Starfleet comrades while Keiko and Molly evacuate. Miles insists that military duty comes before family: "We can't just let the Cardies have the wormhole!" But Keiko is unconvinced: "They can have the whole Gamma Quadrant, for all I care!" (Kolbe 1993b). And soon after the Federation's ominous first contact with the Dominion, Bajoran families begin leaving the station and Keiko closes the school, tutoring the few children who remain (Landau 1994b).

O'Brien Family Values

Miles does everything he can think of to cheer up his wife, whose sense of satisfaction in her formal work has again been undermined. He even asks Commander Sisko about setting up an arboretum on the station. But he still struggles to see Keiko's profession as more than a hobby. As Bashir asks him over lunch, "Would you be satisfied just puttering around in a workshop making nanocircuit boards and playing with tricorders? . . . You're chief of operations, I'm a doctor, and Keiko's a botanist. And until she can be a botanist again, I'm not sure she's ever really going to be happy" (Landau 1993a).

Eventually, Keiko does find quite rewarding work as chief botanist on a six-month survey mission on Bajor. The job also comes with free childcare, but it effectively renders her a full-time single parent when she isn't working on the survey. To make matters even more complicated, Bajor is a three-hour shuttle ride from the station, adding the new stressor of distance to the O'Briens' relationship, and the pressure to make the most out of too-brief visits after a long journey (Brooks 1994c). When the survey mission concludes, Keiko seems to have steady work as an independent scholar, producing scholarship based on the survey data for at least the next three years and working from home well into the evenings as Molly gets older.

If Miles is preoccupied with his wife's career crises, Keiko finds clever ways to manage Miles's crises of social reproduction upon her return, particularly when he finds himself with free time but she has other things to do (Landau 1996a). During Keiko's posting to Bajor, Miles and Bashir become much closer, spending a great deal of free time together on racquetball courts, in the holosuite, and drinking and playing darts at Quark's. When Keiko returns, Miles expects to give up his "regression" into bachelor life altogether, perhaps out of guilt for having thrown Keiko's career into crisis in the first place. But it becomes apparent that what Keiko most desires is time to work quietly. Rather than telling her husband to buzz off, though, Keiko feigns worry about Bashir's loneliness:

KEIKO: Miles, I promised I wouldn't say anything, but it's about Julian.
MILES: What about him?

18. Professor Keiko Ishikawa O'Brien cheerfully getting her husband out of her hair so she can get back to work ("Accession," season 4, episode 17, aired February 24, 1996).

KEIKO: I ran into him the other day, and he seemed depressed. He'd never admit it, but he really misses you.

MILES: Poor guy. No family to come home to every night.

KEIKO: Maybe you should go find him, you know, cheer him up a little.

MILES: Depressed, is he?

KEIKO: Very.

MILES: Maybe I should go spend an hour with him.

KEIKO: Maybe two.

MILES: I'm a lucky man.

KEIKO: [winks]

As soon as her husband is out the door, Keiko contacts Bashir, giving him a different version of the same story. Several scholars (Geraghty 2003; Howe 2017) and a great many fans have remarked on the homosocial "bromance" between Miles and Bashir, a dynamic that develops despite Miles's early distaste for the arrogant young English doctor. Yet homosociality and homoerotics—erotics of all sorts, for that matter—emerge in part from the intimate spaces of social reproduction, which are constantly being made and remade. Rather than a mere proxy for unnamable desires between men, Keiko quite savvily works the dynamics between her husband and his best friend in order to get some peace and quiet.

*

Upon returning to the station from the botanical survey, Keiko also reveals that she is pregnant, a result of one of the couple's furtive reunions during her time on Bajor (Landau 1996a). Both parents are delighted at their growing family. But it also grows in a less expected way. After Keiko is later badly injured in a shuttle accident, Kira asks Bashir to transplant the fetus to her own womb—a spectacular feat of twenty-fourth-century medicine that covered for Nana Visitor's actual pregnancy (Brooks 1996). As Keiko recovers, the O'Briens struggle with respect for Kira's privacy, and ask her to move in with them for the remainder of the pregnancy.

With astonishing generosity, Kira agrees, welcoming Molly to call her "Aunt Nerys," and the three adults live together as an extended family for several months. Miles plays a central role in Kira's prenatal care, giving her massages, helping manage appointments, arguing with her about limits on her activity, and even helping her out of the bathtub. The bond between them grows so intense that Quark snickeringly refers to them as "the other O'Briens, Miles and Kira" (A. Robinson 1996). Keiko seems breezily comfortable with the whole dynamic, but Miles and Kira realize they are starting to develop an attraction to one another, which they agree to repress for the sake of their own, presumably monogamous romantic relationships. After Kira gives birth to the O'Briens' son—named Kirayoshi (Clara Bravo) in his surrogate mom's honor—she privately mourns the return of the child to the nuclear family. Kira confides melancholically in Odo, "I got into this because the O'Briens needed my help. I never wanted a baby. But now? I just wish I could hold him in my arms and never let him go" (Treviño 1997).

Audiences interpret the Kira surrogate pregnancy arc quite differently. Nussbaum (2008) finds Miles's "proprietary" assumptions about his access to Kira's body and health "creepy." But other fans have found the arc "wonderfully poly," representing forms of kinship beyond the constraints of the heteronormative, nuclear family and its presumptions of monogamy and quasi ownership of biological children (OmicronPerseiNine 2012). Literary scholar David Greven (2009) has argued that on TNG, the crew of the *Enterprise-D* comprise a queer extended family (194). If Greven is right, then DS9 takes this experiment in kinship even further. Fans have picked up on and often joke about a web of both depicted and implied romantic and erotic relationships—between Worf and Dax, Dax and Bashir, Bashir and Garak, Bashir and Miles, Miles and Keiko, Miles and Kira, Kira and Odo—that link much of the senior staff in an extended, polyamorous kinship network.

DS9 surely falls far short of the bold reimaginations of reproduction envisaged by SF writers like Octavia Butler, or social theorists like geographer Sophie Lewis (2019), who calls for "open-source, fully collaborative gestation" that "explode[s] notions of hereditary parentage, and multipl[ies] real, loving solidarities" (26). But where American studies scholar Lincoln Geraghty (2003) argues that the show's text parallels the U.S. Democratic Party's embrace of neoliberal "family values" in the 1990s, we might also note how DS9's subtext seems to gesture longingly for "queerer, more comradely modes" of what Lewis calls "doing family" (22).

"O'Brien(s) Must Suffer"

Keiko endures numerous displacements on DS9. She moves across the galaxy for her husband's promotion, loses her job in the process, takes a series of short-term jobs as a teacher and a surveyor, and is often relegated to the position of interstellar, trailing, stay-at-home spouse. Even her pregnancy is relocated to the womb of another person. So it is ironic that it is Miles O'Brien who is depicted as the "long-suffering" one. One of the recurrent motifs on DS9, openly discussed by the show's creators, is that "O'Brien"—meaning Miles—"must suffer" (Memory Alpha n.d.k). Miles is

O'Brien Family Values

cast as the "everyman" on the senior staff, the only white human male in a predominantly extraterrestrial crew, with Keiko's "nagging" compounding his many woes. Behr calls the character "the workingman's hero" (Altman and Gross 2016, 443). All of this suffering is piled onto the well-known plight of the *Star Trek* engineer, who is, to comic effect, constantly asked by the commanding officer to perform tasks in half the time they take or less.

It cannot be denied that Miles endures a parade of misery that continues unabated across the series. In the first season, a group of mysterious extraterrestrials make contact with the crew by embodying figments of their imagination, menacing Miles with a recurring hallucination of the imp Rumpelstiltskin after he reads the German fairy tale to Molly (Legato 1993). Before he and Bashir are really friends, Miles repeatedly injures and exhausts himself squaring off with the doctor in a racquetball tournament, until a device altering the laws of probability on the station momentarily turns things in his favor (Livingston 1994a). Indeed, it seems that Miles is almost constantly injuring and reinjuring his shoulder during recreational activities, kayaking on the holosuite or playing darts at Quark's.

In "Armageddon Game," Miles and Bashir help two extraterrestrial communities that have recently signed a peace and disarmament treaty destroy their remaining stockpiles of biological weapons. Things go awry, and Miles is exposed to the deadly poison (Kolbe 1994a). To make matters worse, the extraterrestrials turn on them, insisting that neither the weapons nor any knowledge of how to create them may survive disarmament, and falsely report to DS9 that Miles and Bashir have been killed in an accident. But Keiko, who knows her husband's diet very well, is able to spot a telling contradiction—coffee in the afternoon?!—in the video evidence of the "accident" provided to Starfleet. Much has been made of Miles and Bashir's bromantic conversation about single and married life as they are on the run in "Armageddon Game" (Geraghty 2003; Howe 2017). But Keiko is, in a way, this episode's hero. Although she turns out to be wrong about her husband's habits in this instance—Miles does, in fact, drink coffee in the afternoon—she is nevertheless right that he and Bashir are still alive, and it is her intuition that prompts Sisko to lead a rescue mission.

19. Miles O'Brien suffering on the station's racquetball court as Julian Bashir, his sparring partner, checks on his health ("Rivals," season 2, episode 11, aired January 2, 1994).

The pain only continues for Miles when a planned romantic vacation with Keiko—the couple's first in five years—is interrupted by Cardassians, who arrest him, falsely accuse him of conspiracy against their state, and sentence him to death (Brooks 1994a). Keiko staunchly refuses to testify against her husband, and the crew manages to get him acquitted. In "Hard Time," Miles is again falsely accused, this time of espionage against the Argrathans, who use a telepathic form of punishment that implants memories of an extended incarceration that never actually occurred (Singer 1996). This punishment, which the Argrathans consider a more enlightened alternative to maintaining actual prisons, proves so severe that it leads Miles to quite seriously contemplate suicide, until Bashir finds a way to counteract the punishment's effects. The episode reminds us that the prison itself was invented as a reform from earlier forms of punishment—and is likewise a cruel, spectacular failure (A. Davis 2003).

O'Brien Family Values

Miles's ostensibly innocent suffering is on especially vivid display in "Whispers," a flashback episode told almost entirely from his point of view, in which the engineer returns to his everyday life on the station only to find that everyone he knows is acting suspiciously (Landau 1994a). Tension mounts as Miles narrowly foils successive attempts to distract, incapacitate, and even incarcerate him, from an inordinately long annual physical examination by Bashir to Keiko's fricandeau stew, which Miles is convinced has been laced with a sedative. "Everybody seems to be getting a head start on me today," Miles remarks, wondering at first if a surprise party of some kind is in the works, despite his birthday being months off.

In a certain light, "Whispers" works as a parody of reactionary persecutory anxieties about so-called political correctness in the 1980s and 1990s; it seems everyone around the "innocent" white everyman Miles is hypervigilant about his capacity to do harm. Only at the end of the episode, when O'Brien successfully escapes the station, do we learn that this is not the real O'Brien at all but a clone, a replicant who has been programmed with all of Miles's experiences but also with instructions to assassinate extraterrestrial dignitaries on their way to the station for peace negotiations.

The trials of Miles O'Brien—those listed here comprise but a few—are told from his point of view. But a systematic approach to Keiko's character arc, in the vein of Fawaz's (2019) affective curation, underscores that she is suffering as well. In "The Assignment"—an acting tour de force for Chao and one of the rare episodes that features her in an A plot—a Bajoran pahwraith takes possession of Keiko, perhaps a poetic revenge for Miles's earlier possession on TNG. Pah-wraiths are sadistic Bajoran demons who rival the Prophets and seek to destroy them. Under control of the pah-wraith, Keiko orders Miles to modify the station's equipment to kill the Prophets, or it will kill Keiko—even throwing her off a balcony and nearly paralyzing her to show Miles its resolve. Luckily, Rom's relationship with Leeta has given him insight into Bajoran spirituality. The Ferengi junior engineer advises a terrified Miles on how to expel the pah-wraith, saving the Prophets and Keiko. Only in the episode's final minutes, once the demon has been exorcised, do we get Keiko's perspective on the terrifying events: "It was more like having something coiled around inside my head. I could see and hear through it, but anytime I tried to do anything, it was like being stuck in sand and squeezed. . . . I don't think it had any intention of leaving either one of us alive" (Kroeker 1996). Some suggest that writers' limited choices for Keiko are a contingent product of Chao's considered decision to take a recurring guest role on DS9, rather than accept producers' offer to become a regular cast member, in order to allow time for other projects and life as a working actor with a family (Spelling 1996). But "The Assignment" makes clear that Chao made superb use of more dynamic script material as a recurring guest when actually given the opportunity.

In "Time's Orphan," another doomed O'Brien family vacation results in Molly getting lost in a cave on a strange planet that accelerates the passage of time and emerging from it as a feral adolescent. Keiko and Miles do an admirable job of attempting to slowly reacclimate feral Molly (Michelle Krusiec) to life on the station, but her longing for the planet where she spent an accelerated, solitary childhood is intense, so much so that she acts violently on the Promenade. Rather than sending Molly to a special care center, the O'Briens reluctantly return her to the planet. Although Molly's facility with language is rudimentary, her sense of attachment to place is strong, and Miles and Keiko recognize that this return, though difficult for them, is the best option for her. Miraculously, feral Molly's return to the cave unexpectedly reunites six-year-old Molly with her parents. While Molly is able to remember the whole affair as a pleasant trip, even drawing a picture of the family picnicking, Keiko and Miles are deeply shaken—so much so that Keiko's next and final appearance, in the series finale, is to discuss the family's return to Earth (Kroeker 1998a, 1999).

Given its focus on Miles's perspective, it is worth asking whether the "O'Brien must suffer" trope is a reactionary one. Cultural theorist David Savran (1998) observes that the trope of "the white male as victim" loomed large in U.S. politics and culture in the 1990s (4). Noting that "there is much symbolic power to be reaped from occupying the social and discursive position of subject-in-crisis," literary scholar Sally Robinson (2000) encourages us to be critical of works of fiction that "positively revel in the spectacle of

O'Brien Family Values

white male bodies in pain, and in the spectacle of a weak masculinity at the mercy of the feminine" (9, 18). Even O'Brien's Irishness could be read as a vehicle for this form of performative self-pity for a mostly white U.S. audience. Historian Matthew Frye Jacobsen (2006) observes that in the late twentieth century, the recuperation of "white ethnic" immigrant identities that were initially persecuted, but assimilated into U.S. whiteness within a generation or two, became a popular means of disavowing white privilege.

Still, there remain good reasons to hesitate before embracing the Miles-as-reactionary thesis. Greven (2009) argues that "without exculpating *Trek* in any way, without attempting to reconcile its own ever-warring impulses toward both progressivism and phobia . . . overall, *Trek*'s greatest contribution to an anti-racist project is its depiction of a denatured, decentered white masculinity" (117). To be sure, Miles harbors a deep-seated bias against Cardassians, a prejudice informed by his experience in the Federation-Cardassian war. Keiko calls him out for such attitudes (Bole 1993). But that an Irish person could resent the Cardassian Empire as a brutal colonial power, or sympathetically identify with Bajorans as fellow historically colonized people (as Sisko also does, to great effect), proves to be less problematic than some have suggested. If anything, it is Miles's views on the Jem'Hadar, on display in "Hippocratic Oath" (see chapter 3), that are completely unredeemable. At the same time, Miles is instinctively supportive of the strike of mostly Bajoran and Ferengi workers at Quark's. He shares his own family lore about an Irish American relative who led a coal miners' strike with the workers, gives up his regular haunt to avoid crossing a picket line, and pressures his friends to do the same (Burton 1996a). Finally, any effort to reduce Miles to some cosmic Archie Bunker is complicated by Colm Meaney's own Leftist political commitments, years of work in Leftist theater, and routine experiences with ethnic profiling as an Irish person in London during the Troubles (see Regan 2020).

But when we read the "(Miles) O'Brien must suffer" trope through the prism of Keiko's experience, we can no longer exceptionalize white male injury at all. Although he clearly wants Keiko to be happy, Miles needs to be challenged to take her career as seriously as he takes his own, even as his career routinely puts him in serious danger and risks making Keiko a widow and single parent. Miles's insecurities about Keiko's love for her work—including the recurrence of fears that she'll leave him for a colleague—get the best of him in at times quite ugly ways (Landau 1994b; Brooks 1994c). Rewatching Chao's appearances in order—making Keiko the deliberate focus of analysis, identification, and study—can elicit strong feelings of frustration with Miles indeed.

If there is a heroic, suffering O'Brien, then, perhaps it is the indispensable Professor Keiko Ishikawa O'Brien, first and foremost. As an engineer, Miles might keep the lights on at DS9, but it is Keiko who, consigned to the position of trailing spouse, champions efforts to collectivize social reproduction on the station, founding and defending the station school and welcoming Kira into her extended family as a brave experiment in collective kinship. Keiko produces scholarship on local botany in collaboration with Bajoran colleagues who are rebuilding agricultural and scientific infrastructure in the wake of the devastating Cardassian Occupation. She does all of this while raising her own children, pushing her husband to be a better person, and abiding the stress of routine threats to her husband's safety as a condition of his work. We only get glimpses of station life from Keiko O'Brien's perspective occasionally. But taking Keiko's geographies seriously challenges fantasies of a future that has automated away the "low-skilled" work of social reproduction or "innovated" away the political problems that surround racialized and gendered divisions of labor.

Keiko's frustrations also offer a cautionary tale, suggesting that if the privatized, neoliberal family values of the 1990s remain the best that twenty-fourth-century humanity has to offer, the same crises of social reproduction and the same racialized and gendered divisions of labor will continue to fester, even in a "postscarcity" Federation economy. In the decades since DS9 aired, this warning has certainly proven prescient. Rather than dismissing Professor O'Brien as "annoying," we might yet learn from her example, finding fairer ways to organize and distribute the joys and burdens of care work and fighting for that work to be valued and supported.

6 Empire's Queer Inheritances

"Evocative Treatment of the *Experience* of Queerness"

From the formation of a station school to the strike at Quark's, from the O'Briens' fights over laundry to battles over the economic personhood of Ferengi women, *DS9* points audiences to struggles over social reproduction as key sites of racial-capitalist contradiction. But social reproduction is also intimately connected to geopolitical contradictions, to the questions of empire and colonization that are likewise at the heart of the series and this book. This final core chapter examines the links between empire and social reproduction by turning to a perhaps-unlikely site: the lives of the station's queers. Social reproduction—which includes but goes well beyond procreation—is often imagined as the natural, authentic province of cis- gender heterosexuals. But feminist and queer social thinkers (Manalansan 2008; Andrucki 2017; Lewis 2019) have pushed the boundaries on this concept, showing that everyone—from the bisexual nanny (who is also a parent) to the gay flight attendant (and his Grindr hookup) to the trans lesbian teacher—has a role to play in the intimate work that makes and remakes social life.

But if everyone's care work makes the social world, it must also be asked what kind of society we are (re)making. Cultural theorist Jasbir Puar (2007) has critiqued what she calls "homonationalism," which describes the U.S. empire's tentative embrace of a diverse, multicultural, and LGBTQ-inclusive range of citizens to shore up its image of enlightenment, democracy, and freedom. Not unlike the use of "Black faces in high places" that historian Keeanga-Yahmatta Taylor (2016) so trenchantly criticizes, homonationalism uses a superficial rendition of diversity to give cover to empire as it continues to enrich the few and immiserate the global many. Puar has emphasized that homonationalism is not an epithet reserved for LGBTQ individuals who publicly espouse imperialist or Islamophobic views. Instead, it is a diffuse discourse, filtering into everyday life and shaping the conduct of "good" liberal multicultural subjects as well as more ardently right-wing ones. What is most compelling about the queer characters examined in this chapter, then, is not the search for an idealized LGBTQ hero but the broader geopolitical contexts and contradictions in which queer identities, desires, and politics are embedded (Stoler 1995).

To be sure, none of the three characters who comprise this chapter's focus—Lieutenant Commander Jadzia Dax, Cardassian tailor and spy Elim Garak, and Doctor Julian Bashir—is ever expressly identified as LGBTQ on the show. But each has been claimed by fans as offering a kind of representation, and for good reason. As a joined Trill, Jadzia Dax is many persons and genders in one—a bright young scientist host (Jadzia) who shares her body and consciousness with a three-hundred-year-old genderless symbiont who has lived as both a man and a woman (Dax). Garak's sexuality—like so many aspects of the character—is subject to endless speculation. Actor Andrew J. Robinson's clever follow-up novel to the events of DS9, A Stitch in Time (2000), suggests attractions to both men and women during Garak's youth as a spy in training. And although he pursues an endless string of women before ending up with Ezri Dax (Jadzia's successor), Bashir enjoys a homosocial "bromance" with Miles O'Brien and is unmistakably the object of Garak's (un)requited affection.

Behr, for his part, is touchingly apologetic about not offering more open LGBTQ representation on DS9 (Behr and Zappone 2019). For LGBTQ Trekkers, myself included, such contrition means a great deal. But when we read the world through a Left queer lens, it becomes clear that although representation matters in both popular culture and politics, it is not the only or even the most important criterion—context, subtext, and content matter too. Queer theory and politics have a long and robust tradition of "subjectless critique," which prioritizes solidarity with society's most abject and marginalized people over strict loyalties solely defined by LGBTQ

Empire's Queer Inheritances

identity (Eng, Halberstam, and Muñoz 2005). Building on that tradition, Greven (2009) argues that, if not LGBTQ, *Star Trek* has always been queer: "If we fail to acknowledge the importance of Trekkian allegory for the representation of homosexuality, we miss out on one of the most remarkable accomplishments of . . . the *Star Trek* monomyth generally: its evocative treatment of the *experience* of queerness in a homophobic, difference-denying culture" (12, original emphasis).

As fan studies scholars (Bacon-Smith 1991; Jenkins 1992; Penley 1997) have demonstrated, Greven's argument is not lost on Trekkers, who have readily detected the franchise's queer allegories. *DS9* is no exception. In "Rejoined," Jadzia Dax comes into conflict with the Trill cultural prohibition against "reassociation," or becoming romantically involved with a lover from a symbiont's previous lifetimes (Brooks 1995b). After a brief, passionate reunion, Dax's lover Lenara Kahn (*Trek* veteran Susanna Thompson) breaks off the romance rather than risk sanction and expulsion from home and homeland (Georgis 2006). Philosopher Judith Butler (2004) observes that grief reminds us of the decidedly queer "ways in which we are from the start, and by virtue of being a bodily being, already given over, beyond ourselves, implicated in lives that are not our own" (22; see also Song and Tan 2020). The sorrow of Jadzia Dax—who is beset with the grief of multiple persons, lifetimes, and genders for love lost twice over—powerfully distills Butler's claim.

"Rejoined" gave audiences the first same-sex kiss in *Star Trek*, airing eighteen months to the day before the famous coming out episode on the sitcom *Ellen* (Junger 1997). It offered an implicit critique of the recently imposed Don't Ask, Don't Tell ban on disclosing LGBTQ identity in the U.S. military (Heath and Carlisle 2020, 53). Avery Brooks, in yet another turn directing a socially consequential episode, refused to sensationalize the kiss between Dax and Kahn, going to great lengths to make Farrell and Thompson feel safe in exploring the characters' relationship (Memory Alpha n.d.o). Farrell movingly describes the sheer volume of fan mail she received over "Rejoined," and cites Leonard Nimoy's Spock as a reference point for portraying Dax as an outsider (Altman and Gross 2016, 519–22;

Behr and Zappone 2019; Gellis 2021). Feminist, queer, and trans scholars continue to celebrate and debate the radical potential of Dax's multiply gendered subjectivity and the Trill reassociation taboo (Ferguson 2002; Kanzler 2004; Song and Tan 2020). "Profit and Lace" aside (see chapter 4), a 2017 survey suggested that DS9 was the most popular *Trek* series among trans Trekkers at the time (Fennell 2017).

Meanwhile, Garak's special friendship with Bashir has become the topic of voluminous queer fan fiction, as well as academic scholarship (e.g., Geraghty 2003; Howe 2017). In 2020 Robinson and Siddig reprised their roles in "Alone Together," a web sequel that catches up with the doctor and the spy twenty-five years after the events of DS9, sustaining the intrigue between them. Bashir reminisces about dating the Dax symbiont's new hosts, both men and women. In an especially droll bit of fan service, "Alone Together" even intimates that Garak once had sex with his hated enemy, Gul Dukat, during the Cardassian Occupation of Bajor (Sid City 2020).

DS9's attention to everyday queer experiences, if not identities, in the context of colonialism and empire directs us to the ways that queer affinities can both reproduce imperial projects and offer departure points for challenging them. We have already seen how the everyday arena of social reproduction can be configured to serve the dictates of capital and patriarchy, but it can also be contested and collectivized, whether by unionizing Quark's, organizing gestation beyond the dyadic couple, or creating a station school. But the social world is, as geographers Cowen and Smith (2009) suggest, both a geoeconomic and geopolitical space; conflicts between forms of life, between colonizer and colonized, suffuse its everyday. How do the imperatives of empire—Cardassian and Federation—come to bear on the psychic lives and ordinary experiences of empire's queer subjects? What forms of queer identity and desire emerge in service and resistance to these dictates?

"I Deserve a Vacation Every Now and Then"

Jadzia Dax provides a fascinating case study of a queer imperial subject. Her immediate Trill predecessor, Curzon Dax (Frank Owen Smith), was a

Empire's Queer Inheritances

mentor to Benjamin Sisko and something of a rumbustious, dirty old man. In more ways than one, Curzon Dax's life echoes that of George Curzon, a Victorian-era British imperial politician, antisuffragist, and geographer. An Orientalist par excellence and a devotee of England's "civilizing mission," George Curzon produced voluminous writing on Russia, Central Asia, and the Middle East before becoming the imperial viceroy of India, where his disastrous push to partition Bengal further stoked local struggles for self-determination (Gilmour 1994). When he returned to Britain, he served as foreign secretary and later as president of the Royal Geographical Society (Goudie 1980). An agent of imperial power and knowledge production through and through, George Curzon was widely held to be an unpleasant and arrogant man, despised by his Indian and British contemporaries alike.

Given Jadzia Dax's charismatic personality and praise from feminist, queer, and trans fans and scholars, drawing a parallel to a hated colonial racist and antisuffragist may be shocking. But for all their differences, there are some striking similarities between George Curzon and Curzon Dax, similarities that also inflect Jadzia and her successor, Ezri Dax, as characters. Both George Curzon and Curzon Dax were, without a doubt, elites. George Curzon was born into massive wealth and served in some of the highest offices in the British Empire. Likewise, only 10 percent of Trill have the honor of being joined with a symbiont, and of course, even fewer Federation citizens serve in Starfleet, much less as ambassadors.[1]

Further, both George Curzon and Curzon Dax were respected by their elite contemporaries as adventuresome experts on Orientalized peoples and places. Curzon Dax spent most of his diplomatic career working closely with Klingons, negotiating a historic Federation-Klingon peace treaty. The parallel here is striking, given the early racialization of the Klingons as Mongolian or Russian (Bernardi 1998) and George Curzon's exploits in Russia and Central Asia. Curzon Dax's intimacy with Klingons also leads to one of the more touching trans allegories in the Dax character arc. In "Blood Oath," Jadzia reunites with some of Curzon's old Klingon pals, Kor (John Colicos), Kang (Michael Ansara), and Koloth (William J. Campbell), characters familiar to many Trekkers from TOS. Jadzia needs only correct them once for the grizzled warriors to internalize Dax's new name and pronouns without batting an eye (Kolbe 1994b). This seemingly minor plot point—the unblinking handling of name changes and transitions between hosts—has been praised as a metaphor for extending courteous decency to trans and nonbinary people (Dale 2020).

Finally, both George Curzon and Curzon Dax were sexually and romantically prolific. One contemporary described George Curzon as "madly reckless with women," including married women (quoted in Gilmour 1994, 108). Even a sympathetic biographer (Gilmour 1994) puts George Curzon's mistress count at a dozen at least. Curzon Dax, for his part, was something of a bon vivant, liaising with numerous women and ultimately dying of ecstatic sexual exhaustion on the Federation pleasure planet Risa, where he spent his final days (Carson 1993b; Bole 1995b; Auberjonois 1996b). Curzon Dax, too, pursued at least one affair with a married woman, and is even posthumously accused of arranging the death of his lover's husband (Carson 1993b).

More than a little of that Curzon sensibility infuses Jadzia Dax, whom Farrell gaily describes as "roguish" (Altman and Gross 2016, 454). Jadzia, too, seems to have a taste for the indulgent, the exotic, and the bawdy. Much to the puzzlement of her colleagues, the collected young science officer regularly gambles with Ferengi and parties with Klingons. When O'Brien, Worf, and Sisko complain that traveling in Dominion territory without a cloaking device to conceal their ship makes them feel exposed, she smirks at "being in the same room with so many naked men" (Landau 1996b).[2] Jadzia Dax delights in the comforts of luxurious hotels with gorgeous views and room service—in being, in a word, "pampered" (Livingston 1998a)—and dates a wide range of men whom others, particularly her good friend Kira, find impossibly different or simply unpalatable (Livingston 1994b). Rejecting the advances of Quark and Bashir, Jadzia sets her sights on Worf from the moment he arrives on DS9, although he is slow to catch on and they do not get together for about a year (Conway 1995; A. Robinson 1996).

In "You Are Cordially Invited . . . ," the celebrated Worf-Dax wedding episode, Jadzia hosts a raucous bachelorette party, featuring a Samoan

Empire's Queer Inheritances

fire-knife dance (*siva 'afi* or *'ailao 'afi*) performance by the muscle-bound Lieutenant Manuele Atoa (Sidney Liufau), a visiting officer of Polynesian descent (Livingston 1997b). Analyzing "popular narratives about Samoan size, strength, and fierceness" in U.S. culture, Pacific studies scholar April K. Henderson (2011) observes that "Samoan bodies—invariably male, invariably big—form an exotic tropical punchline or exclamation point in a text that's really about something else" (270, 288). Jadzia's flirtation with Atoa confirms Henderson's claim, making Atoa an interloper in the Jadzia-Worf relationship, juxtaposing Samoan and Black male bodies but ultimately figuring the Samoan as an ephemeral curiosity. The flirtation, among other transgressions, incurs the rage of Lady Sirrella (Shannon Cochran), Worf's surrogate mother and Dax's would-be mother-in-law. Following Klingon tradition, Sirrella is tasked with vetting Worf's fiancée, and it remains unclear whether Jadzia will pass muster. But true to the episode's romantic-comedy form, love conquers all, and the wedding finally proceeds.

Like Dax's same-sex kiss in "Rejoined," the relationship between Worf and Dax broke ground for the franchise. Although Worf has a brief romance with Commander Deanna Troi (Marina Sirtis) at the end of TNG, *Star Trek* had never before depicted a long-term relationship between characters played by a Black man and a white woman, and cultural anxieties about such pairings inflect the Worf-Dax dynamic (Shabazz 2015; Nast 2000). If Worf, as SF luminary Ursula Le Guin ([1994] 1995) has suggested, is in a constant crisis of kinship, an endless Shakespearean drama of inheritance, then Jadzia Dax seems to be at a carnival, a cheerful cosmopolitan consumer of eclectic pleasures. Gene Roddenberry's liberal multiculturalist vision of *Star Trek* as grounded in "a delight in the essential differences between men and between cultures" seems to infuse Jadzia's libidinal experience of the world (Whitfield and Roddenberry 1968, 40). Worf, by contrast, is considerably more circumspect, hypervigilant about being perceived as a dangerous Klingon.

The differences and tensions between the two lovers are on full display in season 5's "Let He Who Is without Sin . . ." (Auberjonois 1996b). The episode is hardly considered a shining jewel, routinely making worst-of lists. Many involved in its creation—Wolfe, Behr, Moore, Farrell, Siddig, and Auberjonois (who both acted and directed)—have expressed regrets (Erdmann and Block 2000, 392–93). Network censorship foiled the writers' original aim to challenge sexual mores, and the episode that resulted depicted so little sexuality that its transgressive potential remained sadly unrealized (Erdmann and Block 2000, 392–93). Yet for all its limitations, "Let He Who Is without Sin . . ." presents a rich tableau of debates on the relationships between labor, leisure, and geopolitics in Federation life.

Still early in their relationship, Dax convinces Worf to take a vacation together—not on Earth, where Worf was raised, but on Risa, the Federation's "pleasure planet." With the motto "All that is ours is yours," the dominant image of Risa articulates Risian indigeneity with hospitality and sexual availability to a multicultural Federation consumer public, a familiar trope of colonial discourse that persists in the contemporary marketing of numerous "exotic" destinations. Risa is synonymous with *jamaharon*, the name of an unspecified pleasure rite that functions as an innuendo in Starfleet circles. Although the planet's sophisticated weather-modification technology, which keeps the climate permanently tourist friendly, and liberated sexual attitudes are depicted as endogenous to Risian political economy and culture, it is worth noting that the planet is not far from Federation Starbase 12, hinting at the intertwined relationship between the military and the geographies of sex tourism (Enloe 2014). In this episode, the trip is meant to be a private one, but the gregarious Dax convinces the misanthropic Worf to allow Bashir, Leeta, and Quark to tag along on the shuttle to Risa.

Upon arrival, everyone is dressed in civilian clothing fit for the balmy weather—everyone but Worf. "Starfleet uniforms are designed for comfort in even the most extreme environments," he offers. Jadzia chides her boyfriend, encouraging him to enjoy the planet's beauty. But where Dax sees gorgeous landscapes, Worf can only see the unnatural: "It's an artificially created paradise, maintained by the most elaborate weather-control system in the Federation. In its natural state, Risa is nothing more than

Empire's Queer Inheritances

20. Quark gleefully preparing to seek *jamaharon*, making the most of the Risian sex-tourism industry, as Jadzia and an unimpressed Worf check out the scenery ("Let He Who Is without Sin . . . ," season 5, episode 7, aired November 11, 1996).

a rain-soaked, geologically unstable jungle" (Auberjonois 1996b). Leeta, Bashir, and Quark take their leave of the couple, but they are not alone for long, almost immediately running into Arandis (Vanessa Lynn Williams), chief facilitator of their vast resort. Arandis is, to Worf's dismay, an old intimate of Curzon's. In fact, it was intimacy with Arandis that led to the old man's "death by *jamaharon*," which is presented as benign, almost as a form of euthanasia by sexual ecstasy. "I suppose there are worse ways to go," Arandis chuckles, and Jadzia reassures her that Curzon died blissfully. As the two women catch up and flirt, Worf can barely contain his envy and revulsion, and he curtly turns down Arandis's offer of a guided tour.

Jadzia is embarrassed by Worf's bad manners, but he soon meets someone whose disgust at Risa matches his own, a conservative intellectual named Pascal Fullerton (Monte Markham). The leader of the aptly named

New Essentialists Movement, Fullerton preaches that "self-indulgence" is "eroding the foundations of Federation society." Worf eagerly reads the New Essentialist manifesto, persuading Jadzia to come with him to a rally where Fullerton belittles gathered tourists as "pampered, spoiled children," indulged by replicators and holosuites and under constant Starfleet protection. Fullerton explicitly links unrestrained consumption and enjoyment of the Federation's postscarcity economy to geopolitical vulnerability. "If I see you as helpless children," he asks, "then how do you think the Borg see you? Or the Romulans or the Klingons or the Dominion? These empires look at the Federation and they see a prize, a prize that we have forgotten how to protect. And if we don't change our ways, they're going to take it from us." He urges Federation citizens to relinquish "childish things and reembrace the hard work that built the Federation in the first place"—before it's too late. There is an unmistakable masculinism here, both in Fullerton's invocation of the King James Bible ("When I became a man, I put away childish things," 1 Cor. 13:11) and his denigration of the social reproduction at the foundation of the Risian economy as both infantile and dangerous, in stark contrast to the "real," disciplined work of empire building and security.[3]

Dax, whose centuries of life experience in multiple genders provides a longer and more capacious view, is unswayed by the right-wing jeremiad: "People have been predicting the end of the Federation since the day it was founded," she tells Worf. "I've spent lifetimes defending the Federation, and I deserve a vacation every now and then." Arandis, for her part, finds Fullerton's antics "entertaining," a sideshow to Risa's joy-enhancing charms. Yet Worf seriously entertains Fullerton's thesis, citing recent Klingon attacks as evidence that the Federation has gone soft. He is scandalized to find both Bashir and Leeta, who at this point in the show are still a couple, in the arms of other lovers. When pressed, the doctor and the dabo girl explain that they are engaging in the Rite of Separation, the Bajoran equivalent of "conscious uncoupling," and are free to share pleasures with other people. Worf dismisses the Bajoran ritual as "frivolous."

Tension escalates when the New Essentialists stage an armed disruption to demonstrate the resort's lack of military readiness—an illegal act that

21. Jadzia and Arandis enjoying some sensuous clay playtime on Risa ("Let He Who Is without Sin . . . ," season 5, episode 7, aired November 11, 1996).

further convinces the normally by-the-book Worf of the link between putative moral decay and strategic vulnerability. Irritated, Jadzia helps Arandis clean up. Arandis takes it all in stride, joking that "what Mister Fullerton could use is a little *jamaharon*." In a scene that fulfills Gene Roddenberry's intention, unrealized in his own lifetime, for Risa's pleasures to include queer sexualities (Strusiewicz 2019), Worf catches Dax and Arandis sensuously sculpting clay together, not unlike Demi Moore and Patrick Swayze in *Ghost* (Zucker 1990). Flying into a jealous rage, Worf begins actively helping the New Essentialists scale up their efforts, hacking into the planet's weather-control system and causing an unheard-of, days-long tropical storm.

The episode culminates in a confrontation between Dax and Worf that provides psychosocial context for Worf's New Essentialist sympathies. Worf's actions, he confesses, stem from an abiding fear of losing Jadzia, of harming her. His preoccupation with his capacity to do harm stems from a childhood athletic accident, a collision with another child that broke that child's neck, killing him. Adopted by human parents, Worf was the only Klingon in the community where he was raised. In grief and guilt, Worf the child internalized a racist Federation view of Klingon masculinity as prematurely overdeveloped, resonant with Fanon's ([1952] 2008) account of colonial pedagogy's impact on Black children. Fanon called the child's identification with the colonizer "a self-sacrifice loaded with sadism," an apt description of adult Worf's jealous and controlling behavior (126). Dax is perhaps right when she remarks, "I've never known a Klingon who had a tougher time enjoying himself." But it is the socially inflicted trauma of racialization in a Federation environment, and not some innate personal flaw, that makes Worf so different from other Klingons (Wynter and McKittrick 2015). As one of the only Klingons in Starfleet and a hypervisible model minority all his life, Worf simply does not experience the same easy, unscrutinized mobility between pleasures, partners, and lives that Dax does.

Dax plays the role of cathartic interlocutor, helping Worf to come to his senses and turn against the New Essentialists' climate terrorism. When Fullerton and his followers use Worf's security codes to cause a seismic disturbance, Worf springs into action, this time in defense of Risa's tourist industry. Worf reframes Fullerton as a geopolitical antagonist, telling him, "I was [one of you] for a time. But I believe the Federation will survive the Dominion, the Borg, and people like you." An outraged Fullerton slaps Worf, who promptly grabs him by the collar and throws him across the room. "I am on vacation," Worf declares in his typical terse, comic understatement, and the planet's pleasant weather and seismic tranquility are restored. In a final victory for Dax, she convinces her uptight boyfriend to skinny-dip as the couple enjoy their last day of vacation, echoing Worf's earlier reluctant mud-bathing excursion with his son Alexander and the Troi family in TNG (Kolbe 1992).

"Let He Who Is without Sin . . ." stages a fascinating range of articulations of the relationships among sexual morality, social reproduction, and empire. The New Essentialists impose more austere, inhospitable geographies of social reproduction on Risa—geographies that demand macho, frontier

Empire's Queer Inheritances

self-mastery—as an antidote to the alienating dimensions of Federation consumer society and a cure for anxieties about imperial decline and vulnerability. Their vision recalls long-standing U.S. imperial fears that coddled decadence would lead to waning geopolitical dominance (Jacobsen 2001). Fullerton's castigation of Federation citizens as overconsumptive "babies" also echoes the "permissiveness" discourses leveraged against student radicals and the welfare state in the late twentieth century (Ehrenreich [1989] 2020). These narratives wrote off rebellions against imperialism and racial capitalism and demands for redistribution as the products of the failure of middle-class white liberal parents to discipline their children, on the one hand, and the excessive appetites of poor mothers of color on public assistance, on the other (D. Roberts 1997). These are, at their root, spiritual discourses, political theologies of reaction. Fullerton's call for a "new essence" demands a restoration not only of the Federation's work ethic and its military but of its soul.

Worf's reformed stance following his reckoning with Dax, by contrast, radically rescripts Fullerton. The New Essentialists go from restoring dignity and security to the Federation to one of its geopolitical adversaries, a parallel threat to the Borg and the Dominion. Worf espouses a liberal nationalism, articulating personal freedom *with* national security, arguing that Fullerton's right-wing terrorism makes the Risians the true Federation patriots (Puar 2007).

But Dax and Arandis see something quite different in Fullerton—not an unpatriotic geopolitical threat but a sexually repressed patriarch who devalues the work of social reproduction. Helping Arandis clean up after Fullerton's first attack, Dax quips that "Risians aren't as lethargic as the Essentialists would like everyone to believe." Dax understands that facilitating the relaxation of other people—tending to hotel grounds, keeping them clean, administering guests' stays, organizing activities, massaging and having sex with them—is labor, something completely ignored by Fullerton's screeds against the decadent consumption side of the Federation economy on Risa. Arandis's reply that the conservative intellectual needs "a little *jamaharon*—no, a lot of *jamaharon*" calls to mind salacious scandals surrounding various publicly prudish figures on the Christian Right, from Jim Bakker to Ted Haggard to Jerry Falwell Jr. But the joke also resonates with anticapitalist theories that tether sexual liberation to freedom from economic exploitation (e.g., Marcuse 1955).

If the conclusion of "Let He Who Is without Sin . . ." proves to be somewhat formulaic in its individual overcoming of mistrust, Worf's catharsis also points to the formative, fundamentally social role of racism in his interpersonal conflicts (Vande Berg 1996). And Dax and Arandis offer latent feminist alternatives that do not resort to the liberal security politics espoused by Worf. What remains altogether unproblematized, however, is Risa's broader political-economic relationship to the Federation and its military. We now turn to a queer character who is considerably more eager to poke holes in the Federation's pretensions of universality.

"With Sentiments Like Those, You Wouldn't Last for Five Seconds on Cardassia"

Political theorist Corey Robin (2018) advances the perhaps-counterintuitive claim that "from the beginning, conservatism has appealed to and relied upon outsiders" (55). "People who aren't conservative often fail to realize this," Robin elaborates, "but conservatism really does speak to and for people who have lost something" (56). Losers, of course, are generally thought of as the proper subjects and objects of the Left, which positions itself as speaking from and for the perspective of the exploited and the dehumanized. But conservatism, too, is linked with loss; it speaks for those who stand to lose something if challenges to racial capitalism, imperialism, and heteropatriarchy succeed. For conservatism, Robin explains, "the chief aim of the loser is not—and indeed cannot be—preservation or protection. It is recovery and restoration" (56).

ds9 is nothing if not a show about outsiders. But it also makes clear that not all losses are created equal. This book argues that ds9 can be read productively for antiracist Left critiques of liberal multicultural discourses— discourses that lend a kinder, gentler face to imperialism and racial capitalism. The other figures considered in this chapter, Dax the Orientalist and Bashir the technocrat, are in some sense good, queer liberal subjects of the Federation's multicultural—but arguably imperialist—project (Eng 2010). But *DS9* also offers insight into the formation of more explicitly reactionary queer subjects. Nowhere is this clearer than in the character of the station's Cardassian tailor, exiled spy Elim Garak.

Unlike some of the more unfairly maligned characters considered in chapters 4 and 5, audiences tend to relish in Robinson's performance as Garak. Garak is a charming "loser," in the precise sense that Robin (2018) describes. The disgraced former darling of the Cardassian Empire's Obsidian Order intelligence agency, he is deliberately abandoned on Terok Nor in the wake of the Occupation. What Garak wants more than anything is "recovery and restoration"—of the Cardassian Empire's former glory, his position in the Obsidian Order, and the approval of his secret and secretive father, the spymaster Enabran Tain (Paul Dooley). Garak also wants to sleep with Bashir. Andrew J. Robinson, who also portrayed the gay piano icon Liberace in a 1988 television movie (Volk-Weiss 2022), playfully recounts that he simply decided Garak had eyes for Bashir in his audition: "Bashir is really good-looking, so as a character choice I thought, 'What the hell? Why not go for it?' There's a close-up of Garak where it looks like he could eat him alive. And I'm sure that's why I got the job" (Altman and Gross 2016, 441).

Robinson's extraordinary Garak novel, *A Stitch in Time* (2000), attests to the queer potential of fictional practices that innovatively extend *Trek*'s televised universe into other media (see carrington 2016, 177–79). Elaborating on Robinson's thirty-three appearances as Garak, the novel examines how Garak came to be, how his queer desires took reactionary ideological form in the context of Cardassian imperial overreach and decline (Hirschman 1991; Pile 2019). To turn to Garak's backstory is by no means to excuse his oft-reprehensible actions, but to better understand what animates and sustains his queer attachments to family and empire, attachments that reverberate in our own "colonial present" (Gregory 2004). Garak's imperialist melancholy, his longing for reincorporation in the Cardassian sociosymbolic order, has a rather distinct minoritarian logic from that of the Federation's internal others.

What keeps some queer people attached to conservative ideals of family and (imperial) nation—ideals that have often excluded people like them? Critiques of LGBTQ bargains with oppressive power structures are a dime a dozen in queer studies. But what sets apart the work of cultural theorist David L. Eng (2010) is his attention to the deeply felt psychic dynamics of such attachments. Eng turns to Sigmund Freud's ([1911] 2002) interpretation of the case of Daniel Paul Schreber, a German judge who published a memoir ([1903] 2000) on his experiences of mental illness—in particular, his fantasy of experiencing sexual intercourse (with God!) as a woman. Freud holds that self-observation can ordinarily be pleasurable or protective, provided it maintains a healthy distance from self-criticism according to society's most punishing standards. But for Schreber, whose physician father was an outspoken advocate of strict parenting, the inner voices of ordinary self-observation and ruthless self-criticism converge and become confused, even indistinguishable (53).

Both Freud's analysis of such a deep and tortured identification with authority and Eng's queer reading of it resonate, to an uncanny degree, as a description of Garak's inner life. Garak is without a doubt queer, not only in his ostensible bisexuality but also in his estranged relationship to the Cardassian national family. He is the illegitimate and largely disavowed son of Obsidian Order chief Tain and Mila (Julianna McCarthy), a woman who worked in Tain's home as a domestic worker. Garak is raised by his adoptive father, Tolan, who tends the gardens of Cardassia's military monuments and passes on a lifelong fascination with Edosian orchids to Garak. The cover of *A Stitch in Time* bears an image of Garak pensively holding one such flower. Schreber's father, likewise, advocated peri-urban gardens, fresh air, and vigorous exercise in children's early lives (Santner 1996, 3). As an adult, Garak has an affair with a woman married to a prominent military official, and he never marries or has children of his own (A. Robinson 2000). On Cardassia, where "family is everything" and intergenerational households are a point of pride, Garak is an outsider to both familial home and national homeland (Bole 1993; Georgis 2006).

Much as Schreber was subject to an invasive, scientifically rationalized parenting regime at home, Garak is whisked away to the Cardassian Bamarren Institute for State Intelligence when he reaches "the age of emergence" (A. Robinson 2000, 10). Reserved principally for children from elite families, education at Bamarren is, quite literally, punishing. The curriculum consists of martial arts, war games, and espionage exercises that can result in grave injuries; one of Garak's classmates loses an eye. Hazing is practically elevated to the status of an extracurricular activity. Already claustrophobic as a legacy of a routine childhood punishment—being locked in a closet by his "Uncle" Tain for misbehavior—the young Garak suffers a brutal beating in a supply closet at the hands of older students (Landau 1998; A. Robinson 2000). Unaware of his elite parentage, Garak experiences Bamarren as an outsider, the son of a gardener and a housekeeper. In the typical form of a coming-of-age novel, Garak masters many of the school's military disciplines, particularly the art of stealth, only to be befriended and then betrayed by two well-heeled classmates, Palandine and her fiancé, Barkan Lokar. Garak harbors an attraction to both members of the couple but becomes enraged when Lokar passes him over for a promotion within the school's vicious, highly formalized pecking order.

Garak is informed that it is time for him to leave Bamarren and assumes that he has been expelled. But he soon learns that his training will continue at the Obsidian Order under Tain's tutelage. As Garak waits to begin training, Tolan rattles him with the revelation that Cardassians are not indigenous to their home planet but a mestizo, settler-colonial society. Dominant Cardassian ideologies hold that Cardassians are the natural evolutionary superiors and successors to a community called the Hebitians. Garak's adoptive father disputes this narrative, describing the Hebitians as technologically and spiritually sophisticated but unconcerned with accumulation for its own sake. He imparts that Cardassians in fact violently seized the Hebitians' home planet and forced surviving Hebitians into intermarriage and assimilation. But Tolan also intimates that Hebitian culture, religion, and politics are in a state of revival, a prospect that both disturbs and fascinates Garak.

Here, too, there is resonance with Schreber, whose gender-transgressive sexual fantasies were also coded in racialized, anti-Semitic terms as "degeneration" into an effeminate Jewish man (Santner 1996, 108–11). And like Schreber, erotic passion that transgresses the nation's familial bedrock lies at the heart of Garak's downfall. His gift for stealth serves him well as a spy, but Garak lets down his guard when pursuing an affair with Palandine, whose now-husband Lokar is an influential military leader. When the affair is exposed, Garak is passed over by his father for a coveted and long-promised promotion and banished to Terok Nor, where he is given the "emasculating" assignment of repairing Cardassian soldiers' clothes. When the Occupation ends, Garak's fellow imperialists abandon him to the mercy of the vengeful Bajorans.

Garak gets deadly revenge on Lokar. But he is haunted by his betrayal of (and betrayal by) both the empire and his family, embodied in his relationship with Tain, the personification of the Cardassian security state. The very "confusion of voices"—the convergence and indistinguishability of self-observation and self-criticism—that Eng (2010, 53) describes is palpable in Garak's queer reactionary mental map of family, state, and nation. Debating the actions of a literary character with Bashir, Garak insists that the correct ethical choice between family and the state is "protecting the state . . . every time" (Wiemer 1994). Bashir replies, "Before you can be loyal to another, you must be loyal to yourself." Garak mocks Bashir: "With sentiments like those, you wouldn't last for five seconds on Cardassia." In the same episode, Garak gets into a political dispute with Sisko, who questions whether the interests of the Cardassian government coincide with those of the Cardassian military. "Is there a difference?" Garak retorts. When he later agrees to serve as a Federation intelligence asset in the Dominion War, he suffers guilty, claustrophobic attacks over feelings of disloyalty and requires rehabilitation from the station's counselor, Ezri Dax (Landau 1998). While many strands of conservative thought are ambivalent or skeptical about state power, Garak speaks as a conservative "loser," an exiled agent of a racist and extractivist settler-colonial state that has itself lost something: its power to dominate Bajor and the Bajorans. For

216 Empire's Queer Inheritances

Garak's queer conservatism, ruthless self-criticism and self-surveillance in allegiance to an imperial state are idealized as the only conceivable route to self-preservation or pleasurable selfhood.

Given his strong allegiance to Cardassia, Garak regards the prospect of permanent life on the station with grim resignation. While in the Obsidian Order, Garak was implanted with a device designed to protect captured spies from torture. The masochistic gadget triggers a pleasure response when the carrier experiences pain, in direct proportion to the degree of pain inflicted. In his early years on the station, Garak permanently activates the device, because "living on this station is torture for me." When Garak's dependence grows too great, Bashir must guide his enigmatic friend kicking and screaming through a detox process (Friedman 1994a).

Garak also searingly mocks Starfleet's liberal universalist promises and model-minoritarian logics. He asks Worf to sponsor his application to Starfleet Academy, espousing facetious hopes of following trailblazers like Worf and Nog to become the first of his kind in the Federation's multicultural military workforce (Beaumont 1997). And when most of DS9's senior staff is accidentally trapped inside one of Bashir's campy James Bond holosuite programs—and could be killed if the program is prematurely shut down—Garak dispenses with the heroic narrative of self-sacrifice for the collective so axiomatic for *Trek*'s Starfleet characters. Attempting to end the program to save his own life, Garak only relents when Bashir wounds him with a twentieth-century holographic pistol (Kolbe 1997).

Rather than make nice with the Federation, Garak seems to be constantly plotting a triumphant return to his homeland and previous standing. Until the Cardassian Empire joins the Dominion in season 5 under the leadership of his longtime nemesis, Gul Dukat, Garak's "former" bosses in the Cardassian military and intelligence community intermittently dangle out opportunities for him to return home in exchange for various shady deeds. On one occasion, he is ordered to kill Cardassian dissidents visiting the station, including Quark's ex-girlfriend—a mission he nearly completes (Wiemer 1994). On another, he is offered the chance to rejoin the Obsidian Order and his father, Tain, on a reckless, genocidal preemptive strike against

22. An uninvited guest, Garak, dropping in on one of Doctor Bashir's James Bond holodeck fantasies and scaring away the doctor's holographic "lady friend," Caprice ("Our Man Bashir," season 4, episode 10, aired November 27, 1995).

the Dominion. Garak jumps at the chance, insisting, "I never betrayed you—at least, not in my heart!" (Brooks 1995a). He does seem to feel pangs of conscience, independent of the state, when Tain orders him to torture Odo, but he nevertheless complies (Brooks 1995a; Livingston 1995a). After the mission fails and Tain disappears, Garak once again drops everything to bust his father out of a Dominion prison (Beaumont 1997). Reunited with an ailing Tain, Garak begs him to acknowledge his paternity before his death, but the best he gets is an enigmatic remark about Garak's childhood.

Finally, as we saw in chapter 1, Garak is central to the events of "In the Pale Moonlight," carrying out the outsourced, illegal, and immoral dirty work of espionage, including murder, that Sisko cannot undertake himself (Lobl 1998). Garak is at once an enabling queer outsider to the Cardassian imperial family who eagerly serves its shady security state *and* an illiberal,

Empire's Queer Inheritances

enabling outsider to the Federation's liberal multicultural empire who abets it by carrying out the same sorts of unspeakable deeds (Joseph 2002; Agamben 2005). We might even read Garak's work for Sisko as a metaphor for the contemporary alliances between military multiculturalisms and neoconservative imperialisms, alliances increasingly embodied in the U.S. Democratic Party (McAlister 2005; Singh 2017). Moore cites the works of the late spy novelist John le Carré, a vocal critic of British and U.S. imperialisms, as an inspiration for creating Garak (Volk-Weiss 2022; le Carré 2010). And Robinson (2019) has spoken thoughtfully about how DS9 pushed the limits of American exceptionalism, an insight consistent with his own lived commitment to anti-imperialism. As an undergraduate student, Robinson was expelled from the University of New Hampshire for demonstrating against mandatory Reserve Officers' Training Corps enrollment in 1962 (Bonderoff 1977).

Political scientist Kate M. Daley (2014) has offered one of the most compelling scholarly assessments of Garak's role in "In the Pale Moonlight." In an imagined dialogue with the character, Daley asks whether Garak's aim is to expose the contradictions of liberal empire and the hypocritical identifications of liberal audiences—whether his purpose is to challenge viewers who disavow him as an evil exception but continue to revere Sisko and the Federation. Garak replies, "My dear, I am here because I have always been here" (231). Daley's work points to the longer history of constitutive violence at the heart of empires, even liberal, multicultural ones (Morefield 2014). But exposing hypocrisy, Daley (2014) suggests, is not the point of Garak's existence. His use of the present perfect tense—"I have always been here"—speaks to longer histories of imperialism, indifferent to the good intentions of today's "enlightened" audiences. Garak is happy to troll Bashir, Worf, and Sisko along the way, but his fundamental motivation remains to restore what he has lost.

None of this is to say that Garak is an entirely unrepentant advocate for Cardassian imperial brutality. During the Occupation, Garak disobeyed orders, helping Bajoran children escape a shuttle destined for the labor camp on Terok Nor (Friedman 1994a; A. Robinson 2000). On several occasions, he is tempted by (often bad-faith) offers to return to his old life but ultimately rejects them. Garak even works with Major Kira in forming a Cardassian Liberation Front opposed to Dominion rule, building on the Cardassian dissident movement and its opposition to the Occupation of Bajor.

But Garak's episodic critiques of Cardassian colonialism and his antipathy to individual foes within the Cardassian state tend to be limited to "excesses" and personal enemies, rather than offering a more thoroughgoing challenge to the Occupation or the state behind it. Not unlike his work as a tailor, Garak seeks to make alterations to the imperial project, hemming it here or there, rather than tearing it up. He justifies many of his most unpredictable, incongruous, and violent actions in terms of a love of nation, frequently offering "for Cardassia" and "I love Cardassia" as a rationale for eliminating old enemies. Garak's "mental gymnastics" remind us that the psyche is a manifestly social space where the reproduction of violent norms is both resisted and desired (Eng 2010, 56; Oliver 2004). But crucially, Garak's example also makes clear that resistance to state violence *itself* is often resisted, that the harshest agencies of the mind—those aligned with the ideals of family, state, and imperial nation—can discipline more empathetic or radical impulses back into alignment (Rose 2007).

At the end of *DS9*, a mournful Garak remains on Cardassia to help with rebuilding efforts. His home planet's elites, frustrated by Bajoran resistance to their colonial designs and anxious about imperial decline, make a deal with the devil—aligning with the Dominion, a racist and extractivist regime even more powerful than their own. This deal, in turn, wreaks genocidal destruction on the Cardassians themselves. "Aren't you going to congratulate me, Doctor?" Garak asks Bashir, tongue ever in cheek (Kroeker 1999). "My exile is now officially over. I've returned home. Or rather, to what's left of it." On some level, even Garak recognizes that the chickens of Cardassian imperialism have come home to roost: "Some may say that we've gotten just what we deserved. After all, we're not entirely innocent, are we? And I'm not just speaking of the Bajoran Occupation. No, our whole history is one of arrogant aggression." But when Bashir reassures him that his people will rebuild, Garak waves off the doctor's "insufferable Federation optimism."

Empire's Queer Inheritances

"Of course [Cardassia] will survive," he quips, "but not as the Cardassia I knew." Garak mourns the loss of Cardassian culture, "our best people, our most gifted minds." He identifies with the Cardassian state so strongly that only when its institutions are in ruins can he begin to imagine otherwise.

Eng (2010) asks, "How might we imagine a psychic landscape beyond Schreber's mental gymnastics, a social terrain beyond" queer reconciliation to conservative idealizations of family and empire (58)? In *A Stitch in Time*, Robinson (2000) continues the story of Garak's homecoming to a devastated Cardassia. Reluctantly, at first, Garak learns more about indigenous Hebitian politics, culture, and religion, and begins to play a role in a democratic, highly localized form of civilian government. *A Stitch in Time* makes few guarantees as to Cardassia's future. But it does imagine a tailoring role for Garak that goes beyond minor adjustments to the garments of imperial brutality—a role that fashions alternative, more egalitarian and peaceful modes of Cardassian social ordering, cut from an altogether different cloth.

If there is hope in Garak's story, perhaps it lies in the prospect that even the most reactionary queers might yet hear through the "confusion of voices" that aligns their subjective interests with the harsh ideals of conservative institutions (Eng 2010, 53). Letting go of idealized institutions can be especially hard for those already expelled from home and homeland, and for many, mere inclusion may be the best that one feels one can hope for. But as Garak's final letters to his beloved Bashir suggest, there is greater promise in following one's discrepant longings far enough to realize that, as Georgis (2013) puts it, "there is always a better story than the better story" (26).

"He's Passed Himself as Normal"

In *DS9*'s first season, Dr. Julian Subatoi Bashir falls hard for Jadzia Dax. Although Bashir complains that Jadzia only sees him as a friend, he is frankly lucky to count her as one (Legato 1993). Second—not first—in his class at Starfleet Medical Academy, the young physician has a chip on his shoulder, and the character did not have many friends—or many fans—in the early years of the show's run. Actor Alexander Siddig interprets the gifted young character's defining flaw as "his zealousness, his enthusiasm for things . . . a romantic vision of what he's capable of" (Memory Alpha n.d.i). Major Kira, true to form, put the matter more pointedly: "Sometimes he just didn't know when to shut up" (Livingston 1997a).[4] According to Behr, fans initially found Bashir "too green, too arrogant, too wet-behind-the-ears, too fumbling" (Memory Alpha n.d.i). If Wesley Crusher (Wil Wheaton) was the "irritating boy-wonder" of TNG, he found something of a successor in Bashir (Kraemer, Cassidy, and Schwartz 2003, 4).

Bashir certainly had his admirers, though. The handsome, single young doctor was, as actor Max Grodénchik puts it, "the hunk of the show," dating a great many women and pursuing even more (Erdmann and Block 2000, 316). If Bashir's stories about his final examinations at Starfleet Medical Academy, which he presents like trophies of war, are unimpressive to his more senior colleagues, they certainly seem to work on some of his romantic conquests (Lynch 1993b). And as we have seen, Garak, in his character-istically oblique way, also takes a liking to Bashir, and regularly joins the doctor for cryptic flirtations over lunch.

Episodes like "Past Tense," "Armageddon Game," "Hippocratic Oath," and "The Quickening" go a long way in demonstrating the admirable dimensions of Bashir's zeal, which he puts to good use in the service of patients, particularly poor and racialized patients (Badiyi 1995; Kolbe 1994a; Auberjonois 1995c; Auberjonois 1996a). Bashir's arc also clarifies that his casual attitude toward dating stems from histories of romantic loss, painful sacrifices made in the service of his career. But it is not until season 5 that audiences get a fuller sense of Bashir's backstory, so well-developed for many of the other characters. In "Doctor Bashir, I Presume?" the prodigious doctor is selected to provide the template for Starfleet's new Long-term Medical Hologram, a complement to the Emergency Medical Hologram popularized on VOY (Livingston 1997a). Pitching the program to Bashir as "a shot at immortality," hologram engineer Dr. Lewis Zimmerman (Robert Picardo) exhaustively interviews Bashir's colleagues but also writes to his parents, whom Bashir had expressly asked not be contacted.

Much to Julian's horror, Amsha and Richard Bashir (Fadwa el Guindi and Brian George) show up on the station. From them, we learn that Julian's

Empire's Queer Inheritances

intellectual and athletic prowess are not "natural" but the result of illegal childhood genetic treatments that they went to great lengths to obtain. "Illegal" is insufficiently strong here. Eugenics is, like money and religion, among the Federation's cardinal taboos (see chapter 3). In TOS's future history, Earth's population is decimated by wars over eugenics in the 1990s, leading to a strict Federation ban on genetic engineering.

Given this prohibition, Julian is thoroughly ashamed of his secret enhancements, which he worries define him, and he is deeply angry at his parents, particularly his father, whom he regards as a mediocre grifter. Bashir's deep insecurities about his genetic engineering may well constrain his efforts to aid fugitive Jem'Hadar in "Hippocratic Oath" (see chapter 3), informing his view of Ketracel-White addiction as genetic rather than social in origin (Auberjonois 1995c; Wynter and McKittrick 2015). But the elder Bashirs refuse their son's censure, justifying their actions as undertaken out of anxiety, guilt, and love. "You know so much that you can stand there and judge us," Richard remarks, "but you're still not smart enough to see that we saved you from a lifetime of remedial education and underachievement!" When Zimmerman discovers the family secret, Richard takes the fall for his son, agreeing to live in a Federation penal colony for two years so that Julian suffers no penalty to his career or commission.

The Bashirs' tale of parental sacrifice restages and critiques shifting U.S. cultural anxieties about race, class, genetic science, and education as they took on new forms in the neoliberal 1990s. Trek creator Gene Roddenberry's ardent antieugenicism in TOS reflected a post–World War II repudiation of biological racism in Western societies that had previously embraced it (McWhorter 2009). But the 1990s saw a resurgence of public fascination with genetic engineering, from Dolly the sheep to the popular film Gattaca (Niccol 1997), from the Human Genome Project to the troubling return of racial eugenics in U.S. policy and cultural discourse (D. Roberts 1997; TallBear 2013). In a certain light, we might say that Roddenberry's dire prediction of 1990s Eugenics Wars in TOS was not so far off (Wynter and McKittrick 2015). Given this changing zeitgeist, DS9 broke Trek's rules in order to uphold them, suggesting that any hope of achieving Roddenberry's utopian antieugenicist future must address the matter head-on, rather than continue to banish it.

We might also read Julian's augmentations as an allegorical allusion to racist and classist fears of the "overachieving" children of immigrant "tiger parents." In this light, Julian's biological "enhancements" stand in for essentialized notions of "culture"—such as strict discipline and private tutoring—through which immigrant parents are imagined to supplement their children's academic performance and "cheat" a putatively meritocratic system (Ochoa 2013). Hearing from Amsha and Richard Bashir complicates this story. Their fears for a son condemned to a life of middling under-achievement aver Saadia's (2016) observation that even if the Federation is "postscarcity," it is nevertheless a brutally competitive society. The Bashirs struggle to make it in London in much the way many poor and working-class Londoners, including many of postcolonial diasporic extraction, do today. Crucially, the resurgence of eugenics in policy discourse, the racist anxieties projected onto immigrant families, the Bashirs' desperation to help their son, all emerge from contexts in which more social understandings of the causes of inequalities—and collective means of transforming them—seem impossibly out of reach. In this way, DS9 links contemporaneous revivals of racial eugenics and educational xenophobia to scarcity fears conditioned by the rise of neoliberalism, suggesting that the Federation's postscarcity and antieugenic futures are worthy, jeopardized, and neces-sarily interdependent horizons.

Although his father's sacrifice seems to repair the breach between them, Julian's relationship with his parents doesn't get much additional elaboration in DS9. But he does seek out an alternative family with other genetically enhanced people—people who, like his father, live in confinement. In "Statistical Probabilities," Bashir is tasked with rehabilitating four genet-ically enhanced adults who have spent the better part of their lives in an institution and are regarded as incapable of assimilating into Federation society (Williams 1997). This motley crew of gifted eccentrics reads like a list of nineteenth-century images of psychosexual pathology cataloged by philosopher Michel Foucault ([1976] 2012): there is the manic and aggressive

Jack (Tim Ransom); the hysterical Lauren (Hilary Shepard-Turner), who is prone to outrageous expressions of lust for almost any man within her sights; the infantile and rotund Patrick (Michael Keenan), who is a kind of big baby; and the waifish, nonverbal Sarina (Faith C. Salie).

As savants, Bashir's patients are hip to why they are being placed in his care—and ambivalent about their new physician. Jack is especially distrustful of Bashir as a genetically enhanced person who is, for the most part, smoothly integrated into society: "I never saw him at the Institute. He wasn't locked away for being too smart. He's passed himself as normal. He's Mister Normal Starfleet Man. Mister Productive Member of Society" (Williams 1997). Bashir tries to be candid with his patients about the arbitrariness of his comparative privilege of having escaped institutionalization. "There but for the grace of God go I," he confides in the station's senior staff. Jack resents his confinement and rejects Bashir's assimilationist logic, refusing to "be a part of a society that put me away for being too smart." But Bashir soon stumbles upon a course of treatment that stimulates his patients' brilliant minds and proves useful to Starfleet—at least at first. Presented by happenstance with a recording of a recent speech by the Cardassian leader Damar, the patients cannily pore over Damar's body language, correctly discerning highly sensitive security information just by looking at him. Bashir asks Sisko if he can provide his patients with more intel, hoping to boost the Federation's position in negotiations with the Dominion. With cautious optimism, Sisko and Starfleet Intelligence agree.

At first, the analysis produced by this would-be think tank seems sure-footed. The group rightly deduces the centrality of a particular planet to Dominion strategy—it is home to a fungus used to make Ketracel-White. Yet after their initial successes, the group begins making more abstract, grandiose, and long-term calculations and projections, finally recommending that the Federation preemptively surrender to the Dominion to avoid a projected 900 billion casualties over several centuries. Taking pleasure in the community of his fellow smarties, Bashir is increasingly convinced of their position, and some of that early arrogance and zeal resurfaces.

Fortunately, Sisko offers a clear-eyed moral refutation of the confidently defeatist statistical projections of Bashir and his patients. "Even if I knew with a hundred percent certainty what was going to happen, I wouldn't ask an entire generation of people to voluntarily give up their freedom," he tells the doctor. "I don't care if the odds are against us. If we're going to lose, then we're going to go down fighting so that when our descendants someday rise up against the Dominion, they'll know what they're made of." Sisko speaks from the perspective of a centuries-long Black freedom struggle that does not preemptively concede to the forces of racial domination and economic exploitation but boldly resists and prefigures alternatives to them. As Brooks explains, "Because I am brown and American and male—it is important for me—and for our brown children everywhere—to be able to think in the long term. . . . My work has always been about making a way for succeeding generations" (Logan [1994] 1995).

Bashir's ragtag brain trust thus offers a prescient satire of the ascendance of the wonky technocrat in U.S. politics. Scientific and professionalized approaches to public policy date to the early twentieth century, and U.S. culture has long had an ambivalent relationship with intellectuals. But in the 1990s, the apparent global triumph of neoliberal capitalism enabled U.S. elites to rhetorically evict the political itself from mainstream discourse—to claim that (racial) capitalism's contradictions could be transcended altogether with "smart" policy. Bill Clinton (2002) famously called this politics, "the true and ultimate third way, going beyond the exclusive claims of old opponents to a future we can all share." As historian Lily Geismer (2014, 2022) demonstrates, the rise of the third way signaled not the end of class conflict but a longer-term shift in the Democratic Party's core constituency, from an increasingly multiracial working class to a whiter cohort of knowledge workers. This more comfortable, educated constituency preferred technical solutions to more transformative, confrontational politics.

The writers of "Statistical Probabilities" say they based the episode in part on Isaac Asimov's *Foundation* series, which follows the efforts of scientist and "psychohistorian" Hari Seldon to allay catastrophic futures that he has calculated and projected with seeming certainty (Erdmann and Block 2000,

Empire's Queer Inheritances

513). Asimov's work has perhaps no greater a devotee than the economist Paul Krugman (2012), who even penned the introduction to a reprinting of *Foundation*, reflecting, "I grew up wanting to be Hari Seldon, using my understanding of the mathematics of human behaviour to save civilisation." Krugman's Keynesianism is not without its merits. But his repeated attacks on Left alternatives to third-way neoliberalism—repeatedly using his bully pulpit to dismiss Medicare for All as "politically unrealistic," for instance—make plain that any "mathematics of human behaviour" is only as sound as the assumptions of the mathematician (Krugman 2016, 2020). Krugman is quick to note that *Foundation* shows the folly as well as the grandeur of Seldon's psychohistorical approach. But his own performative surety about the horizons of the possible in contemporary U.S. political life actively forecloses still-possible geographies of solidarity and care.

By contrast, in "Statistical Probabilities," Sisko recognizes that the predictive quantitative models offered by Bashir's cadre of experts are not purely objective but reflect particular, often contestable presuppositions. "I'm happy to hear your group's advice on how to win this war," he tells Bashir, "but I don't need your advice on how to lose it" (Williams 1997). Where Bashir's technocrats attempt to take political conflict out of the equation, Sisko reminds them that science is always practiced in a (geo)political-economic context, in the service of moral aims. Sisko's words ring true, both in the neoliberal 1990s and in the present, when wonks, consultants, and pollsters urge preemptive capitulation to the interests of capital and the forces of reaction and dismiss urgent (and often popular) grassroots demands for racial and economic justice as "unrealistic." "Statistical Probabilities" does not so much turn against the utopian investments of earlier SF as it cautions against the prematurity and conservatism of technocratic triumphalisms.

By the end of *DS9*, Bashir has grown up and won the heart of Dax—just not the Dax whom he had pursued so ardently. When Jadzia Dax's young life is brutally cut short by Gul Dukat at the end of season 6, the Dax symbiont moves on to a new host, Ezri Tigan (Nicole de Boer). Unprepared to become a Trill host and a few years younger than Julian, Ezri's youthful zeal and insecurity are as glaring as Julian's were at first, but she proves herself as a capable soldier and an insightful counselor and morale officer. Now a widower, Worf is begrudgingly supportive when Ezri Dax and Julian get together—with an emphasis on "begrudgingly." "He is a child," Worf mutters to Ezri as Julian and Miles labor over a diorama, planning their latest holosuite adventure, this time defending the Alamo (Vejar 1999b). "He gets excited playing with toys."

Worf is not wrong about Bashir's predilection for the holosuite. Bashir's sense of self is forged in significant part through what cultural historian Carly A. Kocurek (2015) calls "the technomasculine": "an idealized vision of youth, masculinity, violence, and digital technology" (xvii). The doctor's holo-adventures typically put him in the role of an imperial spy or colonial frontiersman, from James Bond to Davy Crockett. Given the loss of a clear antagonist or foil for Western identity in post–Cold War Hollywood (Sharp 1998), perhaps Bashir's indulgences in colonial machismo and Cold War camp evince what geographer and James Bond scholar Klaus Dodds (2018) calls a conservative, "nostalgic geopolitics" (224). In moments, it can be easy to read Bashir as a postcolonial subject whose mimicry of the white colonizer comprises repetition with too little difference (Bhabha [1994] 2012).

But gaming and adventure stories are themselves domains of social reproduction, and as Kocurek and geographer Richard Phillips (1997) contend, these cultural forms' political ideologies are contingent and contestable. While social reproduction tends toward the reproduction of the status quo, it can also be interrupted, hijacked to more transformative ends (Katz 2001). In the final ten-part episode arc of DS9, Bashir and O'Brien race against the genocidal machinations of the Federation's own intelligence officials. The two search desperately for a cure to a Federation-created biological weapon, a virus deployed against the Dominion's Founders using Odo as a carrier. Although both engineer O'Brien and physician Bashir are presented as professional-class scientific experts, O'Brien is an avatar for the working class, and he must often remind his younger friend that many of the problems they face require political solutions and cannot

Empire's Queer Inheritances

be resolved with "pure" science. In "Tacking into the Wind," Miles tells Julian, "It's time to face facts. You're not going to pull a rabbit out of your medkit" (Vejar 1999c).

Instead, Bashir and O'Brien lure the Machiavellian Federation spy, Section 31 agent Luther Sloan, to DS9 (see chapter 3). In "Extreme Measures," the two friends put their holosuite gaming skills to work against the racism of the state that purports to represent them by hunting for the cure in a virtual representation of Sloan's mind (Posey 1999b). This episode is often noted for its droll, homoerotic dialogue; convinced that they are dying, the two quibble over Miles's failure to leave a note for his wife before embarking on this dangerous mission, and over Keiko's charge that Miles likes Julian more than he likes her (Geraghty 2003). But it also suggests that technical expertise and even technomasculine adventurism can give way to a practice of queer hacking that confronts and undermines a racist state, rather than contributing to its reproduction and enhancement. When Bashir listens to his better angels—Sisko's repudiation of technocratic defeatism, O'Brien's recognition of the limits of technical solutions, or the fugitive Jem'Hadar Goran'Agar from chapter 3, who demands that genetic science serve a more liberatory purpose—perhaps the doctor's immature, technocratic masculinity can be put to good use.

If social reproduction encompasses the capacious range of ways that people make and remake the world, then the hope of "queering" social reproduction is to remake the world with a meaningful difference (Andrucki 2017). In that sense, a great many efforts to politicize social reproduction— from the strike at Quark's to Professor O'Brien's station school to Arandis's insistence that hospitality is valuable work—might be thought of as queer. But as geographers (e.g., Katz 2001) have insisted, social reproduction is an inherently ambivalent category; the daily and generational terms on which people reproduce the world, replenish and rejuvenate our energies, and seek to remake the world differently could go either way, toward liberation or toward exploitation and reaction. And as Puar (2007) advises, queer subjects can be just as guilty as anybody else of reproducing imperial relations of power, a point amply illustrated by Dax's swashbuckling exoticism, Garak's imperial nostalgia, and Bashir's antidemocratic brain trust. But as Eng (2010) might remind us, guilt itself might be part of the problem. On their best days, there remains a surprising, impish, ludic quality to Dax, Garak, and Bashir, one that might yet win out against the harsh idealization of family and nation, speaking to the queerer voices and possibilities in all of us.

Empire's Queer Inheritances

Conclusion

"This Darker Thing"

"Let's Try to Actually End It"

Star Trek often struggles with endings. Three series (TOS, TAS, and ENT) were abruptly canceled and cannot be said to enjoy rousing conclusions at all. TNG's finale was an award-winning triumph—but it also wasn't really an ending, as four TNG films soon followed, with the first released less than six months after the last episode aired. Living, as we are, in an era of remakes and sequels, 2020 even brought a pensive TNG follow-up series (PIC) and a playful animated series (LD) that spoofs TNG with a loving, nostalgic fidelity.

DS9, by contrast, *really* ends. Its ninety-minute finale, "What You Leave Behind," aired the week of June 2, 1999, and that was it. Behr, ever aware of the show's bastard-middle-child status, reflects, "We knew there wasn't going to be a movie, let's not kid ourselves, and so let's end it. Let's try to actually end it. And that's what we did" (Altman and Gross 2016, 542).

Fundamentally, "What You Leave Behind" is a meditation on the question of home, and on how the geographies of home change after the Federation-Klingon-Romulan alliance defeats the Dominion and the Cardassians (Kroeker 1999). A rejuvenated Odo, cured of the Changeling virus, and a glum Garak return to their respective defeated imperial metropoles, pushing for more just and democratic forms of reconstruction back home. The O'Briens, too, return to Earth, where Miles accepts an engineering professorship at Starfleet Academy, Keiko enjoys abundant opportunities for meaningful work, and Molly and Kirayoshi can grow up in comparative safety. Worf is elevated to Federation Ambassador to the Klingon Empire, a prestigious title finally commensurate with the job he has, in many ways, been doing all along. And Rom and Leeta set out to remake the Ferengi

Alliance in the image of a feminist economic democracy. Remaining on the station are the happy new romantic item, Ezri Dax and Bashir, as well as Kira, Nog, Jake, Kasidy, and Quark. The Ferengi entrepreneur is strangely upset to see his longtime rival, Odo, depart. Kira, who is losing both a lover and a friend in Odo, counsels, "Don't take it hard, Quark." "Hard?" Quark protests. "What are you talking about? That man loves me. Couldn't you see? It was written all over his back" (Kroeker 1999). A rare outtake of this scene features a kiss between Odo and Quark.

But it is Captain Sisko's fate that has proven the most controversial. From the outset of DS9, when he is named Emissary of the Prophets, Sisko's destiny is tied to Bajor. But in season 7, we learn that Sisko's mother, the late photographer Sarah Sisko (Deborah Lacey), was possessed by a Bajoran Prophet at the time of his conception—that Benjamin Lafayette Sisko himself is both a human and Bajoran Prophet. In the finale's final hour, Sisko is called to defend Bajor from Gul Dukat and Kai Winn—who now openly worship the demonic Bajoran pah-wraiths—and return to his people in the Celestial Temple.[1]

There are a litany of objections to this premise: that it echoes a long-standing history of fantasies of "going Native," revealing the outsider Sisko to be an indigenous Bajoran insider (think *Avatar*) (Tuck and Yang 2012; J. Cameron 2009; Arvin 2015); that in elevating a Black man to messianic status, it requires his sacrifice to redeem the world (Lamp 2010; Wilderson 2010); that it evades the possibility that a Black human hero could simply be, as Brooks puts it, "completely human, and brown, too" (Shatner 2013). When the finale was in production, Brooks himself worried about the message it would send for Sisko to leave his young adult son, Jake, and pregnant wife, Kasidy Yates-Sisko, without so much as a goodbye (Altman and Gross 2016, 540). To tell such a story, Brooks worried, would have validated pernicious, dehumanizing misrepresentations of Black fatherhood (Kelley 1998). Thanks to Brooks raising such concerns, Sisko appears to Kasidy in a tender vision, intimating that he must go to the Celestial Temple but that with the Prophets' nonlinear experience of time and space, he will return: "Maybe a year, maybe yesterday. But I will be back" (Kroeker 1999).

23. Benjamin Sisko, Emissary to the Bajoran Prophets, visiting his wife, freighter captain Kasidy Yates-Sisko, from the Celestial Temple and promising to return to his family ("What You Leave Behind," season 7, episodes 25–26, aired June 2, 1999).

24. All my own contradictory inheritances—*Star Trek* among them—in a single photograph taken on a family vacation on Christmas Day, 1998 (photo by Dan Seitz, courtesy of Kristie Kroening and Al Nichols).

It may well be my Lutheran upbringing or lifelong *DS9* fandom talking, but for what it's worth, I believe him.

But if we read *DS9* critically, and generously, in the depressive/reparative vein that this book has advocated and modeled, we might notice still other valences to the Sisko/Bajor arc. Sneed (2021) argues that Sisko's Bajoran spiritual ties give voice to a "prophetic Blackness" (78) conveying "a revelation of the end of oppression" (90) in keeping with liberation theologies. Indeed, Sisko's special connection to the Bajoran Prophets, including a revelatory pilgrimage to the desert planet of Tyree (Kroeker 1998b), recalls the significance of many forms of religious life—and not only Christian ones—to Black freedom struggles. Malcolm X's autobiography ([1965] 1992) powerfully describes how his journey to Mecca exposed him to possibilities for interracial cooperation and solidarity through Islam, an experience that opened him up to a universalist revolutionary politics forged from below (Cone 1991; Saldanha 2015). Insofar as Bajor allegorizes a predominantly Muslim place like Palestine, we might understand Sisko's Bajoran connection not as a disavowal of Black humanness but as an embrace of African Islamic genealogies immanent to Black freedom struggles throughout the Americas and throughout the world (e.g., Crawley 2017).

To a degree never before seen in *Star Trek*, Sisko's arc makes "ongoing black struggles to assert and reinvent black humanity as fantastic" (McKittrick 2017, 98) the origin story for humanity itself, the principal reference point for articulations of connections between another world and Earth (carrington 2016; Barnes 1998). As Bajor remains independent of the Federation, Sisko leaves the Federation behind, at least for now, (re)joining the Prophets in the Celestial Temple. For all *DS9*'s contradictions, its allegorical solidarities—between a Black man from New Orleans and the colonized people of Bajor/Palestine, between Bajoran freedom fighters and dissident Founders and anyone fighting the scourge of galactic imperialism, between Irish and Sudanese British scientists and exploited dabo girls and Ferengi waiters, between a Japanese woman and all the station's exploited and exhausted parents, between Black and Brown time travelers and the poor people of San Francisco—come light-years closer than previous *Treks* to "a hitherto unknown and unknowable ecumenically inclusive version of our human freedom" (Wynter and McKittrick 2015, 62).

"Just a Dot in Space"

Given *DS9*'s critical promise, it remains both curious and revealing that some have read its "darkness" and introspection as necessarily indulging a reactionary isolationism. International relations scholar Barry Buzan (2010), for instance, observes that "the forward-looking, upbeat secular vision of *Star Trek* has been replaced by an inward- and backward-looking religious one. This 'America' has lost faith in its own cultural model, has an increasingly depressed, fearful and militarized outlook on the world, and lives in mortal fear of its mirror image . . . Other. Its sense of progress has been replaced by a fear of technology and a dread of endless repetition of a Manichean conflict cycle" (179).

When viewed through the lens of cultural geography, however, *DS9*'s critical, place-based look at U.S. racial capitalism and empire proves to be neither parochial nor regressive—not in the slightest. The radical, fantastic Benjamin Lafayette Sisko shows us both the limits of "diverse" representation in imperial institutions and the centrality of the Black freedom struggles, both material and metaphysical, to progressive movements for racial and economic justice and international cooperation. Major Kira and her Bajoran comrades make clear that religion and anticolonial attachments to place can be capacious as well as reactionary, that one can remain a particularist while one's "heart for the universal" and communities of solidarity grow (Fawaz 2019).

The Dominion, meanwhile, forces us to confront the unseemliest parts of the U.S. empire—its race and class hierarchies and casual human sacrifice of racialized underclasses to do its dirty work (Gilmore 2017). But the Dominion's allegories also point us to maroon Jem'Hadar who refuse their narrative condemnation (Wynter 1992), and to dissident Founders like Odo, who queerly question their imperial inheritances. The Ferengi, far from anti-Semitic or Orientalist caricatures that can be safely written off as irrelevant to contemporary racial capitalism, lampoon the neuroses of neoliberalism and map the folly and the promise of attempts to survive, escape, or transform an "ownership society." The O'Briens' squabbles teach us that no degree of technical "innovation" will exempt us from the necessary work of social reproduction—and that a fairer division of that labor will only come through struggle that is at once socialist, antiracist, and feminist, "naggy" though it might be. The station's queers, finally, remind us that while no one exists outside unjust power relations, we always have the option of not faithfully reproducing the world as it was presented to us—and of enjoying ourselves along the way, if we can stand it.

Rather than a show that is parochially mired in place, DS9 avers the late geographer Doreen Massey's (1994) claim that "*it is people, not places in themselves, which are reactionary or regressive*" (141, original emphasis). At stake in the finale's impulse to return so many of its characters "home" is not a rejection of difference but an embrace of lessons learned in fraught coalitional spaces (Reagon 1983) and a return home to do what feminist scholar Minnie Bruce Pratt (1984) might call "one's own work" (41).

Perhaps the most delicious irony in dismissals of DS9 as "inward looking" is the show's final image, which is, quite literally, outward looking. Colonel Kira is now the commanding officer of DS9, representing an independent Bajor. She joins Jake Sisko, budding young writer and son of the Emissary of the Prophets, looking out the window toward the Celestial Temple. Both come from peoples with long histories of anticolonial struggle, and both care about the Temple, where Benjamin Sisko now lives, as well as what might be on the other side. Kira's and Jake's fates are linked to each other, to this place they call home, *and* to the spaces beyond it. The script elaborates, "The wormhole goes WHOOSH. Then we pull back and back, until DS9 is just a dot in space as we leave them behind" (Kroeker 1999).

What, exactly, is so frightening about the idea that what we currently call the United States, like DS9, could be just another dot in space, connected to and looking out at other dots but relinquishing the need to dominate the surrounding space? And who is to say that global justice movements must strictly adhere to Western secular humanist models, especially given the outsized role that other cosmogonies play in contemporary, Indigenous-led

Conclusion

25. Colonel Kira and Jake Sisko looking outward from the Promenade, while contemplating the Celestial Temple and the spaces beyond it ("What You Leave Behind," season 7, episodes 25–26, aired June 2, 1999).

movements protecting all Earthly life from extractivism (Estes 2019)? Buzan (2010, 179), who extols the virtues of "American leadership," resists the deidealization (M. Klein [1963] 1975) of the U.S. empire—the same empire that Martin Luther King Jr. ([1967] 2015) called "the greatest purveyor of violence in the world today" (204)—that *DS9* can invite. Klein ([1963] 1975) cautions that deidealization can be "very painful work," particularly for those whose harsh idealizations have long repressed meaningful reflection (306). But the alternative is much worse.

U.S. business and policy elites might have everything to fear in a more multipolar world, which is why they are frantically extracting as much value as they can from the empire and the planet on the way down. But the rest of us have much, if not everything, to gain. At issue here is not fundamentalism, isolationism, or reactionary localism but the promise of forms of cosmopolitanism and ethical cohabitation that exceed capture by liberal imperialism—the kind of "particularism with a heart for the universal" modeled by Kira's capacious, anticolonial sensibilities (Butler 2012; Fawaz 2019).

*

As DS9 turns thirty years old, *Star Trek* enjoys a third golden age, with an unprecedented five series currently releasing new episodes, and more on the way. Contemporary installments take on urgent social questions like mass refugee crises and state surveillance, represent queer and trans life intricately and proudly, offer sensitive and funny portrayals of Black mother-daughter dynamics, feature multiple women of color in command positions, and ace Bechdel and DuVernay tests of many kinds. While *A Different "Trek"* defers examination of these exciting works to those who have subjected them to the careful, sustained analysis they deserve (e.g., Mittermeier and Spychala 2020), one notices in these adventures thoughtful continuities with and expansions upon DS9's transformative contributions to *Star Trek* and SF. There is even talk of a Benjamin Sisko statue going up in New Orleans (Pesola 2022).

In other moments, however, one wonders whether DS9's legacy is undergoing erasure. Although rumors of a DS9 return or reboot have been swirling as this book goes to press, comparatively few DS9 characters and actors have been asked to return to the small screen in current *Treks*. The TNG film *Star Trek: Insurrection* (Frakes 2002) even cut a scene featuring Quark (Carrington 2021). Much *Trek* merchandise currently on the market, from Amazon's "Star Trek T-shirt Club" to the pop-up shop at the Skirball Cultural Center's fantastic 2021–22 Exploring New Worlds exhibition in Los Angeles, draws a straight line between "flagship" series, from TOS to TNG to DIS, omitting other installments altogether. For better and for worse, advertisements for a 2020 "Trek the Vote to Victory" Joe Biden presidential campaign fundraiser did not list a single DS9 actor.

As this book has argued, inclusion in merchandising and tepid neoliberal political programs are hardly the most radical "otherwise possibilities" that DS9 and all good SF dare us to imagine (Crawley 2017). But such occlusions should give us pause if they mean that DS9's warnings, prophecies, and proposed alternatives continue to go unheeded. At stake here is less nostalgia for a lost image of the future (Harding and Rosenberg 2005) than a missed opportunity to learn in the present. As a powerful critique of the racial capitalism and imperialism of the 1990s, DS9 presciently addressed many of the crises we continue to face today, from the deep, racialized crisis of economic inequality in U.S. cities to the ongoing siege on the Gaza Strip. The question, then, is not really whether Sisko's or Garak's faces are on new mugs, but whether we understand that their dilemmas and contradictions, from the busted streets of San Francisco to the twisted mental gymnastics of the U.S. war machine, are very much our own. The question is not whether actors who play Bajorans are invited to speak at a fundraiser for a politician who has little to say about Palestinian human rights anyway, but whether we can connect our admiration for Bajor's decolonization struggles to solidarity with Palestinians fighting to remain in their homes, and with Indigenous peoples protecting their sovereign lands from extractivist projects that threaten all life on Earth. As the Bezoses and Musks of the world promise to make "humanity" a "multispecies civilization"—based not on postscarcity Trekonomics but on levels of inequality that would scandalize even the most rapacious Ferengi—it is clear we have more to learn from the only *Star Trek* series that tarries with "stuckness," that remains progressively committed to place. So many *Trek* installments deserve praise for reflecting, to increasingly heterogeneous audiences, who we are. But DS9 issues an ongoing challenge to Americans to reckon with *where* we are.

What, then, is to be done? To be sure, looking to art alone—whether as responsible for our collective political failures or as an antidote to them—is wrongheaded. Even as DS9 is replete with "otherwise possibilities" (Crawley 2017), cultural geographer Emilie Cameron (2012) sagely warns that there remains a real danger of "reifying possibility itself such that the political work required to achieve the hoped-for state is deferred" (582). Even if DS9 offered some crystal clear road map for revolution, as Brooks tells SF writer K. Tempest Braford (Brooks 2013), the question remains whether we "find a way to integrate these things that we believe into our lives." If writer and activist adrienne maree brown (2021) is correct in the claim that all community organizing is a kind of SF, then, the question requires us to turn to SF creators of a different sort.

A Different "Trek" has emphasized the centrality of the Black freedom struggle to Left internationalisms, the creativity of progressive Jewish artists, the urgency of Palestinian human rights and self-determination, and the necessity of collective provisioning for social reproduction. Given these priorities, all royalties from the book's sale will be split between three organizations doing urgently needed work addressing these concerns: the Black Alliance for Peace, Jewish Voice for Peace, and the Los Angeles unhoused aid and advocacy group Koreatown for All. Each of these exemplary "co-operative human efforts" seeks far-reaching transformations that might yet make Earth a place where all of humanity—conceived in a truly ecumenical way—enjoys the material and political conditions needed to thrive (Gilmore 2007, 241; quoted in McKittrick 2011, 960; Wynter and McKittrick 2015).

I also plan to continue teaching Star Trek for as long as it helps invite my students to consider uses for their science and engineering educations that serve the common good, rather than capital and empire. Occasionally, a student, colleague, or alum will come to my office eager to chat about the technological innovations that Star Trek has anticipated or inspired. When this happens, I smile and listen intently. I am not an incurious person, and many technical aspects of Trek genuinely fascinate me as well. But I also cannot help but think of King's words ([1967] 2015) in "Beyond Vietnam": "When machines and computers, profit motives and property rights, are considered more important than people, the giant triplets of racism, extreme materialism, and militarism are incapable of being conquered" (214).

I then gently advise my fellow Trekkers that what matters most is what people have used Star Trek to do, the radical imaginations it has affirmed and inspired: Nichelle Nichols's vision for a truly inclusive human scientific enterprise; King's civil rights, antiwar, and labor activism; the politically conscientious interventions of DS9's on- and off-screen internal counternarrators; Briahna Joy Gray's dauntless advocacy for democratic socialism; Wallace Shawn's and Michelle Forbes's calls for Palestinian self-determination; and the radical dreams of millions of ordinary *Trekkers*, many of them savvy and critical consumers. More than anything, I hope that *A Different "Trek"* lends a little further coherence, validation, legitimacy, and encouragement to such radical uses and creates the occasion for more of them. In its best moments, as Brooks explains with a laugh, *Star Trek*—and I would argue, DS9 most of all—still enlivens us to "the wonder of being alive, the wonder of possibility. That's what Mr. Roddenberry created, et cetera—not alone, but that's what he did" (Shatner 2013).

"And then," Brooks grins, "the *people* took it!"

To that, I can only add, "Walk with the Prophets."

Notes

Introduction

1. This count includes *Star Trek: The Animated Series* (TAS) as the second installment. On what constitutes *Trek* canon and for compelling readings of TAS, see Kotsko (2016).

1. The Radical Sisko

1. Philip Hayes Dean's script for the 1978 play *Paul Robeson* was panned by many Black artists and intellectuals for failing to do justice to Robeson's complexity and political sensibilities. But journalist Donna Britt (1989) reports that even the play's harshest critics, including Paul Robeson Jr., gave credit to Brooks for his interpretation of Robeson Sr., in excess of the script's limitations.

2. In a way, Matsuda's approach reverberates with the late *Trek* and SF writer Theodore Sturgeon's famous method of "asking the next question," a relentless, extrapolative curiosity fundamental to all insight and transformation (Sturgeon [1979] n.d.).

3. It should be noted that Sisko is a bit of a playboy in DS9's mirror-universe arc, in keeping with that universe's function as a foil. Perhaps the definitive analysis of *Star Trek*'s mirror universe comes from American studies scholar Steffen Hantke (2014), who argues that its reversals, although containing occasional critiques of U.S. imperialism, are more campy fun than anything else, and that the mirror framing tends to protect audiences from invitations to sustained reflection and critique. If nothing else, however, DS9's revival of the mirror-universe plotline introduced in TOS deserves credit for its experiments in sexuality for characters including Sisko, Kira, and Ezri.

4. Geographer Mark Alan Rhodes II (2017) notes two historical incidents that informed "Past Tense": the 1970 National Guard shooting of thirteen unarmed students at antiwar demonstrations at Kent State University in Ohio and the 1971 rebellion of prisoners at Attica Correctional Facility in New York. If the geopolitical referent for the Kent State shooting is obvious, the Attica rebellion was a direct response to the killing of intellectual and activist George Jackson ([1970] 1994), a revolutionary Black Marxist whose writings linked domestic racial oppression to global capitalism and imperialism.

5. Scholars of the long history of U.S. red scares have noted how anti-Blackness, anti-Semitism, and anticommunism have often used one another as proxies, depending on

which framing was most politically expedient in a given time and place. Progressive organizers have long worked to overcome anti-Semitic tropes about progressive Jews as disloyal, rootless cosmopolitans and outside agitators in order to forge working-class solidarities across race, religion, and ethnicity. See Kelley ([1990] 2015), Postone (1980), and Jewish Voice for Peace (2017).

6. Writer Ronald D. Moore (1998) has also compared the initial premise for "In the Pale Moonlight" to the classic Hollywood treatment of the Watergate scandal, *All the President's Men* (Pakula 1976). Although a Watergate narrative was discarded, "In the Pale Moonlight" does share that film's feverish, conspiratorial pacing.

7. Targeted military-recruitment efforts, it must be noted, were redoubled in the wake of the 1992 Los Angeles uprising. These efforts were touted by figures like the late General Colin Powell, to whom the Sisko character has also been compared (*Newsweek* 1993), as bringing moral discipline and uplift to "destructive" urban youth of color (Pérez 2015, 34–35).

2. Cardassian Settler Colonialism

1. Coincidentally, the late *Trek* legend Leonard Nimoy starred in a 1971 production of *The Man in the Glass Booth*.

2. Other scholars have read Cardassia as the Soviet Union (Johnson-Smith 2005; Vuori 2017; Nolton 2008) or a right-wing Latin American military junta (Gonzalez 2015) and Bajor as postcolonial Africa (Winn 2003; Lee 2008), but these readings have likewise been suggested rather than developed.

3. The Trail of Tears refers to the forced evacuation of one hundred thousand Cherokee, Muscogee, Seminole, Chickasaw, Choctaw, Ponca, and Ho-Chunk/Winnebago people from their ancestral lands between 1830 and 1850.

4. Kira's abiding morality makes the characterization of her counterpart in DS9's mirror-universe plot arc as a scheming imperialist and a pansexual libertine all the more fascinating.

5. *A Different "Trek"* uses the terms "military sexual servitude" and "forced sexual servitude" rather than "comfort women," the term that frequently appears in interviews with DS9 creators. "Comfort women" translates a euphemism for a system of coerced sex work used by the Japanese empire in the early and mid-twentieth century. Under that system, women were trafficked from throughout Asia, particularly Korea and China, and forced into sexual servitude of Japanese soldiers. The 1990s are touted by many as the moment when the survivors of military sexual servitude achieved public visibility and the possibility of redress. But scholars emphasize that the history is much more complex (e.g., Kang 2020). They also note that efforts to confront distinct but not incomparable contemporary systems of military sexual servitude involving U.S. military bases in South Korea and elsewhere have struggled to garner comparable levels of attention (Moon 2010).

6. Thanks to the students in section 14 of my spring 2021 *Star Trek* and Social Theory class at Harvey Mudd College for this observation!

3. Jem'Hadar Marronage

1. Historians of whiteness (e.g., Jacobsen 2006) emphasize that it confers social mobility but is also highly variable in its inclusion and exclusion criteria and material and cultural benefits. Scholars of political economy (e.g., Harvey 2005) observe that capital is compelled to grow itself across space-time or die, making its commitments to place likewise highly contingent.

2. Auberjonois, too, played an Oliver North character, the unsubtly named Colonel West, in *Star Trek VI* (Meyer 1991). Another insatiably bellicose cold warrior, West is disgruntled at the prospect of Federation-Klingon peace.

3. Before leaving the station, Talak'talan expresses disappointment in the weakness of Bajoran and Federation combatants and a wish to meet a Klingon in the hopes of encountering a worthier adversary. The mutual fascination and antipathy between Jem'Hadar and Klingons resurfaces when Worf, Bashir, Garak, and Martok must later break out of a Jem'Hadar prison (Landau 1997; Beaumont 1997). To distract the guards, Worf participates in a spectacular series of fights with Jem'Hadar soldiers. Both Jem'Hadar and Klingons blur stereotypes about Blackness and Japanese "warrior" traditions, and the Jem'Hadar are in a subservient position within the Dominion. Might this mutual fascination tell us something important about how the Federation sees the Klingons? About U.S. elite anxieties over Black American sympathies with Japan during World War II?

4. As Gallardo's (2013) analysis suggests, the racialized casting choices for Jem'Hadar characters, as well as their fearsome prostheses and ability to "shroud," or become tactically invisible, recall the *Predator* films (e.g., McTiernan 1987), two of which cast the late actor Kevin Peter Hall as the principal antagonist.

5. Wynter's "we" deliberately begins with people historically excluded from Western definitions of the human. See also McKittrick (2021).

6. In *DS9*'s hypothetical eighth season, many Jem'Hadar convert to the Bajoran religion under Kira's tutelage, seeking an exit from a Dominion political theology that has never valued their lives and finding a spiritual affinity with other historically exploited and dominated people (Behr and Zappone 2019).

7. To the best of my knowledge, *DS9*'s production did not involve any formal cooperation with the U.S. Department of Defense, unlike at least one *Trek* film (Secker 2016).

8. Indeed, between the androgynous aesthetic of the Changelings, the polymorphous nature of the Great Link, the Vorta's alienation from and fascination with sexual reproduction, and the all-male character of Jem'Hadar sociality, it might be asked whether the entire Dominion in some sense figures as queer (see Kanzler 2004; Puar 2007).

4. Defetishizing the Ferengi

1. It is worth noting that Japanese American actor and TNG veteran Clyde Kusatsu was also invited to audition for the Quark role (Yu 2020a). Following Day (2016), we might argue that if the Ferengi are the repository for crude stereotypes about petit bourgeois Asians and Jewish merchants, then tropes about grand bourgeois Asians and Jews as refined, rational, austere, mystical, and cosmopolitan have accreted to the Vulcans, particularly in *Star Trek: Enterprise* (ENT) (see Greven 2009; Gellis 2021).
2. Wayne welcomed this term, making "deliberate efforts to use his screen image as an instrument of political persuasion" in favor of U.S. imperialism, particularly in Vietnam (Slotkin 1992, 520). See Wayne himself (1971) and Wills (1997).
3. Leeta is far from the only woman to tell Quark off. Although Dax deflects his advances more patiently, Major Kira gets spectacular revenge on Quark for some astonishingly creepy behavior (Frakes 1994b).
4. Though Sean O'Brien is fictitious, the successful 1902 Pennsylvania anthracite coal strike really happened (Blatz 1994). Women at Warp contributor and SF scholar Sara Wenger (2021) importantly points out that the Quark's strike also recalls Playboy Bunnies' efforts at unionization in the 1960s and 1970s.
5. Dorn's comedic timing excels in the B plot of "Bar Association," itself a crisis of social reproduction in which misanthropic newcomer Worf decides he would rather live on the tiny but empty *Defiant* than deal with neighbors on the station.
6. An excellent recent Left labor review of "Bar Association" sums up Rom's praxis with the ingenious portmanteau "Rommunism," while the delightful Leftist dirtbags of *Soy Trek* joke that "you haven't read Marx until you've read it in the original Ferengi" (Dirnbach and Fir 2022; Strah and Hoey 2022; Meyer 1991).
7. *Trek* has long speculated about possibilities for reconfiguring gender, from the coerced body-swapping between Captain Kirk and rival Dr. Janice Lester in the TOS finale to the transplantation of Trill symbionts between hosts to the Founders' ability to manifest as various persons, to name a few. As we saw in chapter 2's discussion of "Second Skin" (Landau 1994c), the use of twenty-fourth-century surgery to imagine changes of "species" as an allegory for race is even more common.
8. Ironically, this rule would seem to read as coercively homoerotic in the Ferengi context, given the prohibition on "females" in the workplace. Thanks to Kyle Turner for this observation.

5. O'Brien Family Values

1. Although I am sensitive to the infantilization that can come from referring to people by their first names, because this chapter is focused on the O'Brien family, it uses first names for clarity, equanimity, and brevity.

2. SF writer S. D. Perry's *Unity* (2003), an intriguing original *Star Trek* novel, makes Keiko head of agricultural recovery on the Cardassian homeworld after the Dominion War, and puts Miles in the awkward position of trailing spouse. carrington (2016) has argued for the radical potential of *Trek* novelizations by Black writers to critique and participate in the franchise's imagined futures, and Perry's work points to linked feminist possibilities for the practice.

6. Empire's Queer Inheritances

1. Ezri Tigan, the Dax symbiont's host after Jadzia, had not been preselected as a Trill host and was joined with the symbiont in an emergency surgery following Jadzia's death. But Ezri, too, comes from privilege, as her family owns a competitive mining consortium, although she admirably rejects their cutthroat values (Lobl 1999).

2. Ezri Dax clearly retains some of this "roguish" sensibility, remarking to her host's uptight family that as a newly joined Trill, "there're days when I wake up and I don't even know if I'm a man or a woman until I pull back the covers" (Lobl 1999). Ezri Tigan's mirror-universe counterpart also appears to be queer.

3. The Bible's New Revised Standard Version includes neither the patriarchal gender construction nor the reference to childish "things": "When I became an adult, I put an end to childish ways."

4. Amusingly, Siddig and Visitor were in a relationship at the time this episode was filmed.

Conclusion

1. In "Shadows and Symbols," Captain Sisko gains insight into his Prophetic ties, returning to the vision from "Far Beyond the Stars" (see chapter 1) that he is Benny Russell, the struggling Black science fiction writer living in New York in 1953 (Kroeker 1998b; Brooks 1998). Both episodes turn our gaze back toward the contingent, contested act of Black storytelling in the twentieth century, throwing DS9 into diegetic crisis (Lancioni 2010; Harris 2006). Behr even pitched a series finale that would have returned to the Benny Russell subplot once more, breaking the fourth wall and revealing the contingency of *Star Trek* itself in its entirety, but this prospect was abandoned (Altman and Gross 2016, 426).

References

Adare, Sierra S. 2005. *Indian Stereotypes in TV Science Fiction: First Nations' Voices Speak Out*. Austin: University of Texas Press.

Agamben, Giorgio. 2005. *State of Exception*. Translated by Kevin Attell. Chicago: University of Chicago Press.

Aldrich, Robert, dir. 1967. *The Dirty Dozen*. Beverly Hills CA: Metro-Goldwyn-Mayer.

Alexander, David. 1994. *"Star Trek" Creator: The Authorized Biography of Gene Roddenberry*. New York: ROC.

Alexander, Lisa Doris. 2016. "Far Beyond the Stars: The Framing of Blackness in *Star Trek: Deep Space Nine*." *Journal of Popular Film and Television* 44 (3): 150–58.

——. 2022. "Star Trek: Deep Space Nine." In *The Routledge Handbook of "Star Trek,"* edited by Leimar Garcia-Siino, Sabrina Mittermeier, and Stefan Rabitsch, 37–47. New York: Routledge.

Alford, C. Fred. 1989. *Melanie Klein and Critical Social Theory: An Account of Politics, Art and Reason Based on Her Psychoanalytic Theory*. New Haven CT: Yale University Press.

Allan, Kathryn, ed. 2013. *Disability in Science Fiction: Representations of Technology as Cure*. New York: Palgrave MacMillan.

Allen, Corey, dir. 1993. *Star Trek: Deep Space Nine*. Season 2, episode 2, "The Circle." Aired October 3, 1993, in syndication.

——, dir. 1994a. *Star Trek: The Next Generation*. Season 7, episode 20, "Journey's End." Aired March 28, 1994, in syndication.

——, dir. 1994b. *Star Trek: Deep Space Nine*. Season 2, episode 21, "The Maquis, Part II." Aired May 1, 1994, in syndication.

Altman, Mark A., and Edward Gross. 2016. *The Fifty-Year Mission: The Complete, Uncensored, Unauthorized Oral History of "Star Trek"; The Next 25 Years, from "The Next Generation" to J. J. Abrams*. New York: St. Martin's Press.

American Humanist Association. 1991. "Gene Roddenberry, 1991 Humanist Arts Award." Recorded from the 50th Anniversary Humanist Conference, May 1991. SoundCloud audio, 8:11. https://soundcloud.com/americanhumanist/gene-roddenberry.

Anderson, Ben. 2020. "Cultural Geography III: The Concept of 'Culture.'" *Progress in Human Geography* 44 (3): 608–17.

Andrucki, Max. 2017. "Queering Social Reproduction, or, How Queers Save the City." *Society and Space*, October 31, 2017. https://www.societyandspace.org/articles/queering-social-reproduction-or-how-queers-save-the-city.

Anijar, Karen. 2000. *Teaching toward the 24th Century: "Star Trek" as Social Curriculum.* New York: Falmer Press.

———. 2001. "Klingon Pedagogy and Education for the 24th Century: Interview of Karen Anijar by Peter McLaren." *International Journal of Educational Reform* 10 (2): 176–92.

———. 2008. "A Very *Trek* Christmas: Goodbye." In *The Influence of "Star Trek" on Television, Film and Culture*, edited by Lincoln Geraghty, 218–33. Jefferson NC: McFarland.

Arendt, Hannah. (1963) 1994. *Eichmann in Jerusalem: A Report on the Banality of Evil.* New York: Penguin Books.

Arruzza, Cinzia, Tithi Bhattacharya, and Nancy Fraser. 2019. *Feminism for the 99%: A Manifesto.* London: Verso.

Arvin, Maile. 2015. "Acting like a White Person Acting like a Native: Ghostly Performances of Global Indigeneity." *Critical Ethnic Studies* 1 (1): 103–16.

Asad, Talal. 2007. *On Suicide Bombing.* New York: Columbia University Press.

Auberjonois, René, dir. 1995a. *Star Trek: Deep Space Nine.* Season 3, episode 16, "Prophet Motive." Aired February 20, 1995, in syndication.

———, dir. 1995b. *Star Trek: Deep Space Nine.* Season 3, episode 23, "Family Business." Aired May 15, 1995, in syndication.

———, dir. 1995c. *Star Trek: Deep Space Nine.* Season 4, episode 4, "Hippocratic Oath." Aired October 16, 1995, in syndication.

———, dir. 1996a. *Star Trek: Deep Space Nine.* Season 4, episode 24, "The Quickening." Aired May 20, 1996, in syndication.

———, dir. 1996b. *Star Trek: Deep Space Nine.* Season 5, episode 7, "Let He Who Is without Sin . . ." Aired November 11, 1996, in syndication.

———, dir. 1997. *Star Trek: Deep Space Nine.* Season 5, episode 20, "Ferengi Love Songs." Aired April 21, 1997, in syndication.

———, dir. 1998. *Star Trek: Deep Space Nine.* Season 6, episode 11, "Waltz." Aired January 3, 1998, in syndication.

———. 2011. "Catching Up with *DS9*'s René Auberjonois, Part 1." StarTrek.com, June 7, 2011. https://www.startrek.com/article/catching-up-with-ds9undefineds-rene-auberjonois-part-1.

Bacon-Smith, Camille. 1991. *Enterprising Women: Television Fandom and the Creation of Popular Myth.* Philadelphia: University of Pennsylvania Press.

Badiyi, Reza, dir. 1994. *Star Trek: Deep Space Nine.* Season 3, episode 7, "Civil Defense." Aired November 7, 1994, in syndication.

——, dir. 1995. *Star Trek: Deep Space Nine*. Season 3, episode 11, "Past Tense, Part I." Aired January 8, 1995, in syndication.

——, dir. 1996. *Star Trek: Deep Space Nine*. Season 4, episode 12, "Paradise Lost." Aired January 8, 1996, in syndication.

Baetens, Jan. 2005. "Novelization, a Contaminated Genre?" *Critical Inquiry* 32 (1): 43–60.

Bahng, Aimee. 2018. *Migrant Futures: Decolonizing Speculation in Financial Times*. Durham NC: Duke University Press.

Barba, Michael. 2010. "Somewhere Out Beyond the Stars: Orientalism and *Star Trek Deep Space Nine*." In *One World Periphery Reads the Other: Knowing the "Oriental" in the Americas and the Iberian Peninsula*, edited by Ignacio López-Calvo, 380–92. Newcastle Upon Tyne, UK: Cambridge Scholars Publishing.

Barnes, Steven. 1998. *Far Beyond the Stars*. Star Trek: Deep Space Nine. New York: Pocket Books.

Barrett, Michèle, and Duncan Barrett. 2017. *"Star Trek": The Human Frontier*. 2nd ed. New York: Routledge.

Barthes, Roland. 1977. *Image-Music-Text*. Translated by Stephen Heath. New York: Fontana.

Bastién, Angelica Jade. 2018a. "The Best Episodes of *Star Trek: Deep Space Nine*, Ranked." Vulture, January 4, 2018. https://www.vulture.com/2018/01/star-trek-deep-space-nine -best-episodes-ranked.html.

——. 2018b. "*Deep Space Nine* Is TV's Most Revolutionary Depiction of Black Fatherhood." Vulture, January 19, 2018. https://www.vulture.com/2018/01/deep-space-nine -revolutionary-depiction-of-black-fatherhood.html.

Beaumont, Gabrielle, dir. 1991. *Star Trek: The Next Generation*. Season 5, episode 5, "Disaster." Aired October 21, 1991, in syndication.

——, dir. 1997. *Star Trek: Deep Space Nine*. Season 5, episode 14, "In Purgatory's Shadow." Aired February 10, 1997, in syndication.

Behr, Ira Steven. 1995. *The Ferengi Rules of Acquisition*. Star Trek: Deep Space Nine. New York: Pocket Books.

Behr, Ira Steven, and David Zappone, dirs. 2019. *What We Left Behind: Looking Back at "Star Trek: Deep Space Nine."* Los Angeles: 455 Films. DVD.

Bell, Steve, and Eli Valley. 2013. "Drawing Truth to Power: A Conversation about Cartoons between Steve Bell and Eli Valley." *Jewish Quarterly* 60 (1): 28–33.

Benanav, Aaron. 2020. *Automation and the Future of Work*. New York: Verso.

Benjamin, Walter. (1935) 2007. "The Work of Art in the Age of Mechanical Reproduction." In *Illuminations*, translated by Harry Zohn, 217–52. New York: Schocken.

——. (1942) 2007. "Theses on the Philosophy of History." In *Illuminations*, translated by Harry Zohn, 253–64. New York: Schocken.

Berger, John. 2001. *Selected Essays*. Edited by Geoff Dyer. New York: Pantheon Books.

Berlant, Lauren. 1994. "'68, or Something." *Critical Inquiry* 21 (1): 124–55.

———. 1997. *The Queen of America Goes to Washington City: Essays on Sex and Citizenship*. Durham NC: Duke University Press.

———. 2008. *The Female Complaint: The Unfinished Business of Sentimentality in American Culture*. Durham NC: Duke University Press.

———. 2011. *Cruel Optimism*. Durham NC: Duke University Press.

———. 2013. "On Citizenship and Optimism: Lauren Berlant, Interviewed by David Seitz." *Society and Space*, March 23, 2013. https://www.societyandspace.org/articles/on-citizenship-and-optimism.

Berman, Rick, and Michael Piller. 1992. *Star Trek DS9: Bible*. Rev. ed. June 12, 1992. http://leethomson.myzen.co.uk/Star_Trek/3_Deep_Space_Nine/Star_Trek_-_Deep_Space_Nine_Bible.pdf.

Bernardi, Daniel Leonard. 1998. *"Star Trek" and History: Race-ing toward a White Future*. New Brunswick NJ: Rutgers University Press.

Bhabha, Homi. (1994) 2012. *The Location of Culture*. New York: Routledge.

BigYangpa. 2018. "Why Is Keiko So Resistant to Non-Japanese Food?" *Daystrom Institute* (forum), Reddit, August 15, 2018. https://www.reddit.com/r/DaystromInstitute/comments/97iow4/why_is_keiko_so_resistant_to_nonjapanese_food/.

Bishop, Bart. 2019. "*Star Trek* into Colonialism." In *The Kelvin Timeline of "Star Trek": Essays on J. J. Abrams' Final Frontier*, edited by Matthew Wilhelm Kapell and Ace G. Pilkington, 58–71. Jefferson NC: McFarland.

Black, A. J. 2020. *"Star Trek," History, and Us: Reflection of the Present and Past throughout the Franchise*. Jefferson NC: McFarland.

Black Girl Nerds. 2019. "National Stage Politics with Briahna Joy Gray." *Black Girl Nerds* (podcast), November 13, 2019. https://blackgirlnerds.com/podcast-national-stage-politics-with-briahna-joy-gray/.

Blair, Karin. 1997. "*Star Trek* Old and New: From the Alien Embodied to the Alien Imagined." In *Yankee Go Home (& Take Me with U): Americanization and Popular Culture*, edited by George McKay, 78–88. London: Bloomsbury.

Blatz, Perry K. 1994. *Democratic Miners: Work and Labor Relations in the Anthracite Coal Industry, 1875–1925*. Albany: State University of New York Press.

Bledsoe, Adam. 2017. "Marronage as a Past and Present Geography in the Americas." *Southeastern Geographer* 57 (1): 30–50.

Boehm, Kimberly Phillips. 2012. *War! What Is It Good For? Black Freedom Struggles and the U.S. Military from World War II to Iraq*. Chapel Hill: University of North Carolina Press.

Bole, Cliff, dir. 1993. *Star Trek: Deep Space Nine*. Season 2, episode 5, "Cardassians." Aired October 24, 1993, in syndication.

———, dir. 1994. *Star Trek: Deep Space Nine*. Season 2, episode 24, "The Collaborator." Aired May 22, 1994, in syndication.

————, dir. 1995a. *Star Trek: Deep Space Nine.* Season 3, episode 22, "Explorers." Aired May 8, 1995, in syndication.

————, dir. 1995b. *Star Trek: Deep Space Nine.* Season 3, episode 25, "Facets." Aired June 12, 1995, in syndication.

Bonderoff, Jason. 1977. "Andrew Robinson: After My Dad Died I Started Stealing." *Daytime TV*, September 1977. https://ryanshopesoapopera.proboards.com/thread/595/repost-andrew-robinson-after-died.

Booker, M. Keith. 2018. *"Star Trek": A Cultural History.* Lanham MD: Rowman and Littlefield.

Boulle, Pierre. (1952) 2007. *The Bridge over the River Kwai.* Translated by Xan Fielding. New York: Presidio Press.

Britt, Donna. 1989. "Rekindling the Spirit of Paul Robeson." *Washington Post*, April 6, 1989. https://www.washingtonpost.com/archive/lifestyle/1989/04/06/rekindling-the-spirit-of-paul-robeson/9ad425b1-3fb4-436a-92b0-62551b7ff8f3/.

Britt, Ryan. 2022. *Phasers on Stun! How the Making (and Remaking) of "Star Trek" Changed the World.* New York: Plume.

Britzman, Deborah P. 1998. *Lost Subjects, Contested Objects: Toward a Psychoanalytic Inquiry of Learning.* Albany: State University of New York Press.

Brooks, Avery, dir. 1994a. *Star Trek: Deep Space Nine.* Season 2, episode 25, "Tribunal." Aired June 5, 1994, in syndication.

————, dir. 1994b. *Star Trek: Deep Space Nine.* Season 3, episode 6, "The Abandoned." Aired October 31, 1994, in syndication.

————, dir. 1994c. *Star Trek: Deep Space Nine.* Season 3, episode 10, "Fascination." Aired November 28, 1994, in syndication.

————, dir. 1995a. *Star Trek: Deep Space Nine.* Season 4, episode 20, "Improbable Cause." Aired April 24, 1995, in syndication.

————, dir. 1995b. *Star Trek: Deep Space Nine.* Season 4, episode 6, "Rejoined." Aired October 30, 1995, in syndication.

————, dir. 1996. *Star Trek: Deep Space Nine.* Season 4, episode 25, "Body Parts." Aired June 10, 1996, in syndication.

————, dir. 1997. *Star Trek: Deep Space Nine.* Season 5, episode 19, "Ties of Blood and Water." Aired April 14, 1997, in syndication.

————, dir. 1998. *Star Trek: Deep Space Nine.* Season 6, episode 13, "Far Beyond the Stars." Aired February 11, 1998, in syndication.

————, dir. 1999. *Star Trek: Deep Space Nine.* Season 7, episode 24, "The Dogs of War." Aired May 26, 1999, in syndication.

————. 2002. "Avery Brooks." In *Black Men in Their Own Words*, edited by Patricia Mignon Hinds, 80–81. New York: Crown Publishers.

————. 2008. "A Conversation with Avery Brooks: Meet the Artists Gala 2008." Filmed February 2, 2008, at the Indianapolis–Marion County Central Public Library. *Between the Lines* video, 45:32. Digitized by the Indianapolis–Marion County Public Library, May 2016. http://www.digitalindy.org/cdm/ref/collection/aah/id/2667.

———. 2013. "Far Beyond Deep Space Nine: A Conversation with Avery Brooks." Interview by K. Tempest Bradford. Daily Dragon Online, September 1, 2013. https://www.dragoncon.org/dailydragon/interviews/far-beyond-deep-space-nine-a-conversation-with-avery-brooks/.

brown, adrienne maree. 2021. "adrienne maree brown on Why 'All Organizing Is Science Fiction.'" Vulture, September 10, 2021. https://www.vulture.com/article/adrienne-maree-brown-grievers.html.

Brown, Wendy. 1995. *States of Injury: Power and Freedom in Late Modernity*. Princeton NJ: Princeton University Press.

———. 2006. "Learning to Love Again: An Interview with Wendy Brown by Christina Colegate, John Dalton, Timothy Rayner, and Cate Hill." *Contretemps* 6 (1): 25–42.

Brunk, Samuel. 2008. *The Posthumous Career of Emiliano Zapata: Myth, Memory, and Mexico's Twentieth Century*. Austin: University of Texas Press.

Burden-Stelly, Charisse. 2020. "Modern U.S. Racial Capitalism." *Monthly Review* 72 (3): 8–20.

Burton, LeVar, dir. 1996a. *Star Trek: Deep Space Nine*. Season 4, episode 16, "Bar Association." Aired February 19, 1996, in syndication.

———, dir. 1996b. *Star Trek: Deep Space Nine*. Season 4, episode 23, "To the Death." Aired May 13, 1996, in syndication.

Burton, Orisanmi. 2016. "Attica Is: Revolutionary Consciousness, Counterinsurgency and the Deferred Abolition of New York State Prisons." PhD thesis, Department of Anthropology, University of North Carolina at Chapel Hill. https://doi.org/10.17615/241k-x147.

Bush, George H. W. 1991. "Remarks to the American Legislative Exchange Council," March 1, 1991. In *Public Papers of the Presidents of the United States*, bk. 1, 195–97. Washington DC: U.S. Government Publishing Office. https://www.govinfo.gov/content/pkg/PPP-1991-book1/html/PPP-1991-book1-doc-pg195-2.htm.

Butler, Judith. 1994. "Against Proper Objects: Introduction." *differences: A Journal of Feminist Cultural Studies* 6 (2–3): 1–26.

———. 2004. *Undoing Gender*. New York: Routledge.

———. 2012. *Parting Ways: Jewishness and the Critique of Zionism*. New York: Columbia University Press.

Buzan, Barry. 2010. "American in Space: The International Relations of *Star Trek* and *Battlestar Galactica*." *Millennium* 39 (1): 175–80.

Cameron, Emilie. 2012. "New Geographies of Story and Storytelling." *Progress in Human Geography* 36 (5): 573–92.

Cameron, James, dir. 2009. *Avatar*. Los Angeles: 20th Century Fox.

Camp, Jordan T. 2016. *Incarcerating the Crisis: Freedom Struggles and the Rise of the Neoliberal State*. Berkeley: University of California Press.

Campbell, Joel R., and Gigi Gokcek. 2019. *The Final Frontier: International Relations and Politics through "Star Trek" and "Star Wars."* Lanham MD: Lexington Books.

Canavan, Gerry. 2014. "Far Beyond the Star Pit: Samuel R. Delany." In *Black and Brown Planets: The Politics of Race in Science Fiction*, edited by Isiah Lavender III, 48–64. Jackson: University of Mississippi Press.

———. 2016. "We Have Never Been *Star Trek*." *Sight and Sound*, September 8, 2016. https://www2.bfi.org.uk/news-opinion/sight-sound-magazine/features/star-trek-50 -we-have-never-been-star-trek.

carrington, andré m. 2016. *Speculative Blackness: The Future of Race in Science Fiction*. Minneapolis: University of Minnesota Press.

Carrington, Rachel. 2021. "Two DS9 Cast Members Were Cut from Insurrection." Redshirts Always Die, July 28, 2021. https://redshirtsalwaysdie.com/2021/07/28/two-ds9 -cast-members-were-cut-from-insurrection/.

Carson, David, dir. 1991. *Star Trek: The Next Generation*. Season 5, episode 1, "Redemption, Part II." Aired September 23, 1991, in syndication.

———, dir. 1993a. *Star Trek: Deep Space Nine*. Season 1, episodes 1–2, "Emissary." Aired January 3, 1993, in syndication.

———, dir. 1993b. *Star Trek: Deep Space Nine*. Season 1, episode 8, "Dax." Aired February 13, 1993, in syndication.

Casavant, Michelle Marie. 2003. "To Boldly Go Where No Other Has Gone Before: The Construction of Race and Gender in *Star Trek*." PhD diss., Department of American Studies, University of Kansas.

Césaire, Aimé. (1955) 2000. *Discourse on Colonialism*. Translated by Joan Pinkham. New York: Monthly Review Press.

Chalmers, Chip, dir. 1991. *Star Trek: The Next Generation*. Season 4, episode 12, "The Wounded." Aired January 28, 1991, in syndication.

———, dir. 1997. *Star Trek: Deep Space Nine*. Season 6, episode 10, "The Magnificent Ferengi." Aired December 17, 1997, in syndication.

Chang, Edward Taehan. 1994. "Myths and Realities of Korean–Black American Relations." In *Black-Korean Encounter: Toward Understanding and Alliance*, edited by Eui-Young Yu, 83–89. Los Angeles: Institute for Asian American and Pacific Asian Studies.

Chen, Mel Y. 2012. *Animacies: Biopolitics, Racial Mattering, and Queer Affect*. Durham NC: Duke University Press.

Chin, Frank, Jefferey Paul Chan, Lawson Fusao Inada, and Shawn Wong. (1974) 2019. *Aiiieeeee! An Anthology of Asian American Writers*. 3rd ed. Seattle: University of Washington Press.

Chow, Rey. 1995. *Primitive Passions: Visuality, Sexuality, Ethnography, and Contemporary Chinese Cinema*. New York: Columbia University Press.

Cimini, Kate. 2019. "Black People Disproportionately Homeless in California." CalMatters, October 5, 2019. https://calmatters.org/california-divide/2019/10/black-people-disproportionately-homeless-in-california/.

Clinton, Bill. 2002. "Labour Conference: Full Text of Bill Clinton's Speech (Part Two)." *Guardian*, October 3, 2002. https://www.theguardian.com/politics/2002/oct/03/labourconference.labour2.

Colla, Richard A., dir. 1987. *Star Trek: The Next Generation*. Season 1, episode 5, "The Last Outpost." Aired October 19, 1987, in syndication.

Combahee River Collective. 1983. "The Combahee River Collective Statement." In *Home Girls: A Black Feminist Anthology*, edited by Barbara Smith, 264–74. New Brunswick NJ: Rutgers University Press.

Cone, James H. 1991. *Martin and Malcolm and America: A Dream or a Nightmare*. New York: Orb Books.

Conway, James L., dir. 1988. *Star Trek: The Next Generation*. Season 1, episode 26, "The Neutral Zone." Aired May 16, 1988, in syndication.

————, dir. 1993a. *Star Trek: Deep Space Nine*. Season 1, episode 19, "Duet." Aired June 13, 1993, in syndication.

————, dir. 1993b. *Star Trek: Deep Space Nine*. Season 2, episode 8, "Necessary Evil." Aired November 14, 1993, in syndication.

————, dir. 1995. *Star Trek: Deep Space Nine*. Season 4, episodes 1–2, "The Way of the Warrior." Aired October 2, 1995, in syndication.

————, dir. 1996. *Star Trek: Deep Space Nine*. Season 4, episode 22, "For the Cause." Aired May 6, 1996, in syndication.

Coodin, Sara. 2017. *Is Shylock Jewish? Citing Scripture and the Moral Agency of Shakespeare's Jews*. Edinburgh: Edinburgh University Press.

Cooper, Marc. 1994. *Roll Over, Che Guevara: Travels of a Radical Reporter*. New York: Verso.

Cooper, Melinda. 2017. *Family Value: Between Neoliberalism and the New Social Conservatism*. New York: Zone Books.

Cotter, Padraig. 2019. "None but the Brave: Frank Sinatra's Directorial Debut Was an Anti-War Epic." Screen Rant, October 6, 2019. https://screenrant.com/none-but-brave-movie-frank-sinatra-antiwar-epic/.

Couch, Aaron, and Graeme McMillan. 2016. "'Star Trek: Deep Space Nine'—The 20 Greatest Episodes." *Hollywood Reporter*, September 22, 2016. https://www.hollywoodreporter.com/lists/star-trek-deep-space-nine-930878.

Coulthard, Glen Sean. 2014. *Red Skin, White Masks: Rejecting the Colonial Politics of Recognition*. Minneapolis: University of Minnesota Press.

Cowan, Douglas E. 2010. *Sacred Space: The Quest for Transcendence in Science Fiction Film and Television*. Waco TX: Baylor University Press.

Cowen, Deborah. 2008. *Military Workfare: The Soldier and Social Citizenship in Canada*. Toronto: University of Toronto Press.

Cowen, Deborah, and Neil Smith. 2009. "After Geopolitics? From the Geopolitical Social to Geoeconomics." *Antipode* 41 (1): 22–48.

Crawley, Ashon T. 2017. *Blackpentecostal Breath: The Aesthetics of Possibility*. New York: Fordham University Press.

Cronin, Brian. 2013. "Did Martin Luther King Jr. Keep Nichelle Nichols from Leaving *Star Trek* after the First Season of the Show?" Entertainment Urban Legends Revealed, April 17, 2013. http://legendsrevealed.com/entertainment/2013/04/17/did-martin-luther -king-keep-nichols-leaving-star-trek/.

Csicsery-Ronay, Istvan, Jr. 2003. "Science Fiction and Empire." *Science Fiction Studies* 30 (2): 231–45.

Dale, Laura. 2020. "Jadzia Dax, *Deep Space Nine*, and an Early Sci-fi Trans Allegory Handled with Respect." Syfy Wire, March 9, 2020. https://www.syfy.com/syfy-wire /jadzia-dax-deep-space-nine-and-an-early-sci-fi-trans-allegory-handled-with-respect.

Daley, Kate M. 2014. "Revolting Comfort: Meeting the Shadow's Gaze." *Critical Studies on Security* 2 (2): 228–31.

Darren, James. 1999. "I'll Be Seeing You." Track 16 on *This One's from the Heart*. Beverly Hills CA: Concord Jazz.

Daunt, Tina, and Tina Nguyen. 1994. "Homeless Camp Weighed in L.A. Industrial Area." *Los Angeles Times*, October 14, 1994. https://www.latimes.com/archives/la-xpm-1994 -10-14-mn-50276-story.html.

Davidson, Fiona. 2017. "Owning the Future: Manifest Destiny and the Vision of American Hegemony in *Star Trek*." *Geographical Bulletin* 58 (1): 8–19.

Davis, Angela Y. 2003. *Are Prisons Obsolete?* New York: Seven Stories Press.

——. 2008. "A Vocabulary for Feminist Praxis: On War and Radical Critique." In *Feminism and War: Confronting U.S. Imperialism*, edited by Robin L. Riley, Chandra Talpade Mohanty, and Minnie Bruce Pratt, 19–26. New York: Zed Books.

——. 2015. *Freedom Is a Constant Struggle: Ferguson, Palestine, and the Foundations of a Movement*. Chicago: Haymarket.

Davis, Heather, and Zoe Todd. 2017. "On the Importance of a Date, or Decolonizing the Anthropocene." *ACME* 16 (4): 761–80.

Day, Iyko. 2016. *Alien Capital: Asian Racialization and the Logic of Settler Colonial Capitalism*. Durham NC: Duke University Press.

DeCandido, Keith R. A. 2011. "*Star Trek: The Next Generation* Rewatch: 'The Last Outpost.'" Tor, May 19, 2011. https://www.tor.com/2011/05/19/star-trek-the-next-generation -rewatch-qthe-last-outpostq/.

Decker, Kevin S. 2016. "'The Human Adventure Is Just Beginning': *Star Trek*'s Secular Society." In *The Ultimate "Star Trek" and Philosophy: The Search for Socrates*, edited by Kevin S. Decker and Jason T. Eberl, 326–39. West Sussex, UK: Wiley Blackwell.

De Gaia, Susan. 2003. "Unity and Diversity: *Star Trek*'s Vision of Transcendence." PhD diss., Department of Religion, University of Southern California.

Delany, Samuel R. 1998. "Racism and Science Fiction." *New York Review of Science Fiction* 120 (August). https://www.nyrsf.com/racism-and-science-fiction-.html.

Deloria, Philip J. 1998. *Playing Indian*. New Haven CT: Yale University Press.

Deloria, Vine, Jr. 2003. *God Is Red: A Native View of Religion*. 30th anniversary ed. Golden CO: Fulcrum.

Democracy Now! 2020. "Moms 4 Housing: Meet the Oakland Mothers Facing Eviction after Two Months Occupying Vacant House." January 14, 2020. https://www.democracynow .org/2020/1/14/oakland_california_moms_4_housing.

Dirnbach, Eric, and Ksenia Fir. 2022. "TV Review: Workers of Deep Space Unite!" Labor Notes, March 24, 2022. https://labornotes.org/blogs/2022/03/tv-review-workers-deep -space-unite.

Dittmer, Jason. 2019. "Preface to the First Edition." In *Popular Culture, Geopolitics, and Identity*, by Jason Dittmer and Daniel Bos, vii–xii. 2nd ed. Lanham MD: Rowman and Littlefield.

Dixon, Darius. 2012. "Turner: Obama 'Going John Wayne.'" *Politico*, May 1, 2012. https:// www.politico.com/story/2012/05/turner-obama-going-john-wayne-075785.

Dodds, Klaus. 2018. "The Resilient Agent: James Bond, 'Nostalgic Geopolitics,' and *Skyfall* (2012)." In *James Bond Uncovered*, edited by Jeremy Strong, 243–64. London: Palgrave.

Dorn, Michael, dir. 1997. *Star Trek: Deep Space Nine*. Season 5, episode 25, "In the Cards." Aired June 9, 1997, in syndication.

———, dir. 1999. *Star Trek: Deep Space Nine*. Season 7, episode 21, "When It Rains . . ." Aired May 5, 1999, in syndication.

Douglas, Andrew J., and Jared A. Loggins. 2021. *Prophet of Discontent: Martin Luther King Jr. and the Critique of Racial Capitalism*. Athens: University of Georgia Press.

Dove-Viebahn, Aviva. 2007. "Embodying Hybridity, (En)gendering Community: Captain Janeway and the Enactment of a Feminist Heterotopia on *Star Trek: Voyager*." *Women's Studies* 36 (8): 597–618.

Dozier, Deshonay. 2019. "Contested Development: Homeless Property, Police Reform, and Resistance in Skid Row, LA." *International Journal of Urban and Regional Research* 43 (1): 179–94.

Du Bois, W. E. B. 1903. *The Souls of Black Folk*. Chicago: A. C. McClurg and Co.

———. (1935) 2021. *Black Reconstruction in America*. New York: Library of America.

Dudziak, Mary L. (2000) 2011. *Cold War Civil Rights: Race and the Image of American Democracy*. Princeton NJ: Princeton University Press.

Duggan, Lisa. 2003. *The Twilight of Equality? Neoliberalism, Cultural Politics, and the Attack on Democracy.* Boston: Beacon.

Dunbar-Ortiz, Roxanne. 2015. *An Indigenous People's History of the United States.* New York: Penguin Random House.

Dyson, Stephen Benedict. 2015. *Otherworldly Politics: The International Relations of "Star Trek," "Game of Thrones," and "Battlestar Galactica."* Baltimore: Johns Hopkins University Press.

Edwards, Kirsten T. 2013. "Christianity as Anti-Colonial Resistance? Womanist Theology, Black Liberation Theology, and the Black Church as Sites for Pedagogical Decolonization." *Souls* 15 (1–2): 146–62.

Ehrenreich, Barbara. (1989) 2020. *Fear of Falling: The Inner Life of the Middle Class.* New York: Twelve Books.

Eng, David L. 2001. *Racial Castration: Managing Masculinity in Asian America.* Durham NC: Duke University Press.

———. 2010. *The Feeling of Kinship: Queer Liberalism and the Racialization of Intimacy.* Durham NC: Duke University Press.

Eng, David L., Jack Halberstam, and José-Esteban Muñoz. 2005. "What's Queer about Queer Studies Now?" *Social Text* 23 (3–4): 1–17.

Engelhardt, Tom. 2007. *The End of Victory Culture: Cold War America and the Disillusioning of a Generation.* Amherst: University of Massachusetts Press.

Enloe, Cynthia. 2014. *Bananas, Beaches and Bases: Making Feminist Sense of International Politics.* 2nd ed. Berkeley: University of California Press.

Erakat, Noura. 2019. *Justice for Some: Law and the Question of Palestine.* Stanford CA: Stanford University Press.

Erdmann, Terry J., and Paula Block. 2000. *"Star Trek: Deep Space Nine" Companion.* New York: Pocket Books.

Erevelles, Nirmala. 2011. *Disability and Difference in Global Contexts: Enabling a Transformative Body Politic.* New York: Palgrave Macmillan.

Espiritu, Augusto. 2014. "Inter-imperial Relations, the Pacific, and Asian American History." *Pacific Historical Review* 83 (2): 238–54.

Estes, Nick. 2019. *Our History Is the Future: Standing Rock versus the Dakota Access Pipeline, and the Long Tradition of Indigenous Resistance.* New York: Verso.

Ewing, Jeff. 2016. "Federation Trekonomics: Marx, the Federation, and the Shift from Necessity to Freedom." In *The Ultimate "Star Trek" and Philosophy: The Search for Socrates,* edited by Kevin S. Decker and Jason T. Eberl, 115–26. Sussex, UK: Wiley Blackwell.

Fanon, Frantz. (1952) 2008. *Black Skin, White Masks.* Translated by Richard Philcox. New York: Grove.

———. (1961) 2004. *The Wretched of the Earth.* Translated by Richard Philcox. New York: Grove.

Fawaz, Ramzi. 2016. "How to Make a Queer Scene, or Notes toward a Practice of Affective Curation." *Feminist Studies* 42 (3): 757–68.

———. 2019. "'An Open Mesh of Possibilities': The Necessity of Eve Sedgwick in Dark Times." In *Reading Sedgwick*, edited by Lauren Berlant, 6–33. Durham NC: Duke University Press.

Featherstone, David. 2012. *Solidarity: Hidden Histories and Geographies of Internationalism.* New York: Zed Books.

Fennell, Jack. 2017. "Infinite Diversity in Infinite Combinations: The Representation of Transgender Identities in *Star Trek*." In *To Boldly Go: Essays on Gender and Identity in the "Star Trek" Universe,* edited by Nadine Farghaly and Simon Bacon, 72–89. Jefferson NC: McFarland.

Ferguson, Kathy E. 2002. "The Species Which Is Not One: Identity Practices in *Star Trek: Deep Space Nine*." *Strategies* 15 (2): 181–95.

Ford, John, dir. 1939. *Stagecoach.* Beverly Hills CA: United Artists.

———, dir. 1956. *The Searchers.* Burbank CA: Warner Brothers.

———, dir. 1962. *The Man Who Shot Liberty Valance.* Hollywood: Paramount.

Foucault, Michel. (1976) 2012. *The History of Sexuality.* Vol. 1, *An Introduction.* Translated by Robert Hurley. New York: Vintage.

Frakes, Jonathan, dir. 1994a. *Star Trek: Deep Space Nine.* Season 3, episode 2, "The Search, Part II." Aired October 3, 1994, in syndication.

———, dir. 1994b. *Star Trek: Deep Space Nine.* Season 3, episode 8, "Meridian." Aired November 14, 1994, in syndication.

———, dir. 1995. *Star Trek: Deep Space Nine.* Season 3, episode 12, "Past Tense, Part II." Aired January 15, 1995, in syndication.

———, dir. 1996. *Star Trek: First Contact.* Hollywood: Paramount.

———, dir. 2002. *Star Trek: Insurrection.* Hollywood: Paramount.

Frank, Thomas. 2016. "Bill Clinton's Odious Presidency: Thomas Frank on the Real History of the '90s." *Salon,* March 14, 2016. https://www.salon.com/2016/03/14/bill_clintons _odious_presidency_thomas_frank_on_the_real_history_of_the_90s/.

Franklin, H. Bruce. 1994. "*Star Trek* in the Vietnam Era." *Film and History* 24 (1–2): 36–46.

Freud, Sigmund. (1905) 2002. *The Joke and Its Relation to the Unconscious.* Translated by Joyce Crick. New York: Penguin.

———. (1911) 1922. *Beyond the Pleasure Principle.* Translated by C. J. M. Hubback. London: The International Psycho-Analytical Press.

———. (1911) 2002. *The Schreber Case.* Translated by Andrew Webber. New York: Penguin.

Friedman, Kim, dir. 1994a. *Star Trek: Deep Space Nine.* Season 2, episode 22, "The Wire." Aired May 8, 1994, in syndication.

———, dir. 1994b. *Star Trek: Deep Space Nine.* Season 2, episode 26, "The Jem'Hadar." Aired June 12, 1994, in syndication.

———, dir. 1994c. *Star Trek: Deep Space Nine*. Season 3, episode 1, "The Search, Part I." Aired September 26, 1994, in syndication.

———, dir. 1997. *Star Trek: Deep Space Nine*. Season 5, episode 23, "Blaze of Glory." Aired May 12, 1997, in syndication.

Friesner, Esther. 1994. *Warchild*. Star Trek: Deep Space Nine. New York: Pocket Books.

Frymer, Paul. 2017. *Building an American Empire: The Era of Territorial and Political Expansion*. Princeton NJ: Princeton University Press.

Gallardo, Ximena C. 2013. "Aliens, Cyborgs and Other Invisible Men: Hollywood's Solutions to the Black 'Problem' in SF Cinema." *Science Fiction Film and Television* 6 (2): 219–51.

Geismer, Lily. 2014. *Don't Blame Us: Suburban Liberals and the Transformation of the Democratic Party*. Princeton NJ: Princeton University Press.

———. 2022. *Left Behind: The Democrats' Failed Attempt to Solve Inequality*. New York: PublicAffairs.

Gellis, Eliza. 2021. "Spock's Jewish Hybridity." *Interdisciplinary Literary Studies* 23 (3): 407–33.

Georgis, Dina S. 2006. "Cultures of Expulsion: Memory, Longing, and the Queer Space of Diaspora." *New Dawn* 1 (1): 4–27.

———. 2013. *The Better Story: Queer Affects from the Middle East*. Albany: State University of New York Press.

Geraghty, Lincoln. 2003. "Homosocial Desire on the Final Frontier: Kinship, the American Romance, and *Deep Space Nine*'s 'Erotic Triangles.'" *Journal of Popular Culture* 36 (3): 441–65.

Gerrold, David. (1984) 2016. *The World of "Star Trek."* Rev. 50th anniversary ed. Norwalk CT: Comicmix.

Gilmore, Ruth Wilson. 1998. "Globalisation and U.S. Prison Growth: From Military Keynesianism to Post-Keynesian Militarism." *Race and Class* 40 (2–3): 171–88.

———. 2002. "Fatal Couplings of Power and Difference: Notes on Racism and Geography." *Professional Geographer* 54 (1): 15–24.

———. 2007. *Golden Gulag: Prisons, Surplus, Crisis, and Opposition in Globalizing California*. Berkeley: University of California Press.

———. 2011. "What Is to Be Done?" *American Quarterly* 63 (2): 245–65.

———. 2017. "Abolition Geography and the Problem of Innocence." In *Futures of Black Radicalism*, edited by Gaye Theresa Johnson and Alex Lubin, 225–40. New York: Verso.

Gilmour, David. 1994. *Curzon: Imperial Statesman*. New York: Farrar, Straus, and Giroux.

Goldberg, Jeffrey. 2020. "Why Obama Fears for Our Democracy." *Atlantic*, November 16, 2020. https://www.theatlantic.com/ideas/archive/2020/11/why-obama-fears-for -our-democracy/617087/.

Goldberg, Jonah. 1999. "The Subtext of *Star Trek*; Excuses and New Stuff; Full Disclosure." *National Review*, September 15, 1999. https://www.nationalreview.com/1999/09/subtext -star-trek-excuses-new-stuff-full-disclosure-jonah-goldberg/.

———. 2001. "As *Voyager* Boldly Goes . . ." *National Review*, June 2, 2001. https://www
.nationalreview.com/2001/06/voyager-boldly-goes-jonah-goldberg/.

Columbia, David. 1995. "Black and White World: Race, Ideology, and Utopia in *Triton* and *Star Trek*." *Cultural Critique* 32:75–95.

Gonzalez, George A. 2015. *The Politics of "Star Trek": Justice, War, and the Future*. New York: Palgrave.

———. 2017. *The Absolute and "Star Trek."* London: Palgrave.

———. 2018. *"Star Trek" and the Politics of Globalism*. London: Palgrave.

Gooding-Williams, Robert, ed. 1993. *Reading Rodney King, Reading Urban Uprising*. New York: Routledge.

Gordon, Avery F. 2008. *Ghostly Matters: Haunting and the Sociological Imagination*. Minneapolis: University of Minnesota Press.

Goudie, A. S. 1980. "George Nathaniel Curzon—Superior Geographer." *Geographical Journal* 146 (2): 203–9.

Goulding, Jay. 1985. *Empire, Aliens, and Conquest: A Critique of American Ideology in "Star Trek" and Other Science Fiction*. San Francisco: Sisyphus Press.

Greene, Robert, II. 2017. "Revisiting *Star Trek*'s Most Political Episode." *Atlantic*, October 8, 2017. https://www.theatlantic.com/entertainment/archive/2017/10/star-trek-deep-space-nine-past-tense/542280/.

Greer, Brenna Wynn. 2019. *Represented: The Black Imagemakers Who Reimagined African American Citizenship*. Philadelphia: University of Pennsylvania Press.

Gregory, Derek. 2004. *The Colonial Present: Afghanistan, Palestine, Iraq*. Malden MA: Blackwell Publishing.

Greven, David. 2009. *Gender and Sexuality in "Star Trek": Allegories of Desire in the Television Series and Films*. Jefferson NC: McFarland.

Gross, Edward, and Mark A. Altman. 1996. *Captain's Logs Supplemental: The Unauthorized Guide to the New "Trek" Voyages*. New York: Little, Brown, and Company.

Guynes, Sean, and Gerry Canavan. 2022. "Novels." In *The Routledge Handbook of "Star Trek,"* edited by Leimar Garcia-Siino, Sabrina Mittermeier, and Stefan Rabitsch, 176–84. New York: Routledge.

Gymnich, Marion. 2005. "Exploring Inner Spaces: Authoritative Narratives and Subjective Worlds in *Star Trek: Deep Space Nine, Voyager,* and *Enterprise*." In *Narrative Strategies in Television Series*, edited by Gaby Allrath and Marion Gymnich, 62–79. London: Palgrave Macmillan.

Halberstam, Jack. 2011. *The Queer Art of Failure*. Durham NC: Duke University Press.

Hale, Jordan. 2017. "Records Management in the 24th Century." *Microformed* (blog), February 8, 2017. http://microformed.net/records-management-in-the-24th-century/.

Hall, Stuart. 1981. "The Whites of Their Eyes: Racist Ideologies and the Media." In *Silver Linings, Some Strategies for the Eighties: Contributions to the Communist University of*

London, edited by George Bridges and Rosalind Brunt, 28–52. London: Lawrence and Wishart.

———. 1997. "The Local and the Global: Globalization and Ethnicity." In *Dangerous Liaisons: Gender, Nation, and Postcolonial Perspectives*, edited by Anne McClintock, Aamir Mufti, and Ella Shohat, 173–87. Minneapolis: University of Minnesota Press.

Haney López, Ian F. 2010. "Post-racial Racism: Racial Stratification and Mass Incarceration in the Age of Obama." *California Law Review* 98 (3): 1023–74.

Hantke, Steffen. 2014. "*Star Trek*'s Mirror Universe Episodes and U.S. Military Culture through the Eyes of the Other." *Science Fiction Studies* 41 (3): 562–78.

Harding, Susan, and Daniel Rosenberg. 2005. *Histories of the Future*. Durham NC: Duke University Press.

Harlin, Renny, dir. 1990. *Die Hard 2*. Los Angeles: 20th Century Fox.

Harris, Geraldine. 2006. *Beyond Representation: Television Drama and the Aesthetics of Identity*. Manchester, UK: Manchester University Press.

Harrison, Taylor, Sarah Projansky, Kent A. Ono, and Elyce Rae Helford, eds. 1996. *Enterprise Zones: Critical Positions on "Star Trek."* Boulder CO: Westview Press.

Hartman, Saidiya V. 1997. *Scenes of Subjection: Terror, Slavery, and Self-Making in Nineteenth-Century America*. Oxford: Oxford University Press.

———. 2019. *Wayward Lives, Beautiful Experiments: Intimate Histories of Riotous Black Girls, Troublesome Women, and Queer Radicals*. New York: W. W. Norton and Co.

Harvey, David. 1993. "From Space to Place and Back Again: Reflections on the Condition of Postmodernity." In *Mapping the Futures: Local Cultures, Global Change*, edited by Jon Bird, Barry Curtis, Tim Putnam, George Robertson, and Lisa Tickner, 2–29. New York: Routledge.

———. 2000. *Spaces of Hope*. Berkeley: University of California Press.

———. 2005. *A Brief History of Neoliberalism*. Oxford: Oxford University Press.

Hashimoto, Tul, and Caitlin Henry. 2017. "Unionizing for the Necessity of Social Reproduction." *Society and Space*, November 7, 2017. https://www.societyandspace.org/articles/unionizing-for-the-necessity-of-social-reproduction.

Hassler, Donald M., and Clyde Wilcox, eds. 1997. *Political Science Fiction*. Columbia: University of South Carolina Press.

Hassler-Forest, Dan. 2016. "*Star Trek*, Global Capitalism, and Immaterial Labour." *Science Fiction Film and Television* 9 (3): 371–91.

Hayden, Dolores. 1980. "What Would a Non-sexist City Be Like? Speculations on Housing, Urban Design, and Human Work." *Signs* 5 (3): S170–S187.

Heath, K. M., and A. S. Carlisle. 2020. *The Voyages of "Star Trek": A Mirror of American Society through Time*. Lanham MD: Rowman and Littlefield.

Heller, Joseph. 1961. *Catch-22*. New York: Simon and Schuster.

Henderson, April K. 2011. "Fleeting Substantiality: The Samoan Giant in U.S. Popular Discourse." *Contemporary Pacific* 23 (2): 269–302.

Henwood, Doug. 2015. "Workers: No Longer Needed?" *Left Business Observer News from Doug Henwood* (blog), July 17, 2015. https://lbo-news.com/2015/07/17/workers -no-longer-needed/.

Hickel, Jason. 2020. "Outgrowing Growth: Why Quality of Life, Not GDP, Should Be Our Measure of Success." *Correspondent*, March 19, 2020. https://thecorrespondent .com/357/outgrowing-growth-why-quality-of-life-not-gdp-should-be-our-measure -of-success/413218170519-b4d036a5.

Hirschman, Albert O. 1991. *The Rhetoric of Reaction: Perversity, Futility, Jeopardy*. Cambridge MA: Harvard University Press.

Hodge, Jarrah. 2013. "DS9 6.23 'Profit and Lace.'" *Trekkie Feminist* (forum), Tumblr, August 2, 2013. https://trekkiefeminist.tumblr.com/post/57157375770/ds9-623-profit-and-lace.

———. 2014. "How Does Your Favorite *Star Trek* Series Fare on the Bechdel Test?" Mary Sue, September 1, 2014. https://www.themarysue.com/star-trek-bechdel-test/.

Hodgins, Paul. 2008. "A Career Made from Scratch." *Orange County (CA) Register*, February 1, 2008. https://www.ocregister.com/2008/02/01/a-career-made-from-scratch/.

hooks, bell. 2018. *All about Love: New Visions*. New York: HarperCollins.

Horne, Abigail. 2012. "The Color of Manhood: Reconsidering Pompey in John Ford's *The Man Who Shot Liberty Valance*." *Black Camera* 4 (1): 5–27.

Horne, Gerald. 1995. *Fire This Time: The Watts Uprising and the 1960s*. Charlottesville: University of Virginia Press.

———. 2016. *Paul Robeson: The Artist as Revolutionary*. London: Pluto Press.

———. 2018. *The Apocalypse of Settler Colonialism: The Roots of Slavery, White Supremacy, and Capitalism in Seventeenth-Century North America and the Caribbean*. New York: Monthly Review Press.

Horti, Samuel. 2020. "'Serious Mistake': Biden Ally Larry Summers." *Business Insider*, December 26, 2020. https://www.businessinsider.com/2000-stimulus-checks-a-serious -mistake-biden-ally-larry-summers-2020-12.

Howe, Andrew. 2017. "Deep Space Gender: Miles O'Brien, Julian Bashir, and Masculinity." In *To Boldly Go: Essays on Gender and Identity in the "Star Trek" Universe*, edited by Nadine Farghaly and Simon Bacon, 90–105. Jefferson NC: McFarland.

Huntington, Samuel P. 1993. "The Clash of Civilizations?" *Foreign Affairs*, June 1, 1993. https://www.foreignaffairs.com/articles/united-states/1993-06-01/clash-civilizations.

Immerwahr, Daniel. (2019) 2020. *How to Hide an Empire: A Short History of the Greater United States*. London: Vintage.

Inayatullah, Naeem. 2003. "Bumpy Space: Imperialism and Resistance in *Star Trek: The Next Generation*." In *To Seek Out New Worlds: Science Fiction and World Politics*, edited by Jutta Weldes, 53–75. New York: Palgrave Macmillan.

Inwood, Joshua, and James Tyner. 2011. "Geography's Pro-peace Agenda: An Unfinished Project." *ACME* 10 (3): 442–57.

Iscove, Robert, dir. 1989. *Star Trek: The Next Generation*. Season 2, episode 14, "The Icarus Factor." Aired April 24, 1989, in syndication.

Iton, Richard. 2008. *In Search of the Black Fantastic: Politics and Popular Culture in the Post–Civil Rights Era*. Oxford: Oxford University Press.

JackityJackson. 2019. "Dax Manipulated Sisko in 'In the Pale Moonlight.'" *Daystrom Institute* (forum), Reddit, January 14, 2019, https://www.reddit.com/r/DaystromInstitute /comments/eoxvoe/dax_manipulated_sisko_in_in_the_pale_moonlight/.

Jackson, George. (1970) 1994. *Soledad Brother: The Prison Letters of George Jackson*. Chicago: Lawrence Hill Books.

Jackson, Patrick Thaddeus, and Daniel H. Nexon. 2003. "Representation Is Futile? American Anti-collectivism and the Borg." In *To Seek Out New Worlds: Science Fiction and World Politics*, edited by Jutta Weldes, 143–67. New York: Palgrave Macmillan.

Jacobsen, Matthew Frye. 2001. *Barbarian Virtues: The United States Encounters Foreign Peoples at Home and Abroad, 1876–1917*. New York: Macmillan.

——. 2006. *Roots Too: White Ethnic Revival in Post–Civil Rights America*. Cambridge MA: Harvard University Press.

James, Kendra. 2020. "O Captain, My Captain: On the Importance of Ben Sisko." StarTrek .com, June 7, 2020. https://www.startrek.com/news/ben-sisko-what-we-left-behind -deep-space-nine-finale. Originally published in 2012 on Racialicious.

Jenkins, Henry. 1992. *Textual Poachers: Television Fans and Participatory Culture*. New York: Routledge.

Jenkins, Henry, and John Tulloch. 1995. *Science Fiction Audiences: Watching "Star Trek" and "Doctor Who."* New York: Routledge.

Jerusalem Post. 2018. "Netanyahu to Likud Party: The Occupation of the Palestinians Is Nonsense." November 6, 2018. https://www.jpost.com/israel-news/netanyahu-to-likud -party-the-occupation-of-the-palestinians-is-nonsense-571162.

Jewish Voice for Peace. 2017. *On Anti-Semitism: Solidarity and the Struggle for Justice*. Chicago: Haymarket.

Johnson-Smith, Jan. 2005. *American Science Fiction TV: "Star Trek," "Stargate" and Beyond*. Middletown CT: Wesleyan University Press.

Jones, Mark, and Lance Parkin. 2003. *Beyond the Final Frontier: An Unauthorized Review of the "Trek" Universe on Television and Film*. London: Contender.

Joseph, Miranda. 2002. *Against the Romance of Community*. Minneapolis: University of Minnesota Press.

Junger, Gil, dir. 1997. *Ellen*. Season 4, episodes 22 and 23, "The Puppy Episode." Aired April 30, 1997, on ABC.

Kanar, Hanley E. 2000. "No Ramps in Space: The Inability to Envision Accessibility in *Star Trek: Deep Space Nine*." In *Fantasy Girls: Gender in the New Universe of Science*

Fiction and Fantasy Television, edited by Elyce Rae Helford, 245–64. Lanham MD: Rowman and Littlefield.

Kang, Laura Hyun Yi. 2020. *Traffic in Asian Women*. Durham NC: Duke University Press.

Kanzler, Katja. 2004. *"Infinite Diversity in Infinite Combinations": The Multicultural Evolution of "Star Trek."* Heidelberg: Winter Verlag.

Kapell, Matthew Wilhelm. 2000. "Speakers for the Dead: *Star Trek*, the Holocaust, and the Representation of Atrocity." *Extrapolation* 41 (2): 101–14.

Karera, Axelle. 2019. "Blackness and the Pitfalls of Anthropocene Ethics." *Critical Philosophy of Race* 7 (1): 32–56.

Karuka, Manu. 2019. *Empire's Tracks: Indigenous Nations, Chinese Workers, and the Transcontinental Railroad*. Berkeley: University of California Press.

Kathke, Torsten. 2020. "A *Star Trek* about Being *Star Trek*: History, Liberalism, and *Discovery*'s Cold War Roots." In *Fighting for the Future: Essays on "Star Trek: Discovery,"* edited by Sabrina Mittermeier and Mareike Spychala, 41–60. Liverpool, UK: Liverpool University Press.

Katz, Cindi. 2001. "Vagabond Capitalism and the Necessity of Social Reproduction." *Antipode* 33 (4): 709–28.

Keeling, Kara. 2019. *Queer Times, Black Futures*. New York: New York University Press.

Kelley, Robin D. G. (1990) 2015. *Hammer and Hoe: Alabama Communists during the Great Depression*. 25th anniversary ed. Chapel Hill: University of North Carolina Press.

———. 1996. *Race Rebels: Culture, Politics, and the Black Working Class*. New York: Free Press.

———. 1998. *Yo' Mama's Disfunktional! Fighting the Culture Wars in Urban America*. Boston: Beacon.

———. 2002. *Freedom Dreams: The Black Radical Imagination*. Boston: Beacon Press.

Khalidi, Rashid. 2020. *The Hundred Years' War on Palestine: A History of Settler Colonialism and Resistance, 1917–2017*. New York: Picador.

Kilgore, De Witt Douglas. 2014. "'The Best Is Yet to Come'; or, Saving the Future: *Star Trek: Deep Space Nine* as Reform Astrofuturism." In *Black and Brown Planets: The Politics of Race in Science Fiction*, edited by Isiah Lavender III, 31–47. Jackson: University Press of Mississippi.

Kim, Ju Yon. 2015. *The Racial Mundane: Asian American Performance and the Embodied Everyday*. New York: New York University Press.

King, Martin Luther, Jr. 1967. "The Casualties of the War in Vietnam." Transcript of a speech presented in Los Angeles, February 25, 1967. Investigating U.S. History. https://investigatinghistory.ashp.cuny.edu/module11D.php.

———. (1967) 2015. "Beyond Vietnam: A Time to Break the Silence." In *The Radical King*, edited by Cornel West, 201–20. Boston: Beacon.

Klein, Melanie. (1946) 1975. "Notes on Some Schizoid Mechanisms." In *Envy and Gratitude and Other Works, 1946–1963*, 1–24. New York: Free Press.

———. (1963) 1975. "On the Sense of Loneliness." In *Envy and Gratitude and Other Works, 1946–1963*, 300–313. New York: Free Press.

Klein, Naomi. 2019. "Only a Green New Deal Can Douse the Fires of Eco-fascism." Intercept, September 16, 2019. https://theintercept.com/2019/09/16/climate-change -immigration-mass-shootings/.

———. 2020. "Screen New Deal: Under Cover of Mass Death, Andrew Cuomo Calls in the Billionaires to Build a High-Tech Dystopia." Intercept, May 8, 2020. https://theintercept .com/2020/05/08/andrew-cuomo-eric-schmidt-coronavirus-tech-shock-doctrine/.

Kocurek, Carly A. 2015. *Coin-Operated Americans: Rebooting Boyhood at the Video Game Arcade*. Minneapolis: University of Minnesota Press.

Kolbe, Winrich, dir. 1992. *Star Trek: The Next Generation*. Season 5, episode 20, "Cost of Living." Aired April 20, 1992, in syndication.

———, dir. 1993a. *Star Trek: Deep Space Nine*. Season 2, episode 1, "The Homecoming." Aired September 26, 1993, in syndication.

———, dir. 1993b. *Star Trek: Deep Space Nine*. Season 2, episode 3, "The Siege." Aired October 10, 1993, in syndication.

———, dir. 1994a. *Star Trek: Deep Space Nine*. Season 2, episode 13, "Armageddon Game." Aired January 30, 1994, in syndication.

———, dir. 1994b. *Star Trek: Deep Space Nine*. Season 2, episode 19, "Blood Oath." Aired March 27, 1994, in syndication.

———, dir. 1997. *Star Trek: Deep Space Nine*. Season 4, episode 10, "Our Man Bashir." Aired November 27, 1995, in syndication.

———, dir. 1998. *Star Trek: Deep Space Nine*. Season 7, episode 8, "The Siege of AR-558." Aired November 18, 1998, in syndication.

Kotsko, Adam. 2015. "What Is *Star Trek*'s Vision of Politics?" *An Und Für Sich* (blog), March 16, 2015. https://itself.blog/2015/03/16/what-is-star-treks-vision-of-politics/.

———. 2016. "The Inertia of Tradition in *Star Trek*: Case Studies in Neglected Corners of the 'Canon.'" *Science Fiction Film and Television* 9 (3): 347–70.

———. 2018. *Neoliberalism's Demons: On the Political Theology of Late Capital*. Stanford CA: Stanford University Press.

Kraemer, Ross S., William Cassidy, and Susan L. Schwartz. 2003. *The Religions of "Star Trek."* Boulder CO: Westview Press.

Kramer, Stanley, dir. 1960. *Inherit the Wind*. Hollywood: United Artists.

Kreitzer, Larry. 1996. "The Cultural Veneer of *Star Trek*." *Journal of Popular Culture* 30 (2): 1–28.

Kristeva, Julia. 1980. *Desire in Language: A Semiotic Approach to Literature and Art*. Edited by Leon S. Roudiez. Translated by Thomas Gora, Alice Jardine, and Leon S. Roudiez. New York: Columbia University Press.

———. 1988. *Strangers to Ourselves*. Translated by Leon S. Roudiez. New York: Columbia University Press.

Kroeker, Allan, dir. 1996. *Star Trek: Deep Space Nine.* Season 5, episode 5, "The Assignment." Aired October 28, 1996, in syndication.

———, dir. 1997. *Star Trek: Deep Space Nine.* Season 5, episode 26, "Call to Arms." Aired June 16, 1997, in syndication.

———, dir. 1998a. *Star Trek: Deep Space Nine.* Season 6, episode 24, "Time's Orphan." Aired May 20, 1998, in syndication.

———, dir. 1998b. *Star Trek: Deep Space Nine.* Season 7, episode 2, "Shadows and Symbols." Aired October 7, 1998, in syndication.

———, dir. 1999. *Star Trek: Deep Space Nine.* Season 7, episodes 25–26, "What You Leave Behind." Aired June 2, 1999, in syndication.

Krugman, Paul. 2012. "Paul Krugman: Asimov's Foundation Novels Grounded My Economics." *Guardian*, December 4, 2012. https://www.theguardian.com/books/2012/dec/04/paul-krugman-asimov-economics.

———. 2016. "Weakened at Bernie's." *New York Times* (blog), January 19, 2016. https://krugman.blogs.nytimes.com/2016/01/19/weakened-at-bernies/.

———. 2020. "Overall, Americans took 9/11 pretty calmly." Twitter, September 11, 2020. https://mobile.twitter.com/paulkrugman/status/1304385740063805440?prefetchtimestamp=1599841107702.

Ku, Robert Ji-Song, Martin F. Manalansan IV, and Anita Mannur, eds. 2013. *Eating Asian America: A Food Studies Reader.* New York: New York University Press.

Kubrick, Stanley, dir. 1975. *Barry Lyndon.* Burbank CA: Warner Brothers.

Kwan, Allen. 2007. "Seeking New Civilizations: Race Normativity in the *Star Trek* Franchise." *Bulletin of Science, Technology, and Society* 27 (1): 59–70.

Lacan, Jacques. (1965) 2002. *The Seminar of Jacques Lacan.* Bk. 12, *Crucial Problems for Psychoanalysis, 1964–1965.* Translated by Cormac Gallagher. London: Karnac.

Lamp, Jeffrey S. 2010. "The Sisko, the Christ: A Comparison of Messiah Figures in the *Star Trek* Universe and the New Testament." In *"Star Trek" as Myth: Essays on Symbol and Archetype at the Final Frontier,* edited by Matthew Wilhelm Kapell, 112–28. Jefferson NC: McFarland.

Lancioni, Judith. 2010. "The Future as Past Perfect: Appropriation of History in the *Star Trek* Series." In *Space and Time: Essays on Visions of History in Science Fiction and Fantasy Television,* edited by David C. Wright Jr. and Allan W. Austin, 131–55. Jefferson NC: McFarland.

Landau, Les, dir. 1991a. *Star Trek: The Next Generation.* Season 4, episode 17, "Night Terrors." Aired March 18, 1991, in syndication.

———, dir. 1991b. *Star Trek: The Next Generation.* Season 5, episode 3, "Ensign Ro." Aired October 7, 1991, in syndication.

———, dir. 1992. *Star Trek: The Next Generation.* Season 6, episode 11, "Chain of Command, Part II." Aired December 21, 1992, in syndication.

———, dir. 1993a. *Star Trek: Deep Space Nine*. Season 1, episode 15, "Progress." Aired May 9, 1993, in syndication.

———, dir. 1993b. *Star Trek: Deep Space Nine*. Season 2, episode 10, "Sanctuary." Aired November 28, 1993, in syndication.

———, dir. 1994a. *Star Trek: Deep Space Nine*. Season 2, episode 14, "Whispers." Aired February 6, 1994, in syndication.

———, dir. 1994b. *Star Trek: Deep Space Nine*. Season 3, episode 3, "The House of Quark." Aired October 10, 1994, in syndication.

———, dir. 1994c. *Star Trek: Deep Space Nine*. Season 3, episode 5, "Second Skin." Aired October 24, 1994, in syndication.

———, dir. 1996a. *Star Trek: Deep Space Nine*. Season 4, episode 17, "Accession." Aired February 24, 1996, in syndication.

———, dir. 1996b. *Star Trek: Deep Space Nine*. Season 4, episode 26, "Broken Link." Aired June 17, 1996, in syndication.

———, dir. 1997. *Star Trek: Deep Space Nine*. Season 5, episode 15, "By Inferno's Light." Aired February 17, 1997, in syndication.

———, dir. 1998. *Star Trek: Deep Space Nine*. Season 7, episode 3, "Afterimage." Aired October 14, 1998, in syndication.

Landry, Alysa. 2016. "Theodore Roosevelt: 'The Only Good Indians Are the Dead Indians.'" Indian Country Today, June 28, 2016. https://indiancountrytoday.com/archive/theodore -roosevelt-the-only-good-indians-are-the-dead-indians-oN1cdfuEW02KzOVVyrp7ig.

Larson, Edward J. 1997. *Summer for the Gods: The Scopes Trial and America's Continuing Debate over Science and Religion*. New York: Basic Books.

Lean, David, dir. 1957. *The Bridge on the River Kwai*. Los Angeles: Columbia Pictures.

le Carré, John. 2010. "Exclusive: British Novelist John le Carré on the Iraq War, Corporate Power, the Exploitation of Africa, and His New Novel, 'Our Kind of Traitor.'" Interview by *Democracy Now!*, October 11, 2010. https://www.democracynow.org/2010/10/11 /exclusive_british_novelist_john_le_carr.

Lee, Sander. 2008. "Is Odo a Collaborator?" In *"Star Trek" and Philosophy: The Wrath of Kant*, edited by Jason T. Eberl and Kevin S. Deckar, 105–16. Chicago: Open Court.

Legato, Robert, dir. 1993. *Star Trek: Deep Space Nine*. Season 1, episode 16, "If Wishes Were Horses." Aired May 16, 1993, in syndication.

Le Guin, Ursula K. (1994) 1995. "My Appointment with the *Enterprise*: An Appreciation." *TV Guide*, Spring 1995, 124–25.

Levy, Gideon. 2018. "In U.S. Media, Israel Is Untouchable." *Haaretz*, January 12, 2018. https://www.haaretz.com/opinion/.premium-cnn-firing-marc-lamont-hill-proves -israel-is-untouchable-in-u-s-media-1.6702572.

Lewis, Sophie. 2019. *Full Surrogacy Now: Feminism against Family*. New York: Verso.

Li, Darryl. 2019. *The Universal Enemy: Jihad, Empire, and the Challenge of Solidarity*. Stanford CA: Stanford University Press.

Littlefield NYC. 2020. "The Katie Halper Show X Struggle Session II." YouTube video, 1:27:15. September 10, 2020. https://www.youtube.com/watch?v=XrbNvFtqWpc.

Lively, Robert L., ed. 2020. *Exploring "Star Trek: Voyager": Critical Essays*. Jefferson NC: McFarland.

Livingston, David, dir. 1993a. *Star Trek: Deep Space Nine*. Season 1, episode 11, "The Nagus." Aired March 21, 1993, in syndication.

———, dir. 1993b. *Star Trek: Deep Space Nine*. Season 1, episode 14, "The Storyteller." Aired May 2, 1993, in syndication.

———, dir. 1993c. *Star Trek: Deep Space Nine*. Season 1, episode 20, "In the Hands of the Prophets." Aired June 20, 1993, in syndication.

———, dir. 1993d. *Star Trek: Deep Space Nine*. Season 2, episode 7, "Rules of Acquisition." Aired November 6, 1993, in syndication.

———, dir. 1994a. *Star Trek: Deep Space Nine*. Season 2, episode 11, "Rivals." Aired January 2, 1994, in syndication.

———, dir. 1994b. *Star Trek: Deep Space Nine*. Season 2, episode 20, "The Maquis, Part I." Aired April 24, 1994, in syndication.

———, dir. 1995a. *Star Trek: Deep Space Nine*. Season 3, episode 21, "The Die Is Cast." Aired May 1, 1995, in syndication.

———, dir. 1995b. *Star Trek: Deep Space Nine*. Season 4, episode 3, "The Visitor." Aired October 9, 1995, in syndication.

———, dir. 1996. *Star Trek: Deep Space Nine*. Season 4, episode 11, "Home Front." Aired January 1, 1996, in syndication.

———, dir. 1997a. *Star Trek: Deep Space Nine*. Season 5, episode 16. "Doctor Bashir, I Presume?" Aired February 24, 1997, in syndication.

———, dir. 1997b. *Star Trek: Deep Space Nine*. Season 6, episode 7, "You Are Cordially Invited . . ." Aired November 10, 1997, in syndication.

———, dir. 1998a. *Star Trek: Deep Space Nine*. Season 6, episode 16, "Change of Heart." Aired February 28, 1998, in syndication.

———, dir. 1998b. *Star Trek: Voyager*. Season 5, episode 8, "Nothing Human." Aired December 2, 1998, in syndication.

Lobl, Victor, dir. 1997. *Star Trek: Deep Space Nine*. Season 5, episode 13, "For the Uniform." Aired February 3, 1997, in syndication.

———, dir. 1998. *Star Trek: Deep Space Nine*. Season 6, episode 19, "In the Pale Moonlight." Aired April 15, 1998, in syndication.

———, dir. 1999. *Star Trek: Deep Space Nine*. Season 7, episode 11, "Prodigal Daughter." Aired January 6, 1999, in syndication.

Locke, John. (1689) 1884. *Two Treatises on Civil Government*. London: George Routledge and Sons.

Logan, Michael. (1994) 1995. "Avery Brooks: The Private Commander." In "*Star Trek* Collectors' Edition." Special issue, *TV Guide*, Spring 1995, 122–24.

————. 2016. "Making the Case for *Space*." In "*Star Trek* 50th Anniversary Special." Special issue, *TV Guide*, October 31, 2016, 71.

Loyd, Jenna. 2014. *Health Rights Are Civil Rights: Peace and Justice Activism in Los Angeles, 1963–1978*. Minneapolis: University of Minnesota Press.

Lynch, Paul, dir. 1993a. *Star Trek: Deep Space Nine*. Season 1, episode 4, "A Man Alone." Aired January 17, 1993, in syndication.

————, dir. 1993b. *Star Trek: Deep Space Nine*. Season 1, episode 7, "Q-Less." Aired February 6, 1993, in syndication.

Lytle Hernández, Kelly. 2017. *City of Inmates: Conquest, Rebellion, and the Rise of Human Caging in Los Angeles, 1771–1965*. Chapel Hill: University of North Carolina Press.

MacDonald, Fraser. 2008. "Space and the Atom: On the Popular Geopolitics of Cold War Rocketry." *Geopolitics* 13 (4): 611–34.

Malle, Louis, dir. 1981. *My Dinner with André*. New York: New Yorker Films.

Manalansan, Martin F., IV. 2008. "Queering the Chain of Care Paradigm." *Scholar and Feminist* 6 (3). http://sfonline.barnard.edu/immigration/print_manalansan.htm.

Marcuse, Herbert. 1955. *Eros and Civilization: A Philosophical Inquiry into Freud*. Boston: Beacon.

mario_painter. 2015. "*DS9's* 'Profit and Lace' Is Appalling, Offensive, and Absolutely, Irredeemably Terrible. It Is By Far the Worst Episode of *Star Trek* Ever Produced." *Daystrom Institute* (forum), Reddit, January 13, 2015. https://www.reddit.com/r/DaystromInstitute/comments/2sdl98/ds9s_profit_and_lace_is_appalling_offensive_and/?utm_source=amp&utm_medium=&utm_content=post_body.

Martin, Frank, dir. 2010. *For Love of Liberty*. Agoura Hills CA: Eleventh Day Entertainment.

Marx, Karl, and Friedrich Engels. (1848) 1919. *The Communist Manifesto*. New York: Rand School of Social Science.

Massey, Doreen. 1994. *Space, Place, and Gender*. Minneapolis: University of Minnesota Press.

————. (2003) 2013. "Some Times of Space." In *Time: Documents of Contemporary Art*, edited by Amelia Groom, 116–22. Cambridge MA: MIT Press.

————. 2005. *For Space*. Thousand Oaks: Sage.

Matsuda, Mari. 1991. "Beside My Sister, Facing the Enemy: Legal Theory out of Coalition." *Stanford Law Review* 43 (6): 1183–92.

MatthiasRussell. 2012. Comment on Gul Bones, "Does Anyone Else Dislike Keiko O'Brien?" *The Trek BBS* (forum), May 24, 2012. https://www.trekbbs.com/threads/does-anyone-else-dislike-keiko-obrien.176926/.

McAlevey, Jane. 2014. *Raising Expectations and Raising Hell: My Decade Fighting for the Labor Movement*. London: Verso.

McAlister, Melani. 2005. *Epic Encounters: Culture, Media, and U.S. Interests in the Middle East since 1945*. 2nd ed. Berkeley: University of California Press.

McClintock, Anne. 1995. *Imperial Leather: Race, Gender, and Sexuality in the Imperial Context*. New York: Routledge.

McCormack, Una. 2005. *Hollow Men*. Star Trek: Deep Space Nine. New York: Pocket Books.

McGeough, Kevin. 2016. "Victorian Archaeologies, Anthropologies and Adventures in the Final Frontier: Modes of Nineteenth-Century Scientific Exploration and Display in *Star Trek*." *Science Fiction Film and Television* 9 (2): 229–52.

McKittrick, Katherine. 2011. "On Plantations, Prisons, and a Black Sense of Place." *Social and Cultural Geography* 12 (8): 947–63.

———. 2016. "Diachronic Loops/Deadweight Tonnage/Bad Made Measure." *cultural geographies* 23 (1): 3–18.

———. 2017. "Worn Out." *Southeastern Geographer* 57 (1): 96–100.

———. 2021. *Dear Science and Other Stories*. Durham NC: Duke University Press.

McTiernan, John, dir. 1987. *Predator*. Los Angeles: 20th Century Fox.

McWhorter, Ladelle. 2009. *Racism and Sexual Oppression in Anglo-America: A Genealogy*. Bloomington: Indiana University Press.

Meisfjord, Tom. 2019. "Every *Star Trek* Captain Ranked Worst to Best." Grunge, October 21, 2019. https://www.grunge.com/171086/every-star-trek-captain-ranked-worst-to-best/.

Melamed, Jodi. 2011. *Represent and Destroy: Rationalizing Violence in the New Racial Capitalism*. Minneapolis: University of Minnesota Press.

Memory Alpha. n.d.a. "Bajoran." Accessed September 17, 2022. https://memory-alpha.fandom.com/wiki/Bajoran.

———. n.d.b. "Brunt." Accessed September 17, 2022. https://memory-alpha.fandom.com/wiki/Brunt.

———. n.d.c. "Cardassian Union." Accessed September 17, 2022. https://memory-alpha.fandom.com/wiki/Cardassian_Union.

———. n.d.d. "Dominion." Accessed September 17, 2022. https://memory-alpha.fandom.com/wiki/Dominion.

———. n.d.e. "Emissary (Episode)." Accessed September 17, 2022. https://memory-alpha.fandom.com/wiki/Emissary_(episode).

———. n.d.f. "Far Beyond the Stars (Episode)." Accessed September 17, 2022. https://memory-alpha.fandom.com/wiki/Far_Beyond_the_Stars_(episode).

———. n.d.g. "Ferengi." Accessed September 17, 2022. https://memory-alpha.fandom.com/wiki/Ferengi.

———. n.d.h. "In the Pale Moonlight (Episode)." Accessed September 17, 2022. https://memory-alpha.fandom.com/wiki/In_the_Pale_Moonlight_(episode).

———. n.d.i. "Julian Bashir." Accessed September 17, 2022. https://memory-alpha.fandom.com/wiki/Julian_Bashir.

———. n.d.j. "Let He Who Is without Sin . . . (Episode)." Accessed September 17, 2022. https://memory-alpha.fandom.com/wiki/Let_He_Who_Is_Without_Sin . . . _(episode).

———. n.d.k. "Miles O'Brien." Accessed September 17, 2022. https://memory-alpha
.fandom.com/wiki/Miles_O%27Brien.

———. n.d.l. "Odo." Accessed September 17, 2022. https://memory-alpha.fandom.com
/wiki/Odo.

———. n.d.m. "Past Tense, Part I (Episode)." Accessed September 17, 2022. https://
memory-alpha.fandom.com/wiki/Past_Tense,_Part_I_(episode).

———. n.d.n. "Promenade." Accessed September 17, 2022. https://memory-alpha.fandom
.com/wiki/Promenade.

———. n.d.o. "Rejoined (Episode)." Accessed September 17, 2022. https://memory-alpha
.fandom.com/wiki/Rejoined_(episode).

———. n.d.p. "Rocks and Shoals (Episode)." Accessed September 17, 2022. https://memory
-alpha.fandom.com/wiki/Rocks_and_Shoals_(episode).

———. n.d.q. "Russell Bates." Accessed September 17, 2022. https://memory-alpha.fandom
.com/wiki/Russell_Bates.

Meyer, Nicholas, dir. 1991. *Star Trek VI: The Undiscovered Country*. Hollywood: Paramount.

Michelle. 2017. "Is Keiko O'Brien the Worst? A Discourse Analysis." Women at Warp,
February 21, 2017. https://www.womenatwarp.com/is-keiko-obrien-the-worst-a
-discourse-analysis/.

Minkowitz, Donna. 2002. "Beam Us Back, Scotty!" *Nation*, March 25, 2002. https://www
.thenation.com/article/archive/beam-us-back-scotty/.

Mitchell, David T., and Sharon L. Snyder. 2015. *The Biopolitics of Disability: Neoliberalism,
Ablenationalism, and Peripheral Embodiment*. Ann Arbor: University of Michigan
Press.

Mitchell, Don. 1997. "The Annihilation of Space by Law: The Roots and Implications of
Anti-homeless Laws in the United States." *Antipode* 29 (3): 303–35.

Mittermeier, Sabrina, and Mareike Spychala. 2020. *Fighting for the Future: Essays on "Star
Trek: Discovery."* Liverpool, UK: Liverpool University Press.

Monteith, Ken. 2017. "From Supercrip to Assimilant: Normalcy, Bioculture, and Disabil-
ity in the *Star Trek* Universe." In *To Boldly Go: Essays on Gender and Identity in the
"Star Trek" Universe*, edited by Nadine Farghaly and Simon Bacon, 106–15. Jefferson
NC: McFarland.

Moon, Katherine H. S. 2010. "South Korean Movements against Militarized Sexual
Labor." In *Militarized Currents: Toward a Decolonized Future in Asia and the Pacific*,
edited by Setsu Shigematsu and Keith L. Camacho, 125–46. Minneapolis: University
of Minnesota Press.

Moore, Ronald D. 1998. "Answers." *AOL Chats* (forum), Memory Alpha, April 21, 1998.
https://memory-alpha.fandom.com/wiki/Memory_Alpha:AOL_chats/Ronald_D.
_Moore/ron103.txt.

Moran, Jeffrey P. 2003. "Reading Race into the Scopes Trial: African American Elites,
Science, and Fundamentalism." *Journal of American History* 90 (3): 891–911.

Morefield, Jeanne. 2014. *Empires without Imperialism: Anglo-American Decline and the Politics of Decline.* Oxford: Oxford University Press.

Morrison, Toni. 1987. *Beloved.* New York: Alfred A. Knopf.

Moten, Fred. 2018. *Consent Not to Be a Single Being: Stolen Life.* Durham NC: Duke University Press.

Moten, Fred, and Stefano Harney. 2013. *The Undercommons: Fugitive Planning and Black Study.* Chico CA: AK Press.

Muñoz, José-Esteban. 1999. *Disidentifications: Queers of Color and the Performance of Politics.* Minneapolis: University of Minnesota Press.

Museum of Television and Radio. 1994. "The Museum of Television and Radio's 11th Annual Television Festival in Los Angeles: *Star Trek: Deep Space Nine.*" March 18, 1994. Video recording, VHS, accessed at the Paley Center for Media, Los Angeles. Catalogue ID: T:33176.

Napolitano, Mark. 2012. "Reshaping the Universe in an Amorphous Image." *Science Fiction Film and Television* 5 (2): 201–20.

Nast, Heidi J. 2000. "Mapping the 'Unconscious': Racism and the Oedipal Family." *Annals of the Association of American Geographers* 90 (2): 215–55.

Nazarian, Cynthia. 2018. "The Outlaw-Knight: Law's Violence in *The Faerie Queene, The Man Who Shot Liberty Valance,* and *The Dark Knight Rises.*" *Cultural Critique* 98:204–23.

Neal, Mark Anthony. 2013. *Looking for Leroy: Illegible Black Masculinities.* New York: New York University Press.

Nemecek, Larry. 2003. *"Star Trek: The Next Generation" Companion.* Rev. ed. New York: Pocket Books.

Neumann, Iver B. 2001. "'Grab a Phaser, Ambassador': Diplomacy in *Star Trek.*" *Millennium* 30 (3): 603–24.

Newsweek. 1993. "*Star Trek* Sets a Bold New Course." January 1, 1993. https://www.newsweek.com/star-trek-sets-bold-new-course-192110.

New York Public Library. 2006. "A Tribute to Octavia E. Butler." *Live from the NYPL,* June 5, 2006, transcript and Adobe Flash audio, 1:20:00. https://www.nypl.org/audiovideo/tribute-octavia-e-butler.

Niccol, Andrew, dir. 1997. *Gattaca.* Culver City CA: Columbia.

Nichols, Nichelle. 1994. *Beyond Uhura: "Star Trek" and Other Memories.* New York: Putnam.

Nimoy, Adam, dir. 1992. *Star Trek: The Next Generation.* Season 6, episode 7, "Rascals." Aired November 2, 1992, in syndication.

Nimoy, Leonard, dir. 1986. *Star Trek IV: The Voyage Home.* Hollywood: Paramount.

Nolton, Marnie. 2008. "Cardassian 'Monsters' and Bajoran 'Freedom Fighters.'" In *"Star Trek" and Philosophy: The Wrath of Kant,* edited by Jason T. Eberl and Kevin S. Decker, 185–200. Chicago: Open Court.

Numbers, Ronald L. 1986. "The Creationists." In *God and Nature: Historical Essays on the Encounter between Christianity and Science*, edited by David C. Lindberg and Ronald L. Numbers, 391–423. Berkeley: University of California Press.

Nussbaum, Abigail. 2008. "Back through the Wormhole, Part VI: Ode to Kira." *Asking the Wrong Questions* (blog), February 8, 2008. http://wrongquestions.blogspot.com /2008/02/back-through-wormhole-part-vi-ode-to.html.

Ochoa, Gilda. 2013. *Academic Profiling: Latinos, Asian Americans, and the Achievement Gap*. Minneapolis: University of Minnesota Press.

O'Connor, Mike. 2012. "Liberals in Space: The 1960s Politics of *Star Trek*." *Sixties* 5 (2): 185–203.

Oglesbee, Frank W. 2004. "Kira Nerys: A Good Woman Fighting Well." *Extrapolation* 45 (3): 263–75.

Oliver, Kelly. 2004. *The Colonization of Psychic Space: A Psychoanalytic Social Theory of Oppression*. Minneapolis: University of Minnesota Press.

OmicronPerseiNine. 2012. "*Star Trek: Deep Space 9* Is Reading as Wonderfully Poly to Me Now." *Polyamory* (forum), Reddit, September 3, 2012. https://www.reddit.com/r /polyamory/comments/zbizf/star_trek_deep_space_9_is_reading_as_wonderfully/.

Ono, Kent A. 1996. "Domesticating Terrorism: A Neocolonial Economy of Différance." In Enterprise *Zones: Critical Positions on "Star Trek*," edited by Taylor Harrison, Sarah Projansky, Kent A. Ono, and Elyce Rae Helford, 157–85. Boulder CO: Westview Press.

Ott, Brian L., and Eric Aoki. 2001. "Popular Imagination and Identity Politics: Reading the Future in *Star Trek: The Next Generation*." *Western Journal of Communication* 65 (4): 392–415.

Pakula, Alan J., dir. 1976. *All the President's Men*. Burbank CA: Warner Brothers.

Pareles, Jon. 1996. "Television View: When Aliens Start to Look a Lot Like Us." *New York Times*, May 26, 1996, H26. https://www.nytimes.com/1996/05/26/arts/television-view -when-aliens-start-to-look-a-lot-like-us.html.

Patterson, William L., ed. 2020. *We Charge Genocide: The Crime of Government against the Negro People*. 3rd ed. New York: International Publishers.

Pauwels, Jacques R. 2002. *The Myth of the Good War: America in the Second World War*. Toronto: Lorimer.

Pearson, Roberta, and Máire Messenger Davies. 2014. *"Star Trek" and American Television*. Berkeley: University of California Press.

Peck, Jamie, and Adam Tickell. 2002. "Neoliberalizing Space." *Antipode* 34 (3): 380–404.

Penley, Constance. 1997. NASA/*Trek: Popular Science and Sex in America*. New York: Verso.

Pérez, Gina M. 2015. *Citizen, Student, Soldier: Latina/o Youth, JROTC, and the American Dream*. New York: New York University Press.

Perry, S. D. 2003. *Unity*. Star Trek: Deep Space Nine. New York: Pocket Books.

Pesola, Eric. 2021. "*DS9* Showrunner Still Unhappy over Censored Episode." Heavy, May 14, 2021. https://heavy.com/entertainment/star-trek/ds9-showrunner-still-unhappy -over-censored-episode/.

———. 2022. "The Fan Push to Get *Star Trek*'s Captain Sisko a Statue in New Orleans." Heavy, January 14, 2022. https://heavy.com/entertainment/star-trek/fans-want-sisko -statue-new-orleans/.

Pevney, Joseph, dir. 1967. *Star Trek*. Season 2, episode 15, "The Trouble with Tribbles." Aired December 29, 1967, on NBC.

Phillips, Richard. 1997. *Mapping Men and Empire: A Geography of Adventure*. New York: Routledge.

Pile, Steve. 2019. "Affect and Ideology: The Political Stake of Desire." *Emotion, Space and Society* 31:108–11.

Polk, Khary. 2020. *Contagions of Empire: Scientific Racism, Sexuality, and Black Military Workers Abroad, 1898–1948*. Chapel Hill: University of North Carolina Press.

Porter, Jennifer E., and Darcee L. McLaren, eds. 1999. *"Star Trek" and Sacred Ground: Explorations of "Star Trek," Religion, and American Culture*. Albany: State University of New York Press.

Posey, Stephen L., dir. 1998. *Star Trek: Deep Space Nine*. Season 7, episode 6, "Treachery, Faith, and the Great River." Aired November 4, 1998, in syndication.

———, dir. 1999a. *Star Trek: Deep Space Nine*. Season 7, episode 14, "Chimera." Aired February 17, 1999, in syndication.

———, dir. 1999b. *Star Trek: Deep Space Nine*. Season 7, episode 23, "Extreme Measures." Aired May 19, 1999, in syndication.

Postone, Moishe. 1980. "Anti-Semitism and National Socialism: Notes on the German Reaction to 'Holocaust.'" *New German Critique* 19 (1): 97–115.

Pounds, Micheal Charles. 1999. *Race in Space: The Representation of Ethnicity in "Star Trek" and "Star Trek: The Next Generation."* Lanham MD: Scarecrow Press.

———. 2009. "'Explorers'—*Star Trek: Deep Space Nine*." *African Identities* 7 (2): 209–35.

Pramaggiore, Maria. 2014. *Making Time in Stanley Kubrick's "Barry Lyndon": Art, History, and Empire*. New York: Bloomsbury.

Pratt, Minnie Bruce. 1984. "Identity: Skin, Blood, Heart." In *Yours in Struggle: Three Feminist Perspective on Anti-Semitism and Racism*, edited by Elly Bulkin, Barbara Smith and Minnie Bruce Pratt, 10–63. New York: Firebrand Books.

Prescod-Weinstein, Chanda. 2019. "Seeking Repentance in *Star Trek*." StarTrek.com, October 9, 2019. https://www.startrek.com/news/star-trek-yom-kippur-forgiveness -dukat-neelix.

Prime Minister of Israel. 2018. "The weak crumble, are slaughtered and are erased from history while the strong, for good or for ill, survive." Twitter, August 29, 2018. https:// twitter.com/israelipm/status/1034849460344573952?lang=en.

Puar, Jasbir K. 2007. *Terrorist Assemblages: Homonationalism in Queer Times*. Durham NC: Duke University Press.

Putman, John. 2013. "Terrorizing Space: *Star Trek*, Terrorism, and History." In *"Star Trek" and History*, edited by Nancy R. Reagin, 143–57. Hoboken NJ: John Wiley and Sons.

Rabitsch, Stefan. 2018. "'Wagon Wheels, Sails, and Warp Cores': *Star Trek* and American Culture; Between Allegory and Worldbuilding." In *Set Phasers to Teach! "Star Trek" in Research and Teaching*, edited by Stefan Rabitsch, Martin Gabriel, Wilfried Elmeinreich, and John N. A. Brown, 29–41. Cham, Switzerland: Springer International Publishing.

Raile, Dan. 2014. "20 Years On, a *Star Trek* Writer on How His Vision of a Tech-Ruined San Francisco Is Panning Out." PandoDaily, September 21, 2014. https://pandodaily .com/2014/09/21/a-star-trek-writer-revisits-his-20-year-old-vision-of-a-futuristic-tech -ruined-san-francisco.

Reagon, Bernice Johnson. 1983. "Coalition Politics: Turning the Century." In *Home Girls: A Black Feminist Anthology*, edited by Barbara Smith, 356–68. New York: Kitchen Table Women of Color Press.

Reddy, Chandan. 2011. *Freedom with Violence: Race, Sexuality, and the U.S. State*. Durham NC: Duke University Press.

Redmond, Shana L. 2020. *Everything Man: The Form and Function of Paul Robeson*. Durham NC: Duke University Press.

Reeves-Stevens, Judith, and Garfield Reeves-Stevens. 1994. *The Making of "Star Trek: Deep Space Nine."* New York: Pocket Books.

Regan, Jarlath. 2020. "Colm Meaney." *An Irishman Abroad* (podcast), episode 356, May 9, 2020. https://anirishmanabroad.podbean.com/e/colm-meaney-episode-356/.

Reich, Wilhelm. (1946) 1980. *The Mass Psychology of Fascism*. New York: Farrar, Straus, and Giroux.

Reiner, Rob, dir. 1987. *The Princess Bride*. Los Angeles: 20th Century Fox.

Relke, Diana M. A. 2006. *Drones, Clones, and Alpha Babes: Retrofitting "Star Trek"'s Humanism*. Calgary AB: University of Calgary Press.

Reuters. 2012. "How Barack Obama Killed John Wayne." November 14, 2012. https:// www.reuters.com/article/idUS279323336020121114.

Rhodes, Mark Alan, II. 2016. "Placing Paul Robeson in History: Understanding His Philosophical Framework." *Journal of Black Studies* 47 (3): 235–57.

———. 2017. "Alternative Pasts, Presents, and Futures in *Star Trek*: Historical Engagement and Representation though Popular Culture." *Geographical Bulletin* 58 (1): 29–39.

Rhodes, Mark Alan, II, Fiona M. Davidson, and Hannah C. Gunderman, eds. 2017. "The Geographies of *Star Trek*." Special issue, *Geographical Bulletin* 58 (1): 1–62.

Richards, Thomas. 1997. *The Meaning of "Star Trek": An Excursion into the Myth and Marvel of the "Star Trek" Universe*. New York: Doubleday.

Ring, Deborah A. 2012. "Avery Brooks." In *Contemporary Black Biography: Profiles from the International Black Community*, vol. 98, edited by Margaret Mazurkiewicz, 26–29. Farmington Hills MI: Gale.

Rivera, Mayra. 2021. "Embodied Counterpoetics." In *Beyond Man: Race, Coloniality, and Philosophy of Religion*, edited by An Yountae and Eleanor Craig, 57–85. Durham NC: Duke University Press.

Roberts, Dorothy. 1997. *Killing the Black Body: Race, Reproduction, and the Meaning of Liberty*. New York: Vintage.

Roberts, Neil. 2015. *Freedom as Marronage*. Chicago: University of Chicago Press.

Roberts, Robin. 1999. *"Star Trek": Sexual Generations*. Champaign: University of Illinois Press.

Robin, Corey. 2018. *The Reactionary Mind: Conservatism from Edmund Burke to Donald Trump*. 2nd ed. Oxford: Oxford University Press.

Robinson, Andrew J., dir. 1996. *Star Trek: Deep Space Nine*. Season 5, episode 3, "Looking for par'Mach in All the Wrong Places." Aired October 14, 1996, in syndication.

——. 2000. *A Stitch in Time*. Star Trek: Deep Space Nine. New York: Pocket Books.

——. 2019. "The Deceptive Complication of Elim Garak." Interview by Marcelo Rossi. StarTrek.com, May 25, 2019. https://www.startrek.com/article/andy-robinson-interview -inside-star-trek-magazine.

Robinson, Cedric J. (1983) 2000. *Black Marxism: The Making of the Black Radical Tradition*. Chapel Hill: University of North Carolina Press.

——. 1993. "Race, Capitalism, and the Anti-democracy." In *Reading Rodney King, Reading Urban Uprising*, edited by Robert Gooding-Williams, 73–81. New York: Routledge.

Robinson, Cedric J., and Elizabeth Robinson. 2017. "Introduction." In *Futures of Black Radicalism*, edited by Gaye Theresa Johnson and Alex Lubin, 1–8. New York: Verso.

Robinson, Sally. 2000. *Marked Men: White Masculinity in Crisis*. New York: Columbia University Press.

Robson, Laura C. 2010. "Palestinian Liberation Theology, Muslim-Christian Relations and the Arab-Israeli Conflict." *Islam and Christian-Muslim Relations* 21 (2): 39–50.

Rodríguez, Dylan. 2008. "Inaugurating Multiculturalist White Supremacy." ColorLines, November 10, 2008. https://www.colorlines.com/articles/dreadful-genius-obama -moment.

Rogoway, Tyler. 2015. "That Time Ronald Reagan Visited *Star Trek: The Next Generation* and Took the Captain's Chair." *Jalopnik* (blog), December 5, 2015. https://foxtrotalpha .jalopnik.com/that-time-ronald-reagan-visited-star-trek-the-next-gen-1746411231.

Rose, Jacqueline. 2007. *The Last Resistance*. New York: Verso.

Ruez, Derek, and Daniel Cockayne. 2021. "Feeling Otherwise: Ambivalent Affects and the Politics of Critique in Geography." *Dialogues in Human Geography* 11 (1): 88–107.

Russell, John G. 2013. "Don't It Make My Black Face Blue: Race, Avatars, Albescence, and the Transnational Imaginary." *Journal of Popular Culture* 46 (1): 192–217.

Russell, Marta. 2019. *Capitalism and Disability*. Chicago: Haymarket.

Rutgers University Alumni Association. n.d. "Avery F. Brooks." Hall of Distinguished Alumni. https://alumni.rutgers.edu/awards-recognition/hall-of-distinguished-alumni /avery-f-brooks/.

Saadia, Manu. 2016. *Trekonomics: The Economics of "Star Trek."* San Francisco: Inkshares.

Sadler, William. 2010. "Luther Sloan from *Deep Space Nine*—William Sadler." StarTrek .com, December 22, 2010. https://www.startrek.com/article/luther-sloan-from-deep -space-nine-william-sadler.

Said, Edward W. (1978) 2003. *Orientalism*. New York: Penguin.

———. (1979) 1992. *The Question of Palestine*. New York: Vintage.

———. 1993. *Culture and Imperialism*. New York: Vintage.

Saldanha, Arun. 2015. "Scale, Difference, and Universality in the Study of Race." *Postcolonial Studies* 18 (3): 326–35.

Santner, Eric L. 1996. *My Own Private Germany: Daniel Paul Schreber's Secret History of Modernity*. Princeton NJ: Princeton University Press.

———. 2011. *The Royal Remains: The King's Two Bodies and the Endgames of Sovereignty*. Chicago: University of Chicago Press.

Saunders, Robert A. 2015. "Imperial Imaginaries: Employing Science Fiction to Talk about Geopolitics." *E-International Relations*, June 11, 2015, 1–7. https://www.e-ir.info /pdf/56749.

Savran, David. 1998. *Taking It Like a Man: White Masculinity, Masochism, and Contemporary American Culture*. Princeton NJ: Princeton University Press.

Schreber, Daniel Paul. (1903) 2000. *Memoirs of My Nervous Illness*. New York: New York Review of Books.

Scott, Darieck. 2022. *Keeping It Unreal: Black Queer Fantasy and Superhero Comics*. New York: New York University Press.

Secker, Tom. 2016. "Updated 'Complete' List of DOD Films." Spy Culture. https://www .spyculture.com/updated-complete-list-of-dod-films/.

Sedgwick, Eve Kosofsky. 1993. *Tendencies*. Durham NC: Duke University Press.

———. 2003. *Touching Feeling: Affect, Pedagogy, Performativity*. Durham NC: Duke University Press.

Seitz, David K. 2017a. *A House of Prayer for All People: Contesting Citizenship in a Queer Church*. Minneapolis: University of Minnesota Press.

———. 2017b. "'Most Damning of All . . . I Think I Can Live with It': Captain Sisko, President Obama, and Emotional Geopolitics." *Geographical Bulletin* 58 (1): 19–28.

———. 2017c. "'Second Skin,' White Masks: Postcolonial Reparation in *Star Trek: Deep Space Nine*." *Psychoanalysis, Culture & Society* 22 (4): 401–19.

Serrano, Richard A. 1992. "King Case Aftermath: A City in Crisis." *Los Angeles Times*, May 2, 1992. https://www.latimes.com/archives/la-xpm-1992-05-02-mn-1287-story.html.

Shabazz, Rashad. 2015. *Spatializing Blackness: Architectures of Confinement and Black Masculinity in Chicago*. Champaign: University of Illinois Press.

Shakespeare, William. (1605) 2004. *The Merchant of Venice*. New York: Simon and Schuster.

Shange, Savannah. 2019. *Progressive Dystopia: Abolition, Antiblackness, and Schooling in San Francisco*. Durham NC: Duke University Press.

Sharp, Joanne P. 1998. "Reel Geographies of the New World Order: Patriotism, Masculinity, and Geopolitics in Post–Cold War American Movies." In *Rethinking Geopolitics*, edited by Simon Dalby and Gearóid Ó Tuathail, 116–27. New York: Routledge.

Sharpe, Christina. 2016. *In the Wake: On Blackness and Being*. Durham NC: Duke University Press.

Sharrett, Christopher. 2005. *The Rifleman*. Detroit MI: Wayne State University Press.

Shatner, William, dir. 2011. *The Captains*. Beverly Hillls CA: Metro-Goldwyn-Mayer.

———, dir. 2013. *The Captains Close Up*. Season 1, episode 3, "Avery Brooks." Aired May 16, 2013, on EPIX.

Shaw, Robert. 1968. *The Man in the Glass Booth*. Directed by Harold Pinter. Opening September 26, 1968, at the Royale Theatre, New York. https://www.playbill.com/playbillpagegallery/inside-playbill?asset=00000150-aea6-d936-a7fd-eef62eff0004&type=InsidePlaybill&slide=1.

Shawn, Wallace. 2009. *Essays*. Chicago: Haymarket.

———. 2017. *Night Thoughts*. Chicago: Haymarket.

Shimerman, Armin. 2020. "Quark/Armin Shimerman Interview—'Live with Regis & Kathie Lee.' (June 7, 1993)." Interview by Regis Philbin and Kathie Lee Gifford. YouTube video, 10:41. July 25, 2020. https://www.youtube.com/watch?v=MLpSXOB6ZqQ.

Shrager, Adam. 1997. *The Finest Crew in the Fleet: "The Next Generation" Cast On Screen and Off*. New York: Wolf Valley Books.

Sid City. 2020. "Alone Together Episode 1—Alexander Siddig & Andrew Robinson." YouTube video, 32:42. July 6, 2020. https://www.youtube.com/watch?v=M44QMKWMxuQ.

Siddig, Alexander, dir. 1998. *Star Trek: Deep Space Nine*. Season 6, episode 23, "Profit and Lace." Aired May 13, 1998, in syndication.

Sinatra, Frank, dir. 1965. *None but the Brave*. Burbank CA: Warner Brothers.

Singer, Alexander, dir. 1995a. *Star Trek: Deep Space Nine*. Season 3, episode 14, "Heart of Stone." Aired February 6, 1995, in syndication.

———, dir. 1995b. *Star Trek: Deep Space Nine*. Season 3, episode 26, "The Adversary." Aired June 25, 1995, in syndication.

———, dir. 1995c. *Star Trek: Deep Space Nine*. Season 4, episode 7, "Starship Down." Aired November 13, 1995, in syndication.

———, dir. 1996. *Star Trek: Deep Space Nine*. Season 4, episode 19, "Hard Time." Aired April 15, 1996, in syndication.

Singh, Nikhil Pal. 2017. *Race and America's Long War*. Berkeley: University of California Press.

Slotkin, Richard. 1992. *Gunfighter Nation: The Myth of the Frontier in Twentieth-Century America*. New York: Atheneum.

Smiles, Deondre S. 2020. "The Settler Logics of (Outer) Space." *Society and Space*, October 26, 2020. https://www.societyandspace.org/articles/the-settler-logics-of-outer-space.

Smith, David L. 2006. *Hoosiers in Hollywood*. Indianapolis: Indiana Historical Society.

Smith, Mona Z. 2004. *Becoming Something: The Story of Canada Lee*. London: Faber and Faber.

Sneed, Roger A. 2021. *The Dreamer and the Dream: Afrofuturism and Black Religious Thought*. Columbus: The Ohio State University Press.

Snorton, C. Riley. 2014. *Nobody Is Supposed to Know: Black Sexuality on the Down Low*. Minneapolis: University of Minnesota Press.

Snyder, Terri L. 2015. *The Power to Die: Slavery and Suicide in British North America*. Chicago: University of Chicago Press.

Sobchack, Vivian Carol. 2001. *Screening Space: The American Science Fiction Film*. 2nd ed. New Brunswick NJ: Rutgers University Press.

Song, Lin, and Chris K. K. Tan. 2020. "The Final Frontier: Imagining Queer Futurity in *Star Trek*." *Continuum* 34 (4): 577–89.

Spelling, Ian. 1996. "Rosalind Chao Likes Part-Time Status on 'DS9.'" *Chicago Tribune*, December 26, 1996.

Spillers, Hortense J. 1987. "Mama's Baby, Papa's Maybe: An American Grammar Book." *Diacritics* 17 (2): 64–81.

Stevens, George, dir. 1953. *Shane*. Hollywood: Paramount.

Stevenson, Brenda. 2015. *The Contested Murder of Latasha Harlins: Justice, Gender, and the Origins of the L.A. Riots*. Oxford: Oxford University Press.

Stewart, Patrick, dir. 1991. *Star Trek: The Next Generation*. Season 4, episode 25, "In Theory." Aired June 3, 1991, in syndication.

———, dir. 1994. *Star Trek: The Next Generation*. Season 7, episode 24, "Preemptive Strike." Aired May 16, 1994, in syndication.

Stoler, Ann Laura. 1995. *Race and the Education of Desire: Foucault's History of Sexuality and the Colonial Order of Things*. Durham NC: Duke University Press.

Strah, Britain Ryan, and Pat Hoey. 2022. "'Lower Decks' S3E5 'Reflections' & 'Deep Space 9' S2E14 'Whispers.'" *Soy Trek* (podcast), September 23, 2022. https://podcasts.apple.com/us/podcast/lower-decks-s3e5-reflections-deep-space-9-s2e14-whispers/id1624305896.

Strusiewicz, Cezary Jan. 2019. "Risa and Gene Roddenberry's Unrealized Queer Vision." StarTrek.com, August 13, 2019. https://www.startrek.com/news/risa-and-gene-roddenberrys-unrealized-queer-vision.

Stuelke, Patricia. 2021. *The Ruse of Repair: U.S. Neoliberal Empire and the Turn from Critique*. Durham NC: Duke University Press.

Sturgeon, Theodore. (1979) n.d. "Push from Within: The Extrapolative Ability of Theodore Sturgeon." Interview by David D. Duncan. The Theodore Sturgeon Page. http://www.physics.emory.edu/faculty/weeks//misc/duncan.html. Originally published in the University of Tennessee's literary magazine, the *Phoenix*, 1979.

Sturgis, Amy H. 2013. "If This Is the (Final) Frontier, Where Are the Natives?" In *"Star Trek" and History*, edited by Nancy R. Reagin, 125–42. Hoboken NJ: John Wiley and Sons.

Sukehiro, Hirakawa. 1999. "Prisoners in Burma: The Anglo-Japanese Hostilities from a Cultural Perspective." *Japan Echo* 26 (6): 43–50.

Summers, Tim. 2013. "*Star Trek* and the Musical Depiction of the Alien Other." *Music, Sound and the Moving Image* 7 (1): 19–52.

Sutherland, Hal, dir. 1973. *Star Trek: The Animated Series*. Season 1, episode 7, "The Infinite Vulcan." Aired October 20, 1973, on NBC.

Swyngedouw, Erik, and Henrik Ernston. 2018. "Interrupting the Anthropo-obScene: Immuno-biopolitics and Depoliticizing Ontologies in the Anthropocene." *Theory, Culture, and Society* 35 (6): 3–30.

Takaki, Ronald. 1998. *Strangers from a Different Shore: A History of Asian Americans*. New York: Hachette.

Takei, George. 2007. "Exclusive: George Takei Thanks Fans for 40 Years of 'Star Trek'—Part 2." Interview by Sean Elliott. *iF Magazine*, November 20, 2007. https://web.archive.org/web/20071123012040/http://ifmagazine.com/feature.asp?article=2478.

TallBear, Kim. 2013. *Native American DNA: Tribal Belonging and the False Promise of Genetic Science*. Minneapolis: University of Minnesota Press.

Taylor, Jud, dir. 1969. *Star Trek: The Original Series*. Season 3, episode 15, "Let That Be Your Last Battlefield." Aired January 10, 1969, on NBC.

Taylor, Keeanga-Yamahtta, ed. 2012. *How We Get Free: Black Feminism and the Combahee River Collective*. Chicago: Haymarket.

———. 2016. *From #BlackLivesMatter to Black Liberation*. Chicago: Haymarket.

———. 2019. *Race for Profit: How Banks and the Real Estate Industry Undermine Black Homeownership*. Chapel Hill: University of North Carolina Press.

———. 2020. "Joe Biden, Kamala Harris, and the Limits of Representation." *New Yorker*, August 24, 2020. https://www.newyorker.com/news/our-columnists/joe-biden-kamala-harris-and-the-limits-of-representation.

Thomas, Ebony Elizabeth, and Amy Stornaiuolo. 2019. "Race, Storying, and Restorying: What Can We Learn from Black Fans?" *Transformative Works and Culture* 29. https://journal.transformativeworks.org/index.php/twc/article/view/1562/2121.

Thompson, Todd, dir. 2019. *Woman in Motion*. Hollywood: Paramount.

Tompkins, Kyla Wazana. 2012. *Racial Indigestion: Eating Bodies in the 19th Century*. New York: New York University Press.

Tran, Anh T. 2018. "Policing Loyalty: Comparing the Tal Shiar and the FBI's COINTEL-PRO." In *Exploring Picard's Galaxy: Essays on "Star Trek: The Next Generation,"* edited by Peter W. Lee, 43–49. Jefferson NC: McFarland.

Treviño, Jésus Salvador, dir. 1997. *Star Trek: Deep Space Nine.* Season 5, episode 12, "The Begotten." Aired January 27, 1997, in syndication.

Trivedi, Harsh. 2022. "*Star Trek* and the Annihilation of Caste." Brown History, August 8, 2022. https://brownhistory.substack.com/p/star-trek-and-the-annihilation-of.

Tuck, Eve, and K. Wayne Yang. 2012. "Decolonization Is Not a Metaphor." *Decolonization* 1 (1): 1–40.

Uddin, Lisa. 2015. *Zoo Renewal: White Flight and the Animal Ghetto.* Minneapolis: University of Minnesota Press.

Vande Berg, Leah R. 1996. "Liminality: Worf as Metonymic Signifier of Racial, Cultural, and National Differences." In Enterprise *Zones: Critical Positions on "Star Trek,"* edited by Taylor Harrison, Sarah Projansky, Kent A. Ono, and Elyce Rae Helford, 51–68. Boulder CO: Westview Press.

Vejar, Mike, dir. 1997a. *Star Trek: Deep Space Nine.* Season 5, episode 11, "The Darkness and the Light." Aired January 6, 1997, in syndication.

———, dir. 1997b. *Star Trek: Deep Space Nine.* Season 6, episode 2, "Rocks and Shoals." Aired October 6, 1997, in syndication.

———, dir. 1999a. *Star Trek: Deep Space Nine.* Season 7, episode 15, "Badda-Bing, Badda-Bang." Aired February 24, 1999, in syndication.

———, dir. 1999b. *Star Trek: Deep Space Nine.* Season 7, episode 20, "The Changing Face of Evil." Aired April 28, 1999, in syndication.

———, dir. 1999c. *Star Trek: Deep Space Nine.* Season 7, episode 22, "Tacking into the Wind." Aired May 12, 1999, in syndication.

Vine, David. 2015. *Base Nation: How U.S. Military Bases Abroad Harm America and the World.* New York: Metropolitan Books.

Visitor, Nana. 2021. "Nana Visitor Is Writing a *Star Trek* Book That Goes Where No Woman Has Gone Before." Interview by Laurie Ulster. TrekMovie, October 7, 2021. https://trekmovie.com/2021/10/07/interview-nana-visitor-is-writing-a-star-trek-book-that-goes-where-no-woman-has-gone-before/.

———, ed. 2022. *"Star Trek": A Woman's Trek.* New York: Hero Collector.

Volk-Weiss, Brian, dir. 2022. *The Center Seat.* Season 1, episode 3, "Dancing with Syndication in the Pale Moonlight." Aired February 13, 2022, on the History Channel.

Vuori, Juha A. 2017. "To Boldly Torture Where No One Has Tortured Before: *Star Trek* and the Transformation of the 'Progressive' Social Imaginary of Torture in the United States." *Global Discourse* 7 (2–3): 309–26.

Wagner, Jon, and Jan Lundeen. 1998. *Deep Space and Sacred Time: "Star Trek" in the American Mythos.* Westport CT: Praeger.

Wang, Wayne, dir. 1993. *The Joy Luck Club*. Burbank CA: Hollywood Pictures.

Ware, Lawrence. 2020. "*Deep Space Nine*'s Radical Depiction of Black Love." StarTrek.com, July 30, 2020. https://www.startrek.com/news/deep-space-nines-radical-depiction -of-black-love.

Warf, Barney. 2001. "The Way It Wasn't: Alternative Histories, Contingent Geographies." In *Lost in Space: Geographies of Science Fiction*, edited by Rob Kitchin and James Kneale, 17–38. New York: Bloomsbury.

Waring, Marilyn. 1999. *Counting for Nothing: What Men Value and What Women Are Worth*. 2nd ed. Toronto: University of Toronto Press.

Washington Post. 1967. "A Tragedy." April 6, 1967.

Wayne, John. 1971. "John Wayne: *Playboy* Interview." Interview by Richard Warren Lewis. *Playboy*, May 1971.

Weinstock, Jeffrey A. 1996. "Freaks in Space: 'Extraterrestrialism' and 'Deep-Space Mul- ticulturalism.'" In *Freakery: Cultural Spectacles of the Extraordinary Body*, edited by Rosemarie Garland-Thompson, 327–37. New York: New York University Press.

Wenger, Sara. 2021. "'I Don't Want to Like Her': Dabo Girls, Playboy Bunnies, and the Importance of Sex Work." Women at Warp, June 24, 2021. https://www.womenatwarp .com/i-dont-want-to-like-her-dabo-girls-playboy-bunnies-and-the-importance-of -sex-work/.

West, Cornel. 1982. *Prophesy Deliverance! An Afro-American Revolutionary Christianity*. Louisville KY: Westminster John Knox.

———. 2015. "The Radical King We Don't Know." Introduction to *The Radical King*, by Martin Luther King Jr., ix–xvi. Boston: Beacon.

———. 2017. "Pity the Sad Legacy of Barack Obama." *Guardian*, January 9, 2017. https:// www.theguardian.com/commentisfree/2017/jan/09/barack-obama-legacy-presidency.

West, Jonathan, dir. 1995. *Star Trek: Deep Space Nine*. Season 3, episode 24, "Shakaar." Aired May 22, 1995, in syndication.

———, dir. 1996a. *Star Trek: Deep Space Nine*. Season 4, episode 14, "Return to Grace." Aired February 5, 1996, in syndication.

———, dir. 1996b. *Star Trek: Deep Space Nine*. Season 5, episode 6, "Trials and Tribble- ations." Aired November 4, 1996, in syndication.

———, dir. 1998. *Star Trek: Deep Space Nine*. Season 6, episode 17, "Wrongs Darker than Death or Night." Aired March 28, 1998, in syndication.

Whalen, Andrew. 2016. "Are Ferengi Jewish? 'Star Trek: Deep Space Nine' Actor Armin Shimerman Answers." Player.One, September 2, 2016. https://www.player.one/are -ferengi-jewish-star-trek-deep-space-nine-cast-quark-armin-shimerman-118548.

Whitfield, Stephen E., and Gene Roddenberry. 1968. *The Making of "Star Trek."* New York: Ballantine.

Whyte, Kyle Powys. 2017. "Indigenous Climate Change Studies: Indigenizing Futures, Decolonizing the Anthropocene." *English Language Notes* 55 (1–2): 153–62.

Wiemer, Robert, dir. 1991. *Star Trek: The Next Generation*. Season 4, episode 11, "Data's Day." Aired January 7, 1991, in syndication.

———, dir. 1994. *Star Trek: Deep Space Nine*. Season 2, episode 18, "Profit and Loss." Aired March 20, 1994, in syndication.

Wilcox, Clyde. 1992. "To Boldly Return Where Others Have Gone Before: Cultural Change and the Old and New *Star Treks*." *Extrapolation* 33 (1): 88–100.

Wilderson, Frank B., III. 2010. *Red, White, and Black: Cinema and the Structure of U.S. Antagonisms*. Durham NC: Duke University Press.

Williams, Anson, dir. 1997. *Star Trek: Deep Space Nine*. Season 6, episode 9, "Statistical Probabilities." Aired November 22, 1997, in syndication.

———, dir. 1998. *Star Trek: Deep Space Nine*. Season 7, episode 10, "It's Only a Paper Moon." Aired December 30, 1998, in syndication.

Wills, Garry. 1997. *John Wayne's America: The Politics of Celebrity*. New York: Simon and Schuster.

Winn, J. Emmett. 2003. "Racial Issues and *Star Trek's Deep Space Nine*." *Kinema*, Spring 2003. https://doi.org/10.15353/kinema.vi.1046.

Wolfe, Patrick. 2006. "Settler Colonialism and the Elimination of the Native." *Journal of Genocide Research* 8 (4): 387–409.

Women at Warp. 2015. "The Ferengi Feminist Revolution." *Women at Warp* (podcast), episode 7, May 24, 2015. https://www.womenatwarp.com/ferengi-feminist-revolution/.

Wong, K. Scott. 2005. *Americans First: Chinese Americans and the Second World War*. Cambridge MA: Harvard University Press.

Woods, Clyde. 1998. *Development Arrested: Race, Power, and the Blues in the Mississippi Delta*. New York: Verso.

Wright, Willie Jamaal. 2020. "The Morphology of Marronage." *Annals of the American Association of Geographers* 110 (4): 1134–49.

Wu, Judy Tzu-Chun. 2013. *Radicals on the Road: Internationalism, Orientalism, and Feminism during the Vietnam Era*. Ithaca NY: Cornell University Press.

Wynter, Sylvia. 1992. "No Humans Involved: An Open Letter to My Colleagues." *Forum N.H.I.* 1 (1): 42–73.

———. 2003. "Unsettling the Coloniality of Being/Power/Truth/Freedom: Toward the Human, after Man, Its Overrepresentation—An Argument." CR 3 (3): 257–337.

Wynter, Sylvia, and Katherine McKittrick. 2015. "Unparalleled Catastrophe for Our Species? or, To Give Humanness a Different Future: Conversations." In *Sylvia Wynter: On Being Human as Praxis*, edited by Katherine McKittrick, 9–89. Durham NC: Duke University Press.

X, Malcolm. (1965) 1992. *The Autobiography of Malcolm X: As Told to Alex Haley*. New York: Ballantine.

Yeğenoğlu, Meyda. 1998. *Colonial Fantasies: Towards a Feminist Reading of Orientalism*. Cambridge: Cambridge University Press.

Yeh, Livian. 2022. "What Keiko O'Brien Taught Me about Belonging." StarTrek.com, March 16, 2022. https://www.startrek.com/news/what-keiko-obrien-taught-me-about -belonging.

Yu, Phil. 2020a. "Clyde Kusatsu." *All the Asians on Star Trek* (podcast), episode 4, September 15, 2020. https://www.alltheasiansonstartrek.com/2020/09/04-clyde-kusatsu.html.

———. 2020b. "Rosalind Chao." *All the Asians on Star Trek* (podcast), episode 11, December 4, 2020. http://blog.angryasianman.com/2020/12/all-asians-on-star-trek-11-rosalind -chao.html.

Zillow Research. 2017. "Highlights from Research on Rents and Homelessness." Zillow, August 3, 2017. https://www.zillow.com/research/highlights-rent-homelessness-16131/.

Zucker, Jerry, dir. 1990. *Ghost.* Hollywood: Paramount.

Index

Page numbers in italics refer to illustrations.

Asimov, Isaac, 226–27
"The Assignment" (*DS9* episode), 195–96
Atoa, Manuele, 204–5
Attica Correctional Facility uprising
  (New York, 1971), 46, 243n4
Auberjonois, René, xxxii, 134–35, 140,
  245n2
Avatar (film), 105–6, 232

Bacon's Rebellion (1676), 80
Bahng, Aimee, 179
Bajor (planet), 1, 86, 95, 96
Bajoran Orbs, 58, 72
Bajoran Prophets, xxix; Benjamin Sisko
  and, 14–15, 37, 39–40, 51, 90, 93, 232;
  Black Christianity's prophetic tradition and, 52; in "Far Beyond the Stars"
  episode, 51, 52; Indigenous spiritualities and, 103; Kira and, 86, 87–89, 97,
  98; liberation theologies of, 16, 17, 144;
  Orbs for communication with, 58, 72;
  Quark and, 167; secular Federation
  name for, xxix, 93, 188. *See also* Celestial Temple; religion
Bajorans: anticolonial story line and,
  103–8; decolonization of, 1–2, 71–74,
  81–86; description of, xxix, 81; and
  independence from the Federation, 85,
  100; in military sex trade, 18; postcolonial development of, 95–99; prostheses
  for, 102, 107; whitewashing of, 102. *See
  also* decolonization of Bajor; Indigenous peoples; Palestine
Baker, Ella, xviii
Bamarren Institute for State Intelligence, 215
Bandung Conference, 56
"Bar Association" (*DS9* episode), 162–66,
  246n6
Barba, Michael, 63
Bareil Antos (character), xxxiii, 94, 97

Barnes, Steven, 57–59
Barrett, Duncan, 72
Barrett, Michèle, 72
Barry Lyndon (film), 130–31
Barthes, Roland, 30
Bashir, Julian Subatoi (character), xxxii;
  backstory of, 221–25; in "Hippocratic
  Oath" episode, 125–29; Miles O'Brien
  and, 180, 189–93, 200; in "Our Man
  Bashir" episode, 218; in "Past Tense"
  episode, 42–43; queerness of, 213,
  223–30
Bastién, Angelica Jade, 38
Batten, Cyia, xxxv
BC (character), 43–45
beauty, 102
"The Begotten" (*DS9* episode), 136
Behr, Ira Steven, xxxvi; on Bajoran
  independence, 100; documentary by,
  7; on *DS9* within *Star Trek* franchise, 7,
  231; on Ferengi, 144–45, 172; on LGBTQ
  representation, 200; on "Past Tense"
  episode, 46–49; on specific characters,
  45, 130, 193, 222; on war, 148, 158
Beimler, Hans, xxxvi
Bell, Gabriel (character), 42, 44–51
Benjamin, Walter, 29, 97
Berger, John, 3
Berlant, Lauren, 181–82. *See also* affect
  theory
Berman, Rick, xxxvi, 102, 119
Bernardi, Daniel Leonard, 20, 115, 180
Beyond Uhura (Nichols), xv
"Beyond Vietnam" (King), xvi–xviii, 34–
  35, 62–63, 134, 240
Bhattarcharya, Tithi, 170
biblical literalists, 22
Biden, Joe, xviii, 238
Biggs, Casey, xxxiii, 99
Bin Laden, Osama, 67

Darren, James, xxxv, 158–59
Darrow, Clarence, 90
Data (character), 116, 178–79, 182
Davidson, Fiona M., 79
Davis, Angela Y., xviii, 67, 78
Dax, Curzon (character), xxxii, 202–4
Dax, Ezri (character), xxxi, 157–58, 161, 200, 216, 227–28, 232, 247nn1–2
Dax, Jadzia (character), xxxii, 42–43, 117, 200–212, 221, 227
Day, Iyko, 149–50, 246n1
Dean, Philip Hayes, 243n1
de Boer, Nicole, xxxi, 200
DeCandido, Keith, 144
decolonization of Bajor, 1–2, 71–74, 81–84. *See also* anticolonialism; Bajorans
Deep Space Nine (series). See *Star Trek: Deep Space Nine* (DS9)
Deep Space Nine station, 1–4, 16–18, 52–53, 74, 139, 143, 146, 186–87. *See also* Terok Nor
deidealization, 114, 142, 158, 237. *See also* depressive/reparative reading; Klein, Melanie
Deloria, Philip J., 103
Deloria, Vine, Jr., 16, 34, 88
democracy: grassroots experiments in, 40–41, 43–50, 60, 104–00, 173, 221, 231, 232; U.S. image of, 25, 69, 85, 100, 109, 199
Democratic National Convention, xviii
Democratic Party, xviii, 8, 41, 164, 192, 219, 226
democratic socialism, 8–9, 32, 35, 241
depressive/reparative reading, 26–28, 31–32, 105, 115, 141, 234. *See also* deidealization; Klein, Melanie; Sedgwick, Eve Kosofsky
Desilu Studios, xv
disability, 17, 161

disidentification, 107. *See also* affect theory
"Doctor Bashir, I Presume?" (DS9 episode), 222–24
Dodds, Klaus, 228
Dogon people, 58
Dominion, xxx, 109–15, 117–20. *See also* Changelings; Jem'Hadar; Ketracel-White (drug); Vorta
Dominion War, 58–59, 111–12, 129, 138, 216, 220, 231; "In the Pale Moonlight" episode on, 61–62, 68; "The Siege of AR-558" episode on, 157–58
Dooley, Paul, xxxiii, 213
Dorn, Michael, xxxiii, 52, 116–17, 246n5
double consciousness, 157
Douglas, Andrew J., 34–35
drug addiction, 121–23. *See also* Ketracel-White (drug)
DS9 (series). See *Star Trek: Deep Space Nine* (DS9)
DS9 (station). *See* Deep Space Nine station
Du Bois, W. E. B., 45, 49, 56, 57, 59, 157
"Duet" (DS9 episode), 77, 84, 91
Duggan, Lisa, 144
Dukat, Gul (character), xxxiii, 81–84, 94, 99, 202, 217, 227, 232
Dürer, Albrecht, 119
Dyson, Stephen Benedict, 63, 101

Echevarria, René, xxxvi, 46, 71, 101
ecofascism, 139
Eddington, Michael (character), xxxiv, 81
education, 89–90, 186–88, 215. *See also* school, DS9
Ehrenreich, Barbara, 153. *See also* professional-managerial class
Eichmann in Jerusalem (Arendt), 77
Eisenberg, Aron, xxxiv, 59, 146
Ellen (TV show), 5, 201

Ellington, Duke, xv

Ellison, Ralph, 57

"Emissary" (*DS9* episode), 1, 3, 4, 14–15, 39, 85

Eng, David L., 154, 158, 214, 221, 230

Enloe, Cynthia, 18

"Ensign Ro" (*TNG* episode), 72, 107. *See also* Ro Laren (character)

ENT. See Star Trek: Enterprise (ENT)

Erdmann, Terry J., 63, 124

Espiritu, Augusto, 85–86

ethical cohabitation, 76, 135–36, 237–38

eugenics, 8, 50, 90, 110, 112, 223–24

extractivism, 71–74, 84, 95–99, 111–12, 216, 220, 237, 239. *See also* capitalism; settler colonialism

"Extreme Measures" (*DS9* episode), 229

family: Blackness and, 9, 38, 232; capitalism and, 155, 168; Cardassians and, 214; neoliberalism and, 180, 192, 198. *See also* fatherhood; feminism; gendered division of labor; pregnancy and childbirth; queerness; social reproduction

"Family Business" (*DS9* episode), 169

fan fiction, 202

Fanon, Frantz, 55, 123, 129, 210. *See also* Wynter, Sylvia

fan studies, 105, 201, 202–4

"Far Beyond the Stars" (*DS9* episode), 36, 51–61, 63, 64, 68, 247n1

Farrell, Terry, xxxii, 200, 201, 204

fatherhood, 1, 9, 37–39, 41, 232

Fawaz, Ramzi, 74, 86, 181, 195. *See also* affect theory

FCA. *See* Ferengi Commerce Authority (FCA)

Federation. *See* United Federation of Planets (UFP)

feminism: bourgeois, 169–174, 177; family and, 155; social reproduction theory and, 16–17, 164–64, 172, 179–82, 199; *Star Trek* and, 23, 85, 106–7, 202–3, 232, 247n2

Ferengi Alliance, xxx, 143–45, 235–36; *DS9* ending and, 231–32; fetishization of characters in, 143, 149–53; Kira on, 144

Ferengi capitalism, 17; "Bar Association" episode on, 162–66; "Body Parts" episode on, 167–69; feminism and, 169–74; vs. humans, 175–77; "It's Only a Paper Moon" episode on, 158–61; Noh-Jay Consortium subplot on, 146–49; "Prophet Motive" episode on, 167

Ferengi Commerce Authority (FCA), 143, 163–65, 167–68

The Ferengi Rules of Acquisition, 144–45, 153, 167, 168, 174, 175, 246n8

fetishism, 106, 149–53, 155, 156, 158–59, 160, 174–75, 177

Fields, Peter Allan, xxxvi, 146

First Intifada (1987–93), 104

Fletcher, Louise, xxxv, 89, 187

Fontaine, Vic (character), xxxv, 158, 159

Forbes, Michelle, 72, 102, 107–8, 241

Ford, John, 24, 65, 67, 159

Forester, C. S., 24

"For the Cause" (*DS9* episode), 79

Foucault, Michel, 224

Foundation (Asimov), 226–27

Founders. *See* Changelings

Fraser, Nancy, 170

free trade, 7, 98, 164

Freud, Sigmund, 149, 152, 159, 214

frontier: space race and, 24; *Star Trek* and, 20, 23, 210–11, 228; U.S. imperialism and, 67; western genre and, 39, 160

Fullerton, Pascal (character), 207–8, 210–12

Immerwahr, Daniel, 147, 148–49

imperialism, xvii, 12–13, 35, 78; British, 24, 165, 203; Cardassian, 79, 81–84, 213–221; Dominion, 110–11; Federation, 15, 85–86, 117; Japanese, 128, 244n5; multiculturalism and, 13, 20; queerness and, 200–202; Roman, 114; social reproduction and, 199; U.S., 49–51, 56, 61–69, 90, 146–48, 211, 237, 243n3. *See also* anticolonialism; capitalism; militarism; settler colonialism

Inayatullah, Naeem, 27, 68

Incredible Tales (fictional publication), 52, 53, 56–57

Indigenous peoples: anti-imperialist perspectives of, 84, 137–38; and concepts of place, 16; cultural appropriation and, 103–6; depiction of, in *TNG*, 80; forced relocation of, 81, 244n3; land extractivism and, 13, 95, 239; marronage and, 125; military discourse on, 67; religious heterogeneity of, 88, 101; social movements of, 50, 105, 236–37. *See also* Bajorans; Palestine; settler colonialism

Inherit the Wind (film), 89–90

interdisciplinarity, 19–21

inter-imperial conflict, 85–86

interracial romance, 34, 180, 205–10, 212

intertextuality, 30

"In the Hands of the Prophets" (*DS9* episode), 89, 188

"In Theory" (*TNG* episode), 178–80

"In the Pale Moonlight" (*DS9* episode), 61–69, 218–19, 244n6

Iran-Contra, 113, 116, 245n2

Iraq, 20, 49, 69, 85, 102. *See also* antiwar movements

Irishness, 177, 183, 185, 197, 237

Ishka (character), xxxiv, 169–70, 172–74, 177

Islam, 72, 88, 94, 234

Islamophobia, 72, 101, 116, 200

Israel: democratic image of, 100; formation of state of, 75–77; internal and external criticism of, 103–7; settler colonialism and, 81, 83. *See also* Jewish Voice for Peace; settler colonialism

"It's Only a Paper Moon" (*DS9* episode), 158–61

Jackson, George, 243n4

Jacobsen, Matthew Frye, 197

jamaharon, 206–7, 209, 211

Japanese Americans, 184–85, 246n1. *See also* Asian Americans

Japaneseness, stereotypes of, 116–17, 127–28, 132–33, 185, 245n3

Jem'Hadar, xxx; in "The Abandoned" episode, 120–24; in "Hippocratic Oath" episode, 124–27, 128–29; in hypothetical eighth *DS9* season, 245n6; race and class positioning of, 110–11, 118–19, 245nn3–4; in "Rocks and Shoals" episode, 131–34; in "To the Death" episode, 129–31

"The Jem'Hadar" (*DS9* episode), 118

Jemison, Mae, xvi

Jenner, Barry, xxxv, 112

Jens, Salome, xxxiii, 135

Jerald, Penny Johnson, xxxiv, 52, 79–80

Jewish Voice for Peace, 75, 240

Johnson, Lyndon, 63

"John Wayne syndrome," 160, 246n2. *See also* Wayne, John

Joseph, Miranda, 155, 168

"Journey's End" (*TNG* episode), 80

Kahn, Lenara (character), 201

Kang (character), 203

Kapell, Matthew Wilhelm, 76–77, 112

Karera, Axelle, 139

Palestine: allegories for 31, 73, 75–78,
79, 83–84, 103–7, 239; Black freedom
struggles and, 50; religion and, 101,
234. *See also* anticolonialism; Israel;
Jewish Voice for Peace; Khalidi,
Rashid; *nakba*; Orientalism; Said,
Edward W.; settler colonialism
"Paradise Lost" (*DS9* episode), 112
Paramount, xv, 28, 41
particularism, 73–74, 86, 235, 238. *See also*
Fawaz, Ramzi; Massey, Doreen; place
"Past Tense" (*DS9* episodes), 36, 41–51,
63–64, 222, 243n4
Patton, Cindy, 32
Paul Robeson (Dean), 243n1. *See also*
Robeson, Paul
Pel (character), 170
Peters, Brock, xxxiv, 33, 52
Phillips, Richard, 228
PIC. See Star Trek: Picard (*PIC*)
Picard, Jean-Luc (character): about, 8–9,
10, 41, 93; Benjamin Sisko and, 15, 85;
Borg and, xxix, 15, 174; on Federation
economics, 145, 149; Q and, 7, 178
Piller, Michael, xxxvi, 6, 75–76, 100
place: Bajorans and, 75–77, 81, 84, 86, 88,
96, 108; Black geographies and, 40–41,
48, 93, 123; as context for *DS9*, 1–5, 70,
72, 186, 234–39; in cultural geography,
11–12, 16–19; Dax and, 203; Molly
O'Brien and, 196; white capitalism
and, 245n1. *See also* Massey, Doreen
police violence, 2, 24, 49, 52–53, 60,
80, 175
political theologies, 73, 93, 126, 144, 175,
211, 245n6. *See also* Bajoran Prophets;
Black Christianity; Christianity; Islam;
liberation theologies; religion
Polk, Khary, 67
polyamory, 192

post–Cold War geopolitics, 49, 100, 109,
115, 158, 228, 245n1. *See also* Cold War
Postone, Moishe, 149, 150
postscarcity economy, 20, 50, 145, 153–54,
198, 208, 224, 239. *See also* capitalism;
United Federation of Planets (UFP)
Pounds, Micheal C., 2
Powell, Colin, 244n7
Pratt, Minnie Bruce, 236
pregnancy and childbirth, xix, 86, 121,
183, 191–92, 232
Prin, Silaran, 86–87
professional-managerial class, 22, 42, 124,
141, 153, 180, 228. *See also* capitalism;
class; Starfleet
"Profit and Lace" (*DS9* episode), 170–73,
202
"Progress" (*DS9* episode), 95–97, 99,
145–49, 156
Promenade, 2–5, 17, 39, 84, 138, 186, 196,
237
"Prophet Motive" (*DS9* episode), 167, 177
Puar, Jasbir, 199–200, 229–30

Q (character), 6–7, 178
Quark (character), xxxiii, 52, 138, 144,
162–77, 207, 232, 246n1, 246n3
Quark's (establishment), 17–18, 146, 167–
77, 197, 199, 202, 229, 246n2
queer fan fiction, 202
queerness: of Bashir, 180, 189–91, 193,
200; of Dominion, 245n8; exile and,
139–40, 201, 214; of Ezri Dax, 243n3,
247n2; of Ferengi, 246nn7–8; of Garak,
200, 213–21; and gender reconfigura-
tions, 170–71, 246n7; and homonationalism, 199–200; of Jadzia Dax, 5,
117, 200–212; of mirror-universe Kira,
243n3, 244n4; of Odo, 139–40
queer studies, 29, 200–201, 214

"The Quickening" (*DS9* episode), 222

Rabitsch, Stefan, 112
racial capitalism: and Anthropocene as concept, 137–39; Avery Brooks on, 55–57; Cedric J. Robinson on, xx, 12–13; Charisse Burden-Stelly on, 13–14; Dominion and, 110–15, 140–42; Ferengi and, 144–52, 175–77; homelessness and, 47–48; Martin Luther King on, 34–35; Ruth Wilson Gilmore on, 47, 49. *See also* capitalism; imperialism; racism
racial profiling, 41, 154, 197. *See also* police violence; racism; state violence
racism: "The Abandoned" episode and, 121–24; Black radical tradition against, 12, 57–59; in "Far Beyond the Stars" episode, 51–61; Jem'Hadar and, 110–11, 118–19, 245nn3–4; against Klingons, 116, 208, 210; by NBC, 183; in "Past Tense" episode, 41–51; police violence and, 2, 4, 49, 243n4; in U.S. military, 59; and violence against Asian Americans, 176. *See also* anti-Blackness; militarism; nationalism; Orientalism; racial capitalism; settler colonialism
Randolph, A. Philip, 59
Reagan, Ronald, 66, 97, 113, 116, 151, 169
Reddy, Chandan, 32
Redmond, Shana, 36
Red Summer (1919), 59
Regehr, Duncan, xxxv, 98
"Rejoined" (*DS9* episode), 5, 201–2, 205
religion: of Bajorans, 72, 73, 87–89, 93–95, 100–101; Christianity, 35, 52, 88, 89, 94, 212, 234; Islam, 72, 88, 94, 234. *See also* Bajoran Prophets; Black Christianity; liberation theologies; political theologies; secularism
Remata'Klan (character), 132–34

representation: vs. allegory, 105; of Blackness, 11, 60, 232; of LGBTQ identities, 20, 172, 200–202; as politically insufficient, xviii, 19, 23, 66–67, 235; as radical intervention, 46, 63, 235
Republican Party, 41, 175
rhinoceros, 119
Rhodes, Mark Alan, II, 243n4
Risa (planet), 204, 206–12
"Rivals" (*DS9* episode), *194*
Roberts, Dorothy, 121–22, 124
Roberts, Neil, 125
Robeson, Paul, 10, 33–34, 36, 56, 66, 79, 83, 243n1
Robin, Corey, 212–13
Robinson, Andrew J., xxxiii, 61, 63, 200, 202, 213–16, 219, 221
Robinson, Cedric J., xx, 12, 50, 57, 125
Robinson, Sally, 196–97
"Rocks and Shoals" (*DS9* episode), 131–34
Roddenberry, Gene: *DS9* and, 6, 60, 72–73, 186, 223–24, 241; muses of, 24; politics of, xv–xviii, 25, 205–9; religion and, 72–73. See also *Star Trek (The Original Series; TOS)*
Rodríguez, Dylan, 67
Ro Laren (character), 72, 79, 102, 107
Rom (character), xxxv, 153–54, 161–66, 174–77, 187, 195, 231–32, 246n6
Romulans, xxxi, 61–62, 68
Roosevelt, Theodore, 83
Ross, William (character), xxxv, 112
Rozhenko, Alexander (character), 117
"Rules of Acquisition" (*DS9* episode), 170
Russell, Benny (character), 51–61, 68, 247n1. *See also* Sisko, Benjamin Lafayette (character)
Russell, John G., 103, 122

Saadia, Manu, 152–53, 154–55, 179, 224

Strode, Woody, 65
Sturgeon, Theodore, 243n2
suicide, 110, 118, 133, 194
Sukehiro, Hirakawa, 127–28
Sulu, Hikaru (character), 6
Summers, Larry, 134
surrogacy (pregnancy), 191–92

"Tacking into the Wind" (DS9 episode),
    229
Tain, Enabran (character), xxxiii, 213–18
Takei, George, 6, 25
Talak'talan (character), 117–18, 245n3
TAS. See Star Trek: The Animated Series
    (TAS)
Taylor, Keeanga-Yamahtta, xviii, 67, 172,
    199–200
technomasculine adventurism, 228–29
Terok Nor, 2, 4, 74, 84, 134, 213, 216, 219.
    See also Deep Space Nine station
terrorism, DS9 depiction of, 1–2, 5, 84,
    102, 104, 152, 211
textualism, 22–23
Thích Nhất Hạnh, xvii
Thompson, Bradley, xxxvi
Thompson, Susanna, 201
"Ties of Blood and Water" (DS9 episode),
    92–93
Tigan, Ezri. See Dax, Ezri (character)
"Time's Orphan" (DS9 episode), 196
TNG. See Star Trek: The Next Generation
    (TNG)
Todd, Tony, 38, 117
Tompkins, Kyla Wazana, 184
TOS. See Star Trek (The Original Series;
    TOS)
"To the Death" (DS9 episode), 129–31, 133
Trail of Tears, 81, 244n3
trans identities, 171–72, 201–2, 203–4
trek (term), 24

"Trials and Tribble-ations" (DS9 epi-
    sode), xix–xx
Trill, 200–203, 227, 246n7, 247nn1–2
Troi, Deanna (character), 205, 210
"The Trouble with Tribbles" (TOS epi-
    sode), xix
Trump, Donald, 67, 174–75
Tuck, Eve, 76
Turner, Nat, 33
TV Guide, 5
Tyree (planet), 234
Tzu-Chun Wu, Judy, 68

Uddin, Lisa, 119
UFP. See United Federation of Planets (UFP)
Uhura, Nyota (character), xv–xx
United Federation of Planets (UFP), xxx,
    25; Bajoran relations with, 85, 100,
    146–48; Cardassian relations with,
    78–79, 197; and Dominion War, 58–59,
    111–12, 129, 138, 216, 231; vs. Ferengi,
    174–76; as geopolitical stand-in, 13,
    115, 141; Klingon relations with, 115–17,
    203–4, 210, 245n2; and Maquis con-
    flict, 78–81. See also humanity; liberal-
    ism; postscarcity economy; Starfleet
U.S. Department of Defense, 133, 245n7
U.S. Dirty Wars (conflicts in Latin Amer-
    ica), 113, 152, 245n2
U.S. Navy, 59–60, 133
USS Defiant, 5, 42, 44, 156, 246n5
USS Enterprise (TOS), xv–xx, 1–3
USS Enterprise-D (TNG), 118, 142, 178, 182,
    183, 192
USS Odyssey, 118

Vande Berg, Leah R., 117
Vesey, Denmark, 33
Vietnam War, xvii–xviii, 20, 25, 35, 63, 69,
    134, 246n2. See also antiwar movements

Visitor, Nana, xxxii, 7, 41, 52, 71–73, 84–85, 191, 247n4
Voortrek (term), 24
Vorta, xxx, 110–11, 113–15, 119, 124–26, 129–32, 141, 245n8
VOY. See *Star Trek: Voyager* (VOY)

wage discrimination, 56–57
Wagner, Jon, 6
Wagon Train (TV series), 24
"Waltz" (DS9 episode), 81–84
Warf, Barney, 22
Wayne, John, 30, 65–67, 85, 135, 160, 246n2. See also "John Wayne syndrome"
We Charge Genocide (Patterson), 83
Weddle, David, xxxvi
Weinstock, Jeffrey A., 29
Wenger, Sara, 246n4
West, Cornel, 10, 52, 67
western genre, 24, 30, 65–67, 159–60
Weyoun (character), xxxv, 52, 129–31, 141
What We Left Behind (film), 7, 47, 63
"What Would a Non-Sexist City Be Like?" (Hayden), 187
"What You Leave Behind" (DS9 episode), 231–36, 237
"Whispers" (DS9 episode), 195
whiteness, 45, 60, 102–4, 110–12, 159, 192–98, 245n1. See also racial capitalism
Wilderson, Frank B., III, 48
Williams, Clarence, III, 130
Wills, Garry, 66
Winn, J. Emmett, 154
Winn Adami (character), xxxv, 89–90, 97–98, 187–88, 232
Wolfe, Patrick, 12, 76
Wolfe, Robert Hewitt, xxxvi; on Dominion, 109–11, 113–14, 118–19, 122–24, 136; on DS9 within *Star Trek* franchise, 3, 50; on sources of inspiration, 46, 98, 151

Wolf 359 battle, 15, 39–40
women: Bechdel test and, 188, 238; as "dabo girls," 18; Ferengi view of, 143, 170–73; in military sex trade, 18; pregnancy of and childbirth by, 183, 191–92; social reproduction and, 185–86, 188–90. See also feminism; gendered division of labor
Women at Warp (podcast), 169–70, 181, 246n4
women's rights, 169–74. See also feminism
Woods, Clyde, 40–41
Worf (character), xxxiii, 52, 116–17, 183, 204–12, 227–28, 231, 246n5
working class: Avery Brooks's sensibilities as, 41; coalitional solidarities among, 35, 44–45, 47, 162–66, 243n5; Miles O'Brien as stand-in for, 228; Nog as stand-in for, 155–56. See also capitalism; labor unions; social reproduction
"The Work of Art in the Age of Mechanical Reproduction" (Benjamin), 29
world-building, 19, 29, 71, 78, 115, 142, 178
World War II, 78, 81, 147, 158, 175, 223, 245n3; Hollywood and, 30, 60, 112, 127, 132, 158. See also Holocaust
"wormhole aliens" (term), xxix, 93, 188. See also Bajoran Prophets
Wright, Herbert J., 151
Wright, Richard, 57
Wright, Willie, 125
"Wrongs Darker than Death or Night" (DS9 episode), 94
Wynter, Sylvia, 14, 48, 89, 123–24, 129, 234–35, 245n5. See also Fanon, Frantz; humanity; McKittrick, Katherine

Xhosa (freighter), 79–80

In the Cultural Geographies + Rewriting the Earth series

Topoi/Graphein: Mapping the Middle in Spatial Thought
Christian Abrahamsson
Foreword by Gunnar Olsson

Negative Geographies: Exploring the Politics of Limits
Edited by David Bissell, Mitch Rose, and Paul Harrison

Animated Lands: Studies in Territoriology
Andrea Mubi Brighenti and Mattias Kärrholm

Mapping Beyond Measure: Art, Cartography,
and the Space of Global Modernity
Simon Ferdinand

The Begging Question: Sweden's Social
Responses to the Roma Destitute
Erik Hansson
Foreword by Don Mitchell

Psychoanalysis and the GlObal
Edited and with an introduction by Ilan Kapoor

A Place More Void
Edited by Paul Kingsbury and Anna J. Secor

Abysmography: A Grand Tour through the Taken-for-Granted
Gunnar Olsson

A Different "Trek": Radical Geographies of "Deep Space Nine"
David K. Seitz

To order or obtain more information on these or other
University of Nebraska Press titles, visit nebraskapress.unl.edu.